A GUIDE TO THE NATIONAL ROAD

THE ROAD AND AMERICAN CULTURE

Drake Hokanson, *Series Editor*
George F. Thompson, *Series Director*

Published in cooperation with the
Center for American Places, Harrisonburg, Virginia

A Guide to the National Road

EDITED BY KARL RAITZ

Project Director and Director of Photography

George F. Thompson

Photography by

Charles Walters

Gregory Conniff

Bob Thall

Michael Putnam

CARTOGRAPHY BY GYULA PAUER

THE JOHNS HOPKINS UNIVERSITY PRESS

BALTIMORE AND LONDON

This book has been brought to publication with the
generous assistance of the Pioneer America Society
and the National Endowment for the Humanities.

The Johns Hopkins University Press
2715 North Charles Street
Baltimore, Maryland 21218-4319
The Johns Hopkins Press Ltd., London

Photo credits will be found at the end of this book.

LIBRARY OF CONGRESS CATALOGING-IN-PUBLICATION DATA

A guide to the National Road / edited by Karl Raitz ; project director
    and director of photography, George F. Thompson ; photography by
    Charles Walters . . . [et al.] ; cartography by Gyula Pauer.
        p.   cm. — (The road and American culture)
    Includes bibliographical references and index.
    ISBN 0-8018-5156-4 (alk. paper)
    1. United States Highway 40.   2. Cumberland Road—United States.
3. Roads—United States.   I. Raitz, Karl B.   II. Thompson, George F.
III. Series.
HE356.C8G85   1996
388.1′0977—dc20   95-44726

A catalog record of this book is available from the British Library.

In Memoriam

HENRY W. DOUGLAS

1906–1989

and for the American people

Contents

Preface

IN VOLUME 2 OF THIS TWO-VOLUME WORK WE EXAMINE THE FORMATIVE role of roads and highways in American life within the context of one highway, the National Road, now US 40, the nation's first federally funded and planned roadway. Both volume 1, entitled *The National Road,* and volume 2, *A Guide to the National Road,* are based upon the premise that transportation has been of critical importance in the development of American society and economy and that the National Road therefore represents several chapters in the American cultural autobiography. Each evolutionary step in transportation technology has affected the countryside, towns, and cities through which routes passed, creating new landscapes from old. Primitive trails and traces became macadamized roads. Roads were superseded by canals and then railroads, which were themselves replaced by concrete highways and interstate freeways.

Although roads were the product of innovation and engineering, their construction was fostered by political and economic interests. The process of conceiving, funding, building, and using the National Road incorporates a complex web of links between national political objectives and regional economic development; between evolving construction and travel technology and their practical application and geographic effects; between the meaning the Road had for local people and how it also contributed to the development of a national identity, and thus became a part of the process of creating a national culture. And a national culture does not develop without linkage of its constituent regional parts. Engineers did not simply build improved roads or refine the vehicles that used them. Manufacturers did not simply produce commodities for delivery to distant markets by way of these roads. Migrants, travelers, and salespeople did not move along roads without effect. Many such events brought people and their ideas from one region to another and cumulatively produced modifications in traditional ways of doing things, and in the landscapes along which they passed.

Unlike shorter pikes, which connected towns along the eastern seaboard, the National Road (1808 to 1850) was intended to foster national economic development by tying empty land of great potential wealth in the Old Northwest and emerging Middle West to established eastern cities and markets. The road would traverse wildly differing topography from the developing coastline, across high forested ridge lands and a rugged mountain chain, to remote prairie plains. Construction of parallel routes would be attempted by transcontinental railroads decades later, but the National Road's founders had no model to refer to as an example. The National Road was conceived before the widespread deployment of steam-powered boats and railroads, and those who oriented themselves to the Road could not anticipate such technologies and would become entangled in the cycle of development and abandonment that accompanied the expansion of these new transport modes.

Volume 2 is a practical field guide that incorporates the geographical and historical perspective of volume 1. The introduction places the National Road corridor within the context of the highway as a key to access and movement, two linchpins of American culture and economy. A portfolio on the National Road as depicted in art then follows. The subsequent seven chapters offer detailed vignettes that describe the landscape along the Road's individual segments. Chapter 1, for example, covers the section from

Baltimore to Cumberland, Maryland; chapter 2, the original section from Cumberland to Wheeling, West Virginia, and so on into chapter 7, which describes the westernmost section from Vandalia, Illinois, to East St. Louis and Alton. Each vignette documents and interprets roadside landscapes as well as the towns and cities; each vignette reflects upon some of the ideas that produced landscape artifacts, such as Federal-style architecture, the Pennsylvania Town plan, and the prototype for the Middle West Corn Belt farm.

With the adoption of a national highway-numbering system in 1926, the old National Road became US 40, a concrete ribbon that engineers regraded to bypass those sections with difficult curves and slopes. The route was soon linked with an increasingly efficient national road network to serve the emerging transportation era of automobiles and trucks. This process added new layers of road-related artifacts to the National Road's landscape: truckstops, gas stations, and motels, automobile sales lots and showrooms, bridges and bypasses. The Road became a composite landscape, a collection of elements from decades of changing technologies and interests, the archetype of a process that is repeated on thousands of other roads across the country. The Interstate Highway System, conceived by Pres. Dwight D. Eisenhower, spawned more change, including a new abandonment cycle along the old Road, and new urban forms, such as the galactic city and the interchange village. This volume illustrates, by way of roadside examples, how all this happened.

The original National Road has been bypassed and even obliterated by subsequent highway construction in many places; it is sometimes difficult to find. The vignettes follow the original Road in some places and its successor, US 40, in others, and reference is often made to Interstates I-70 and I-68, which run parallel to the Road for most of the route. The term "road corridor" is used in several chapters. The meaning varies, but a convenient standard is that the corridor refers to the roadbed proper, including the original Road and subsequent US 40 beds, the interstate bed, and the land extending on either side to the visual horizon.

This volume, as well as volume 1, is written in a manner that will allow you to envision the grand process of national development that the Road represents. May it serve you well as you travel along the nation's first "interstate" highway.

Acknowledgments

I AM INDEBTED TO MANY INDIVIDUALS AND INSTITUTIONS WHO CONtributed impetus, knowledge, records, and ideas, or critically reviewed our interpretations of roadside historic events and geography. This project began in the mind of Mr. Henry H. Douglas, founder of the Pioneer America Society, and National Road devotee. In 1981, Mr. Douglas and photographer Wm. Edmund Barrett, of Shepherdstown, West Virginia, conceived a photo-essay project that would commemorate some of the historic structures erected beside the National Road. When Mr. Douglas died, he left a substantial bequest to the Pioneer America Society to carry the project forward. That idea grew to the two volumes now presented, prepared by nineteen contributing authors and four professional photographers. In addition to the bequest by Mr. Douglas, I am very pleased to acknowledge that these two books were supported by a substantial grant from the National Endowment for the Humanities, an independent federal agency. Everyone affiliated with this project has done everything in his or her power to ensure that these books are enduring legacies for the American public.

Special thanks to George F. Thompson, president of the Center for American Places, whose inspired insights into the management of a project of this scope were invaluable. "Saint" George, as he came to be known, directed the project's photography and editorial development. Not only is he a gifted editor and keen observer of landscape, but he is probably without peer in his zeal to encourage original writing, research, and photography about the American scene. In addition, I am grateful to Thomas J. Schlereth of the Department of American Studies at the University of Notre Dame, who carefully and critically reviewed the manuscripts of both volumes and made numerous suggestions for corrections and improvements. He was later engaged to prepare the two portfolios, for which I am most grateful.

We wish to acknowledge the following for their permission to publish maps and photographs: Houghton Mifflin Company for permission to reprint the Erwin Raisz maps from George R. Stewart's *U.S. 40* (pp. 66–67, 70–71, 84–85, 112–13 (Copyright © 1953 by George R. Stewart, © renewed 1981 by Theodosia B. Stewart, all rights reserved); to Jean Yeshilian of Raisz Landform Maps for permission to reprint portions of Erwin Raisz, *Map of the Landforms of the United States*, 6th ed., 1956; to Douglas Meyer for permission to use photographs from the Mack Wilson Collection; to the Maryland Historical Society for George Beck's *View of Baltimore from Howard's Park*, and Thomas Cole Ruckle's *Fairview Inn or Three Mile House on Old Frederick Road*; to the University of Illinois at Chicago for John Melish's *Map of National Road Between Cumberland and Wheeling*; to the Federal Highway Administration for Carl Rakeman's *1823—First American MacAdam Road*, to the Rutherford B. Hayes Presidential Center for Carl Rakeman's *1839—Our First Iron Bridge* and Carl Rakeman's *Adoption of Uniform Signs*; to the George Washington Hotel, Washington, Pennsylvania, for Malcolm Stevens Parcell's *Henry Clay's Visit to Washington, Pennsylvania*; to the Indiana Historical Society for *Indianapolis Motor Speedway, Greatest Racecourse in the World*; to the Missouri Historical Society for *Bird's-Eye View, St. Louis, Missouri*; to the Carnegie Museum of Art for David Gilmour Blythe's *The Post Office, Pittsburgh*; to the Friends Collection, Earlham College, for Marcus Mote's *Indiana Yearly Meeting of Friends, 1844*; to Houghton Mifflin for Ross Lockridge Jr., *Raintree County* and *Town of Waycross* maps; to the Indianapolis

Museum of Art for Theodore Groll's *Washington Street, Indianapolis at Dusk;* to the Indiana State Library for the anonymous pamphlet *U.S. 40 National Old Trails Road;* to the National Geographic Society for John Matthew Heller's *Vandalia, Illinois;* and to the Mariner's Museum of Newport News for E. Sachse and Company's *St. Louis, Missouri.*

Thanks also to Carol Mishler at the Center for American Places, to Sonya Simms for valuable research assistance, and to the expert staffs of the Geography and Map Division at the Library of Congress, the Newberry Library, the Mercantile Library, the Ohio Historical Library, the Indiana State Library, the Hagley Museum and Library, the University of Kentucky Library and Special Collections, and the Illinois State Historical Library; to the Miami Conservancy Office in Dayton, Ohio, and the Dunbar Library Special Collections and Archives, at Wright State University in Dayton; to James R. Bertsch of Cambridge City, Indiana; to Mary Burtschi of Vandalia, Illinois; to Tom Thomas, National Park Service at the Denver Service Center; to Daniel Reedy, dean of the Graduate School, University of Kentucky, who contributed an extended interview with his father, Ralph Reedy. The Reedy family lived beside the Road in Livingston, Illinois, and Mr. Reedy worked as a brick carrier when the Road was resurfaced in the early 1930s; to Carol Stewart, a Columbus, Ohio, preservationist for information on the Scioto River bridge and Veterans Park; to Helen Felton of Lewisburg, Ohio, for information on Lewisburg; to Chris Robinson of London, Ohio, for piloting an aerial photography flight; to David Halman of Capitol Manufacturing and Patrick Smith of Toagosei America, Inc., both of West Jefferson, Ohio; and to Glenn Harper of the Ohio Historic Preservation Office at Wright State University and Mary Ann Olding Brown of the Cincinnati Preservation Association for their contributions to the project in general, but especially to chapter 4.

I also wish to make a special acknowledgment to Gyula Pauer, director of the University of Kentucky Cartography Laboratory, who designed the maps and diagrams, and directed the cartographic work; and to Derran Broyles and Phillip Stiefel for their cartographic production work. This volume and its companion contain numerous original photographs by Charles Waters of Colorado Springs, Gregory Conniff of Madison, Wisconsin, Bob Thall of Chicago, and Michael Putnam of New York City. These photographers worked within the parameters of the project—to provide informative illustrations—but they went well beyond the call of duty in making works of art. In so many ways does their vision and effort hearken back to the photographers of the Farm Security Administration, like the National Road another federally funded project. The nation is forever grateful to these photographers for their spectacular work.

A Message to the Reader

TRAVEL, NOT BASEBALL, IS THE NATIONAL PASTIME. HARD-SURFACED roads have allowed Americans to embrace travel as their muse and the automobile as their fetish. We drive to work and to shop. The favored mode of family vacation is car-enclosed and highway-bound. We sometimes prefer to "go for a drive" just "to relax." Yet, while Americans are among the most traveled people in the world, we are also notoriously poor travelers. Summer vacations are often destination-oriented; a theme park is the target, or a mountain ski resort, or a coastal golf course with adjacent condos, or an antique-besotted village—so outfitted by local business people to attract "Heritage Tourism." The trip is a pelt down the interstate, punctuated only by a series of stops at "highlights," or tourist traps that manufacture "attractions" sufficiently bizarre to attract the naive "adventurer."

Many Americans prefer their travel in the form of the guided tour led by well-meaning "experts" who make stops at "historic sites" and destination restaurants. But other than direct the innocents to the largest collections of roadside truck, or to the newest "factory outlet" cluster, or to the world's tallest windmill, such trips allow the grand tableau of ancient physical environments to slide past unexamined, such trips purvey little understanding of how the roadside landscape has been put together, or how the complex arrangements of open country farms, small towns, and large cities that align the road interrelate in time and place to form distinctive regions.

The informed traveler, on the other hand, is path-oriented and aware of countryside and community along the highway. Pathway travel is hard work, which is probably the reason we seldom commit the time and effort required to do it properly. Skillful travel requires locally scaled information on history and geography of the kind rarely found in common travel-club literature. One must be willing to read more than the roadside historical markers whose pretense is to declare what places and which slices of time are historically significant, which "great men" (women are rarely honored) were responsible for certain "historic" events, or accept the fallacy that the hired hands who operate the corporate "attractions" also "know the local history," understand local and regional geographies, and if asked can impart understanding to the visitor. Important history is more often aligned with the experiences of common people and common events than the sporadic episodes commemorated by plaques bolted to building fronts, or the statue troupe convened about the courthouse steps. The trick is to learn about the everyday landscapes that "common folk" create, and to realize that the structures people build and the uses they make of their land reflect not only an economy, but also a deep ancestral heritage, a changing amalgam of historic and contemporary geographical contexts, and environmental nuance.

Americans might look to Europeans as examples of informed and sophisticated travelers. They begin learning about landscapes early; most European school systems mandate that students study geography beginning in the elementary grades and continuing through graduate study, if pursued. They move through a landscape understanding the purpose and pattern in what they see beyond the hiking path or roadside. They question what they cannot decipher.

This book is a field guide to America's National Road, its cities and communities, the countryside through which it passes, and the physical environments it encounters. We have chosen to order the chapters from east to west, because this is the same direction that the Road was built and the land was settled. But we have also tested the guide from St. Louis to Baltimore so that, with minor adjustments, one can also follow the text from west to east. Should you choose this latter option, we still suggest that you read the introductory chapter before proceeding.

Whether you read this book in the comfort of an armchair, or in your motor vehicle, you will find that we have not recorded or explained every building, every street, or every landscape detail. No portable guide book could do that. Instead, we describe the physical geography to give a sense of the lay of the land and the humanly constructed places that were important in the building of the National Road, the common places that represent changes that have taken place along the Road across the subsequent decades, and the sites that represent the great processes that lie behind the making of landscape—technological changes, population growth, migration, and political policy. Great historic events are not slighted nor are important individuals ignored; instead we place them within a larger context, that of common people and common landscapes. To orient yourself for the Road's seven segments, begin by studying the strip maps that introduce each vignette (chapters 1 through 7).

To augment your National Road traverse we suggest that you consider obtaining some supporting materials. Although this book contains many maps, diagrams, and photographs, we suggest you acquire additional maps. The most useful are the U.S. Geological Survey topographic quadrangles, scale 1:24,000 or 2.6 inches per mile, which are perfect for studying towns, cities, and landscapes in detail. To order these maps directly, write to the USGS, Washington Distribution Section, 1200 South Eads Street, Arlington, Virginia 22202. The DeLorme Mapping Company, in Freeport, Maine, produces state atlases filled with maps at 1:150,000 or 0.4 inches per mile; each map contains a wealth of information on secondary roads, wooded areas, streams and lakes, place names, railroads, museums, and important historic sites. And at the national scale, you can write to Raisz Landform Maps, P.O. Box 773, Melrose, Massachusetts 02176, for a copy of Erwin Raisz's "Landforms of the United States" (27″ × 42″). This treasure is hand-drawn with an oblique perspective and presents the land surface, streams, and city locations in delicious visual relief. You will also find binoculars or a spot glass invaluable for watching a farmer guide a $100,000 tractor across an Indiana soybean field, for example, or to examine the Doric details atop a Greek-columned Pennsylvania courthouse portico.

The skillful traveler need not be disappointed by "bad weather." The key is to anticipate the range of weather that one might expect, given the season, and then make appropriate preparations. For example, the four climate graphs instruct us that Baltimore (elevation 90 feet above sea level) has mild winters—in no month does the average temperature fall below 32 degrees Fahrenheit. But summer temperature averages soar into the upper 70s and, during July and August, one can expect more than four inches of rain per month, usually in the form of thunderstorms. Traveling all sections of the Road in mid-summer might require an air-conditioned automobile, whereas spring trips are more temperate and fall trips are somewhat drier, except when the occasional late summer or autumn hurricane might imperil travel with heavy rain and wind. In the winter, caution mounts with altitude and distance from the coast. Frostburg, Maryland, at 2,035 feet above sea level, receives three or more inches of precipitation in December and January, and because the average temperatures during those months are below freezing one might expect to encounter heavy snow should a storm strike. This is true for other mountain locations. Travelers at all times, but especially during winter, should pay close attention to weather conditions. The Weather Channel on cable television is now available at many hotels and motels on the route.

From Columbus, Ohio, to Greenville, Illinois, the seasons tend toward more uniformity, although hundreds of miles separate these places. At Greenville, only about forty-five miles east of East St. Louis, springtime temperatures climb rapidly from March through June, accompanied by an equally steep climb in rainfall as the warm, moisture-laden air from the Gulf of Mexico begins to invade the Heartland, and afternoon thundershowers and storms bring the rains that grow middlewestern corn and soybeans. By mid-summer, the risk of rain subsides, although August temperatures rival those of Baltimore. But even if the weather is variable, recognizing its regional patterns and reveling in spectacular cloud formations is part of the fun, and education, of travel.

We recommend that you eat in local restaurants and avoid the national franchise places. Maybe you will notice the regional changes in food as you make the transition from Maryland crab cakes, to Pennsylvania pirogis, to

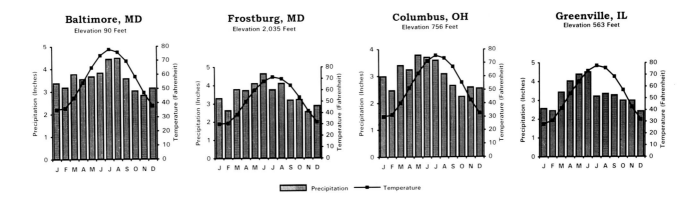

Baltimore, MD
Elevation 90 Feet

Frostburg, MD
Elevation 2,035 Feet

Columbus, OH
Elevation 756 Feet

Greenville, IL
Elevation 563 Feet

Precipitation — Temperature

Ohio blue-plate specials, to Indiana country ham and cornbread, to western Illinois catfish. You may be able to tell where the Maryland cruller becomes the Pennsylvania fat-cake and eventually the Ohio doughnut, and where soda turns into pop. Dozens of fine-quality locally owned restaurants can be found in the towns along the National Road: the Lone Star in Markleysburg, Pennsylvania; Angelo's in Washington, Pennsylvania; Schmidt's in German Town, Columbus, Ohio; and Niemerg's Steak House in Effingham, Illinois, are stellar examples. And accommodations are easy to find. Because Interstate 68/70 parallels the Road for most of its length, one can expect to find modern motels run by familiar national chains at most interstate interchanges in the larger towns. But we also recommend that you seek out the fine old city hotels that have been refurbished and updated, such as Failinger's Hotel Gunter in Frostburg, Maryland; the Great Southern Hotel in Columbus, Ohio; the Leland Hotel in Richmond, Indiana; or the Archer House in Marshall, Illinois. You see, the rewards that accrue to the informed traveler come in many forms and guises.

Also, we make a special request. Please pay particular attention to the photographs in this volume. We consciously chose to engage photographers who read landscapes as amateur geographers and as professional artists. The photographs are not necessarily intended to document architectural detail or topographic form. The photographers were asked to view the road and roadside as an ensemble of cultural pieces in a vast humanistic puzzle, and to try to record some of the cultural attributes that they found most evocative of the Road and the roadside. Their photographs portray the National Road landscape and life at a local scale in a manner that travelers seldom have time to grasp or assemble into an image that reflects the place. Rather than search only for documentation, the photographers

Embracing the weather

Climographs (*left to right*) of Baltimore, Frostburg, Md., Columbus, Ohio, and Greenville, Illinois.

looked to make works of art. As a result we can see, through their work, a kind of literary nonfiction. Different cameras were used, among them 8″ × 10″ and 4″ × 5″ view cameras; 6″ × 9″, 6″ × 7″, and 6″ × 6″ cameras; and occasionally the 35mm.

Cotton Mather, one of America's eminent geographers who is a direct descendant of the famous Puritan, and who, we might as well add, is indirectly related to Stephen Tyne Mather, the first director of the National Park Service, has taught thousands of students and citizens worldwide about the value and importance of being in the field. Recently, in the book *Landscape in America*, he was quoted as saying that "the original source of all geographical knowledge is in the field." By traveling the open road, walking the fence line, and strolling up and down our city streets, and by paying attention to everything in view, we learn to read a landscape and to understand the relationships between land and culture, history and geography, art and science, regions and nation-building. As you travel along the National Road, we encourage you to read the landscape, to see what we as a nation have become in the intervening years since construction began on the National Road in 1808.

A GUIDE TO THE NATIONAL ROAD

Introduction: The National Road and Its Landscapes

KARL RAITZ

As highway, U.S. 40 may be complex as the body of a [person] is complex—developing or deteriorating, always changing. But as route it is complex after the manner of a [person's] personality, in that it cannot be weighted, or even defined clearly—though it is highly interesting, and can be talked about indefinitely.

GEORGE R. STEWART
U.S. 40

THIS VOLUME SERVES TWO DISTINCT PURPOSES. AS A TRAVELOGUE, IT organizes information about America's National Road and encourages readers to travel the National Road corridor, either vicariously from a comfortable chair or as "explorers on the ground." Whether tracing vestiges of original Road segments, the US 40 concrete ribbon that replaced it, or sections of I-68 and I-70 that parallel it, one finds along the roadside a record of change—nearly two centuries' worth in some sections. The book also employs the National Road as a cross-sectional example that illustrates the highway's place in American life. In reading this book, and its companion volume, one can become "traveled," an experience that should help one recognize that while the Road and its landscape embody a tangible and accessible record of historic events and geographic processes, they also represent more abstract cultural structures that comprise American life.

The American road and roadside landscape are a product of our social system, an extended linear space where we contend for access, where we build and organize places, where we declare social priorities and cultural attributes. This landscape accumulates new artifactual strata through time, yet it is much more than an unconsolidated agglomeration of remnants from bygone eras that are gradually submerged beneath new accretions. The road and its landscapes are synecdoches, parts that represent the whole, places that should be interpreted as signatures or as signifying a system that encapsulates great chunks of America's being. By probing the roadside for meaning we find revealed the vestiges of American values and preferences, cultural and social processes, and the people who created them. This highway corridor contains evidence, for example, that political actions, economic strategies, and social interactions leave evidence, a representational residue upon the land. Knowing this, one should no longer travel any highway as a flaneur whose aimless and uninformed wandering is directed by little more than the desire to sense motion and experience movement, or to witness the odd or outrageous. Instead, for the informed traveler, the roadside is a tableau of places and structures laden with meanings that vividly represent the product of many political and social actions that collectively comprise important segments of American cultural history and geography.

American society is predicated upon movement. Farmers, foresters, manufacturers, miners, and other entrepreneurs move their products from hinterland or port to market. Villages and cities grow up at crossroads or at places where roads can be built to harbors or riverbanks, or at strategic interregional locations. River flatboats, canal boats, or steam trains could all move bulky cargo cheaper than road-bound wagons. Some movement is casual, some critical to business success or even human survival. Some movements are large-scale, local, and cyclical; others are small-scale, national, and unidirectional. Since 1808 and the National Road's first decade, Americans have used roads to move east to west, south to north, from farm to city, from city to suburb, from Rustbelt to Sunbelt. Movement's common denominator—the place where it begins and ends—is the road. Donald Meinig's quote of a Spaniard visiting America in 1847 illustrates this preoccupation with movement: "If God were suddenly to call the world to judgement," the visitor said, "He would surprise two-thirds of the population of the United States on the road like ants."[1]

Certainly roads, like the physical environment, do not determine human behavior but offer opportunities and options. To know America one has to

KARL RAITZ

understand how people have built their lives around the road, the access it provides and the activities it stimulates. Therefore, to know the road is to progress a long way toward knowing America. Passing along an old road, one sees history in landscape cross-section and witnesses how past values and ideas represent themselves in artifact or material form. The roadside landscape is a record of how American culture and economies developed, complex and difficult to interpret though that may be. The best place to search for the archetypal road that will illustrate how life becomes landscape is an old road—not a simple track, abandoned and backwatered, but a road with purpose, a road built in the context of nation-building, a road that would become a key part of the national highway network. That road is the National Road.

THE NATIONAL ROAD, ITS SUCCESSORS, AND THE MODERNIZATION OF AMERICA

American culture is characterized by change and transformation, and improvements in technology or alterations in political priority dramatically influence transportation. Overland travel on America's nineteenth-century roads was by carriage, coach, wagon, horse, mule, or foot. Travelers' needs were met by people who made the roadside into a trial ground for business experimentation. No one knew how many taverns and drovers' stands could be supported by National Road traffic or where, exactly, the best roadside business locations would be. People built where it suited them, the logic of travelers' needs the only direction they had. Farmers' concerns were more circumspect; by building their farmsteads adjacent to the Road they had the best possible access to the region's best highway—in poor repair and near impassable at times—and would not be vulnerable to abysmal back-country tracks. Nor did town and city residents have the advantage of planners who might advise them concerning the appropriate place for stores, churches, or residences. Only infrequently did architects provide high-style building designs and plans. More often people decided these things for themselves and the structures and land uses that resulted were a corporate product of vernacular expression.

The railroad introduced a new cycle of changes to the transportation landscape, especially within larger urban places. Livestock brokers built stockyards at rail sidings. Rail companies built passenger depots near downtown, and Main Street merchants could go to a new freight depot for daily or weekly shipments of dry goods from distant suppliers. Seeking more space to expand, and backed by a generation of business success, merchants pulled down old frame and clapboard buildings and replaced them with two- to four-story brick structures, often faced with popular Revival-style facades. Regional architects might be commissioned to design important structures: schools, libraries, banks, churches, public buildings, or private residences for the local elite. Vernacular houses and farm buildings usually remained but they were now augmented by popular or high-style structures.

Trucks and automobiles introduced another cycle of landscape change. Use railroad-oriented structures declined into abandonment. Old roadside buildings were converted to auto-related services. Blacksmiths might transform their shops into auto repair garages, for example. Businesses selling food, fuel, and lodging appeared in strips near the edge of town—vernacular structures at first, but gradually replaced by national franchises, until one could travel the length of the old National Road corridor and patronize the same restaurants, gas stations, and motels for the entire distance.

If highway engineers realigned US 40 around a town, the Road-oriented businesses often relocated to the bypass, leaving the old strip and business district to stagnate. Storefronts retained the same nineteenth-century facades but interiors lay vacant or occupied by a nontraditional business—someone might convert the old jewelry store to a shop selling antiques. Second and third floors had been apartments, professional offices, or retail space, but now stood empty, the street-front windows painted white or papered over. Should a building burn down or an unhappy owner raze an empty structure to reduce taxes, the empty lot lay unbuilt. The remaining buildings presented a gapped-toothed, vacant-eyed facade to the few Main Street passersby. When the interstate bypassed most sections of the entire National Road–US 40 corridor in the 1960s, this process was repeated, but on a grander scale. Merchants vacated 1950s automobile strip shopping centers in favor of new locations along the roads that connected to interstate interchanges, and franchise businesses dominated those places. Meanwhile, the old roadside was revernacularized and began to slide down the retail hierarchy. Once again, local people reinvented uses for abandoned roadside buildings. Few alterations to building design or form would be made; the old structure would still be recognizable as a former gas station or motel, but the property now entertained different clientele.

Conversion and reconversion—from local vernacular to national franchise or national taste, and back again to vernacular—is a predominant theme along the National Road. The roadside is temporally dynamic, a place where land use is contested, mistakes in anticipation or interpretation by local business people are confirmed by failure, or cleverness and correct guesses underwritten by success and longevity. To deny access to the highway is to enforce an isolation that is the nemesis of a dynamic national culture and economy. Change the scale and a similar process is operating—the villagers that found their settlement bypassed by the new road either moved to the new roadside or made their livings doing things that did not require direct access to modern transport lines.

Most Americans are beneficiaries of highways and so it is more useful to conceive of roads not as patronized by one American public but by many, each perceiving its relationship to roads from different perspectives and different contexts. Each group has different criteria for road use and road development and so employs a distinct "language" to articulate those interests. Each constitutes an agency that participates in the creation of road landscapes and contributes to the social life that springs up along the road and is nurtured by its continued use. How many constituency groups and how many roads can one identify? The list is lengthy but a few will suffice to illustrate the theme.

The Politicians' Road

For the eighteenth- and nineteenth-century politician serving in national office, the road was a means to consolidate national power and to take control of resource flows, gained through penetration into the country's rich interior, back east to coastal ports and power centers. Seen from a less cynical perspective, a National Road into the interior would help direct a straightforward transfer to the Northwest Territory's young and virtuous agrarian population a flow of Jeffersonian ideals upon which an American political economy could be based. Roads were tools politicians could employ to override the vagaries of Nature's geography—rivers were "natural" routes into the continent's heart but rivers did not always follow courses convenient to the direction of national expansion. The politician employs the fabulist's language; facile if need be, or allegorical and allusive if dreams are to be implanted and opinion swayed. Words like *facilitate, unite, strengthen, perpetuate, secure, imperative,* and *community of interest* found their way into the nineteenth-century political discourse about road-building. Politicians directed surveyors to take the National Road across the Appalachians by the most direct route in lieu of a suitable river. Some state or local politicians, aware of their constituents, argued to redirect the Road toward old established settlements out of self-interest, recognizing that to deprive a territory of a road was to retard, or even exclude, the process of development. The federal treasury has become an attractive target for those seeking largess, and highway construction companies, seeking to glean contracts from the government, have been cultivating their relationships with purse-controlling politicians since the National Road's inception.

The Engineers' and Laborers' Road

Highway engineers are empowered by politicians. The engineer's task is to invent and apply technologies to overcome topographic and geologic barriers. The highway engineer's language is glib and technical; it seeks to marry concerns for load and compression, shrink and expansion, angle, radius, and camber, to the building materials at hand—macadam, concrete, brick, asphalt—and reconfigure natural slopes with cuts, fills, and grades. Early-nineteenth-century engineers worried about roadway durability, resistance to erosion, and the crushing effects of wagonwheels and iron-shod horses' hooves. Twentieth-century engineers speak of superelevation, down-ramp speeds, prestressed concrete, and four-tiered interchanges whose sight-angles and speed-to-radius ratios mandate junctions that consume land in forty-acre consignments.

Laborers, on the other hand, are an anonymous group. Nineteenth-century road construction employed local men and their teams of heavy horses to move dirt and rock. Irish, English, and German immigrants were often the most numerous construction-crew members. They might follow the Road into the interior, settling in towns and on farms along the route where they raised families whose descendants still reside in those settlements. A century later, when the Road's dirt, gravel, and broken limestone surface was concrete-surfaced—about 1922 in eastern Illinois, for example—construction companies again hired local farm and town men as laborers, although they brought their own "bosses" and skilled workers from elsewhere.[2] Modern highway construction requires an experienced engineering staff, large and efficient equipment, and an experienced labor force, things a small, local construction company may not be able to muster. Consequently, large regional firms usually are successful in obtaining contracts to build new highways, and their construction crews travel long distances to reach the site. As transients, the crews often eat in local restaurants and stay in local motels (the cheap ones are on the old highway) for the project's duration.

The People's Road

Access to a highway democratizes transportation; people can travel to (or from) almost anywhere if it has a road. At the turn of the twentieth century, railroads linked major cities but served open farm country and small towns poorly. In the twenty-five years from 1904 to the eve of the Depression, over half a million miles of roads were built in the United States. Although those roads were poor, trucks and affordable automobiles soon solved the problem of short-range transportation. Highways—not trains— allowed cities to extend their trade hinterlands into the countryside.[3] The National Road was initially a linear traverse between metropolitan centers, but between 1900 and 1930 the Road was linked into a national highway net that connected cities around the compass.

While early-twentieth-century roads increasingly provided short-distance access for short-duration trips, they also became the routes of choice for great migratory movements by common people. European immigrants moved inland from coastal ports along roads. African-American migrants moved out of the South to Northern cities, many following bus routes; others drove farm vehicles and well-used cars along the road net. Great Plains Dust Bowl migrants moved to the California cornucopia in a similar manner. Appalachian migrants, too, moved out of the mountains by following the roads leading north to hoped-for industrial jobs. Their language is one of common experiences, hard times, simple pleasures, separation from family and place. Their lives, like the laborers that built the nation's roads, are seldom recorded in biographies, but are remembered in folk stories and the words of John Steinbeck (*The Grapes of Wrath*), Harriet Arnow (*The Doll Maker*), and Dwight Yoakam (*Readin,' Ritin,' Rt. 23*). "Highway 66 is the main migrant road . . . ," Steinbeck wrote. "The people are in flight, and they come into 66 from the tributary side roads, from the wagon tracks and the rutted country roads. 66 is the mother road, the road of flight." Such permanent movement constitutes personal revolution and entails high costs, especially if one is unprepared. Steinbeck continued. "Two hundred and fifty thousand people over the road. Fifty thousand old cars—wounded, steaming. Wrecks along the road, abandoned."[4]

The costs that common people incur to use the nation's highways are relative to context, but one irony in such large population movements—or day-to-day travel, for that matter—is that they would not have been possible without Henry Ford's cheap cars, nor would those cars have been practical without cheap fuel. The people's access to the American highway is tempered by the nation's Cyclopean petroleum reservoir. Cheap fuel continues to underwrite ubiquitous access; it permits long commutes, weekend trips, and Sunday drivers; it allows truck companies to function in place of railroads. And it reinforces the entrepreneurship of business folk who wish to experiment with antique shops or ethnic restaurants in small towns where the local clientele for such places is exceedingly small.

The Commercial Traveler's Road

Before the automobile and the truck, salespeople called on retailers and other clients by train or interurban, and wholesalers supplied goods via freight depots. Cars and trucks gave them much greater temporal flexibility and geographical access. "Business as travel" might have been the commercial travelers' creed. The Society of Commercial Travelers, founded in the late nineteenth century, was apparently concerned that time spent away from home might lead business travelers to stray from their ecclesiastical moorings—the society supported the Gideon Bible movement from the beginning, a Bible in every hotel and motel room. The commercial travelers' relationship with roads was couched in their language: guaranteed freshness, West Coast product, time-to-delivery, shipment date, our truck (or, simply, the Truck), overnight. Good highways meant easier travel, which shrank distance and conserved time. Such savings would soon change American geography. Any product that required special care to maintain purity or freshness, for example, could be delivered over much longer distances by hard-surface highway. Small-town bakeries enjoyed local monopoly over the supply of fresh baked goods until the highway and the truck. Regional bakeries in larger cities enjoyed the economies that accrue from automating bread production and baking thousand-loaf lots. When the bread truck delivered still-warm loaves to small-town grocery stores at dawn, at prices lower than those charged by the local bakery, the result was predictable. Small towns would stagnate without access to highways, but when the link was made their businesses would have to weather competition from a much broader area.

The Waysider's Road

Waysiders do not travel the highway but engage the people who do. To the waysider, "travel is business." They recognize travelers' needs for food, fuel, and lodging, and place themselves along the road in parasitical positions where they might minister to road users. Other waysiders position themselves at the roadside to capitalize upon the driver's preference for convenient shopping—a place to park a car without paying a fee or putting change in a meter. So many waysiders gathered at town gateways—the points where open land gave way to the first residential districts—that they created a strip of similar, competing businesses. To grab the traveler's attention, waysiders developed a simple language that they then communicated by way of imagery, signs, and symbols: Food, Eat, Gas, Motel, Shop, Store, Mart.

No one planned the auto business strip, it was a place of experiment, of trial and error. Outside larger towns the strip grew longer over time—1950s drive-ins close to the city, 1990s postmodern shopping centers at the distant periphery. Mom-and-pop vernacular roadside businesses gradually gave way to patently commercial firms controlled by regional or national management. If the highway department elected to build a bypass around the town to reduce congestion, the franchise businesses moved to the bypass, creating a new strip. Restaurant, motel, and retail chains gave more thought to proper location and placement within the strip. McDonald's became a locational bellwether—when this franchise built a new restaurant, competitors flocked to the courthouse to find the owners of adjoining property. Because traffic volume has a direct relationship to roadside land value, prices dropped along the old highway strip. Waysiders along the strip had struggled to learn the "laws" that would explain how to conduct business—which product, presentation, or position was required to be successful. The bypass changed their rules. One either moved to regain access to the high-traffic roadside (interchange or bypass) or business withered. The old strip stagnated, property values fell. Local people began to revernacularize the roadside, buying discounted buildings for creative reuse. These businesses were often no longer road-oriented, and the owners did not need to be place- or position-conscious but simply clever enough to adapt the old structure to new uses.

If this first group of waysiders purposefully sought out appropriate business locations along vital highways, there is a second group, the farmers, who no doubt constitute the largest group if measured in amount of land held along the road. Farmers tended to be ambivalent about living next to the highway. On the one hand the highway had the great advantage of being a "hard road," all-weather access to farm-related businesses—the lumberyard, hardware, machinery dealer, hatchery, creamery, egg buyer, co-op fuel dealer, grain elevator, stockyard, tire shop—in the nearby town. Otherwise, road frontage meant little to the farmer and, in the early years of auto touring, was often a major disadvantage. Before roadside parks were common, Sunday drivers ("tin-can tourists" was the derisive term for them) had the uncouth habit of parking along the road in front of a farmer's home and picnicking on the yard under a shade tree, leaving their garbage behind for the farm family to remove. Since World War II, farmers have found their highway frontage will bring a better return than corn or soybeans, and many have sold road-frontage lots to commuters. Across long sections of US 40 in Ohio and eastern Indiana, the density and form of these "rural, nonfarm" residences recalls similar linear villages in rural Quebec or southern Louisiana.

The Adventurers' Road

The canon recording the "American Experience" places adventure in chapter 1, and Americans have long associated roads and trails with adventure and exploration. In the nineteenth century, travel to distant places always bore some risk; robbers frequented some remote sections of the National Road, coaches overturned when badly driven across deep ruts, and lodging at a roadside tavern might entail all manner of discomforts. The reward was a new experience that could be encapsulated in tales told to envious friends, a new opportunity to pursue an individual dream.

The automobile put adventure further into one's own hands, and control of speed made risk a condition one could invoke by simply ignoring warning signs and admonitions from passengers, and depressing the accelerator. Traveling for adventure is not necessarily to cover a given distance or to reach a certain destination or to begin anew. It is travel for discovery, to see new places and people, to employ the freedom inherent in a surfaced road. When manufacturers installed batteries and lights on automobiles, night driving became a new and adventurous experience, and by the 1920s leisure driving, night and day, had become an American pastime.

The contemporary highway is alive with adventure drivers. Natural mechanics—those people who can fix anything without a manual—buy 1950s

The National Road in Illinois

What constitutes adventure often depends upon the context. In July 1915, the Albert M. Wilson family set out to drive the Road from St. Louis to Riley, Indiana, southeast of Terre Haute. Shown here, in the midst of their adventure, the family stops their new Paige automobile to consider the Illinois mud ahead. Telephones and electricity have come to the countryside but local people and travelers alike still struggle with roads that seem little more than tracks.

No match for the mud and standing water, the Wilsons became stuck and had to be pulled free by a nearby farmer's mule team. The steel-wheeled wagon may have been the farmer's primary utility vehicle.

or 1960s vintage cars and restore them for nostalgic highway cruising. Some are retirees who spend their pensions guiding sheet-metal houses-on-wheels from one campground to another, "seeing the country." Some hibernate until June when they appear on the highway with no itinerary other than an intent to "go north," or "head for the mountains," and so consume their hard-won vacation days with maps across their laps in rapid pursuit of "fun." Still others are bikers on Harley "Hogs," whose hippie-length hair and skull-and-crossbones appliqued jackets personify a kind of irresponsible freedom and go-to-hell attitude that modern-day station wagon–borne family folk find too wild to take seriously. Or an adventurer might urge her Porsche 911 turbo to 150 miles per hour on an isolated stretch of Indiana interstate highway just to see if the factory installed speed limiter works.

The one thing that the highway adventurer is not is a hitchhiker. The contemporary American road does not welcome those without a car or truck. If speed is a modern religion of the road, the person on foot is a heretic. We do what we can to avoid the stigma. A $30,000 automobile encumbers us with the same magnitude of debt that would have garnered a fine home a generation ago. We pay insurance premiums that, if aggregated nationally, would no doubt retire the national debt within a decade. We renew our driver's licenses punctually. We must do this for as Andrei Codrescu has observed, "The truth is that an American without a driver's license doesn't have an identity."[5] Establishing our identity requires pledging allegiance to the road so that we might enjoy the access to the opportunities, freedoms, and pleasure-seeking that it provides. We all want to be adventurers.

The National Road in Art

THOMAS J. SCHLERETH

> [The National Road affords] first-class scenes for the American painter—who . . . seizes original and really picturesque occasions of this sort for his pieces.
>
> WALT WHITMAN
> Collected Works, 1:186

WHITMAN'S OBSERVATION, BASED ON A STAGECOACH TRIP BETWEEN Cumberland, Maryland, and Brownsville, Pennsylvania, proved true throughout the National Road's history. As early as 1829 artists such as Thomas Ruckle captured the activities at Three-Mile House on the Old Frederick Road on canvas. By 1844, Marcus Mote had documented the Indiana Yearly Meeting of Friends in Richmond.

The National Road corridor has also prompted artistic re-creations of past times and places. Included in the visual portfolio that follows are Edwin Willard Deming's historical painting of Gen. Edward Braddock's defeat (1755) by the French and their Indian allies; John Matthew Heller's depiction of Abraham Lincoln meeting with Stephen Douglas; plus three other works by Carl Rakeman focused on innovations in highway technology in America.

George Beck
(1748?–1812)
View of Baltimore from Howard's Park (1796)
Oil on canvas 37" × 46¼"
Maryland Historical Society, Baltimore
Gift of Robert Gilmor

A ROMANTIC EIGHTEENTH-CENTURY LANDSCAPE LOOKING SOUTH TO THE Baltimore harbor and depicting the extensive landholdings of Col. John Howard—Revolutionary War hero, Maryland governor, U.S. senator—whose family estate, Belvedere, is pictured on the far right. Two structures, the courthouse and St. Paul's Episcopal Church, dominate the painting's middle ground. While this pastoral setting is one of Baltimore prior to National Road development, Howard's real estate holdings on the city's west side (known as Howard's Addition) would become the site of numerous hotels, liveries, warehouses, and taverns serving the National Road trade.

THOMAS J. SCHLERETH

A BUSY ENCLOSURE FRAMED BY a VIRGINIA SNAKE FENCE AND AN 1801 stone tavern with a string of outbuildings (barns, granaries, wagon sheds), the Three Mile House services stagecoach passengers, teamsters both arriving and harnessing up, and single riders—watering horses at the inn's pump, heading for breakfast, or discussing routes. Drovers move hogs, sheep, and cattle eastward to slaughter in city markets. On a spring morning (fruit trees blossoming next to the inn), a quartet of farmers work out their road tax in the left foreground while a menagerie of goats, turkeys, chickens, and dogs—plus draft animals (mules, oxen, horses)—animates processions east and west.

Thomas Coke Ruckle
(1808–91)
*Fairview Inn, or Three Mile
House on Old Frederick
Road* (c. 1829)
Watercolor on paper
25″ × 39½″
Museum and Library of
Maryland History, Maryland Historical Society,
Baltimore

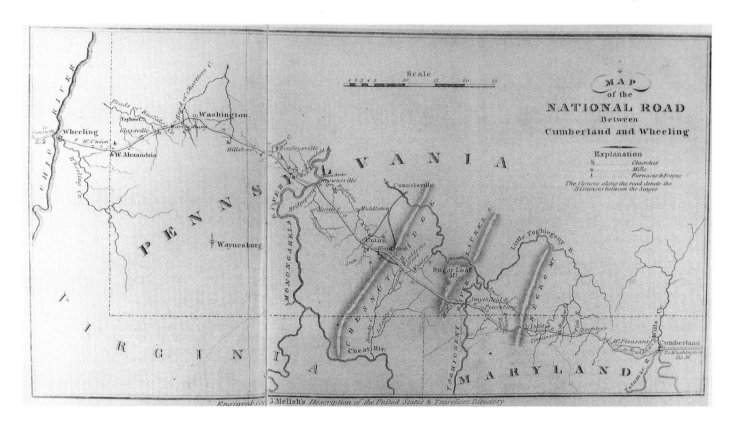

John Melish (1771–1822)
Map of the National Road between Cumberland and Wheeling (1926)

Published in John Melish, *A Geographical Description of the United States* (New York: A. T. Goodrich, 1826)

8″ × 16″

University of Illinois at Chicago

MELISH'S DELINEATION OF A NATIONAL ROAD SEGMENT IN ITS HEYDAY provided travelers with readable yet detailed topographical and cultural information. Evident are major rivers (for example, "Yo[u]ghiogeny," Monongahela, Ohio), creeks, and runs, as well as mountains (particularly Sugar Loaf and Chestnut Ridge). In addition to major settlements, one can identify western Pennsylvania's iron and glass industry (riverine forges and furnaces), saw- and gristmills, plus local churches and historical sites (Braddock's grave). Orienting the Road east (135 miles to Washington) and west (80 miles to Zanesville), the map denoted mileage figures between stage stops.

THOMAS J. SCHLERETH

To renew their state charters, several Maryland banks agreed in 1822 to finance, through a turnpike company, the completion of a ten-mile National Road segment between Boonsboro and Hagerstown. Built according to John Loudon McAdam's *Remarks on Road Making* (1816), using stone "not to exceed six ounces or to pass through a two-inch ring," the new twenty-foot-wide roadbed had three strata—each compacted with a cast-iron roller, raked, and dressed. A second National Road section was constructed (1825–30) according to McAdam's principles by the U.S. government between Canton and Zanesville (Ohio).

Carl Rakeman
(1878–1965)
*1823—First American
Macadam Road* (1926)
Oil on canvas 52″ × 40″
Federal Highway Administration, Washington, D.C.

Carl Rakeman
(1878–1965)
*1839—Our First Iron
Bridge* (1926)
Oil on canvas 52″ × 40″
Rutherford B. Hayes Presidential Center, Fremont,
Ohio

BUILT DURING THE FEDERAL GOVERNMENT'S REPAIR OF 131 MILES OF
the National Road in Pennsylvania in the 1830s, a cast-iron bridge over Dunlap's Creek proved feasible because of numerous foundries in the vicinity.
Sandstone abutment walls, an arch of nine elliptical voussoir sections, and
a macadam floor surface comprised the span. Completed on July 4, 1839,
the new bridge surpassed the technology of the covered bridge in the background. Once the Baltimore & Ohio Railroad was opened to Wheeling
(1853), the bridge's traffic was eclipsed until automotive transport gave the
span a second life in the twentieth century.

THOMAS J. SCHLERETH

With two contrasting diagonals of action—one showing British Redcoats commanded by Gen. Edward Braddock caught in a withering crossfire in open daylight; another depicting French and Indian forces firing from a foreground of forest darkness—history painter Deming dramatized the Battle of the Monongahela of 1755. Braddock, who had several horses shot out from under him during the three-hour battle, here is fatally wounded in the arm and lungs. He died four days later. George Washington, who took command of the retreat, buried him in the middle of the military road (Braddock's Road) that he and his troops had cut through the Pennsylvania wilderness and that parallels the National Road at Great Meadows.

Edwin Willard Deming
(1860–1942)
General Braddock's Defeat (1755); also known as *The Death of General Braddock* (1903)
Oil on canvas 41″ × 61″
State Historical Society of Wisconsin, Madison, Wis.

Malcolm Stevens Parcell
(1896–1987)
Henry Clay's Visit to Washington, Pennsylvania (1935)
Wall mural (detail) 4′ × 8′
George Washington Hotel (now the Pioneer Grill), Washington, Pa.
Michael Bennett, photographer

ONE OF SEVEN LARGE MURALS BY LOCAL ARTIST PARCELL DEPICTING National Road history in southwestern Pennsylvania in the dining room of the George Washington Hotel. Here Henry Clay, an ardent supporter of the National Road's extension westward and a frequent traveler to Congress through towns such as Washington, is greeted by that community's local gentry—whose likeness Parcell modeled after his family and friends from Washington County.

THOMAS J. SCHLERETH

David Gilmour Blythe
(1815–65)
The Post Office, Pittsburgh
(1859–63)
Oil on canvas 24″ × 20″
The Carnegie Museum of
Art, Pittsburgh
Purchased 1942

IN A MAJOR CITY THAT THE NATIONAL ROAD BYPASSED, EVERYONE SELF-ishly jostles everyone else, each either completely self-centered (absorbed in their own reading) or self-serving (pushing and shoving; picking pockets—one rogue with his hand in a man's trousers worn backwards). A monkey-like urchin, chewing a cigar, suggests a degenerate newsboy. Atop the General Delivery window (there was also a Gentleman's Delivery window) in the Pittsburgh post office, a classical bust of a generic Founding Father looks down on this contest of what Blythe called the urban "washed, unwashed, and unterrified."

Carl Rakeman
(1878–1965)
1925—Adoption of Uniform Signs (1926)
Oil on canvas 52″ × 40″
Rutherford B. Hayes
Presidential Center,
Fremont, Ohio

IN A SCENE REPEATED OFTEN IN TWENTIETH-CENTURY AMERICAN HIStory, the vernacular succumbs to the national as workmen uproot local, frequently hand-lettered, directional road signs, replacing them with standardized federal route (R) markers in the form of the U.S. shield. In 1925, a Joint Board of State and Federal Highway Officials numbered what had previously been named. With numerical priority given to East Coast roads, the federal system imposed a grid of even-numbered (east/west) and odd-numbered (north/south) highways on the country. The National Road became US 40.

THOMAS J. SCHLERETH

Drawn by Marcus Mote in 1844.
Repainted & enlarged 1885.
INDIANA YEARLY MEETING OF FRIENDS. 1844.
Copyright & all rights reserved.

PIONEER PORTRAIT AND PANORAMA PAINTER MOTE, ORIGINALLY FROM Lebanon, Ohio, began attending Society of Friends annual meetings in Richmond, Indiana, in 1836. Here he documents the morning arrival, via buggy and wagon, of his plainly dressed coreligionists for the year's major spiritual and social gathering. Along the National Road in Indiana, Quakers established thirty-nine meetinghouses, such as this one in Richmond, and also founded the towns of Knightstown, Philadelphia, Greenfield, Pennsville, and Plainfield along the route.

Marcus Mote (1817–98)
Indiana Yearly Meeting of Friends (1844, 1885)
Oil on canvas 18″ × 28″
Earlham College,
Richmond, Ind.

Ross Lockridge Jr.
Raintree County and *Town of Waycross* (1948)

Published in Ross Lockridge Jr., *Raintree County* (Boston: Houghton Mifflin, 1948)

Courtesy Penguin Books USA, Inc.

Rᴇᴍɪɴɪsᴄᴇɴᴛ ᴏꜰ ᴏᴛʜᴇʀ Aᴍᴇʀɪᴄᴀɴ ᴡʀɪᴛᴇʀs ᴡʜᴏ ᴄʀᴇᴀᴛᴇᴅ ꜰɪᴄᴛɪᴏɴᴀʟ geographies such as Edgar Lee Masters (Sangamon and Spoon Rivers) and William Faulkner (Yoknapatawpha), Hoosier author Lockridge located his most famous fictive work on a section of the National Road. His 1948 novel, based in part on Indiana's Henry County, provided readers with both regional and community cartography. The National Road town of Waycross, its Midwest typicality configured by a railroad station, grain elevator, post office, general store, school, and several churches, served as the stage setting for his literary portrayal of small-town life.

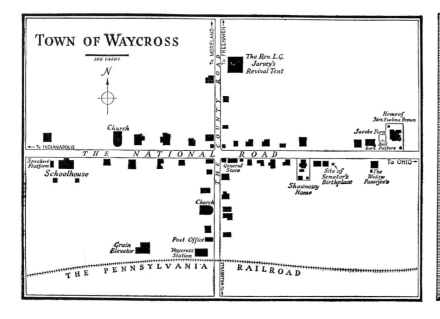

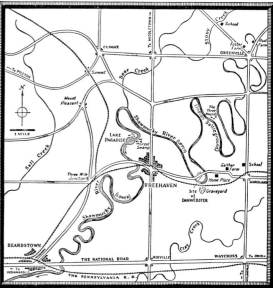

Tʜᴏᴍᴀs J. Sᴄʜʟᴇʀᴇᴛʜ

USING THE CITY'S MAIN THOROUGHFARE (NAMED FOR THE PRESIDENT and the capital city to which it led), German artist Groll choreographed its varied denizens and their activities along several blocks of the National Road to evoke the nocturnal tempo of Indianapolis in the 1890s. New city features such as electric lights, paved streets, public transit lines, telephone service, and drugstores, coexist with traditional elements of urban life: the city hall, theaters, stores, saloons, plus street vendors and newspaper hawkers, loiterers, commuters, onlookers, and shoppers.

Theodore Groll
(1857–1913)
Washington Street, Indi-anapolis, at Dusk
(1892–95)
Oil on canvas 76″ × 98½″
Indianapolis Museum of Art, Indianapolis
Gift of a Couple of Old Hoosiers

Otis Lithograph Company
*Indianapolis Motor
Speedway* (1909)
Chromolithograph
40″ × 20″
Private collection

JUST OFF US 40 IN A COMMUNITY CALLED SPEEDWAY, WITH STREETS NAMED
Firestone, Fisher, Auburn, and Hulman, is "The Brickyard," site of America's most famous competitive auto race run every Memorial Day weekend.
Founded in 1909 by Carl G. Fisher, owner of Prest-O-Lite, an auto-lamp
company in Speedway, the two-and-one-half-mile track fielded its first 500-
mile endurance test in 1911 with a winning average speed of 74.59 MPH. Indiana's most famous tourist attraction has evolved into an international
Race Week Festival that celebrates the road and those who drive it the
fastest.

THOMAS J. SCHLERETH

COMBINING TWO OF THE NATIONAL ROAD CORRIDOR'S EARLY TWENTIETH-century identities—the 1913 private highway association transcontinental route (National Old Trails Road) and the 1925 federally numbered thoroughfare (US 40)—this tourist road-guide cover also promoted progress: the triumph of mechanized, safe (no need to bear firearms), gasoline-powered (oil companies were major organizers of American private highway organizations), comfortable (no tree stumps to avoid), even chauffeured automotive transport and travel.

Anonymous
U.S. 40 National Old Trails Road (1926)
Lithographed road guide cover 8″ × 14″
Indiana State Library, Indianapolis

John Matthew Heller
(n.d.)
Vandalia, Illinois, in 1836
(n.d.)
Original painting destroyed
by fire. Image reproduced
here from Kodachrome by
Ralph Gray in *National Geographic* (December 1966)
National Geographic Society, Washington, D.C.

PAINTED TO RECREATE ILLINOIS'S FIRST CAPITOL AS RESIDENTS AND TRAVelers would have known it during the 1930s, this image no longer survives in its original mural form. A bird's-eye perspective, which once hung in Vandalia's Hotel Evans, the view depicts the city's capitol square with the state legislature (to which a columned portico has been added) in its center. In the foreground two of the state's (later nationally known) politicians meet as Abraham Lincoln, arriving in the stagecoach, greets Stephen A. Douglas, his fellow Illinois representative.

THOMAS J. SCHLERETH

One of the few chromolithographs done of St. Louis from the west with an Illinois town (later East St. Louis), the Mississippi River, and the eventual route US 40 in the background. Focusing on the fashionable Italianate mansions (center foreground) and rowhouses of the city's first private street (Lucas Place, now Locust Street), the Sachse one-point perspective also provides an idealized view of a cityscape of churches (First Presbyterian, Basilica of St. Louis), schools, and the Old Courthouse (site of the Dred Scott decision in 1846) prior to St. Louis's postbellum economic boom and its bridging the Mississippi with the Eads Bridge in 1874.

Edward Sachse and Company
View of Lucas Place in St. Louis, Missouri (1865)
Chromolithograph
18½″ × 30⅛″
The Mariners' Museum of Newport News
Newport News, Virginia

Baltimore and Washington, D.C., to Hagerstown

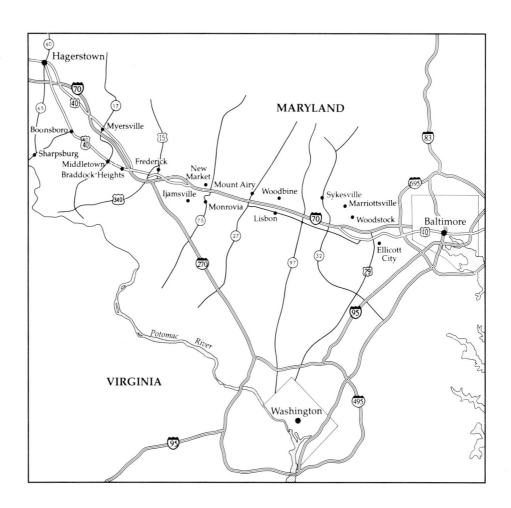

Hagerstown to Cumberland

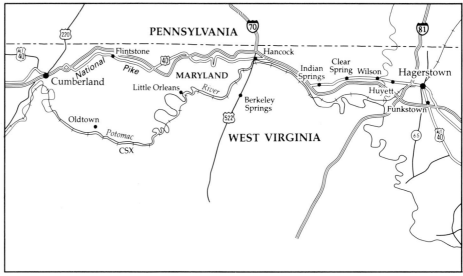

From Baltimore to Cumberland, Maryland

CHARLES J. FARMER

I was soon asked how I liked the crab; when I replied that I could get along better with him than I did with the oysters, though I could not say that I was fond of either; but if ever Mr. Holland should visit Allegany I would take great pleasure in treating him to a fine piece of a bear, or a fat buck, which I thought, if he could divest himself of prejudice, he would find to be preferable to anything that could be taken out of the salt water.

MESHACH BROWNING
Fourty-four Years of the Life of a Hunter

THE EASTERN AND WESTERN EXTREMITIES OF THIS EASTERN CONNECtion take form in the bay and the mountain. The extremes between those environments and the variations in people's attitudes and perceptions from one place to the other remain, albeit in different forms than those expressed by mountain hunter and trader Meshach Browning while dining in Annapolis, Maryland, in 1827. The Eastern Connection linking Baltimore to Cumberland was not part of the federal legislation that created the National Road. The several earlier roads that composed this 140-mile section were hurriedly upgraded to conform to the newer western road's specifications. Because these projects were financed by private capital, primarily Maryland banks, they were incorporated into the National Road system as toll roads.

The unity of the Eastern Connection has been expressed primarily through its close relationship with Baltimore. But it is also the most diverse section along the National Road's entire reach. Four themes emerge to link this unity and diversity in historical and contemporary contexts—east-to-west continuity and variation, north-to-south influences and competition, transport evolution, and topographic influences.

BALTIMORE: THE URBAN ROAD

To begin a National Road traverse in downtown Baltimore almost seems a heretical act. The National Road has traditionally been depicted more as an open, stable, rural, small-town landscape characteristically viewed from the low-angle perspectives one finds on hard-rock hills and glacial moraines. But Baltimore was the National Road's focus and profited the most from its construction. Because of this link to the Road, Baltimore expanded its trading hinterland to surpass that of its long-time mid-Atlantic rival, Philadelphia. The city's population increased from 16,000 in 1790 to over 80,000 in 1830, bringing it to parity with that of Philadelphia. The new wealth fostered by the Road during this formative period provided the basis for founding seven new banks.[1]

Although the many layers of urban modernization have obviously modified what was no more than a country road, the alert traveler may still follow the Road through the streets of present-day Baltimore. Frederick Avenue, or Maryland Route 144, is the only direct link to the original route and today seems engulfed in a maze of streets. Although not always consistent, the designation "Route 144" seems to be Maryland's way of recognizing the National Road's route where it is not supplanted by more recent highways.

From Baltimore's western city limits, Frederick Avenue is a two-way street that follows the original Baltimore-Frederick Turnpike. As Frederick Avenue nears the downtown area, it becomes two one-way streets. Pratt Street continues into the city to Harborplace; Lombard Street brings traffic out of the downtown back to Frederick Avenue. The original route into the city proper, which followed Market Street (now West Baltimore Street), cannot be followed today because of these one-way designations.

Contemporary Baltimore shares much with the National Road–era city; both periods represent important times of revitalization for the city. A true renaissance has taken place in downtown Baltimore during the past fifteen years. The city's postindustrial downtown is dominated by entertainment and tourism as exemplified by the transformation of the old Inner Harbor area into Harborplace. From the corner of Pratt and Light Streets—very close to the junction of the Coastal Plain and Piedmont—it is a short walk

CHARLES J. FARMER

to the postmodern food and shop pavilions that form the Harborplace centerpiece, to numerous new hotels and small shopping malls behind the pavilions, and to the high-rise World Trade Center, the National Aquarium, the Baltimore Arena, the Convention Center, the Maryland Science Center, and the financial district's urban canyons. It is only a slightly longer walk to the now culinary-based neighborhood of Little Italy and the Lexington and Cross Street Markets; to Federal Hill Park, overlooking the harbor, and some of the most successful gentrification projects in the United States; and to the Baltimore & Ohio Railroad Museum and the magnificent Oriole Park at Camden Yards.

The National Road brought the city sufficient wealth for its first important western expansion. Several blocks northwest from Pratt and Light, hotels, taverns, and warehouses collected to service the Road trade along present-day Paca Street between Franklin and Pratt in the Lexington Market area. The prominent hotel-taverns included the Maypole Tavern at Paca and German (now Redwood) Street, the Hand in Hand on Paca between Lexington and Saratoga Streets, the General Wayne at Paca and Baltimore, and the Indian Queen at Baltimore and Hanover Streets.[2]

Following Lombard Street and Frederick Avenue west toward the city limits one passes block after block of rowhouses, Baltimore's signature residential form. Whether housing the more affluent in the gentrified neighborhoods of Pratt and Lombard near the downtown area or the poor population that dominates much of Frederick Avenue, rowhouses present a stark yet functional high-density urban landscape. Where neighborhoods have declined—residences deteriorated and businesses boarded up—the rowhouse evokes a strong sense of unfamiliarity, which fuels the widespread fear of the modern American city.

But Frederick Avenue also has several distinctive neighborhoods that share a sense of community. The streets are usually filled with people; there are small, busy shopping centers; floating street vendors ply their trades and hawk their wares within close proximity to boarded-up businesses. The Catholic Church, with its orders, schools, and several large cemeteries, has helped retain diversity and green space, which softens urban edges.

CATONSVILLE AND ELLICOTT CITY: THE SUBURBAN ROAD

Frederick Avenue becomes Frederick Road as it exits the city and enters the Baltimore County town of Catonsville. Maryland 144 and Frederick

Turnpike are a part of this same route. Catonsville, like other western suburbs of Baltimore, is primarily a middle- and upper-middle-class community of attractive residences on well-manicured properties. The older business section, restricted primarily to a narrow strip along Frederick Road, is composed of small businesses in two- and three-story buildings.

Present-day Catonsville is the product of a long relationship with Baltimore in which business and residential neighborhoods have been shaped primarily by changing transport technology. Catonsville was originally a service point on the Frederick Turnpike. Horsecar tracks were added to the Pike in 1862. The addition of a commuter railway in 1884, the completion of trolley tracks in 1895, and the advent of the automobile in the 1920s brought the town progressively into the day-to-day activities of the city.[3]

The first arrivals from Baltimore were the very wealthy, who were attracted to the little town by its physical amenities and the cooler country setting, 400 to 500 feet higher in elevation than downtown Baltimore. This is Fall Line and Piedmont topography, which Baltimore's elite chose for their elaborate summer and permanent country estates. Although the more accessible transportation afforded by electric streetcar lines and the automobile enabled the middle class largely to supplant the elite population in most Catonsville neighborhoods after the turn of the century, their money bestowed a legacy of open park lands on the town's older sections.

The National Road leaves Catonsville, descends the Devil's Elbow to the narrow Patapsco River valley, which defines the Baltimore County and Howard County line, and follows the river briefly before abruptly crossing it into Howard County and the Ellicott City main street. Ellicott City's business district occupies a narrow, shallow gorge cut by Tiber Creek near its junction with the Patapsco. It is flanked by Courthouse Hill on the north, an acropolis site of residences, churches, and the Greek Revival seat of government; and Quaker Hill on the south, the location for additional residences and churches.

The business district is the result of the very successful union of late-twentieth-century consumerism with an early-nineteenth-century mill-town developed at the site of the falls that separate

Catonsville, Maryland

The old Hawes Inn and wagonyard stood about seven miles from Baltimore on Frederick Road. From here, wagoners could haul a load to downtown markets, unload and reload, and return to stay the night before embarking on the long trip west.

CHARLES J. FARMER

the Piedmont and the Coastal Plain. (Other Fall Line cities are Wilmington, Delaware, Philadelphia, Washington, D.C., Richmond, Virginia, and Columbia, South Carolina.) A plethora of contemporary businesses dispense a cornucopia of boutique items, specialty goods, antiques, crafts, food, and books to shoppers with sizable disposable incomes. The shops are housed in granite and brick buildings squeezed in between the narrow main street and the steep granite cliffs. We are not yet in the sedimentary limestone country of the Road's Ridge and Valley section, but in the Piedmont where the granite rocks lie just under the surface.

In 1772 Joseph, Andrew, and John Ellicott, Quaker industrialists from Bucks County, Pennsylvania, moved their entire milling operations to this Patapsco valley wilderness then known as "The Hollow." Their many industrial innovations placed the Patapsco on the cutting edge of the American industrial revolution. Fall Line rapids meant abundant water-power potential. This and the successful Ellicott mills attracted new industries. Company towns to house the rapidly increasing number of workers grew up nearby. Oella, a nearby company town founded in 1808, closed the doors on its last textile mill during the 1970s. It is now rapidly making the transition toward upscale residential real estate. The village, with its steep slopes, narrow and curving roads, and long history of water and sanitation problems, is no longer considered inaccessible and undesirable; it is now picturesque and pricey.[4]

Industrial development at Ellicott Mills, as Ellicott City was known prior to 1867, also had a powerful impact on the development of this Eastern Connection to the National Road. Initial road construction was both political and practical. The Ellicotts constructed a five-mile road to Doughoregan Manor, the country home of Charles Carroll (best known as the longest surviving signer of the Declaration of Independence), to court Carroll's support for expanded wheat production on the Piedmont. (Carroll died in 1832; the manor is not open to the public and appears to be increasingly removed from life along the Road.) The Ellicotts were also responsible for the extension of

Ellicott City, Maryland

The grain mill at the Fall Line rapids in Ellicott City provides a backdrop for boutique, craft, and antique shops along Main Street just around the corner.

Ellicott City, Maryland

Ellicott City's main street in 1936. The stone and brick buildings remain today but the first-floor shops that stood empty during the Depression are now filled with businesses that attract weekend tourists and shoppers.

Ellicott City and the Patapsco Valley, Maryland, 1859

Artist E. Sachse illustrates the popular perception of the National Road in the era of railroad dominance. The artist has removed the Road from the landscape west of Ellicott City (*left center*) and reduced the Road heading east toward Baltimore (*right center*). The business district is strikingly similar to that of present day.

CHARLES J. FARMER

that road west to Frederick to capture the interior wheat trade, and the development of Frederick Road eastward to their dock facilities in Baltimore. During the construction of the road to Doughoregan, the Ellicotts converted a wagon into a mobile kitchen to feed the road workers. They also developed a larger wagon brake to increase the safety of travel on downhill grades.[5]

Despite the many changes over time—the destructive floods that are endemic to the region, new industrial technology, and economic cycles—Ellicott City's appearance changed little between the mid-nineteenth century and the 1960s. It reached its peak industrial development as the dominant flour-milling center in the United States during the first half of the nineteenth century and then began a long decline. The city had become a seedy town with a bad reputation when a redevelopment plan was initiated during the 1960s to capitalize on its early-nineteenth-century landscape that had been frozen in time. The plan's success was assured with the rapid expansion of Baltimore's upscale western suburbs and the development of Columbia, a nearby planned community developed during the mid-1960s by the Rouse Company, which later renovated Baltimore's Inner Harbor. Columbia did not exist when the plan to revive Ellicott City was launched; today it has over 85,000 inhabitants and is internationally known for its design and planning schemes.

Frederick Road continues west from downtown Ellicott City through a high-density modern residential area and joins US 40, also known as the Baltimore National Pike, for a short distance before breaking off to become a separate road, the National Pike, heading west across the Maryland Piedmont toward Frederick. The strip development of shopping centers, service stations, and fast-food establishments along US 40 suggests that the contemporary Ellicott City is more than a nineteenth-century milltown with a 1990s business district dominated by tourists and boutiques. US 40 is the primary commercial area for a growing town of more than 40,000 people, an almost fivefold increase in only twenty years; Ellicott City will continue to boom for a long time, it seems.

Several roads have been built across the west Baltimore suburbs to link with or supplement the original National Road. One can best sort them out by following their courses from upper Ellicott City back into Baltimore. US 40 crosses the Patapsco River and enters Catonsville's commercial strip, a place very different from the venerable residential park setting a few blocks south on Frederick Road. The strip's centerpiece is the Double T Diner,

West Edmundson Avenue, Baltimore

The rowhouse was a popular plan in East Coast cities from the late eighteenth to the mid-nineteenth century because it conserved space and presented a uniform facade that exuded the Democratic ideal of equality. Most red-brick rowhouse blocks in Baltimore have small businesses in the first-floor corner buildings.

which has been on the northwest corner of US 40 and Rolling Road for more than 40 years. When US 40 enters Baltimore, it becomes Edmondson Avenue and eventually divides into Mulberry Street for traffic going into the city, and Franklin Street for traffic exiting the city. Interstate 70, immediately north of US 40, follows a course generally parallel to that highway before connecting with Interstate 695, the Baltimore Beltway.

The Old Frederick Road, the original east-west road that connected the backcountry to Baltimore, is immediately north of I-70. After crossing the Patapsco near Ellicott's Upper Mills, a place known as Hallofield today, it becomes Johnnycake Road ("Johnnycake" was the name of a tavern apparently known for its cornbread; it stood on the present site of Catonsville and provided the original name for that Baltimore County town), which closely follows the interstate until it veers sharply south to join US 40 in Catonsville. It follows 40 into Baltimore, then reemerges as Old Frederick Road and follows a separate and diagonal southeastern course to connect with Frederick Road at the intersection of Caton and Hilton Avenues. Another Old Frederick Road designation, separating from Frederick Road in the Devil's Elbow area to follow Rolling Road into US 40, suggests that the two early

CHARLES J. FARMER

roads between Baltimore and Frederick originally became one road for the descent across the Fall Line into Baltimore.

ELLICOTT CITY TO FREDERICK: PARALLEL LINES AND PAIRED PLACES

The National Road enters its more characteristic landscape as it moves westward from Ellicott City toward Frederick. This is an expansive country partially filled with farms and distinctive linear road villages that reside on the rolling plain and gentle hills that have developed on the Piedmont's ancient igneous and metamorphic rocks. Although pleasant, even peaceful, this is not a simple pastoral landscape. Widely scattered housing developments featuring massive houses on large properties and a proliferation of horseriding stables and academies are the harbingers of extended suburban expansion from Baltimore.

The numerous roads that radiate from the National Road in Baltimore and its suburbs reappear in the countryside. The Road breaks from its short union with US 40 in Ellicott City and continues alone as the National Pike and Maryland 144 through the villages that it helped develop. Cooksville, Lisbon, and Poplar Springs are Pike towns that lie within the southeast-flowing Patuxent drainage system; Mount Airy is at the divide between the Patapsco, the Patuxent, and southwestern flowing Monocacy systems. New Market, farther west, is on the Monocacy drainage. I-70, north of and parallel to the National Pike, links with US 40 just past the Ellicott City strip and they continue as the same road throughout this section. Old Frederick Road, although modified considerably (now Maryland 99), is on the north side of I-70. It parallels the other two roads until it crosses the interstate and intersects the National Pike at Poplar Springs. It does not appear as a separate highway after this point, apparently following the same course as the National Road all the way to Frederick.

The Baltimore & Ohio Railroad track (now CSX) is farther north along the Patapsco Valley, and completes the complement of parallel transport lines. This is the original route the track followed beyond Ellicott City and its promise of economic development stimulated town development much like the National Road had fifty years earlier. Woodstock, Marriotsville, Sykesville, and Woodbine on the railroad were paired with Cooksville, Lisbon, and Poplar Springs a mile or two south on the Road; and railroad villages Monrovia and Ijamsville were paired with New Market on the Road still farther west. Both village groups had modest summer resort functions for a short time which were presumably supported by Baltimoreans seeking relief from the city's oppressive heat. Unlike their roadside counterparts, the railside villages also had industries, primarily flour mills and sawmills, capitalizing on the proximity of water power and railroad.

Although predisposed to eventual stagnation and decline, the presence of these Road and rail village pairs worked against the long-term development of larger towns in the area. The rail settlements siphoned business from the Road towns, reducing their trade areas, but could not accomplish a complete takeover because the older places serviced the trade traffic that continued along the Road.

Today, the Road town's character—physical dimensions and number of structures—varies little from its mid-eighteenth-century counterpart. Cooksville, whose 500 inhabitants may be attributable only to suburban expansion, has only one business, a tavern. Ironically, it is located adjacent to the structure that contained Robert's Tavern, a former stopover on the Pike. The original tavern is now a residence. Poplar Springs, with a population of 200, has only one remaining business. Lisbon, laid out on one of the more extensive level areas along the Pike, has retained more of its service functions. Its size, 900 people, suggests stability, a characteristic not shared by the abandoned and badly deteriorated Lisbon Hotel, a remnant from wagon days. Open farmland along this Road section is often given over to small hobby farms where Baltimore residents keep horses for recreational riding.

When Maryland 144 intersects with Maryland 27, turn right; go under the I-70 bridge; turn left at the first traffic light, past the McDonald's restaurant and the old watertower on the hill into Mount Airy. Turn left (or west) at the first light onto Ridgeville Boulevard, which is the old National Pike. The Baltimore & Ohio rail line appears on the left and parallels the high-

New Market shops

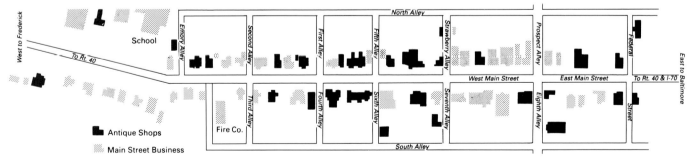

way on and off. The Road remains organic here, that is, it emulates the land surface's every contour. Just east of New Market, at Pleasant Valley Road, the Highway 144 sign appears.

The concept of paired places is not restricted to the relationship between Road and railroad settlements. Both Lisbon and New Market have new, larger shopping areas beyond their village limits which provide goods and services to an expanding commuter population. Primarily because of topography and possible flooding, the railroad towns of Sykesville and Woodbine have long had separate commercial and residential districts similar to those in Ellicott City. In recent years, primarily in response to new residential areas created by Baltimore commuters, both villages have also developed small shopping centers on adjacent uplands.

New Market, Maryland

Blooming dogwoods and daffodils, boxwood hedges, and wrought iron fences all add refinement to New Market's historic West Main Street neighborhood.

Although new commercial development has generally avoided the Road and railroad towns, there are nevertheless two important exceptions—Sykesville, the rail town that is attempting to emulate Ellicott City's rehabilitation, and New Market, the consummate nineteenth-century Road town. Sykesville is the largest Patapsco rail town, and has begun to make some progress toward attracting the type of consumers that now frequent Ellicott City. New Market is the most specialized place in Maryland west of Ocean City, the coastal resort. It is all about antiques, especially antiques for the serious collector unafraid of market prices. And no place along this Road segment has so aggressively taken advantage of its National Road location.

New Market seems little changed from a nineteenth-century Pike stop and local rural trade service center. The entire village is on the National Register of Historic Places. Both row- and detached frame and brick houses contain specialized collections of furniture, jewelry, toys, and books. Other associated businesses—general antiques with a variety of goods and price ranges, quaint bed-and-breakfast establishments, restaurants, and specialty shops—illustrate how small towns can reestablish links with urban and suburban populations by specializing their medium of consumerism to include place as well as commodities.

New Market is an element in what Peirce Lewis has called the "Galactic

Metropolis" that is sweeping across this National Road countryside.[6] Superficially, it retains the image of a place frozen in time, and every effort is made to prevent any thawing. Residents and business owners protect its presentation as a classic nineteenth-century Road town just as vigorously as Williamsburg guards its "authenticity" as an eighteenth-century colonial capital. New Market has managed economic growth without building structures or increasing population. The population, hovering just above three hundred for the past fifty years, is less than during its period of decline during the late nineteenth century.

FREDERICK TO MIDDLETOWN: PLACE PIRACY

The National Road had traditionally been defined in terms of its role as an east-west route linking Baltimore to its central Maryland hinterland and beyond. Although there have been numerous past instances of important north-south linkages across the Road—the Civil War, for instance—there had never been a serious threat to the traditional city and hinterland relationships along the Road's alignment until recently. But an invader from the south has now captured important sections of the Road and is on the brink of stealing much more of this traditional Baltimore trade area. The invasion has come from Washington, D.C., to the southeast, and the focus of succession has been Frederick.

During the past twenty years, Washington has expanded much faster than Baltimore, a triumph of political consultants over blue-collar industrial workers perhaps. I-270 is the primary expansion route to Frederick. The expansion is best illustrated by new, large, multipurpose service centers that have grown up around regional shopping malls at suburban freeway interchanges. Joel Garreau calls these centers "edge cities"; Jon Teaford and other scholars call them simply part of the twentieth-century American city, which here extends from central Washington to exurbia. Recent population growth in outlying areas such as Frederick reflects more the expansion of nearby edge cities than spillover from the more distant central city. Montgomery is the affluent county between Washington and Frederick. It has six edge cities. The western Baltimore suburbs have one, Columbia, and its trade is not directed west.[7] Recent population increases in the Frederick area have been substantial. From 1980 to 1990, the town increased from 28,000 to 40,000; Frederick County reached 150,000, a gain of 35,000 for the decade.

The National Road, still disguised as Maryland 144, crosses the low Pied-

CHARLES J. FARMER

mont hills and the Monocacy River as it approaches Frederick from the east. One of the most notable stone bridges in Maryland carried the Road over the river. The Road enters Frederick via East Patrick Street. Old Frederick lies just beyond the Frederick County fairground. As the focus of a prosperous wheat and cattle (beef and dairy) farming area, Frederick has had an agricultural fair since 1822 and has used this particular place since 1867. The fairground, with its unique Spanish Revival pavilion, also provides a link with the strong agrarian traditions of the original settlers, Germans from the Palatinate and nearby Pennsylvania. Half the county's population in 1790 was German and, until the recent population influx, the Lutheran Church had the most members.[8]

As East Patrick Street enters the business district it becomes apparent that recent population growth is having an effect on the renewal of a town once in decline. Although most recent growth—and it has been extreme—has been in suburban housing and strip developments at the town's edges, downtown has followed the rejuvenation pattern that was so successful in New Market and Ellicott City. East Patrick Street, in the downtown section, is the focus of renewal, and has been renamed "Antique Walk." One block south, Carroll Creek has been ducted into cement channels to create a park-like character within the downtown; it is being extended to the east as a greenway. Beyond the creek, the old warehouse district has been revived by combining businesses from different levels of the same family—antique shops and flea markets. Although the Frederick renaissance is concentrated in a relatively small area and its functions are limited, there is a significant rejuvenative fallout throughout the rest of downtown. Frederick is also home of the Keys (after Francis Scott Key, who wrote the National Anthem), a single-A baseball team affiliated with the Baltimore Orioles, a recent reconquest of some of the port city's former hinterland.

One block west of center city, at the juncture of Patrick and Market Streets, stands the modern Frederick County courthouse. With the exception of the Allegany County courthouse in Cumberland to the west, courthouses along this Eastern Connection are usually not grand edifices for which the population holds great reverence. There are no downtown courthouse squares, for example. In Hagerstown, the next county seat west, one is likely to walk by the courthouse without recognition. The acropolis site for the Howard County courthouse here does not create a sense of prominence, only separation from the real source of power back east along the

The Jug Bridge, Monocacy River, Frederick, Maryland

A hill crest Pennsylvania barn overlooks Jug Bridge, named for the decorative "jug" (*lower right*) that contains the names of important contributors to the development and construction of the bridge and the National Road in 1807. This scene, looking west toward Frederick in 1910, captures the bridge 113 years later. The local toll house was in a building on the Road's right side.

By 1933, the Road, then US 40, had been widened with concrete shoulders and surfaced with asphalt. And although the bridge was straightened and repaired, it collapsed in 1942. The decorative jug was relocated in a park on Maryland 144 on Frederick's east side.

CHARLES J. FARMER

Patapsco and in the Tiber gorge of Ellicott City. Today, most of the administrative work, typical of an expanding suburban county, takes place in new county office buildings.

Less than a block west of the courthouse is the home of Barbara Fritchie, arguably the most famous name associated with the Eastern Connection. According to the poem by John Greenleaf Whittier, Fritchie vigorously waved the Stars and Stripes at Stonewall Jackson as he led his gray-clad troops into town. Jackson, out of respect for her loyalty and courage, and the suggested personal guilt of betrayal to his true flag, took no action to confiscate the flag or punish this brave woman. The authenticity of this story has never been proven, but native residents of Frederick hold it to be fact.

The most relevant part of the poem rests in the first few stanzas. They explain the positive perception of Frederick over the course of time, and especially the recent growth that has attached it to Washington.

> Up from the meadows rich with corn.
> Clear in the cool September morn.
> The clustered spires of Frederick stand
> Green-walled by the hills of Maryland.
> Round about them orchards sweep
> Apple and peach tree fruited deep.
> Fair as a garden of the Lord
> To the eyes of the famished rebel horde.

At its intersection with US 15 North (the road to Gettysburg) on the west side of Frederick, the National Road becomes the sole possession of US 40, which has left its long union with I-70 to return to slower traffic as the Baltimore National Pike. But instead of returning to the pastoral countryside as the Pike leaves Frederick, one meets with another edition of modern urban sprawl. Along the Pike's first mile as US 40 lies the "Golden Mile." The Pike here is a six-lane "Main Street" highway and it traverses the most intensely developed modern commercial strip in the Eastern Connection west of Baltimore. Traffic intensity is increased by numerous subdivisions that provide a backdrop to the varied and tightly packed businesses along the Pike. Until the 1970s, the Golden Mile was a two-lane highway accompanied only by pasture land and—a sure sign of impending suburbanization—a large nursery. It is appropriate that Frederick's westward expansion follows, as it were, Braddock's Road, which originated here.

At the Golden Mile's western edge the Road becomes Alternate 40 (take Alternate 40 toward Braddock Heights), which follows a more southerly route across Catoctin Mountain—a low eastern arm of the Blue Ridge—to Middletown through a 200-year-old Euro-American cultural landscape. US 40 (not Alternate 40) follows a more direct northerly course across the mountain. Here is the Barbara Fritchie Restaurant, a diner-type restaurant situated just beyond the "Golden Mile." I-70 follows a middle course across Catoctin Mountain.

Braddock Heights, with a population approaching 5,000, stands at the summit of Catoctin Mountain on Alternate 40. The present town is the product of the mountain site's physical amenities and urban sprawl from Frederick. Braddock Heights began as a planned resort in 1896. The development of an interurban trolley line that linked the site with Frederick and Hagerstown to the west provided the impetus for the development of this narrow, breezy ridge, with its spectacular views and wholesome fresh produce from the farms of the Middletown Valley to the west. Only the large two- and three-story cottages, with their expansive wraparound porches and abundant windows, and the skating rink remain from the complex that included hotels, an observatory, and a large amusement park. Today, the cottages are residences that stand among more recent homes in a very attractive residential setting that suggests a smaller version of Catonsville, a place with similar site and situational credentials.[9]

Suburban sprawl continues along Alternate 40 the three miles into Middletown, the Middletown Valley's primary focus since its creation in the 1760s. Middletown, a neat and attractive place of 1,800 inhabitants, presents a Norman Rockwellian image of the ideal American small town. At its eastern end stand several prominent and well-maintained homes of varied architectural styles, although predominantly Victorian, whose size suggests the presence of nineteenth-century robber barons. The Lutheran church spires loom above the business district and the many small businesses suggest a decades-long commercial decline. The town's west side contains primarily plain, well-maintained frame houses, although a new housing development attests to the range of commuter expansion from Frederick to Washington D.C., and Baltimore.

Most suburban development and sprawl in the Middletown Valley occurs along the Frederick-to-Middletown corridor on Alternate 40. Development along US 40 and I-70 is restricted to the valley's extreme eastern edge and

CHARLES J. FARMER

Catoctin Mountain along these routes remains undeveloped. Farther away from Alternate 40, the battle between developers pushing suburban expansion and farmers trying to control their rural landscape is, for the moment, being won by the dairy farms.

MIDDLETOWN TO HAGERSTOWN: A MIDDLE GROUND

The Road from Middletown to Hagerstown is a geographic and ideological middle ground. Because it lies roughly halfway between Baltimore and Cumberland, it shares the archetypal landscapes from the countryside both east and west from this section. But individual landscape elements here exhibit a blending of influence rather than the pure form, and so the composite is more muted in tone. Its position as middle ground between north and south, however, is more sharply defined.

Four miles beyond Middletown, Alternate 40 ascends South Mountain, which is the Blue Ridge's westernmost arm (Catoctin Mountain was the eastern arm), and crosses the Appalachian National Scenic Trail at the summit before descending into the limestone-floored Great Valley, which extends from eastern Tennessee to New York's Lake Champlain and beyond into Canada. The valley provided a broad north-south routeway along the Appalachians through Washington County. Germans from Pennsylvania followed the valley southward to settle and develop the valley's fertile soils, and by 1790 Germans comprised more than half of the county's population.[10]

This section was also geographic and ideological middle ground during the Civil War. Settlements, most with divided loyalties between the Union and Confederacy, were captured and relinquished almost daily as the two armies moved back and forth between northern Virginia and southern Pennsylvania. The county was the site of a major confrontation—"Bloody Antietam" National Battlefield is just ten miles south of Hagerstown.

US 40, Alternate 40, and I-70 continue across this section to Hagerstown. Although each route continues independently across the Middletown Valley, over South Mountain, and into the Great Valley, they possess very different personalities.

Alternate 40, the National Road here, follows a more winding course characteristic of an older road, and attendant to it is a more developed landscape. The National Road crosses South Mountain at Turner's Gap, the site of several points of interest—the first monument to George Washington, the Appalachian Trail, and South Mountain Inn. The inn, built of local sand-

East of Funkstown, Maryland

Family businesses and their vernacular signs abound along the National Road. A [Christ]mas Tree Farm—the handcarved sign has been broken off—on the limestone-floored Great Valley. The admonishment to call to purchase a sheared white pine is enforced by a woven-wire fence topped by a strand of barbed wire.

Restaurant in Hagerstown, Maryland

The vernacular reclaims the commercial. The roadside is a place for business trial and error. The locally owned El Paso 2 Mexican restaurant converted a former Rax chain restaurant building and added a spectacular wall mural.

stone, was a former National Road service point. Although it is very old, perhaps constructed in the late eighteenth century, and has undergone numerous changes, today it is a beautiful upscale structure whose services are not readily affordable to the same type of transient population that supported it in the past.

Boonsboro lies just west of South Mountain, where it marks the last settlement on the Baltimore and Frederick Turnpike and the beginning point for the Hagerstown and Boonsboro Turnpike.[11] (Travelers who follow the National Road west to Indiana will notice a resemblance between Boonsboro's overhanging porticoes and those in Greenup, Illinois.) The latter Pike, the first macadam road in the United States, provided the final link in the Eastern Connection of the National Road when it was completed in 1823. Although Boonsboro's population, now at 2,500, has been increasing steadily for several decades and many new housing developments have been spawned, the business district does not appear to share fully that growth.

Six miles beyond Boonsboro, and adjacent to the southern city limits of Hagerstown, stands Funkstown, whose entire history has been marked by political and economic competition with Hagerstown. Funkstown's fate was sealed when Hagerstown was made the seat of government for Washington County at its creation in 1776. Originally known as Jerusalem, Funkstown's street grid suggests its early ambitions to county-seat status; all the other small towns and villages along the Road have the simpler linear street pattern characteristic of National Road towns. Approaching Funkstown

CHARLES J. FARMER

from the east one will notice limestone outcropping in the fields, the steeply pitched beds generally paralleling the trend of the ridges; also notice the Pennsylvania-German bank barns with limestone-faced gable ends, and the smaller English-style barns, as well as occasional limestone walls built to form animal lots around the barns. Funkstown's main street (Baltimore Street) is very handsome indeed. Alternate 40 is a left turn at Baltimore Street.

US 40, the northernmost of the three roads, follows a more direct though hilly course across the Middletown Valley. After its brief encounter with the valley's more developed eastern section, this road is usually flanked by woodland, suggesting that it was constructed through farm woodlots, which created a park-like setting in the process. US 40 bypasses all towns and only rarely does one find along it a cluster of houses or a stream-side farmstead. At the western base of South Mountain, the road is accompanied by a more developed cultural landscape that ranges from late-eighteenth- and early-nineteenth-century communities, focused on streams and fringed by woods

Locust Point Market, Hagerstown, Maryland

When roads follow metes and bounds survey lines, sharply angled field and town lot shapes are one result. The mansard-roofed market building stands at a "point" where the road to Antietam joins the city's street grid. This scene, looking north on Maryland 65 (Hagerstown Pike) is visible on one's return from a side trip one might take to Antietam Battlefield.

Antietam Battlefield Diptych—Confederate Perspective

The Burnside Bridge as seen from the Georgia side.

and fields, to the treeless plains and hills of recent housing developments. Finally, at the eastern entrance to Hagerstown, it becomes an auto-oriented business strip.

I-70 follows a direct middle course westward. Unlike US 40 and Alternate 40, it follows a more open landscape. From the base of South Mountain westward across the Great Valley to Hagerstown, the road passes a large number of early-nineteenth-century farmsteads with attractive stone farmhouses and bank barns that have been converted to commuter homesteads. Several large functioning farms contain older farmhouses and barns, but also have silos and other modern additions to support the demands of contemporary agriculture.

Hagerstown, originally known as Elizabeth Town, is best entered through the US 40 portal rather than the ill-defined Alternate 40. Follow Alternate 40 out of Funkstown, crossing Antietam Creek just outside of town. After entering the Hagerstown corporate limits, take the first right beyond the railroad track onto Eastern Boulevard. Bear right at the first intersection onto Memorial, which will intersect with US 40, here a dual highway. US 40

CHARLES J. FARMER

follows the one-way Franklin Street west through blocks of blue-collar brick rowhouses that serve both as residences and small businesses. The business district aligns with Washington Street, which also carries the east branch of US 40 through town. At first glance, the commercial district appears attractive and prosperous. But many buildings are unoccupied, even on the downtown square formed by the intersection of Washington Street with Potomac Avenue. Hagerstown has lost most of the industry that brought its past prosperity. The most critical losses have been in truck and aircraft manufacturing that employed large numbers of workers. Yet it does not suffer from the isolation and economic depression of its Appalachian neighbors to the west. It occupies a middle ground, between Frederick and Cumberland, and its location at the junction of two major interstates (70 and 81) is a drawing card for future prosperity.

This section of the Great Valley also was a middle ground during the Civil War. For the Confederate and Union armies the valley was a corridor that allowed relatively rapid movement and they fought bloody battles here to

Antietam Battlefield Diptych—Union Perspective

The Burnside Bridge as seen from the Union side.

control strategic sites. The Antietam National Battlefield lies about twelve miles south of Hagerstown along Maryland 65, the Sharpsburg Pike. A side trip to visit the site will help place into context the landscapes through which the National Road passes.

HAGERSTOWN TO CLEAR SPRING: COMMUNITY THROUGH SPACE AND TIME

Despite being bypassed by I-70 and competition from nearby places where groceries and services can be found, the ten-mile stretch of the Road between Hagerstown and Clear Spring is not a bypassed society. Some structures along this densely populated section are commuter residences—termed "rural nonfarm" by the federal agricultural census—which tightly hug the National Pike. Others may be residential or one of a variety of businesses that, despite diversity, maintain a strong sense of community. Farm pastures and fields open the landscape and separate its elements, further diversifying this portion of the western Great Valley. Culturally, this is a very rich section of the Road, one that maintains a palpable sense of early settlement. Numerous surviving eighteenth- and nineteenth-century farmhouses and taverns of Georgian-inspired, Classical Revival, and Victorian architecture sit beside twentieth-century split-levels, ranches, ramblers, and Cape Cods. Interspersed are well-maintained modern taverns, restaurants, grocery stores and markets, and other small businesses. The past is not being pushed aside or destroyed for progress. But neither are older buildings set aside as special, sterile museum pieces. They are occupied as residences or businesses.[12]

Most, but not all, older structures are concentrated in relatively short stretches along the Road separated by longer expanses of primarily twentieth-century structures. Older buildings are concentrated in three communities—from east to west, Huyett, Wilson, and Shady Bower.

Huyett is immediately west of the Maryland 144–US 40 junction, about three miles from Hagerstown. US 40 replaces 144 at this point. As US 40 continues west along the National Road into Huyett, it passes several important old stone structures—a large, immaculate mid-nineteenth-century farm, several well-maintained early-nineteenth-century residences, and Newcomer's Tavern, a service point during wagon days, now a craft and sewing shop. Amid the old buildings is a 1950s restaurant with an attendant small motel. Across the Road from the restaurant is a modern tavern.

CHARLES J. FARMER

Wilson Bridge

The Conococheague Creek flows south across the limestone-floored Great Valley and, a few miles below the Wilson Bridge, joins the Potomac River at Williamsport, a Chesapeake & Ohio Canal town. The bridge linked two separate turnpike companies and is a reminder of the high level of esthetics, engineering, and craftwork associated with the Road's construction.

The Huyett community's focus is the intersection of US 40 with Greencastle Pike. At the intersection's northwest corner stands Sheetz's—found from western Pennsylvania to Harrisonburg, Virginia—a regional version of the 7-Eleven convenience store chain. Although one finds a blend of old and new along this Road section, this particular business is really a reincarnated equivalent to a tavern on the early Pike. But its bold red, yellow, and orange colors are intended only to attract potential customers. The color explosion on this simple square form in concrete block, glass, and plastic stretches one's aesthetic tolerance to the limit.

Wilson, three miles west of Huyett, contains three impressive historical institutions. The primary one is the stone, five-arch Wilson Bridge, constructed in 1819 to span Conococheague Creek and to connect the Hagerstown and Boonsboro Turnpike with the Cumberland Turnpike. Although functionally replaced by a new bridge on US 40 during the 1930s, Wilson Bridge continued to carry traffic until 1972, when it was closed for safety reasons. The bridge narrowly escaped demolition in the summer of 1983, but preservationists rallied to save it. In an unusual turn of events, the money set aside for its destruction became the seed donation to support its renovation.

Shady Bower east of Clear Spring, Maryland

Sheafs in brick. To ventilate the hayloft and threshing floor in a Pennsylvania forebay barn, the bricks in the gable ends were often spaced in decorative patterns. The triangle, diamond, and sheaf of wheat (at the bottom just above the attached shed roof) were popular designs.

A reincarnation of an old institution stands adjacent to Wilson Bridge on the Road's north side. The renowned Hagerstown Speedway, billed as the "fastest dirt track in the East" for "midget" racecars, continues a tradition that began when carriage owners once raced their horses on roadways and flat tracks throughout the region. Races attract drivers from several adjoining states and fans begin arriving the day before important races to claim camping spaces.

On the southwest side of Wilson Bridge is the Wilson Country Store, established during the 1850s and still operating. It sits on an original strip of National Road that was bypassed when the highway was straightened during the 1930s, the same process that bypassed Wilson Bridge in the 1970s. The store stands in a building cluster that includes residences, a bank barn, a church, a school, and a post office.

Approximately three miles west of Wilson is Shady Bower. US 40 enters the community by following a narrow course between two early-nineteenth-century taverns; both the white brick structure on the north side and the stone building on the south are now private residences. East Stafford Farm, with a brick residence and a large bank barn, is a working farm at the intersection of US 40 and Cohill Road. The community's primary commercial structures are a grocery store and gas station.

On the Road's south side, between Wilson and Shady Bower, stands an incredible farmstead owned by the Hamby brothers, its eighteenth- and nineteenth-century features still largely intact: springhouse, summer kitchen, garden, brick Federal-style house, and a brick-end Pennsylvania bank barn. Just beyond, St. Paul's Church stands on a hill. The church, organized in 1747 at a location closer to Conococheague Creek, is an example of community consolidation; both United Church of Christ (Congregational) and Lutheran congregations hold their services in the building.

Although Clear Spring is the last village on the Road in the Great Valley, it seems disconnected from the smaller communities to the east, a role appropriate to its transitional location between Road sections. This village of approximately 500 inhabitants continues to reflect its early association with the Pike. Brick and frame rowhouses, duplexes, and detached structures,

CHARLES J. FARMER

both residential and businesses, stand together in a very tight linear pattern along the main street. Although an interchange just to the south links this place with I-70 and provides the local population with easy access to larger towns, the village contains only small businesses and thankfully sends no significant sprawl into the countryside.

CLEAR SPRING TO SIDELING HILL: TRANSITION ZONE

The Pike section from Clear Spring to Sideling Hill is a transition zone between the east—with its more developed open lowlands and sense of community—and the west—with its less developed, mountainous topography and greater separation of population. There is also a strong historical precedent for this section's transitional character. It was a transition zone during the French and Indian War when forts were constructed in this area to defend settlers from potential Indian attacks that would come from the western mountains. Fort Frederick, a large structure with impressive stone walls, stood a few miles south near the Potomac. It has been reconstructed and now stands in a state park named for it.

US 40 west of Clear Spring moves into the eastern part of the Ridge and Valley, a region of intensely folded sedimentary rocks that form north-south trending sandstone and quartzite ridges and shale and limestone valleys. West of Clear Spring the region's mountainous topography is less pronounced, and only Fairview Mountain stands out. Fairview was an important place of refuge for Clear Spring residents during the Civil War. When Confederate troops occupied the village, Union sympathizers headed for the safety of the mountain; when Union troops took possession, Confederate supporters sought the mountain's protective heights. With support equally divided between adversaries, and with the constant movement of troops in the area, there was a lot of traffic on the Pike.[13]

Fairview Mountain was also the site of several facilities that serviced Road travel and some of these have survived. The Old Stone House, constructed of local sandstone, stood immediately west of the summit on the north side of the road; it is a private residence today. On the summit's east side are a few remaining sandstone tourist cottages from the early automobile era.

US 40 unites with I-70 west of Indian Springs. Together they follow the defile cut by the Potomac River. Across the river to the south is West Virginia. Just to the east of Hancock the roads again separate at Stanley (take I-70, exit 3). Maryland 144, revived once again, follows the National Road through Hancock. I-70 bypasses Hancock and turns north into Pennsylvania to join the Pennsylvania Turnpike at the Breezewood portal. The newly constructed I-68, the National Freeway, carries interstate traffic from here westward. The designation "National Freeway" originally referred to US 48, named in 1976 as the constantly modified transition highway representing the evolution of old US 40 into I-68.

Hancock, with a stable population of 1,900, stands at the narrowest north-to-south point in Maryland's western panhandle, only one and one-half miles wide. It has been an important transportation center throughout most of its almost 250 years. Both the original National Road and the Chesapeake & Ohio Canal pass through town, and the CSX Railroad is just across the river in West Virginia. With the decline or displacement of these transport lines, and with a limited hinterland in the far western part of Washington County, Hancock is not likely to experience any renewed growth, thereby

CHARLES J. FARMER

extending its pre–World War II downtown into a new generation. This seems acceptable compared to the conditions that one traveler experienced in 1879 as the decline of the National Road had descended over the community. "Hancock, which was one of the busiest villages on the road, is now lugubriously apathetic, and the citizens sit before their doors with their interest buried in the past. The main street is silent, and the stables are vacant."[14]

Maryland 144 follows the old Pike's path west of Hancock through four miles of hilly country that sustains numerous apple orchards. An old toll house sits on the highway's north side opposite Locker Road, the entrance to Tonoloway State Park. Farther west, also on the north side, is the extensively altered version of "Old Mr. Flints House," where, of course, George Washington stayed overnight in 1769. The Oliver House, possibly an early inn, three miles west of Hancock, opposite Orchard Road, is a 2½-story structure whose original construction probably dates to the early nineteenth century. It now serves as a shelter for migrant workers in the apple orchards.

Maryland 144 once again disappears as it emerges from beautiful apple country and joins US 40 alongside I-68. As I-68 and US 40 head west toward the Sideling Hill cut-through, Scenic 40 appears for the first time. Scenic 40, designated a separate road during the mid-1960s when extensive route changes to US 40 were initiated, follows the course of the original US 40 constructed during the 1930s, almost two miles south of "Sideling Cut," where I-68 crosses the mountain. (Get on I-68 long enough to experience the Sideling Cut and its visitors center; then return to Scenic 40 at exit 72.)

The National Road's original course follows a narrow country road called Western Pike south of Scenic 40. At a point before Western Pike crosses Sideling Hill along a lower course than its successors stands a gate and a "No Trespassing" sign; the old Pike is closed to traffic. Part of the Road's closed portion may be viewed from the scenic overlook on Scenic 40 west of Sideling. At the point where the Road's course has been truncated is a large residence, known as Mountain House or the Harvey House, which was formerly an inn on the Pike. The original log structure was built in 1815.

FROM FRONTIER TO OUTBACK: SIDELING HILL TO CUMBERLAND

Maryland's far western mountains have always been the most isolated and the least developed part of the National Road's Eastern Connection. Although the mountains in this thirty-five-mile stretch do not approach 2,000 feet, they have nevertheless been the most critical factor in the landscape's development. The valleys in this section of the Ridge and Valley are very narrow. Valley soils here derive from shale and are much less productive than the limestone soils to the east. The first roads to Fort Cumberland avoided this area in favor of routes south of the Potomac. These roads reentered Maryland at Old Town, a few miles southeast of Fort Cumberland, a frontier settlement developed by Thomas Cresap. This section of road, then, and the countryside through which it passes, was associated with wily frontiersmen such as Cresap, fledgling military leaders such as the young George Washington, and National Road traders such as Meshach Browning, an early-nineteenth-century version of Cresap, who transported his deerskins and venison on the Pike to eastern markets. This section would see no German farming communities, nor stone farmhouses, bank barns, and pleasant linear Road villages. There was no Braddock's Road to establish a transport precedent in this area; the general and his army avoided the area entirely.

Because this section afforded the least potential for settlement and economic development its landscape is primarily a product of the Road's travelers. Changes in Road construction and alignment, and competition from the railroad, completed to Cumberland in 1842, had a greater impact here than along any other Road segment. In 1879, a traveler noted that because of a decline in road travel no hotels or taverns between Hancock and Cumberland were operating, toll houses were abandoned, and most of the population had left the area.[15]

During the 1920s, when long-distance automobile traffic came to the Road, the regrading and other improvements that accompanied the highway's designation as US 40 began to revive the region. Service centers—usually with a gas station, restaurant, and hotel—were built on the summits of each ridge to service the still-unreliable automobile. The old Road's steep grades and tight curves would quickly find the cantankerous radiators and fragile brakes and clutches. So mechanical fragility coupled with the early automobile's relatively slow speeds provided roadside entrepreneurs a captive cadre of weary and wary travelers. The spectacular views from these heights and the cool summer temperatures created a small-scale resort business here that is now expanding.

Within a few decades, a new combination of technical and social changes again forced the region into a severe decline. Initially, during the 1960s, US 40 was realigned to a straighter course or moved entirely to locations that

CHARLES J. FARMER

Sideling Hill, Maryland

Cut, fill, and bridge are the bywords of modern highway construction. The work of engineers to level a route for I-68 reveals the product of natural mountain-building processes.

bypassed mountain summits so that faster automobiles might be accommodated. The completion of I-68 dramatically finished what the bypasses of the 1960s had initiated. Not only did all the old service centers close, but most disappeared from the landscape. Today, even the reason for their existence seems a terribly archaic notion. The region's primary landowner, the state of Maryland, has converted much of the land to state forests and wildlife management areas.

That this section of the Road differs from those further east is also suggested by its magnificent portal through Sideling Hill. Here, in cutting a new route for I-68 through the Hill, engineers have exposed the Ridge and Valley's hidden structural secret and in so doing have also revealed some of nature's beauty. The cut's original hues of blues, greens, yellows, and oranges have faded to grays and rusts with exposure to the air. The Ridge and Valley mountains represent horizontal sedimentary rocks that have been warped into anticlinal or synclinal folds, like accordion pleats. Only in a cutthrough such as this one is the symmetrically folded rock revealed. Here stands a textbook example of a syncline, or U-shaped downfold, of multi-

Crest of Town Hill, Maryland

A scalloped metal roof shades benches where tourists once sat to gaze south from Town Hill. Three ridges loom in the distance. The Potomac River flows through the water gap of Sideling Hill (to the east) and away toward the Atlantic.

colored sandstone and quartzite layers. (Pull off at the visitors center for a closer view.)

One can also read a sense of foreboding in this landscape. The magnitude of the cut suggests that this topography has been a formidable adversary for a long time, especially to those who would attempt to cross it with wagons in tow. This rugged land could also be a redoubt. During the French and Indian War, forts stood along the eastern flank of Sideling Hill to guard the settlers from native attack. As you pass through the cut, the western horizon presents what appears to be an endless line of barrier ridges, with only a trace of human presence.

Scenic 40 provides access to I-68 and US 40 on the western flank of Sideling Hill and then temporarily disappears. And here the National Road reappears again as McFarland Road. Scenic 40 also reappears to parallel I-68 for a short distance and then moves north to follow the original courses of the Road and US 40 across Town Hill and Green Ridge. The restored Town Hill

CHARLES J. FARMER

Hotel is in excellent physical condition and is the best reminder along this section of the highway traffic that once followed this route. The interstate follows a more direct route through a water gap cut into the two ridges by Fifteen-Mile Creek, an easier route that surprisingly was not taken by the original highways.

Shipways once stood on Green Ridge at the junction of Scenic 40 and Green Ridge Road, and was probably the largest service center on this Road section. It was razed years ago and there is no surviving memorial to its existence.

After its seven-mile wandering across Town Hill and Green Ridge, Scenic 40 returns to I-68 at Fifteen-Mile Creek. The interstate and Maryland 144 both follow Pratt's Hollow, the short, winding valley between Green Ridge and Polish Mountain.

Near the Polish Mountain summit, a side road diverges from 144 and follows higher ground westward; this is the route followed by the original

Town Hill Hotel, Maryland

Although atop Town Hill, the restored hotel was built not to overlook one of the great views in the eastern United States, but to face the Road. Mobil gas pumps once dispensed fuel under a canopy where the sign now hangs.

The Yonkers gas station,
restaurant, and observation
tower atop Polish Moun-
tain during the early automobile era.

National Road. Today, it is a country road without a number and with vegetation threatening overgrowth from both sides. Between the 1920s and the
mid-1950s, Yonkers, a service center with restaurant and observation tower,
stood here.

The summit and west side of Polish Mountain provide a rare example of
juxtaposed roads that reveal different highway construction techniques. At
the summit, I-68 follows a deep cut through the mountain, although less remarkable compared to the Sideling Cut. The 1930s' version of US 40 (144
here), built without benefit of modern earthmoving technology, follows a
more elevated course immediately south of the I-68 cut. The older highway
follows an even more elevated path south of 144. On the ridge's flank, both
I-68 and Maryland 144 follow direct courses to the valley below while the
older route takes a more leisurely serpentine track to the bottom. In the valley the topographical positions of the three roads have been reversed. Massive amounts of fill were used to reduce the I-68 grade as it descends the
ridge. Maryland 144 follows an intermediate course; the Old Road is considerably lower than the other two routes.

Maryland 144 brings together the Old Road and the original US 40 as it
follows the narrow gap in Warrior Mountain into the village of Flintstone,
which was settled during the late eighteenth century and developed as a service point on the National Pike. The Flintstone Hotel, which opened in
1807, was built for this trade and briefly provided the primary housing for

a local springs resort. The hotel, a large structure of stucco over brick over wood, has been abandoned for years, although its exterior has not suffered appreciably.

From Flintstone, the roads follow predictable courses. The interstate follows a curving path that cuts through Martin's Mountain, an anticline composed of layers of resistant limestone. Maryland 144 generally follows the courses of the two older highways as it takes a more elevated path that curves around the mountain's edge. A small portion of the original National Road follows the general course of West Wilson Road for a short distance along a lower contour before halting abruptly at a garbage collection site. Returning to 144 from this point is accomplished by following the short span of Street Road. Maryland 144 exposes the anticline, but whether for financial or engineering reasons the new road does not expose any dramatic complement to Sideling Hill's exposed syncline. The rock quarry between the two roads, created to supply fill for I-68 construction, exposes a complex fold sequence: large anticline–small syncline–small anticline.

From Martin's Mountain summit to the Cumberland city limits, a distance of approximately twelve miles, the National Road and I-68 routes follow a sequence of compatibility, separation, and reunification. Along the way, a state park—Rocky Gap—and two wagon-era hotels, one abandoned and the other partially disguised as a modern motel-restaurant complex at the junction of I-68 and US 220 North, are the major landmarks.

Flintstone, Maryland

Where travelers were once welcomed, three "No Trespassing" signs now try to protect the aging and fragile Flintstone Hotel.

CUMBERLAND: THE END OF THE ROAD

Along a relatively flat stretch of I-68, Cumberland appears abruptly on a ridge lined with the white-frame houses of a blue-collar neighborhood. But except for the obligatory road signs, there is little indication that a city is nearby.

Traffic may enter Cumberland from the east by way of two routes. I-68 cuts through the ridge and descends into the narrow north-south valley that contains the city. Once in the valley, the interstate actually passes over the city on a long cross-town bridge. Although providing a good view of the city, the traveler should be more aware of the steep slopes and tight curves that make this section a serious candidate for the most dangerous stretch of interstate highway in existence. The danger is real, palpable, and is symbolized in Cumberland's dominant scent, the smell of burning truck brakes.

The second and preferred entry into Cumberland, Alternate 40, leaves

East of Cumberland, Maryland

The irony of bypass and replacement. The only way to appreciate the graceful line of a new I-68 bridge is from below on the old National Road (Maryland 144).

CHARLES J. FARMER

the interstate at the outskirts of town and follows the traditional National Road and US 40 routes down the ridge through a high-density blue-collar neighborhood that shows evidence of decline. This narrow, curving stretch of Baltimore Street provides the key to interpreting a complex city. Along the curving descent the traveler confronts three views that reveal the city's past, present, and possible future.

The first view, nearer the top, overlooks the smokestacks of the abandoned Kelly-Springfield tire plant—the symbol of past prominence as a manufacturing city; the city of 39,000 inhabitants in 1940, not the 21,000 of today; the primary factory and home base for several giants of industry that included the Amcelle plant of Celanese Corporation; a major rail center with tracks, roundhouses, and switching yards scattered all over town; two magnificent train stations; and more than twenty passenger trains daily as late as the 1950s.

Halfway down the hill, a second opening reveals the large and impressive courthouse—Richardson Romanesque save for the one dominant tower— and the spires of several churches on a hill beyond the downtown district. Fort Cumberland stood on this site where one now finds the symbols of community that represent the order and continuity that transcend cyclical economies. Entire blocks of Washington Street, the focus of the hill area, are on the National Register of Historic Places. The massive houses, with their varied architectural styles, provide present evidence of Cumberland's dynamic and, for some, lucrative past.

At the bottom of Baltimore Street stands the downtown mall that represented hope for the future. It appears that the city will not generate sufficient business to justify the investment. Although the area is attractive, with its brick walkway and luxuriant vegetation, many of its buildings have no occupants and there are few shoppers. Several prominent businesses have closed since the mall opened. The business district has shrunk to half its 1950s dimensions and is likely to diminish further.

Cumberland today is challenged by a heady addiction to the nostalgia of a prominent past and an inferiority complex created by several decades of economic decline. The city has interstate highway accessibility and mountain amenities, prime factors for potential economic development. And given the cacophony of ills arising from the coastal urban belt to the east, one wonders if Cumberland's residents are not fortunate to find themselves with time to assess and plan, and the resources with which to build a future.

Cumberland to
Uniontown

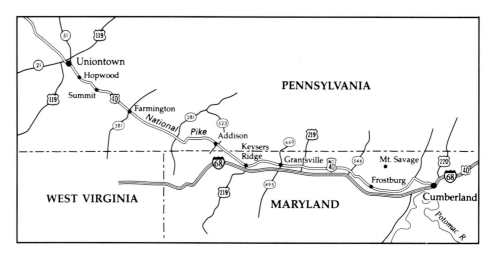

Uniontown to Wheeling

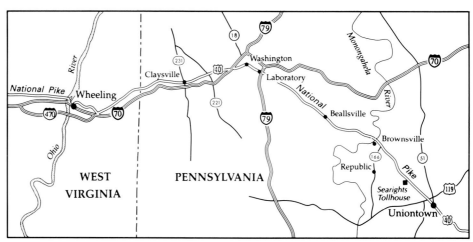

From Cumberland to Wheeling, West Virginia

KAREN KOEGLER AND KENNETH PAVELCHAK

The spirit of emigration is great, people have got impatient, and tho' you cannot stop the road, it is yet in your power to mark the way; a little while and you will not be able to do either.

GEORGE WASHINGTON
letter to Richard Henry Lee, 1784

No other section of the route, perhaps no section of any of our other highways, has been so closely connected with the great events of our history, or has surpassed this one for its actual influence upon the course of history.

GEORGE R. STEWART
U.S. 40

THIS PART OF THE NATIONAL ROAD BEGINS IN MARYLAND'S PANHANdle and ends in West Virginia's panhandle. It begins at the bottom of a sheer-walled water gap outside of Cumberland and ends on a bridge above the Ohio River, arriving in Wheeling after climbing and plunging through the corridor's most dramatic corrugations. Most of the mileage covered in this segment cuts through Pennsylvania's southwestern corner. Although not marketed as the "historic" Pennsylvania—the Liberty Bell, Valley Forge, Gettysburg, or Lancaster County's Amish—this corner of Pennsylvania forged an important part of the national identity.

In southwestern Pennsylvania, the National Road encounters the French and Indian War and the Whiskey Rebellion. The Road also connects the different theaters in which George Washington's proto-Revolutionary and post-Revolutionary careers were shaped. In this region, he became a surveyor, land speculator, transportation planner, diplomat, military strategist, landlord, and, during the Whiskey Rebellion, an uncompromising Federalist.

The Road rims the crucible of American industry—from the earliest glassworks, pottery kilns, oil wells, and iron furnaces to the plants producing Allied armaments during World War II. In one of America's most worked-over landscapes, extraction and abandonment occurred on a scale never before imagined. If these were throwaway landscapes, what of the people who worked them? The Road curves through hills pitted with company towns. Ethnic churches and cemeteries invoke images of Eastern and Southern European immigrants toiling on Monongahela River barges or in front of banks of blazing coke ovens. Places along this segment share the cycles of use, abandonment, and reuse common to the National Road, but there is an important difference. Perhaps nowhere else on the Road are landscapes of work and play, or rich and poor, so jarringly juxtaposed. All of which raises the issue of commemoration along the Road. The National Road is also a highway of memory—lined with monuments, plaques, and cemeteries. What is marked and remembered? What is the nature of the remembrance? Do the federally administered sites associated with Washington's career impart the Road's historic course, or do scattered unmarked sites connected to Uniontown coal baron J. V. Thompson better represent the region's identity? Does the National Road's story in this region remain untold in the official memorialization? If historic preservation is an effort at collective biography, perhaps this segment of the National Road traverses a region unsure of how to write its autobiography.

INTO APPALACHIAN MARYLAND: FROM CUMBERLAND TO FROSTBURG

After the National Road leaves Cumberland, it cuts through Maryland's Appalachian wedge. This is a place apart. Western Marylanders root for the Pirates and the Steelers just like their West Virginia compatriots at this stretch's other end. Settlers began penetrating the rugged tableland in the 1820s. In contrast to southern Maryland's manorial English Catholic settlement, these were German Protestants from the Palatinate and eastern Pennsylvania. Once-cleared hills are laced with company towns left from lumbering and coal ventures. The National Road pushes across the grain of the terrain, contradicting the rail short lines to the coal that wove valley settlements into a larger community. Maryland still doesn't know quite what

KAREN KOEGLER AND KENNETH PAVELCHAK

to make of western Maryland and the feeling is mutual. "Maryland doesn't want us, West Virginia won't have us, and we don't want Pennsylvania. We want a state of our own," exclaims a Garrett County car dealer.[1]

Leaving Cumberland, the decision faced is the same one faced by the Road's engineers: to proceed through the Narrows (locally pronounced "Narz"), a water gap, or climb over Haystack Mountain. The first trails— Nemacolin's track, Braddock's Road, and the National Road—climbed the mountain. After the National Road passed into the states' hands, the gap worn through the mountain by Wills Creek was used. One of Braddock's officers—a naval lieutenant, oddly enough—is usually credited with the "discovery" of the water-gap route, but surely the Indians were aware of it.

Different transport routes have sorted themselves out in this steep-sided valley on a first-come, first-served basis. The creek lies at the lowest elevation, bordered by the National Road. The B&O Railroad, forced across the

Cumberland, Maryland

Angles of transport. The B&O tracks (*right*) slice through the water gap on the way to Pittsburgh while concrete-encased Wills Creek flows south to nearby Cumberland.

creek to its opposite bank, then used Wills Creek to head north to Pittsburgh. The Cumberland & Pennsylvania (C&P) Railroad swung north of the Road, tracing Jennings Run to Frostburg and the Georges Creek valley. The Western Maryland line arrived last in the valley and climbed higher on the slope, carving its own looping contour into the hillside above the Road. A 1910 steel double-truss bridge that carried the Western Maryland cars crosses the brick C&P bridge and provides present-day excursion-train riders with a valley view.

When Cumberland's streetcar system pushed westward, farm fields became National Road front-yards. Two centers drew people from the city to the countryside in the 1890s, Narrows Park and Allegany Grove. A rural trolley ride carried revelers to the midway amusements of Narrows Park, while excursion trains transported city dwellers to Allegany Grove, a Chautauqua-influenced religious revival camp. The Road became increasingly peripheral to the web of rails that brought the "best-dressed miners"[2] of Allegany County together for work and play (though the streetcar ran on its surface between Cumberland and Frostburg). A developer bought a half-mile strip along the Road in 1909 and Cumberland's first streetcar suburb, LaVale, grew out of the farm furrows.[3] Not a bandstand or ferris wheel or board-and-batten cottage remains of Narrows Park and Allegany Grove.

Craftsman-style bungalows along a streetcar line connoted a fashionable middle-class family suburb in the early twentieth century. This is LaVale. The bungalow, a low-slung house born in California in the early 1900s, met the need for inexpensive and democratically informal housing. Along the National Road in LaVale these houses exhibit the characteristic one-and-a-half-story profile; multiple low-pitched roof lines with broad overhangs and exposed roof rafters; large porches supported by trunk-like posts; and Craftsman surfacing materials like wood shingles, brick, stone, and stucco.

Once the farmland became suburb, there was no turning back. The National Road between Cumberland and Frostburg became a corridor for development. The Road was repaved and widened during the 1950s and early 1960s and LaVale's residential expansion quickened. A full-blown strip with

KAREN KOEGLER AND KENNETH PAVELCHAK

all businesses of recent vintage—no remnants, all replacements—reflects access to nearby Interstate 68. Two 1960s shopping centers testify to the passenger car's ability to reshape land use: LaVale Shopping Center, and LaVale Plaza, which advertises itself as "On Historic Old Route 40—Your Road to Savings!" Country Club Mall on a flattened mountain top off I-68 has superseded these aging centers.

The LaVale Toll Gate House, the National Road's sole remaining toll house in Maryland, flanks a mile marker about six miles out of Cumberland. The tollkeeper collected tolls in this 1836 gatehouse until the early 1900s. An old alignment transcribes a gentle curve off the Road between the seven- and eight-mile markers as the road ascends the Allegheny Front's hummocky hills. The road's older alignment threads through tiny Clarysville, where the columned and graceful Clarysville Inn (c. 1806) and the Clarysville Motel (since 1948) bear witness to two widely separated eras. The inn served as a wagonstand and stage house to early travelers and teams. The motel—with its kidney-shaped poured-concrete pool, large sixteen-panel bay window, and soaring roof line over the office, all reminiscent of Las Vegas's growing influence on vernacular architecture throughout the United States—catered to the vacationing public of the 1950s. Most Maryland motels catered to only one segment of that public until desegregation in the 1960s. The original alignment continues west of the inn to cross Braddock Run on a single-span stone-arch bridge ("By J Murray" and "Supt J

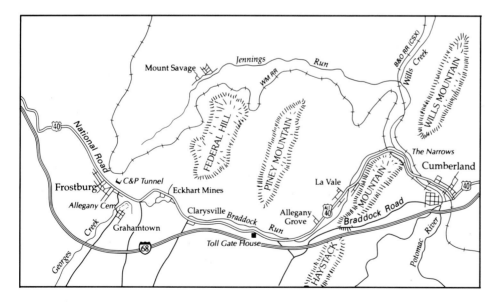

Cumberland to Frostburg

Huddleston"), rebuilt in the 1830s on Maryland's insistence that all bridges and culverts be of stone before the state would assume control of the Pike.

Proceeding uphill, Eckhart or Eckhart Mines, huddles in another crook of the road. The presence of "cole-mines" was noted as early as 1736 on a survey map. Known as the Georges Creek Coal Basin, these synclinal beds contain typical Appalachian low volatile bituminous coal renowned for steam production. The "Big Vein," a high-quality fourteen-foot Pittsburgh seam, was exploited by local farmers by 1810 and significant exports began moving by river, rail, and canal in the 1850s. When the Maryland Mining Company bought "Mr. Eckhart's pit," the scale of production changed and an influx of workers needed housing. After reaching peak production in 1907, activity declined in the basin in the 1930s when most deep mines closed. The gob piles and head frames are gone, but small stone cottages and larger frame duplexes remain in Eckhart and other Georges Creek towns as markers of this dynamic past.

FROSTBURG: A PICTURESQUE COLLEGE TOWN

Frostburg, formerly a summer resort and commercial center of the bituminous coal field, is now promoted in tourist publications as a picturesque college town. The satisfying mesh of town and site results from several factors. The town sits on a mountain spur and the National Road is its spine. The steeples of several churches located on Main Street, which the National Road becomes, buttress this verticality. The commercial center remains remarkably intact: few "holes" punched in the urban fabric, little alteration in the handsome brick facades above street level, and a pleasing sense of enclosure as the buildings ascend the hill. Most of the commercial buildings and churches are brick. An important early local industry, brickworks operated both in town and in the valley to the north. The Mount Savage inventor who discovered a one-step process for firing and glazing brick—a prizewinner at the 1904 St. Louis World Fair—took the secret to the grave, but some Frostburg buildings and pavements sport the glossy bricks.

Horizontal mineshafts follow coal seams beneath Frostburg and completely undermine the area. The C&P railroad tunnel also bores directly under Main Street, connecting mines in the Georges Creek district with the B&O in Cumberland and markets to the east. Beginning in 1795, Josiah Frost presciently selected parcels to plat the town in the National Road's path. Josiah was also among the first to recognize the area's industrial potential, for his 1813 will tells his heirs of a coal mine.

KAREN KOEGLER AND KENNETH PAVELCHAK

Frostburg, Maryland
Field of daydreams. Far from the unremitting urbanism of Camden Yards in Baltimore, small towns luxuriate in openness, overgrown ditches, and unassigned space.

Entering Frostburg from the east on Alternate 40, the road first passes through a residential section fronted by a WPA-built stone retaining wall with sawtooth coping. Turreted residences and Greek Revival houses once occupied by mine officials date from the coal industry's heady days. A right turn at Depot Street, at a former Buick dealership with a canopied entry (now D & S Cleaners), and a steep plunge down the hillside leads to the newly restored 1891 depot. The depot serves as a terminus for the Western Maryland Scenic Railroad operating out of Cumberland since 1989. Near the depot are a tunnel, turntable, and the restored Tunnel Hotel. In contrast to the Gladstone Hotel above on Main Street, the Tunnel Hotel catered to the more unsavory element of townies and travelers and housed a 1920s moonshining operation. Back up on the Road, the brick dealership, originally the Frostburg Motor Company, cantilevers down Depot Street. The garage offered parking for travelers staying at the adjacent St. Cloud Hotel, but some Main Street business owners, even those within walking distance of their homes, would rent space by the month because their homes had no garages.

A quartet of brick buildings associated with St. Michael's Parish marks the heart of Frostburg. Maryland's early settlement stemmed from Catholics seeking religious freedom and circuit-riding priests from Cumberland ministered to the mountain counties until the mines attracted larger popu-

Frostburg, Maryland

The National Road as civic center. Near the downtown intersection of Main and Water, prior Frostburg generations met at the drugstore, the post office, and the trolley waiting room. In lieu of a park or monument, three plaques to the city's war dead are affixed to the exterior of the American Legion Post.

lations of Irish and Italian immigrants. The church (1868), rectory (1871), school (1891), and convent (1906) were built on the site of Highland Hall, the tavern and home of town founders Catherine and Meshach Frost. The monument over their graves in front of the church describes Frost as "a successful farmer, coal operator, and land speculator." This unholy trinity of endeavors came to be the formula for success in the Appalachian Highlands, whether in Maryland or in Pennsylvania.

Adjacent to the church property is the 1876 opera house, followed by several commercial buildings with elaborate pressed-metal cornices. The Durst Building, the Kline Furniture Company, and Griffith's Fashions all feature the black Carrara glass panels and Moderne signage of the 1940s. These remodelings signal the point at which Allegany County's small manufacturing diversity, which kept the economy healthy even during the 1920s, plummeted. Main Street's current visual cohesion stems in part from minimal subsequent storefront remodeling.

Important civic and ecclesiastical buildings mark the western edge of Frostburg before frame residences replace the brick streetscape. The gable-fronted Ward mansion was built by an early millionaire who owned brickyards, lumber mills, and coal lands, as well as twenty-nine slaves. Sidewalks appear sunken, but instead indicate the extent of road resurfacing over the

KAREN KOEGLER AND KENNETH PAVELCHAK

years. A left turn on any of the tree-named side streets, a practice begun in Philadelphia's grid, and another left leads to Frost Avenue, which became the finer residential address during the Road's eclipse. Appropriately, the founding Frosts sold their property on Main Street and rebuilt here in brick in the mid-1800s. Their heirs, in turn, added six rooms and the mansard roof in the late 1800s to create a summer hotel serving tourists from Baltimore and Washington. With its incarnation as a funeral home, a cycle common to such large residences is complete. Brick sidewalks, shed-like garages, and double-rut driveways with grassy medians can be glimpsed on Frost Avenue and other residential streets parallel to Main.

Although Frostburg was never the county seat, it was more cosmopolitan than Allegany County's mining towns. The state placed both the miners' hospital and the "normal school" for teacher training (now Frostburg State University) here in response to public demand. The university, with a student enrollment of about 5,000, is a popular alternative for Maryland students who prefer rural settings. A sizable black community, unusual for western Maryland, resided near the college on Park Avenue and built the frame African Methodist Episcopal Church (1881) on West Mechanic Street to replace their first church. The Jewish community was large enough to support a synagogue in Frostburg, though the Torah returned to Cumberland in the 1950s when that population ebbed. Suburban expansion extends on highlands north of Main Street and to the south where an earlier, and separate community, Grahamtown, has been engulfed.

FROM FROSTBURG TO THE PENNSYLVANIA STATE LINE

Heading out of Frostburg, the traveler comes upon the gateposts that marked the second toll house thirteen miles from Cumberland. The summit of Big Savage Mountain and a panoramic view coincide with entry into Garrett County. Named for an official of the B&O Railroad, this county is the coldest, highest, and most sparsely populated in the state. The last area settled in Maryland, it remains the state's most forested county. When the B&O passed through southern Garrett County, scenic glades attracted resort development. A sawn-wood building boom began as communities like Deer Park, Mountain Lake Park, and Loch Lynn draped summer hotels and cottages in board-and-batten Gothic.

Still part of the Appalachian "second home" region, Garrett County draws one-quarter of its property tax base from sojourners. After the rail-

The Savage River at Big Savage State Park, west and south of Frostburg, Maryland

In 1989 whitewater enthusiasts from around the world came to the Savage River to compete in the world championship. The river also serves as a training ground for American Olympians. The river was named for a surveyor named Savage; in 1736, he was almost "Donnered" by his frozen and starving campmates.

road resorts declined, summer pilgrims began using the National Road to get to the panhandle. Beginning in the 1920s, vacationers from the East Coast and western Pennsylvania gravitated to Deep Creek Lake, the largest freshwater lake in Maryland, created to provide power for a Pennsylvania electric company's customers.

After descending Big Savage Mountain (elevation 2,900 feet), the ascent of Little Savage Mountain (elevation 2,810 feet) begins. Both mountains and the mining town northeast of Frostburg take their names from the Savage River, a favorite of whitewater enthusiasts worldwide. The moniker invokes neither wildness nor the presence of Native Americans. These places commemorate a surveyor named Savage who, as a member of the 1736 Mayo Expedition, sought the headwaters of the Potomac and boundary clarification with Virginia. Like Frostburg, Grahamtown, Eckhart Mines, Clarysville, and Grantsville, the name follows from a surname as do the majority

KAREN KOEGLER AND KENNETH PAVELCHAK

of Maryland's toponyms. Even LaVale was not named for the valley of Braddock's Run, but for the developer's family farmstead in Pennsylvania. Some Native American toponyms survive—in particular, Allegany in its different spellings, from an Algonquin root for "lapping water."

At the mountain's base, the Road divides weathered farm buildings that mark Savage River Camp, Braddock's third stop on the way to Fort Duquesne. This farmstead, with a Second Empire farmhouse and forebay barn on the Road's north side and two other barns to the south (pictured in George Stewart's book), belonged to the Johnson descendants of Maryland's first governor. Beyond the barns, the famous "Long Stretch" of the National Road begins. Although the grades are up and down, the road follows an unusually straight line for two and a half miles. Visible in the distance is Meadow Mountain. South of the road, I-68 follows Braddock's old route, the newest retracing the oldest. Across Meadow Mountain, just before the US 40 and US 219 intersection, the Road passes the stone Tomlinson Tavern at Little Meadows.

Dairy herds and cropland testify to active but limited farming on the plateau once mantled in a great white pine forest. Past the simple Zion Church with handsome stained-glass windows, the Road became the "Shades of Death," a spooky enclave where the branches of towering pines hid robbers who preyed on National Road travelers. Early water-powered sawmills operating on the little tributaries made quick work of that dense pine forest.

West of Piney Grove, Maryland

Little Meadows near Meadow Mountain and Meadow Run. Whitewashed Tomlinson's Tavern has shed its porches, but sits astride a site where General Braddock made his fourth camp on the way west to his fatal battle. Searight reported President-elect Polk addressing the locals in the tavern as he followed the National Road to his inauguration.

Casselman River, Maryland

The Little Crossings stone bridge (1813) soars across the Casselman River, anticipating canal boats that never came. The C&O Canal's extension was not dug and the span need not have been this high, but the masons' skills transcend the (f)utility of it all.

Casselman River Bridge, Maryland

From the apex of the historic arched stone bridge (*foreground*), designs for the spans carrying US 40 (*middle*) and I-68 (*background*) traffic become increasingly sedate.

The stand of white pines with specimens four or five feet in diameter extended from Little Savage Mountain to the summit of Meadow Mountain and north into Pennsylvania's Somerset County. The 10,000 to 50,000 feet of lumber that each acre produced were hauled off for everything from mine prop lumber to railroad bridge supports. Automobile travelers in the 1920s could still glimpse stump-studded farm fields and tentacled fences fashioned from uprooted stumps. (A large white pine stump often required a century to decompose.) Now all traces of the virgin forest have vanished. A post-and-rail fence on the Road's north side and a snake rail fence on the south stand out today, but old photos show some sort of fencing along much of the Road's frontage.

The Casselman River, a tributary of the Youghiogheny, marks the point at which Maryland's watersheds drain toward the Gulf of Mexico via the Ohio and Mississippi rather than toward the Atlantic Ocean via the Potomac. Settlers seized the Casselman's water power early on, grinding grain in the 1797 gristmill and selling lumber ripped in a nearby sawmill along the National Road. The centerpiece of the tourist village is the Little Crossings stone-arch bridge. Built in 1813 with an unusual fifty-foot clearance, the bridge was closed to traffic in 1953. A 1913 steel bridge now carries US 40 traffic over the

KAREN KOEGLER AND KENNETH PAVELCHAK

Casselman. A third bridge supporting I-68 is visible from the other two. The 1818 stagecoach tavern (Penn Alps Restaurant), first updated to the Italianate, has been remodeled to Alpine heights. Most of the surrounding vintage log buildings with crafts shops were relocated to this site in the 1970s.

Grantsville, a classic linear town strung along the Road, has a movable past. Settlers moved ten houses from a village of the same name from Braddock's Road to this site on the National Road. When Garrett County split off Allegany in 1872, its northern and southern portions competed for the county seat. Grantsville lost and remains a one-blinking-yellow-light town, a small hub for the surrounding farms. Main Street homes—a variety of bungalows, foursquares, and I-houses—are set back from the road and widely spaced. The Casselman Inn is the community's focal point. South of Grantsville (at the light on US 219) is another linear village and agricultural trade center, Accident. Surveyors for different land speculators "accidentally" claimed the same tracts of mountain land after Lord Baltimore opened his charter lands west of Cumberland to settlement. Field shapes, property lines, and township boundaries in Maryland, Pennsylvania, and West Virginia reflect the irregular survey that predated the Middle West's Township and Range checkerboard.

Grantsville, Maryland

Standing sentinel at curbside, a mile marker (*lower right*) points to Grantsville's pivotal building, the county's earliest surviving Georgian plan and a rare house built of brick when most Garrett Countians were chinking their log houses.

West of Grantsville, Maryland

Near Braddock's fifth camp, the official welcome to Grantsville from the west still includes a log house built as a companion to the National Road. Renovation is under way.

Negro Mountain, Maryland

Built by accretion, burned by the fire department for practice in 1983, Ashby's Tavern was an all-purpose roadhouse with associated cabins that mirrored the Road's shift from horses to cars.

KAREN KOEGLER AND KENNETH PAVELCHAK

Braddock's soldiers left the heavy artillery behind at his fifth campsite near a log house on the western edge of Grantsville. Fill from the interstate walls off the valley, canyoning the National Road. A tipple with a truck dump above on the Road's north side points to coal stripping further up the valley. At the top of the hill past Little Shade Run, the telephone poles soldier along with the old alignment as it swings off to the right. The summit of Negro Mountain, named for a black servant of the Ohio Company's Thomas Cresap, is the highest point of elevation on the National Road—3,075 feet. A piece of the abandoned roadbed and an old high-arch bridge are visible on the Road's north side as it passes over Puzzly Run. "Run" is a popular generic for small streams in Maryland and Pennsylvania. Keyser's Ridge, a bald mountain, once notorious for snowdrifts that forced travelers down off the crest into the glades, was later capped by several taverns, but now road-related services reveal the proximity of I-68. The State Line Methodist Church of restrained Gothic style, pictured in Stewart's book, strides the Mason-Dixon Line. In Stewart's photo, the highway surface changed color—each state's maintenance making "one of the most famous abstractions in American history" black and white.

Keysers Ridge, Maryland

Masons mark the run. A finely chiseled arch of irregularly coursed stone arcs over Puzzly Run. One approach remains intact, the other crumbles.

ADDISON: THE NATIONAL ROAD'S THREE FACES

After crossing into Pennsylvania, the Road's original alignment veers south to traverse the linear town of Addison. The distinctive sandstone toll house heralds the east-end turnoff to Addison (formerly Petersburg). Now a small hamlet with no commercial services, Addison includes three vignettes that recall life on the Road during its early years, its eclipse in the second half of the 1800s, and its rebirth during the auto touring era. The toll house, one of six erected in Pennsylvania, marks the highest point in the hamlet. When the states took over the Road's maintenance, they erected toll houses approximately every fifteen miles. The DAR's involvement insured survival of this heptagonal one with a two-story tower.

Women have involved themselves as "culture-preservers" along this historic route: memorializing dead heroes (rarely heroines) and past events in monuments and plaques as well as preserving historic structures. The toll house is a perfect example. Although clearly associated with the National Road and the epitome of picturesque, even these distinctive structures were endangered and only two of the original six Pennsylvania toll houses remain.

Once identified and "roped off" in the landscape, however, the structure's

Addison, Pennsylvania

Sacred space. Marking the high ground of Addison's linear village, the cut sandstone toll house no longer funnels the backcountry's commerce, but guards a welter of commemorative plaques and monuments.

"sacred space" attracted other commemorative efforts. In Addison, three additional memorials have been placed near the toll house. The DAR's 1924 bronze plaque is dedicated to Somerset County soldiers who "served the cause of world liberty in the Great War and in memory of those who made the supreme sacrifice." A large sandstone wall erected in 1943 stands across the Road with a tablet honoring Addison's Honor Roll, the veterans and dead of World War I, World War II, and the Spanish-American War. The oldest monument, commemorating the crossing of the Youghiogheny River by Washington and Braddock, was placed on the Great Crossings stone bridge four miles west by the DAR in 1912, but was removed to this location when that valley was flooded. This conflation of war and remembrance is a striking aspect of memorialization along the National Road in Pennsylvania—for example, further down the Road in Addison, toll-house gateposts flank the cemetery entrance with a Civil War cannon just inside.

After leaving the toll house, the sense of the Road's built environment during the wagon and stagecoach era can be recaptured by proceeding to a trio of buildings on the street's south side. The tavern, a white-painted five-bay frame structure, housed travelers until the 1850s. Beside the tavern stands the only remaining wagon shop on the Road in Pennsylvania. This red-painted plank building with its gable facing the Road was built at mid-century. Just beyond the tavern, a frame building with large windows on the first floor and an attached garage with a Western-style false front housed the town's undertaker and cabinetmaker and his hearse.

A very different cluster of buildings summons the Road's image during the "Old Trails" era (c. 1912–25) when private promoters took over the highway's management. The Old Trail Garage (1920), a concrete-block building with a large second-story porch, offered auto sales, service, gas, and parking for the Rush Hotel next door (50 cents a day in 1924, according to the *Hobbs Guide*). The yellow-brick Rush Hotel (1914) was the last successor in a long line of hotels on this site since 1832. In 1924, the *Hobbs Guide* called it "a new brick building, clean and well maintained," with rooms for $1.00

KAREN KOEGLER AND KENNETH PAVELCHAK

Addison, Pennsylvania

The National Road was a good address in the county seats and the best address in the small towns. The Mitchell-Augustine house.

Addison, Pennsylvania

The Gilded Age descends upon Addison in a confection of sawn woodwork. The Mitchell-Augustine carriage house.

to $1.50 per person or $3.00 on the American plan. The red-brick garage with arched window hoods behind the hotel dates from 1924, when it offered auto repair and service, though the gas pumps are vintage 1940s.

The last property glimpsed before leaving Addison is the time-worn Mitchell-Augustine farm, and it is a knockout. The white-painted, five-bay brick house sits on an early tavern site. A gazebo and water trough stand beside the house, though what was a dance pavilion has been converted to a residence. The showpieces are across the road: a Queen Anne Revival carriage house and barn. Augustine was a Mennonite farmer and coal speculator. The family's wealth brought the Gilded Age to somnolent Addison in a pair of utilitarian buildings unlike any others on this section of the Road. The massive barn rises three levels above a sandstone foundation and features a front gable, elaborate shingles in the gables, diamond-shaped ventilation windows with lattice, and the remnants of decorative bargeboards in the eaves. The carriage house is even more exuberant. A canopied entry supported by ten Ionic columns once sheltered buggies and phaetons, though an old gasoline pump suggests later conversion to a garage. The cross-gabled roof is embellished by dentils and brackets. Alternating scalloped and plain shingles animate the gables. Elaborate hoods crown louvered windows while star-shaped panes divide the gables' round windows. Even the tin roof is patterned with an inverted Y shape.

Beyond the Augustine farm, sugar maples form a canopy over the National Road, imparting a feeling of enclosure. Wild white roses dot both sides of the highway in June as this segment rejoins US 40 to descend at a 9 percent grade to the Youghiogheny valley.

RECREATION ON THE LAND: FROM ADDISON TO FARMINGTON

The Youghiogheny (pronounced "*Yahk*-ah-gainy") is the largest river the Road crosses until the Monongahela at Brownsville; its valley marks the lowest point of elevation since Cumberland and until Uniontown on the other side of Chestnut Ridge. What had been the river's Great Crossings became an artificial lake when dam construction inundated five communities. The marina lies to the south while rental cottages and trailer housing are visible near the public launch on the north. The Yough Dam concentrates benefits seasonally and spatially, residents note, as few locals profit from boat storage, rentals, and the marina. Most vacationers are from

Maryland and western Pennsylvania, so the chief competitors are older, more established Deep Creek, Maryland, and posh new Nemacolin Woodlands, six miles west on the National Road.

When crossing the bridge over Yough Lake in the winter, the former Great Crossings Bridge—three stone spans built by National Road contractors Kinkead, Beck, and Evans in 1818—and Somerfield's foundations appear through the low water. The bridge crossing coincides with entry into Henry Clay Township, Fayette County—names drawn from two of the Road's most famous travelers. As the Road ascends the ridge, the heavily wooded landscape falsely imparts a sense of the original forest cover. That oak and hemlock forest is gone, though the hemlock remains Pennsylvania's state tree. Now the sumac signals second-growth forest. About halfway up the ridge, the Road crests and offers an interesting view of the route to the west with the sandstone Brown Tavern (c. 1826) at mid-slope. One of many stone taverns on the Road in Pennsylvania, this L-shaped building served as the official polling place for Henry Clay Township, illustrating the centripetal role these structures played in the rural landscape.

Viable small-scale commercial enterprises that would have been visible during the auto touring era appear: ice cream shops, sandwich shops, bakeries, auto repair, and gas stations. This stretch is also the best place to observe the cabin camp phenomenon. Occupying a middle ground between the tent camps of early automobile tourists and the motels of the 1940s, most cabin camps provided detached units around an owner-occupied office/restaurant. Over half a million cabin camps were built in the early 1930s. Some traces of nine camps remain on Pennsylvania's portion of the National Road, five of them near the settlement of Flat Rock—those of the Hi Top Motel, the Leber Brothers, the Traveler's Rest Motel, the classic short-order Lone Star Restaurant (since 1936), and Flat Rock Park. Their very survival confirms the backwater nature of this Road section. The most intact cluster can be observed on the Road's north side after entering Flat Rock. The Leber brothers built their log-cabin camp by hand in the 1930s and travelers can still rent from the family. The scattered cabins are of round log construction on sandstone foundations. The building housing the office and restaurant once had a store and ice cream shop.

Just as Frostburg and Garrett County resorts provided mountain air for Tidewater residents, Pennsylvanians have long associated recreation with these sandstone-capped ridges. Fayette County is currently packaging itself as part of the Laurel Highlands (along with Somerset, Cambria, Westmoreland, and Greene Counties) tourist region. Recreationalists are attracted to eastern Fayette County by state game lands, forests, and wilderness parks like Ohiopyle. Tourists who stay at Uniontown's Holiday Inn and go whitewater rafting on the Yough or tour Frank Lloyd Wright's Fallingwater are the successors of those who traveled the National Road to see Fort Necessity or water-carved Laurel Caverns and spent the night at the Mount Summit Inn decades earlier.

The National Trail Motel on the Road's north side is a typical 1950s design with two parallel banks of rooms. As each unit is set apart by a small porch and a jog in the roof line, the effect is of conjoined houses. Current print ads for this motel show a Conestoga pulled by oxen. After crossing into Wharton Township, the newly recontoured grounds of Nemacolin Woodlands appear. This luxurious resort and spa, revamped by the 84 Lumber chain's founder, added a second eighteen-hole golf course (designed by Pete Dye) in 1995 to attract major pro tournaments. Further ahead is the elaborate entry with water feature, gatehouse, and electronic signboards. The resort invokes the name of Nemacolin, the Indian guide whose trail preceded Braddock's wagon road.

The rambling white-sided resort on the south, Gorley's Lake Hotel, dates from an earlier time. The original farmhouse forms the roadside corner of the structure, but by the 1920s the facility had grown to 100 rooms overlooking a lake. Never a luxury hotel, Gorley's was set apart from other lodgings by the opportunities for fishing, boating, and swimming. A German communal group, the Hutterite Brethren, who drained and moved the lake in 1965, now occupy the hotel and grounds.

The Rush Tavern, at Farmington, was built by a local judge in 1837 on the site of an earlier stone tavern. The brick facing on a stone building is unusual. Twin doorways led to the tavern and the rooms; the more gullied threshold suggests that the thirsty outnumbered the sleepy. Across the road is the Rush Service Station of 1918–20, a two-story, rock-faced concrete building. A builder could produce the blocks on site using patented molds. Commonly used in commercial buildings, the technology was also intended for residential use. At the National Park Service sign for Fort Necessity the Road crosses a stone bridge built in 1895 over a tributary to Meadow Run. This bridge, with date stone and initials, replaced one of the original National Road bridges.

WAR AND REMEMBRANCE ON THE LAND: THE WASHINGTON AND BRADDOCK SITES

The National Park Service sites related to Washington and Braddock along the National Road raise issues of commemoration. Modest markers—mostly plaques and a reconstructed fort—represent the hearth of the French and Indian War in North America. Yet it is an unknown war, poorly fixed in the national consciousness because it predated the national period. Further, these were losing campaigns: Washington surrendered, Braddock was routed.

Control of the Ohio Valley fur trade and the French desire to consolidate their hold west of the mountains fired the conflict. Washington's initial forays into western Pennsylvania to represent Virginia's business and political interests were more trail-blazing than military maneuvers. The war began with the seizure of an unfinished fort at Pittsburgh in April of 1754, but Washington's force shed the first blood at Jumonville Glen, north of the Road on Chestnut Ridge. Fort Necessity, a sorry little stockade hastily built by tired, starving men, was surrendered by Washington to the French after a day-long battle in the rain in July of 1754. He then retreated to Cumberland, Maryland.

The procession of Braddock's army from Maryland the following year widened Washington's trail into a proper military road. It was slow going. Little wonder that Braddock perceived the forest and the mountains as greater enemies than the Indians.[4] Defeated south of Fort Duquesne (Pittsburgh) in the Battle of the Monongahela, the British and colonial troops were decimated. Most of the officers died. Braddock had five horses shot from under him before he suffered a mortal wound. The soldiers were also victims of what has been called the "hallucination of the displaced terrain." "The Redcoats fall, expecting at any moment to enter upon the true battlefield, the soft rolling greenswards prescribed by the canons of their craft and presupposed by every principle that makes warfare intelligible to the soldier of the eighteenth century."[5] When Washington assumed command of the retreat, he became the saga's central figure. Braddock's dying words— "We shall know better how to deal with them another time"—allude to the alien landscape's disorienting power. Washington had him buried in the Road and ordered the wagons to roll over the unmarked grave to protect the body. Braddock's defeat left the frontiers of western Pennsylvania porous until Forbes's march to the forks of the Ohio River and the Fort Stan-wix Treaty established new borders in 1768.

The first site is the Fort Necessity Battlefield. It is tempting to second-guess Washington's decision to encamp at Great Meadows. The exposed po-sition looks ripe for entrapment. But the very bogginess that precluded tree growth signaled fresh water—an important consideration for men and beasts slogging over these mountains. In Stewart's 1953 book *U.S. 40,* he de-scribed Fort Necessity as "a quadrangle in the midst of a quagmire." Later excavation revealed that the true fort was smaller and circular, so the Park Service razed the square reconstruction that Stewart saw and built a new fort. Additional monuments at the site include a rock wall, the Washington Tavern, and a marker noting Braddock's original track. A series of tablets in the meadow south of the fort invokes "Manifest Destiny" rhetoric in trac-ing Braddock's route. A visitor center offers a general introduction to these events.

Western Pennsylvania preoccupied George Washington throughout his life. He eventually bought the land that witnessed his only military surren-der—the ground on which he built Fort Necessity—and held it until his death. In his will he describes the parcel's "local situation" on Braddock's Road as valuable for an inn, but the Washington Inn was not built until the National Road went through. After a local judge built the inn from brick made on the site, it served as a stage stop on the Good Intent line. By con-trast, the judge's Rush Tavern (a mile to the east) was a wagonstand. Like many National Road inns, the Mount Washington Tavern was not associ-ated with a town, but played a central place function to the surrounding rural areas. National Road taverns also sheltered spaces where frontier women—those traveling and those working within—could break the boun-daries of their assigned social sphere. Many taverns were husband-and-wife enterprises and taverns were judged by their food and ambience. Women even became sole proprietors in some instances.[6]

The Braddock retreat sites lie one mile west on the Road's north side in Braddock Park. The National Road follows the general thrust of Braddock's Road, but rarely its roadbed. Braddock's Road parallels the National Road to the south at Great Meadows, but at Braddock's grave it crosses the road to splay north to Pittsburgh. There are two monuments in Braddock Park, erected in 1913 and 1931. *Hobbs Road Guide* of 1924 admonishes: "Brad-dock's grave; interesting; read the tablets." The 1913 monument marks

KAREN KOEGLER AND KENNETH PAVELCHAK

Braddock's grave and alludes to Washington reading the burial service. When Braddock's skeleton was unearthed from the Road in 1812 to be reburied, some bones were taken as relics. The monument itself is simple—an equestrian statue would have been inappropriate, after all—and may reflect confusion over what exactly is being memorialized here: Braddock's life? Braddock's death? Braddock's defeat? Or does the monument mark a man whose death allowed us a view of the proto-Revolutionary George Washington under fire? In this conception, southwestern Pennsylvania serves as proving ground for later greatness. The event becomes significant only in light of subsequent events.

The second marker, a bronze tablet set into a rock, floridly recounts the sanctioned saga of "The Old Braddock Road." "Nemacolin and his associates" are credited with blazing the trail. The associates' skin color might remain unknown were it not that frontier scout Christopher Gist's property is then identified as the "first Anglo-Saxon settlement" west of the mountains. George Washington is initially cited in his role as "youthful ambassador." The French and Indians are described on their way to Fort Necessity as is the

West of Flat Rock, Pennsylvania

The mountain ridges yielded sandstone for the taverns that line the National Road in southwestern Pennsylvania. Small family-operated businesses across the road from the stone house continue the tavernkeeping tradition.

return of "the bleeding remnant" of Braddock's army after its defeat. Federal troops extinguishing the Whiskey Insurrection are depicted as using the road—a broad interpretation of their actual route. The monument's text concludes: "This wheel worn chasm is a veritable monument to a past age, the last span through a mountain fastness that linked the east with the west."

With these words, the tablet unlocks the evocative power of this site. The sunken scar that cuts diagonally across the park is the real legacy of Braddock and Washington. Descending into this depression as it disappears into the trees, with traffic buzzing above, imparts some sense of the literal carving of road from forest. Over this track went a commander profoundly out of step with the time of this place. His death ultimately allows others to conquer the distance he fought.

CHESTNUT RIDGE TO HOPWOOD: DESCENDING INTO THE FRONTIER

Beyond Braddock's grave the roadside establishments and signage on the way to Chestnut Ridge continue to advertise the recreational nature of settlement in this part of Fayette County. The Fayette Springs Hotel, a large stone inn sited on a narrow stream valley terrace (c. 1822), was alternately occupied as a residence and a tavern during the wagon-road era. Later it advertised its proximity to mineral springs. Guests could also bowl and play billiards in the expansive hotel. A sign advertising Laurel Caverns recalls how common billboards once were along the nation's highways. At Chalk Hill (its name derived from a white clay uncovered by National Road workers), a road to the north leads to Deer Lake, a second home development veneered on an earlier lakeside resort. The Downer house (c. 1823) on the Road's south side illustrates some of the dilemmas of adaptive reuse: as a thriving commercial concern, it is occupied, but altered. This wagon-tavern owner's residence, with Flemish bond brick and corbelling, is unusual in that few tavern owners lived off their premises.

As the Road ascends Chestnut Ridge, one sign notes the turn for Laurel Caverns, another alerts drivers to the "Dangerous Mountain," and the distinctive brown-and-white National Park Service sign directs tourists to Jumonville Glen to the north. The glen and Washington Spring remain particularly evocative because there is little intrusion other than signage, allowing the visitor unmediated contemplation.

The chestnuts that gave the mountain its name fell victim to blight by the

KAREN KOEGLER AND KENNETH PAVELCHAK

1920s. Still, though newer growth replaces the original oak-hemlock forest, the effect of these forested hills upon the earliest travelers can easily be imagined. The extensive tree cover with few clearings and fewer vistas produced a disorienting effect, similar to the placelessness of an ocean voyage. One traveler, writing in 1796, called the mountains "a sea of woods" while another described the view of "the lower country" from the Allegheny Ridge as having "all the sameness of the surface of the ocean."[7] The hallucinatory power of these forested hills affected others besides Braddock and his soldiers. William Faux, writing of his crossing of the Allegheny Mountains in 1819, opined, "All here is wild, awfully precipitous, and darkly umbrageous, high as the heavens, or low as perdition."[8]

At the top of Chestnut Ridge is the Mount Summit Inn, a complex of seven buildings, a 1930 swimming pool, and a golf course. Located in a largely unaltered setting on the site of two former resorts, these structures date from 1907. *Hobbs Guide* pronounced it a "beautiful tourist hotel" in the 1920s with single rates two to four dollars and doubles three to seven dollars. As a tourist hotel, the Summit was open in those days only from April through November. The main hotel building, with an Alamo-silhouette parapet flanked by two towers and a sweeping sandstone-anchored porch, wraps around the hillside. The lobby, through which passed Edison, Ford, and Firestone, among other celebrities, retains its rustic beamed ceiling and stone fireplaces. In the evenings, young scions of Uniontown and Pittsburgh industrialists could drink and dance on this porch, looking out over the glow of hundreds of coke ovens blazing in the valleys below.

The descent from the summit to Hopwood, the town at its base, is formidable. Signs for "Sharp Curves" and "Steep Grade" and a gravel runaway truck ramp (engage parachute now) attest to the hill's incline. As on Great Savage and Negro Mountains, horses could develop "sprung knees" from holding back as they descended Chestnut Ridge. In the early twentieth century, motorists would hire experienced drivers to drive them over the mountains.[9] Two dozen automobile manufacturers tested models for brakes and power on this hill in the 1920s and drag-racers also tested their mettle / metal. Follow Business 40 into Hopwood and avoid the new 40 bypass to Uniontown.

Hopwood, a small town at the foot of Chestnut Ridge, marks an important transition. Throughout the early settlement of western Pennsylvania, Chestnut Ridge delineated not only a topographic barrier, but also an economic and social barrier. People living west of Chestnut Ridge were described as living "in the settlement," and that world had its own circulatory pattern of commerce and specie. The National Road taverns in the settlement paid farmers the best prices for their products. Farmers who risked driving wagons of produce back East over the ridge were called "sharpshooters." Hopwood also marks the intersection of the National Road with a northeast-southwest line of early Fayette County charcoal-fired iron furnaces. Native Americans first etched this rough X through Fayette County: just as the National Road's nascent roadbed here was Nemacolin's Trail, this mountain-skimming route traces the Catawba Trail.

This northeast-southwest line divides roughly square Fayette County into two triangular parts. In the sparsely settled, heavily wooded southwestern triangle, recreation and commemoration characterize the land's use. This was an area to be gotten through in the pioneering phase of settlement and the National Road taverns, as regularly spaced as the mile markers, were outposts of civility. The more densely settled northeastern portion had a different history: people farmed, but farming was always "skimpy business."[10] The real resource lay under the marginal fields: the world's finest coking coal beds. Its overburden now includes a myriad of "patch" towns and two major cities, Uniontown and Brownsville.

KAREN KOEGLER AND KENNETH PAVELCHAK

Building in stone was a rare practice. Hopwood has the most concentrated display of stone buildings on the National Road. The first, the German D. Hair Tavern, with an unusual street-level, diamond-shaped 1818 date stone, was reportedly built for a mason who worked on many National Road bridges. The 1838 Hayden building on the opposite side of the street, clearly intended as a commercial storefront from the start, sports distinctively tooled ashlar masonry. Set back from the Road on Church Street to the south is a stone stable that was associated with still another stone tavern, since demolished. The wagonyard lay between the National Road tavern and this rare stone stable (only one other survives in Pennsylvania). It is now used as a garage. Another stone tavern on the street's south side, altered with large display windows, was an A&P (Atlantic & Pacific) grocery store in the 1920s when the National Road was Main Street and supermarkets unimagined. The Moses Hopwood house, opposite Ruse's Roost, a small takeout-food eatery advertised by a giant revolving fiberglass chicken, is another statement in stone. This five-bay house, with stone spring house and frame carriage house, built in the 1790s, signals the founding family's anticipation of the National Road's path. President Monroe slept here and the town briefly changed its name to Monroe in his honor.

Southwestern Pennsylvania possesses an unusual concentration of stone buildings dating from the last quarter of the eighteenth century through the first half of the nineteenth century. Fayette County was central to this tradition. Coal measure sandstones could be obtained in massive beds and in an abundance of float rock. Builders in Fayette County utilized several different sandstones: gray when fresh, weathering to brown, now black with soot. The Waynesburg sandstone, for example, varies from massive to flaggy in deposition and from coarse to fine in grain. At its finest, it possesses the characteristics masons seek: it "works well, both in lifting from the bed and in dressing to shape" and though "soft when freshly quarried . . . the surface hardens in time and preserves tool marks indefinitely."[11] Although sandstone was commercially quarried, in most places people worked farm quarries for a single house and barn foundation. Stonework varied, then, both from the mason's touch and the variety of sandstone. About three hundred of these buildings still stand in southwestern Pennsylvania. Fayette County claims one hundred of them, many on or within a mile or two of the National Road.

Leaving town, the Road crosses a small single-span stone bridge over Bennington Spring Run with chiseled radiating voussoirs, dating from the re-

Hopwood, Pennsylvania

Wanted: an architecture to pull the motoring public off the road. Found: in the synthesizing vision of Howard Johnson. Just as Howard Johnson combined elements of colonial (translation: homey) with streamlined (translation: sanitary) in his orange-roofed restaurants, this vintage sign marries moderne lettering to the Simple Simon and the Pieman trademark. Motel operators cannily located their enterprises near HoJos.

pair and replacement era. The National Road between Hopwood and Uniontown features several good examples of roadside restaurants, small independent motels, and vacant porcelain-enameled metal-clad "box" gas stations of the 1940s and 1950s.

Kovach's beer distributorship occupies a structure conjoining a post-Road brick I-house with lovely Italianate brackets to a pre-Road stone house. The I-house's attenuated profile, one-room deep, announces a folk-housing type particular to Pennsylvania that diffused into the Middle West. Several more of these houses are visible along the section between Union-town and Brownsville. As the character of the Road becomes more residential on the fringes of Uniontown, a singular example of a streamlined house appears. At the intersection of the Road and Roosevelt Avenue stands a flat-roofed white-brick house with porthole windows, glass block, frameless windows, and curved aluminum railings. This residential use of the Moderne is unusual. That it exists here on the National Road promotes the idea of the Road as a good address. While some towns had a better residential street—Frost Avenue in Frostburg, Ben Lomond in Uniontown,

KAREN KOEGLER AND KENNETH PAVELCHAK

Front Street in Brownsville—the National Road was a good address in the cities and the best address in the small towns.

UNIONTOWN: COKING COAL CAPITAL

Early travelers usually described Uniontown, the county seat of Fayette County, as the "most flourishing" town west of the mountains outside Pittsburgh and Wheeling. Uniontown was a market center and transshipper for regional agricultural products in the early 1800s. The stage lines that competed on the National Road were headquartered in Uniontown and major coach works were located here. Connected to the Monongahela River by the Road, the city did not woo the railroad so the B&O went south through West Virginia. Uniontown also served as the financial and managerial nucleus for the renowned Connellsville coke region, beds lying nearly horizontally under eastern Fayette County outcropping on the Monongahela River. "The rambling city of narrow streets has an appearance of prosperity," opined the WPA writers in 1940, but no observer of today's moribund Main Street could agree.

Fayette County's lost prosperity can still be read in Uniontown's fine Romanesque courthouse, elaborate storefronts, impressive bank buildings, large churches, handsome mansions, and many hotels. Uniontown was once a popular stop for travelers. A county historian described the National Road in Uniontown in the 1830s as "thickly studded with public-houses on both sides and from end to end."[12] Only one tavern from that era remains, but additional Main Street hotels trace the gamut of styles. The gray-painted brick building on the corner of Moran and Main Streets across from the courthouse is the Fulton House/Moran House, the sole survivor of that "thickly-studded" street. At the corner of Gallatin and Main, next to the State Theatre, a terra-cotta fantasy, is the Gallatin Hotel (1905), a narrow five-story Renaissance Revival building with vertical lines capped by a modillioned cornice. The Gallatin served auto tourists in the early twentieth century. By contrast, just past the theater on the other side of the street is the earlier Hotel Exchange, which catered to railroad travelers. Completely altered on the first floor, the 1891 brick building's asymmetrical facade incorporates balconies and turrets to modestly interpret the Queen Anne revival on the upper stories.

Here on Main Street is Uniontown's first skyscraper: the First National Bank Building (now the First Commerce Bank Building), built by J. V.

Thompson. The region's most famous coal baron, Thompson was a local farm boy who made good. His fortune and influence rivaled that of Carnegie and Frick. As in many of the Middle West's small cities, the first skyscraper proclaimed a town that thought it was going somewhere. Sometimes the first was the only one ever built. After Thompson's beloved wife died, little interested him until the planning of this building. He invested himself and his fortune. Built in 1902 at a cost of over $1 million with eleven stories (Thompson's lucky number), the bank's interior sported marble, mosaic, mahogany, and bronze, while the exterior was yellow brick and limestone. Four elevators carried tenants to the upper floors, many of which housed independent coal operators. "My father wanted me to build a little one," Thompson once said, "but I said, 'No. When we build we'll build big and the town will grow to it.'"[13]

Three more hotel buildings survive on West Main Street. The Hotel Titlow, a restrained Renaissance Revival brick building of the 1890s, had businesses below and flats above. Across the street is the White Swan Hotel, a U-shaped Colonial Revival building from 1925, with a name derived from the original log tavern's sign. The hotel is now an apartment building. Keystone Auto Company, which stood next door, served the White Swan's guests with a 160-car capacity. Keystone Auto's garage stood on the site of a wagon and carriage works, which, in turn, had replaced a blacksmith shop. Although this 1910 garage was borderline historic, it was razed to make way for a new park honoring George Marshall. A plaque beside the Road commemorates Marshall, whose nearby home was torn down. A World War I doughboy statue guards a wedge of park across the street.

It is no accident that the Mount Vernon Inn, located at Uniontown's stellar intersection, the "Five Corners," has grown by accretion. This complex began as a brick residence built by one of Uniontown's Beeson founders (formerly Beesons Mills). Then the property became "Ben Lomond," the home of Lucius Stockton, manager of the National Stage Company that had the U.S. Mail contract on the National Road. In the 1940s, the home became an inn and restaurant, its piecemeal additions common to urban motor hotels.

At this intersection, a turn back up Fayette Street, which parallels Main, reveals where the automotive-associated usages clustered in support of the hostelries on Main. Fayette Street alternates vintage automobile dealerships and repair shops with large Colonial Revival houses, in the familiar reuse

KAREN KOEGLER AND KENNETH PAVELCHAK

guise of funeral parlors. J. V. Thompson worshipped at the Presbyterian Church at the corner of Fayette and Morgantown. Contributions from his father, Jasper Thompson, helped build this edifice, modeled on Boston's Trinity, with exceptional ornamental ironwork on the doors.

A right past the Mount Vernon Inn and a left on Ben Lomond Street unveils the millionaire row of mansions that once belonged to Fayette County's coal entrepreneurs. After three blocks, another left on Mont View Street returns one to US 40 facing Uniontown Cemetery's Gothic caretaker's house. This large cemetery, lying portentously below the city hospital, was for the people on Ben Lomond Street—not the mineworkers with the unpronounceable last names. Their ethnic cemeteries are located beyond the city margins. A section fronting on the Pike features an elaborate Civil War memorial, clearly sited to address the National Road. Just beyond this obelisk are the Thompson graves. An elevated sarcophagus with a portrait of Jasper Thompson almost enables him to transcend his earthen bier. This monument, erected when his son J. V. still had money, contrasts with the simple graves of J. V. and his first wife located just below.

After passing US 119, the south side of 40 becomes fast-food row with every major eatery represented, fronting Uniontown Mall on the leveled hill behind. Across the road stands J. V. Thompson's estate, Oak Hill, where he died a pauper after his creditors ruined him. The sisters of the Order of St. Basil purchased the estate after his death. Now called Mount St. Macrina, the religious center prepares women for vocations in the Eastern Orthodox rite and draws pilgrims from all over the United States.

FROM UNIONTOWN TO BROWNSVILLE

As the Road undulates over the corrugated plateau between Uniontown and Brownsville, relict gas stations appear in its dips, I-houses top the hills, and stone taverns crowd the curves. Redstone Creek and its tributaries provided fine milling and agricultural sites for the earliest settlers. High assessments in late-eighteenth-century tax records reveal the prosperity of these Monongahela River townships in northwestern Fayette County. The frontier's movers and shakers built stone houses during the pioneering years and settlers in townships such as Redstone built more of them than in any other part of southwestern Pennsylvania. Many of the sixteen surviving stone taverns on Pennsylvania's section of the Road lie along this stretch.

Woody overgrowth obscures this agrarian past just as it softens what had

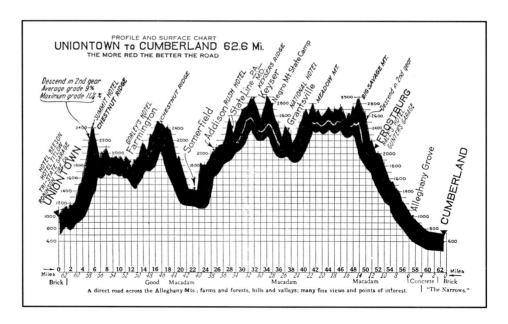

been a burnt-over environment of mining towns and coke production. As one inhabitant recalled: "It seemed natural and right to me that the world should consist of coal mines, coal trains, coal houses, coal taverns, coal trees, coal streets, coal children, coal everything."[14] Any right or left turn off the Pike through here inevitably leads to a patch town. The Road also exhibits some self-consciousness along this heavily traveled section: the Route 40 Diner, the Mid-City Motel, and an auto junkyard called Route 40 Sales and Salvage. Today, businesses continue to invoke the National Road's name.

On the left, the octagonal Searight's Tollhouse heralds the approach of a significant junction, Searight's Crossroads. Where Searight's Tavern stood at the northwest corner of the crossroads (across from the extant four-bay double-door stone house) only some foundation stones remain. As indicated earlier, National Road taverns were nodal in their agricultural communities. Citizens from Uniontown, Brownsville, and Connellsville held Democratic meetings and conventions in Searight's large H-chimneyed tavern. Searight, the proprietor, was a settlement unto himself. One of the wealthiest men in Menallen Township in the 1800s, he owned a wagon shop, a blacksmith shop, a livery stable, and a general store. He ran the post office and served as Road commissioner for a decade. No wonder his name is plastered everywhere. The road to the south goes to Searight's mining town, as a sign for Searight's Crossroads Coalyard suggests.

Two early auto-related buildings with characteristically restrained, utilitarian design replaced the wagon shop, blacksmith shop, and stable, demonstrating that this crossroads continued to be important for early-twentieth-century wayfarers. The Searight Garage (c. 1920), its horizontal facade accented by a white-brick beltcourse and small window panes above the large plate windows, functions as the OK Body Shop. Across the Road, Searight's Service Station, with vintage pumps and Coca-Cola signs, combines a garage, filling station, and auto sales into a two-story building with recessed entry and beaded board walls.

South of the Searight tavern site stands a four-bay stone house connected to Josiah Frost, son of that Maryland town's platter, who may have been a mason or a blacksmith at the Searight site. The pattern of people relocating westward on the Road to engage in related commercial opportunities is one that repeats itself. The brick Abel Colley house, set back on the north side of the Road, sat opposite his tavern. The racial and gender diversity of Colley's household at mid-century illustrates how taverns served as urban portals for the countryside. The stone tavern two miles ahead at Brier Hill, built by Colley's father, predated the Road.

Just before Brier Hill is a stuccoed, two-story canopy gas station, unusual for its size and living space in the canopy. Inheriting the taverns' centripetal pull on the countryside, Null's Service Station, built in the early 1920s, added innovations to draw the public. Null opened a private airfield behind the station and offered airplane rides. In the 1930s, he used wood from a dis-

Abel Colley Tavern Household
National Road, Menallen Township, Fayette County, 1850

Name	Age	Sex	Occupation	Birthplace
Abel Colley	59	M	Farmer and innkeeper	PA
Mary Colley	57	F	—	PA
Searight Colley	22	M	Farmer	PA
Maryjane Colley	18	F	—	PA
Anne Bagley	35	F	—	PA
William Bagley	3	M	—	PA
Louise Ross (Mulatto)	15	F	—	PA
Charles Colstickle (Black)	15	M	—	PA
Jack Scott (Black)	45	M	—	VA
Pateriol(?) Thompson	35	M	Farmer	IRE

Source: U.S. Census, 1850

Brier Hill, Pennsylvania

The Peter Colley Tavern.
Listing on the National
Register of Historic Places
affords a measure of pro-
tection, but does not necessarily preserve. The Colleys
anticipated the Road's
course and made a barrel
of money.

mantled hangar to construct a dance-hall addition.[15] Gathered at the settlement of Brier Hill are the new post office, followed by the Peter Colley
tavern and barn, followed by a 1943 soldier and sailor war memorial of folk
expression, followed by a tricolor building that housed the Brier Hill post
office when it was one of the smallest in the United States. Brush cloaks the
remains of Brier Hill, the mining patch, its banks of coke ovens, and its
cemetery.

The green swath of Lafayette Memorial Park swings into view. The
flush-type markers indicate the newest iteration of the burying ground—
the memorial park. As in Uniontown's cemetery, the flagged veterans'
graves cluster around a large war memorial at the Road side. The memorial park's placement here suggests that National Road frontage is not pricey.
Further ahead on the same side of the road are two older burial grounds,

KAREN KOEGLER AND KENNETH PAVELCHAK

St. Peter's Cemetery and Redstone Cemetery, for the Eastern and Southern European populations brought to this region by the mines. Slavic names, Italian names, and Byzantine crosses—some of the earliest in weathered wood—identify the ethnic "neighborhoods" within the cemeteries.

On the outskirts of Brownsville, a still functional drive-in theater competes for space with a computer store. Drive-ins boomed in the 1950s, but began to decline in the 1960s when shopping malls competed for the land and television competed for the attention span. In this region, the drive-in's appeal persisted longer. To enter Brownsville by the Road's old alignment, one must continue straight through the intersection at the top of the hill and past Redstone Cemetery. Large boxy houses with double chimneys—company housing—are visible on the opposite hill across US 40's new alignment.

Brier Hill, Pennsylvania
Veterans Day at Lafayette Memorial Park. War and remembrance are everywhere combined on the National Road. The flush-type markers signal a society no longer willing to manicure individual plots.

BROWNSVILLE: MONONGAHELA RIVER PORT

Before the Pennsylvania legislature objected, the Road was to arc north of Uniontown and south of Washington, but still pass through Brownsville. Like Pittsburgh, there was no denying this site's centrality and the necessity for transshipment of people and goods where the Road crossed the river. Many wagons moving on the Road switched venue here for "the gleaming bosom of the Monongahela signified travel less hazardous and far less wearying than that over the mountains," noted the 1940 WPA guide to Pennsylvania. The Road's emigrants took to the water, lashing brigades of keelboats together and poling downstream. Brownsville, as a break-in-bulk site, became a center of flatboat and keelboat construction. Later, the many steamboats built in Brownsville, including the *Comet* (1813), subverted Pittsburgh's monopoly. A series of locks begun in the 1840s enhanced slackwater navigation. A century later, these locks were handling more tonnage than the Panama or Suez Canals.

Most of what was moving on the Monongahela was as dark as its depths. The Pittsburgh Seam, rising and falling in low-amplitude synclines and anticlines, opens on the river. In the nineteenth century, miners simply dug

Brownsville, Pennsylvania

Market Street in Brownsville: the Upper Town makes a stately procession to the Monongahela River. Where once Lafayette addressed the citizens of Brownsville, a drive-through beer distributorship punches a hole in an historic tavern. Hard liquor, however, is available only in "state stores" in Pennsylvania.

into the hillsides. From Brownsville north to Pittsburgh, there was no point on the river at which one could not see a mine, tipple, or loading dock. The Republic and Jones & Laughlin tipples were north of Brownsville, while those of Pittsburgh Steel, Weirton Steel, Crucible Steel, Henry Clay Frick Coke Company, Frick Mine Light, Duquesne Light Company, and many others lay to the south. Most of these structures were razed during the 1970s, as were hundreds of others in the Rustbelt region.

Brownsville's form tells of its past. The upper town (Market Street) is the National Road town, the lower town along the Monongahela is the rail/coke city of the early twentieth century, and West Brownsville, across the river, is the industrial/blue-collar residential area. As the Road's wide pavement descends into Brownsville from the east, the vista across the river beckons and Market Street's buildings reflect the immigrants' trail through this river port. Anchored by a stone stage tavern on the corner, a row of brick commercial buildings stairstep down the hill to the Monongahela, culminating in an onion-domed yellow-brick Greek Catholic church.

Paralleling Market Street to the north is Church Street, where assorted churches reflect different nationalities' desire for priests who could speak

KAREN KOEGLER AND KENNETH PAVELCHAK

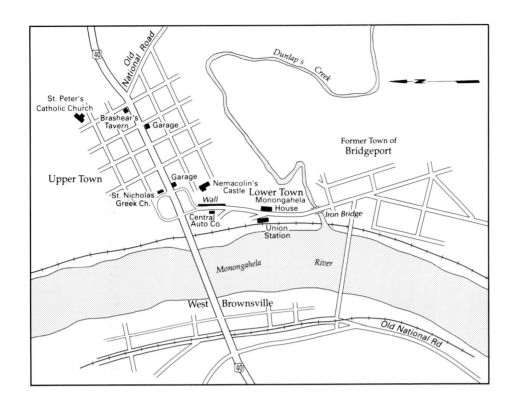

their languages. At the top of Church Street rises St. Peter's Catholic Church, the town's Irish church, resembling a British stone parish church nestled in its burying yard. Paralleling Market Street to the south is Front Street, the premier residential address. Brashear Street, between Market and Front and tied to those streets by alleys, shows how the Front Street residents have housed their vehicles through the decades.

Automobile-related buildings replaced earlier structures on the Road's south side. The brick National Garage (1918) was one of the earliest repair shops operating on the Pike. Garlett's Garage on the corner, described by *Hobbs Guide* as "never closed," was one of the largest in Pennsylvania. In the late 1920s when the owner added a dealership, it became Max Goldman's Modern Garage. An indented corner entry with a curved canopy calls attention to another dealership/repair garage on Market Street. In this rare example of art Moderne, a decorative beltcourse patterns the smooth wall surfaces and metal-framed windows enclose curved glass.

In Lower Town, a stone retaining wall dates from the original construction of the Road (c. 1816–20) and includes a plaque about "Redstone Old Fort," the stone house trading post that formed the nucleus of Brownsville (now Nemacolin Castle). Across from the wall, the dark brick Central Auto Company (c. 1910–20) adjusts to the topography as it backs down the hill to the Monongahela. Its undulating front signals its functions: showroom on the right, garage and sales in the indented center, and auto access on the left. It served local and nonlocal patrons, some of whom stayed at the nearby Monongahela Hotel, the third largest in Pennsylvania along the Road in the late 1920s and early 1930s.[16] Some of these travelers entered Uniontown through the Union Terminal. Looking at the empty shop windows on the terminal's first floor, it is difficult to imagine sidewalks so crowded with people that they had to walk in the streets to get by. Today, Fayette County's use of food stamps and public assistance is outstripped in Pennsylvania only by the city of Philadelphia. Further, outside of the anthracite region, Fayette County receives the greatest state investment to reverse degradation from abandoned mine lands.[17] The vacant storefronts of Brownsville and Uniontown mirror the bust of a boom-and-bust economy.

The arched cast-iron bridge that crosses Dunlap's Creek is a national Historic Civil Engineering Landmark because it was the first such bridge in the United States (1836–37). Henry Clay reputedly spurred appropriations after a carriage spill in the creek led him to announce that "Clay and mud" would never mix again on that spot. This span is called "the Neck" because the bridge's narrowness caused a traffic bottleneck in Brownsville's more halcyon days. To enter Washington County, the Road crosses the Monongahela on another landmark: a 519-foot-long steel bridge built in 1914. It stands on two of the sandstone piers that supported the 1833 covered wooden tollbridge. This steel bridge is only the second bridge at this site: a ferry was the only way to cross the river prior to 1833.

FROM THE MONONGAHELA RIVER TO CENTERVILLE, BEALLSVILLE, AND SCENERY HILL

West Brownsville's industries included the Thompson Distillery, of which several structures remain along the river, though the associated hog lots are gone. The second story of a stone house with a paint-store sign is all that is visible after decades of fill and highway resurfacing. On the Monongahela River side, the house, once linked with Krepps's Ferry, evidences finely shaped keystone lintels over the windows and door. After this old routing of US 40 ascends a hill, the Malden Inn looms into view. This massive stone tavern is one of the most spectacular of the forty-five taverns that remain

KAREN KOEGLER AND KENNETH PAVELCHAK

on the Pennsylvania segment of the Road, and its stone stable is unique. The inn's intricately carved date stones with an eagle and sheaves of wheat proclaim the builder's desire for a settlement with his name—Kreppsville. The settlers who followed chose Malden instead. Across the street is the Malden drive-in theater, still functioning, though no one sells tickets at the brick booth.

After this section, one rejoins the current surface of US 40 until the original alignment proceeds up a hill to the Taylor Cemetery. The ruins of a stone house belonging to Jonathan Knight, the Road's surveyor, can be seen on the north side of US 40, appended to a mansarded brick mansion built by a later owner. The most prominent marker next to the Taylor Church belongs to a miserly farmer named McCutcheon who seems to have been provoked by the "you can't take it with you" sentiment. His children were dressed in feed sacks while all of McCutcheon's assets went into the construction of the 85-foot-tall central obelisk and four flanking shafts completed after his death in 1902. Lightning truncated the McCutcheon "spite" monument, but it still dwarfs General Braddock's stone.

The old roadbed transcribes an S as it crosses US 40 to enter Centerville, illustrating how much the road has been straightened. Laid out in 1821 as a Pike town, Centerville's name stems from its location midway between Uniontown and Washington. Undulations and changes in elevation mask the settlement's stringtown morphology. Houses set back from the road and woven into the slopes, I-houses and taverns among them, deny Centerville the business-like frontality of the "Pennsylvania town." An unusual "house with canopy" gas station (c. 1918–20) beckons. Several stations of this form remain on the Pike, including two others between Centerville and Beallsville, but this stuccoed example with a vaguely Oriental flair retains enough of its original fabric to be a time machine. It features a tin and tile roof, stucco window and door moldings, beadboard under the canopy, and light sockets for bulbs around the canopy's perimeter. West of town, the sign for the Joseph Yablonski Memorial Clinic represents another instance of memorialization—this time the figure is the reforming United Mine Workers president murdered by contract in 1969.

A right (north) turn off US 40 into Richeyville unveils a former company town, though the Richeyville post office's location on US 40 signals that the Main Street functions of Richeyville and Centerville have migrated to the modern alignment. After passing a war memorial (World War II, Korea, and

Vietnam) that lists an unexpectedly large number of names for such a small settlement, rows of identical gable-fronted houses appear. Owners have customized the houses with paint and siding and added garages, but the company-built look prevails. Some privies survive at the back of the lots.

The golf courses south of the Road belong to the Nemacolin Country Club, which draws members from Pittsburgh's wealthy South Hills suburbs. The Indian symbol on the signs provides the visual clue for the name. Across from the country club, World War II–era brick houses exhibit different solutions to linking up with the small single garages—attached, separate, in the basement, or connected by a breezeway. The figure of the Madonna of the Trail, following so closely after the Nemacolin signs, provokes reflection on which groups are absent in roadside memorialization. Erected in 1928 by the Daughters of the American Revolution in connection with the National Old Trails movement, this statue is one of a dozen placed on the Road. While women have been instrumental in perpetuating these patriotic shrines, they are rarely depicted on memorials. This figure represents all pioneer women, just as Nemacolin has been summoned to stand in for western Pennsylvania's aboriginal population. Further, it appears that the only concession sculptor Leimbach made to his subject's gender was to add breasts to a sinewy, square-jawed masculine figure.

Beallsville (pronounced "Bellsville") arose at a crossroads and a right turn at the Federal-style Beallsville Hotel (c. 1819–21) allows one a view of some rolling fields and substantial four-over-four farmhouses—houses in which the two-room-deep floor plan doubles the space of the I-house. An Amish buggy traffic sign at the west end of Beallsville provides a clue as to who is farming the area. In Beallsville, the houses are close to each other and to the National Road, imparting a sense of the businesslike Pennsylvania town. During the auto touring era, this town offered its schoolgrounds for campers.

FROM SCENERY HILL TO WASHINGTON'S COUNTY SEAT

Scenery Hill boasts a fine assortment of taverns, clustered at the crest of a ridge, most built in the 1820s. It continues to attract travelers and tourists. The brick Beck-Ringland Tavern, operated for a year by one of the National Road contractors, has a saltbox roof line atypical of this region. The Zephania Riggle Tavern, stucco over brick, is currently painted green with pink trim. Its 1860s remodeling to the Gothic style with a center gable is also re-

Scenery Hill, Pennsylvania

A tavern could become the nucleus for a community. The oldest continuously operated tavern on the National Road, Hill's Tavern crowned Scenery Hill before the Road crested it. At heart a typical western Pennsylvania vernacular stone house, almost organically one with the site, it has taken on stylish airs with dormers and brackets.

gionally rare. The Century Inn (1794), or Hill's Tavern, is the settlement's nucleus and the oldest continuously operating tavern on the National Road. Once again, some entrepreneurs predated the Road and anticipated its path. Because the site drops off on each side of the road, the wagonyard was in front of Hill's Tavern, and the banked barn is down a side street, Swagler Street. A trip down Swagler Street (right turn) provides dramatic vistas of farmsteads and a distant view of Cokeburg's company housing, which is wonderfully intact (via Pennsylvania 917 north from US 40). Cokeburg is on the western edge of coke country, with Uniontown, the coking coal capital of the area, to the east on 40.

Adjacent to Hill's Tavern, a 1929 one-story building housed a Chrysler-Plymouth dealership and Esso gas station until the 1970s. Its simple facade is patterned with terra-cotta coping, yellow-brick diamonds, and black tiles under the windows; the sides are constructed of rusticated concrete. Its current reuse in this picturesque village raises the question, why is there so little "ye olde gift shoppe" conversion and antiquing in these historic National Road towns? Antique dealers consider southwestern Pennsylvania a kind of antiques "black hole" between eastern markets and the Midwestern agglomeration that begins in Ohio.

Cokeburg, Pennsylvania

Cokeburg. Duplexburg. A recycled company town just off the National Road and visible to the north when the trees are defoliated.

After leaving Scenery Hill, spectacular valley views with active farming abound. Commodious barns testify to past agricultural prosperity. The Road's current alignment strands several crescents of the old road. At South Strabane, a half-moon called Anderson Road crosses a rare stone bridge with sandstone walls and a brick barrel. Anderson Road also sports a canopy-style gas station, an Italianate brick house with a projecting front pavilion, and the only surviving blacksmith shop on the National Road in Pennsylvania.

"LITTLE WASHINGTON"

Those who organized Washington County during the Revolution named it for the Continental Army's general. Ironically, though Washington remained a landowner and millowner in this county when he was president of the United States, he was unable to use that clout to extract rents from his tenants and eventually disposed of these troublesome holdings. Pittsburgh-area residents call the county seat "Little Washington" to distinguish it from the nation's capital.

When the National Road enters Washington from the east, it becomes Maiden Street, where large houses proclaim a fashionable residential address throughout the 1800s. Gaps and infill on this residential street can be traced to automotive-related enterprises, such as the 1930s garage with six service bays on the corner of Maiden and Main. Maiden Street (US 40) passes Washington and Jefferson College (founded 1781) with its unusual iron fence of interwoven ovals and, in another block, the LeMoyne stone house, built in 1812 and rumored to be a stop on the Underground Railroad. Dr. Francis Julius LeMoyne, the son of the builder, was an outspoken abolitionist. A right turn onto Main Street reveals the domed courthouse at the top of the hill and immediately on the left, an historic marker calls attention to the David Bradford two-story stone house built in 1788 and featuring distinctive twelve-over-twelve windows. A lawyer and land speculator, Bradford fled this property in advance of federal troops because he was a major instigator of the Whiskey Rebellion. Frontier settlers perceived the federal tax on whiskey as discriminatory. Because of shipment difficulties over the mountains, whiskey was at least six times more valuable than corn of the same bulk. Although the plotters met in Brownsville, several sites in western Pennsylvania were attacked and the U.S. Mail stage was robbed. Interpreted by some as a test of the new federal government's power, the rebellion was quelled by troops dispatched by President Washington. Many farmers were imprisoned, yet most of the local politicos who had supported them escaped punishment or censure. Bradford left behind a great deal: this property was one of the most highly assessed in Washington County in the late eighteenth century. Perhaps Bradford would delight in the irony of the "state store" (Pennsylvania's form of a liquor store) now located next door!

The town's tallest building is not the courthouse but the ten-story George Washington Hotel, on the corner of Main and Cherry, built specifically to cater to the motoring tourist. Before it was built, local residents put up visitors in their homes because the city lacked hotel rooms, so the Chamber of Commerce led the building drive, encouraging the city's women to buy hotel stock. The largest hotel on the National Road in Pennsylvania, with 210 guest rooms and private baths, it was seen as a symbol of the town's modernity and vitality. Guests who stopped in Washington included Henry Ford and Lou Gehrig. When the hotel opened on February 22, 1923, more than 800 citizens who had supported construction were feted with a lavish dinner. Before the guests could be seated, a figure portraying George Washington appeared as the hotel orchestra played the National Anthem. He read a diary of his impressions of the hotel, the town named in his honor, and western Pennsylvania.

Main Street has been refurbished, not exactly "mall-ified," but sharing some of the trappings such as street trees and planters, though the first stories on the Italianate commercial buildings retain their modernized facades. A left turn on Chestnut Street follows the Road out of town. Where Chestnut meets the downtown bypass, a massive resculpting of the landscape has occurred, with parking lots, government housing, shopping mall, post office, and Goodyear Tire Center replacing earlier structures. A mixture of residences, mom-and-pop repair shops, and defunct vintage gas stations line the route. A handsome yellow-brick service station with a brown-tile pent roof and a stepped parapet houses Chappy's Auto Electric. The Gantz oil-well marker for the county's first well at the side of the Road underscores the longevity of oil production as an economic mainstay in Washington County.

FROM WASHINGTON TO CLAYSVILLE AND NEW ALEXANDER

After passing under the B&O line, the modern strip oriented to I-70 begins: gas stations, fast-food eateries, motels, and building-supply stores leave behind the husks of buildings that housed similar enterprises. Once the Road passes under the interstate, its character recedes a few decades once again with a carwash, laundromat, and older motels. Pugh's, a U-shaped motel now rents as apartments, while across the street an arrow-shaped neon sign pointed 1950s travelers to the Noce Motel. An older alignment swings off to the south. At the end of this up-and-over section, the identical houses of the Lincoln Hill Mining Camp, described as "a model mining town" by Howard Hobbs in 1924, curve down the hillside.

After the Sugar Hill intersection in Buffalo Township, the Road passes several large brick houses and taverns. Frontier farmers who could make the transition from log housing chose brick in most areas of Washington and Greene Counties. Because of heavier settlement from Maryland and Virginia, these counties were originally more English than Fayette and Westmoreland, where the German and Scots-Irish proportions were larger. Stone as a building material predominated in the townships adjacent to the Monongahela River, reflecting the influence of Brownsville where stone-

KAREN KOEGLER AND KENNETH PAVELCHAK

masons clustered at the middle of the nineteenth century, but Washington County evidences greater use of brick away from the river.

The large barns reflect the continued agricultural prosperity of Washington County. With most farmland devoted to dairy and livestock, Washington County is still among Pennsylvania's leading counties in total number of farms—all of the other leading counties (Adams, Berks, Bucks, Lancaster, York) are on the fine Piedmont soils outside Philadelphia. Also contributing to the generally more prosperous feel of this county—in contrast to Fayette—is its commuting proximity to Pittsburgh. Old farmhouses have been recycled into weekend homes.

The highway department truncated the only S-bridge remaining on the Road in Pennsylvania. Pieces of the old roadbed, some deadending, veer off to the south: One crosses an intact stone culvert with radiating voussoirs that dates from the Road's construction. Another sliver, appropriately called Spur Road, arches past a brick house and over the National Pike Body Shop, an old gas station appended to an earlier roadhouse. The Road then plunges downhill into a flat-bottomed valley, and past Sunset Beach Park, a recre-

Claysville, Pennsylvania
On the beach, near the border. More than a heroic-sized swimming pool, Sunset Beach and its surrounding attractions is really a road-side country club, despite the austere security measures.

ation area complete with a huge public swimming pool, picnic pavilions, park, and drive-in theater.

CLAYSVILLE AND WEST ALEXANDER

Claysville is a National Road crossroads town, founded in 1817 and named for one of the Road's progenitors. The Road enters town paralleling the abandoned right-of-way of the B&O line to Wheeling. The Claysville Cemetery's hilltop siting provides a dramatic vantage of I-70 and US 40 and the town from winding pavements lined with cypress and buckeye (horse chestnut). What may be the nation's oldest monument-maker, White's Sons, located in a frame building off Main on North Alley, obtained stone from a quarry at a nearby farm. Claysville's tight street scene—frame houses and brick taverns close to the road with scant side yards—is that of the Pennsylvania town.

Even when the railroad eclipsed the Road during the second half of the nineteenth century, Claysville continued building. The mansard-roofed Claysville Hotel was built in the 1890s. Another Second Empire structure on Main Street evidences the carpenter-owner's delight in wood: elaborate brackets, prominent window hoods, and porch gingerbread. Adjacent is a Gothic Revival cottage with thin pointed windows, dripping brackets, and lacy bargeboard. Next door is an I-house with sawn woodwork on the porch to keep up with the Joneses. Across Main Street, a frame Italianate house topped by a belvedere is set back in the trees on a large lot. These fashionable facades and the cemetery date from the late 1800s, so for Claysville there was life after the Road: productive agriculture and small-scale oil production. Main Street remains a busy hub today.

The Road's original alignment to the west passes under I-70 and through bridge abutments from the old B&O line. Just past the abutments, the trees' canopies interlace overhead, imparting some sense of what many sections of the National Road would have been like in the early wagon days and early motoring days. The Pike takes the high road, overlooking I-70 to the north, crossing two bridges: the first a well-preserved arch of tooled sandstone blocks, the second, about three-tenths of a mile beyond at a humble settlement called Coon Island, a concrete span dating from the automobile-improvement era (c. 1915–29). Coon Island grew around a popular wagon- and stage stand; the railroad called the settlement Vienna on its timetables, but the more elegant name never stuck.[18]

KAREN KOEGLER AND KENNETH PAVELCHAK

Until West Alexander, the road winds along the tops of ridges revealing sheep-raising and hay-baling, as cleared land alternates with allees of heavy tree cover. Among the frame taverns passed is the white-columned Valentine Tavern with a 1790s three-bay log section that predates the Road. One of the tavernkeeper's brothers had a tavern in Washington and another brother was a National Road teamster.

The road crosses I-70 to enter West Alexander at an angle, then lines up with Main Street. Like Frostburg, the hillside falls away on each side of Main Street and, like Frostburg, the railroad tunnels under Main Street. West Alexander overlooks West Virginia to the west. The founder, who served under Lafayette in the Revolution, used his wife's maiden name for the town. Lafayette stopped here during an 1824 trip that reverses this itinerary with stops at Scenery Hill, Brashear's stone tavern in Brownsville, and the Moses Hopwood house.

Located at the site of the last tollgate in Pennsylvania, West Alexander was a way station on the Underground Railroad. Craft and gift shops occupy some of the early houses, taverns, and commercial buildings. West Allegheny Cemetery, dating from the late 1800s, is outside of town on the 40 bypass. This cemetery's location and curvilinear layout represent the rural cemetery movement, begun with the 1831 opening of Mount Auburn Cemetery in Cambridge, Massachusetts.

INTO WEST VIRGINIA

Tall pillars on a railroad bridge where the B&O crossed the National Road mark the state line. The Road then sashays across the floodplain of Little Wheeling Creek, passing through the settlements of Valley Grove, Roney's Point, and Triadelphia. The Road crosses and recrosses the creek as it downgrades off the Allegheny Plateau. Today small farm fields and vegetable gardens utilize the floodplain soils where the Road and the railroad once competed for flat land. Vernacular farmhouses, bungalows, and mobile homes crowd the roadside, some with walkways or bridges over the creek. Reuse of older structures occurred during the auto touring era. At Roney's Point, the 1820 stone stagecoach stop has been augmented by the Stone House Motel, perpendicular to the Road. This unusual stuccoed motel offered motorists individual garages tucked under their rooms.

Entry into Elm Grove coincides with the confluence of Little Wheeling Creek and Wheeling Creek. The density of Wheeling's built environment

Ohio County, West Virginia

Empty lightbulb sockets dimple a once-bright-on-Saturday-night sign. Supper clubs drew their clientele from a local hinterland, not from highway-borne passersby.

begins to be palpable. Foursquare and bungalow residences precede the core of Elm Grove's business district with its substantial bank buildings. An interurban rail line connected Elm Grove's Main Street, the National Road, with downtown Wheeling. Then the street becomes more discordant with spaces between buildings. Just before the Madonna of the Trail statue, the residential predominates again with some Victorian and Craftsman designs and more modern split levels. The Madonna of the Trail backs up to Wheeling Park's golf course. An important public recreation area since 1925, Wheeling Park was founded as a privately owned amusement park accessible to city dwellers by steam train and streetcar. As with Narrows Park outside Cumberland, the location stimulated ridership on weekends and in the evenings. Additional greenswards surrounded the city. Mozart Park, a hilltop resort run by a brewing company president, was reached by an incline between 1893 and 1907 and then by streetcar. Oglebay Park, once the 1,500-acre country estate of Great Lakes ore shipping baron Earl Oglebay, passed into public hands in 1928. Its Speidel Golf Course was designed by Robert Trent Jones.

When the city's population outgrew its riverside bench in the late nineteenth century, the Wheeling Creek valley along the National Road was a natural avenue for residential expansion. Wheeling's old social geography— "the people who lived on the bottom looked down on the people on top"— typified urban places throughout the state until the automobile era. The automobile turned this social ladder upside down. The elites moved off the bottom land onto the hillsides near the parks and cemeteries.

Cemeteries and large estates line this portion of the Road. Mount Calvary Cemetery includes impressive monuments centered on a Gothic stone caretaker's house. Greenwood Cemetery, its mausolea and obelisks visible on the Road's south side, is this segment's finest example of the rural cemetery. Even the name announces its era; this was once rural Wheeling.

As the road ascends into the Edgewood neighborhood, fabulous estates

Roney's Point, West Virginia

The pike's creeky roadbed concentrates commerce and transport at Roney's Point and other meandering West Virginia settlements. (*Above*) The B&O line has been abandoned and the track removed. (*Left*) Tooled ashlar masonry updated by Italianate frosting at the cornice creates a stately facade for this Roney's Point tavern.

with equally monumental garages appear, followed by commercial enterprises such as Hampton Inn and Fostoria Glass outlet before the mile marker (two miles to Wheeling). The Road ascends Wheeling Hill, with vegetation on both sides and a view down into the valley. The Road could have been routed around this hill, but such an alignment would have required additional bridge-building. The figure of an Indian crowns the hilltop, with the valley of the Ohio River below. Erected by the Wheeling Kiwanis in 1918–23, the plaque on the statue's base reads, "The Mingo, original inhabitant of this valley extends greetings and peace to all wayfarers." The interwar time period coincides with almost all of the other memorials on this Road segment. Feelings of nationalism were running high and traveling families crowded the highways looking for historic America. The Indian figure and the text are unusual: the vanquished are usually not memorialized.

Before the National Road descends into downtown Wheeling, a road to the right at the Mingo statue leads to the Mount Wood Overlook and the 1848 Mount Wood Cemetery—both clinging to the hillside where local legend McCullough leapt on horseback in 1777 to evade an Indian party. Washington's prescient comments on Pittsburgh's siting for a fort are echoed in his journal entry on Wheeling: "This is a fine place for a fort, the banks be-

Wheeling, West Virginia

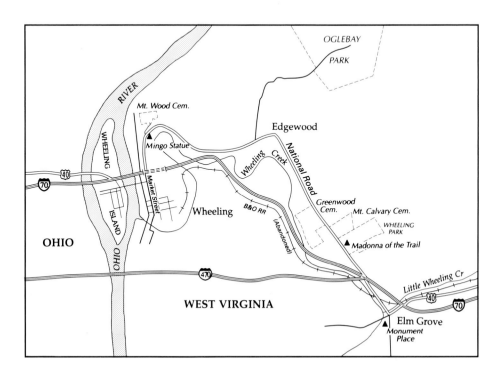

KAREN KOEGLER AND KENNETH PAVELCHAK

ing high and the bottom land level and the hills running gradual to the summit."

WHEELING

Founded by Ebenezer Zane in 1793, Wheeling's ascendancy as an Ohio River port was assured when the Road was rerouted from rival locations such as Charlestown (Wellsburg) to Wheeling. Lydia Boggs Shepherd Cruger, a prominent Wheeling political hostess, pressured Henry Clay on this decision and at considerable extra expense the Road was routed past her property. She later erected a monument to Clay on her estate, Monument Place. When the first mail stage arrived in Wheeling in 1818, it heralded the linking of river and road.

The natural layercake of coal, limestone, sandstone, and fire clay along the banks of the river and Wheeling Creek, a tributary to the Ohio from the east, gave rise to glass and steel industries. Wheeling was known as the "Nail City" until wire nails replaced hand-cut ones. One of the cut-nail plants evolved into a steel-pipe manufacturer and thence to Wheeling Steel (the employee-owned company's roadside billboard reads: "Iron-willed and steel proud"). Wheeling's location at the head of low-water navigation on the Ohio made it a nineteenth-century boat-building center like Brownsville. Several tobacco plants congregated on Water Street: Marsh Tobacco Company manufactured the "stogies" smoked by Conestoga teamsters and Bloch Brothers produced Mail Pouch tobacco.

Urban rowhousing and commercial facades of the mid- to late 1800s with fine architectural details crowd the streets that parallel the river, heirlooms of past manufacturing wealth. Market Street, the key commercial avenue, held two farmers' markets, the Lower between 22nd and 23rd Streets, and the Upper, between 10th and 11th, where slaves were sold. The Wheeling Jamboree, a rival to Nashville's Grand Old Opry, was held every Saturday night in the old Capitol Theater, a block south from the suspension bridge on South Main. Some facilities that required more expansive tracts of land located on Wheeling Island—two miles long and a half mile wide. Parks,

Wheeling, West Virginia

Contemporary Mount Wood overlook above Wheeling's propitious site. After the National Road climbs Wheeling Hill, it jackknifes back down to the Ohio River.

Wheeling, West Virginia

Foursquare and stalwart: a turn-of-the-century patchwork of housing on Wheeling Island.

fairgrounds, a drive-in theater, and a minor league baseball stadium shared the island. Baseball was played until 1932 on the island: the Wheeling Nailers, representing the city in the late nineteenth century, were succeeded by the Stogies. The horsetrack, Wheeling Downs, an "opportunity track" sited to lure bettors from adjacent states, converted to dog-racing in 1976.

The arrival of the Baltimore & Ohio Railroad in Wheeling in 1853 is generally taken as the watershed date in the National Road's demise. Nor was the railroad's routing the advantage it initially appeared to be. As the B&O's middlewestern connections became more important, its southern branch

KAREN KOEGLER AND KENNETH PAVELCHAK

eclipsed the Wheeling line. Wheeling remained well connected, but was never a true rail center.

When Wheeling became the National Road's terminus, it was in Virginia. The state of West Virginia was born in the custom house at Market and 16th, which served as the state capitol from 1861 to 1863. George Washington's vision of a Potomac-Monongahela linkage was finally realized in the two-handled outline of West Virginia's border that grasps both ends of the B&O corridor. This was critical geography for a state created in the midst of the Civil War.

The idea that Wheeling could have ever challenged Pittsburgh for economic dominance of the Ohio Valley may seem implausible in hindsight, but the city's backers foresaw a different future in the 1800s. The suspension bridge over the Ohio from Wheeling to Wheeling Island created fric-

Wheeling, West Virginia

Wheeling into Wheeling. The tracery of a cyclist on the side of a commercial building (*above*) presages Wheeling's annual Christmas holiday incarnation as "The City of Lights." Glass-blocked, but bayed and unbowed, this commercial facade is typical of the fine nineteenth-century structures on streets paralleling the river. (*Left*) Signs advise National Road motorists on Wheeling Island to go easy on the old bridge.

Wheeling Island, West Virginia

People built settlements at National Road river crossings to capitalize on the rare merger of these two transportation venues, but the price of convenience was high. A local prince of tides keeps a vernacular flood record on a Wheeling Island wall. A prophecy of high water can also be read in the eight-foot raised foundations under island houses, visible throughout the island.

tion between Pittsburgh and Wheeling, spawning a lawsuit that went to the Supreme Court. When the bridge opened in 1849, it was the world's longest. The length of the bridge was not the issue; it was the height. Jockeying for Ohio River dominance, Pittsburgh's river interests thought the bridge blocked some of its steamboats. Wheeling eventually won. Congress declared the Road an essential military and postal route. But the importance of both the National Road and the steamboats had already faded. Today both cities share the dislocations and abandonment of the Rustbelt region, though their large parks, cemeteries, public buildings, and suburban estates bear mute witness to the glory days of the industrial past.

KAREN KOEGLER AND KENNETH PAVELCHAK

From Wheeling to Columbus, Ohio

HUBERT G. H. WILHELM AND ARTIMUS KEIFFER

The road crept west section by section; it reached Zanesville
in 1826, Columbus in 1833, and Springfield in 1838. . . .
The State of Ohio was now neatly bisected—and
conveniently tied together—East to West.

WPA
The National Road in Song and Story

FROM BRIDGEPORT TO COLUMBUS, A DISTANCE OF 135 MILES, THE NAtional Road and its adjoining highways, US 40 and Interstate 70, cross from the unglaciated to the glaciated Appalachians and, finally, into the Central Plains. Beyond the Ohio River, the land rises rapidly to Ohio's prominent eastern sandstone bluff, the Flushing Escarpment. Near its top is St. Clairsville, where, on July 4, 1825, ground was broken for the continuance of the Road through Ohio.[1] St. Clairsville is one of some thirty towns and lesser settlements that flank the Road between Bridgeport and Columbus.

West of St. Clairsville the terrain is a jumble of irregular ridges and valleys, typical of the long-time effect of stream erosion on the horizontally lying sedimentary bedrock. There are, however, extensive areas where the contours have been softened by recent efforts to reclaim strip-mined land. Stands of broadleaf forest vie in prominence with open farmland and the

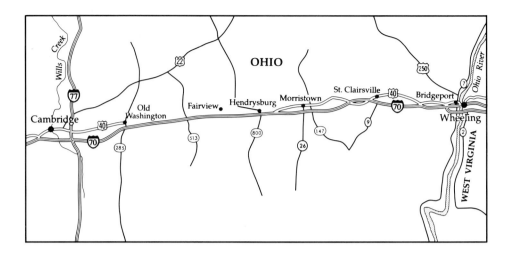

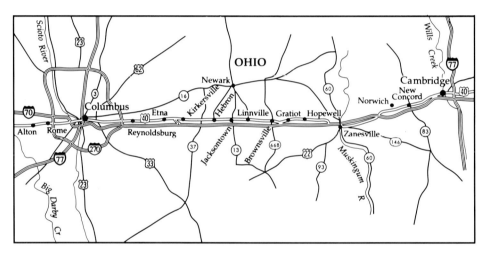

grassy knolls and vales of reclaimed areas. Except for livestock grazing, there is little agricultural activity.

The transition from unglaciated to glaciated hill country is not obvious, but occurs near the Road town of Gratiot. One landscape hint is that more land is in agriculture, including the ubiquitous corn fields. After Jacksontown in Licking County, the terrain flattens as hills were worn down and valleys filled in by glacial action. Finally, near Reynoldsburg, on the east side of Columbus, the Road leaves the Appalachians and enters the Central Plains.

The Road was completed to Columbus in 1833 and by then had crossed an already well-settled area. Columbus had a population of about 2,000 when it became the state's capital in 1816, after it had been moved back and forth between Zanesville and Chillicothe.[2] Zanesville, with a population of 3,000, was the most important settlement on this stretch between Bridgeport and Columbus when the National Road reached the town in 1826.[3] Those who walked or rode on this section of the Road during its early days through Ohio probably were aware that in Belmont and Guernsey Counties it crossed one of the country's most historic areas, Ohio's Seven Ranges. In 1785, Thomas Hutchins, Geographer of the United States, had surveyed this part of the state according to a new land division system of rectangular parcels, including townships and sections, which eventually would cover most of the United States and Canada. Land sales were conducted in one of Ohio's earliest land offices (1800), upriver from the Road, in Steubenville. The combination of officially surveyed and available land and the completion of the National Road must have been an important incentive to buy a lot and settle down. Irish immigrants who worked in large numbers on the Road also took up land alongside it, forming a settlement wedge that extends from Belmont through Guernsey, Muskingum, and Licking Counties.

The unglaciated and glaciated parts of Ohio's eastern hill country form a logical division for our traverse. In addition, Road towns will form a basis for further subdivision of the route. Let the traveler beware: in eastern Ohio the National Road and its modern-day cousin, US 40, rarely coincide. But this should make for an exciting traverse because it allows for orienteering and exploration.

BRIDGEPORT TO ST. CLAIRSVILLE: BETWEEN VALLEY AND PLATEAU

At Wheeling, I-70 enters Ohio on an elevated bridge span that takes traffic rapidly and high above the buildings of Bridgeport toward the west. With the exception of a few exits, I-70 follows this built-up roadbed without so much of a glance of the valley below and its tightly packed homes, churches, and businesses. Do not use the I-70/US 40 route but follow the Old Road across the suspension and truss bridges. After crossing the suspension bridge to Wheeling Island, turn right or north on York Street for three full blocks from the bridge; then go one block left on Zane Street. Follow the 40 West signs at Madison School to the truss bridge and cross into Bridgeport. This route will take you across the flood-prone Ohio River island where grand old houses stand on stilts that raise them off the flood plain. At the island's south end, Wheeling Downs has been strategically placed at the state's western border so that tax monies from horserace gambling might be drawn from both West Virginia and Ohio residents.

Across the Ohio, the Old Pike used the valley of Wheeling Creek, hug-

The Belmont Bridge, truss-built in 1893, carried old US 40 from Wheeling Island to Bridgeport, Ohio, a boat-building center in the early nineteenth century. The toll to cross in the 1930s was 5 cents. This view is to the east toward Wheeling.

ging its northern side, as it passed from its lowest point in the state, right next to the Ohio River (elevation 660 feet), toward the interior uplands and plains. US 40, on the other hand, tends to follow the National Road path, only closer to the valley bottom, on fill, so not to deviate too much from a straight course.

US 40 is one of three major roads that intersect in Bridgeport. The others are Ohio Route 7, the River Road, and US 250. Bridgeport is directly opposite from Wheeling Island and prospered at the confluence of Wheeling Creek and the Ohio River. The truss-type iron bridge links Bridgeport with Wheeling Island. A few nineteenth-century commercial structures survive in downtown Bridgeport, but most buildings are a hodgepodge of older and newer structures that form a continuous urban strip for several miles between Bridgeport and Blaine. Three other towns—Brookside, Wolfhurst,

HUBERT G. H. WILHELM AND ARTIMUS KEIFFER

and Lansing—are part of this strip, which consists primarily of residential subdivisions and the kinds of stores and businesses that spring up wherever people cluster. Today, this valley area is very different from the days when the National Road and its later transportation companion, the Baltimore & Ohio Railroad, contributed to local linear development. Then, "gristmills, sawmills, tanneries, and woolen mills lined the creek's banks," which by the early 1900s were replaced by "huge slack piles and tiers of miners' houses."[4] Coal, iron ore, and steel had become the resource triumvirate of the "Valley."

At Blaine, approximately five miles from the Ohio River, the strip development ends and US 40 leaves Wheeling Creek Valley and begins its ascent of the Flushing Escarpment. This is Ohio's prominent eastern sandstone ridge, which forms the divide for rivers that come off its steeper eastern slope and flow into the Ohio River, and those that flow westward and eventually end up in the Tuscarawas or Muskingum Rivers. Here, at Blaine, US 40 replaces the Old Pike. At the western edge of town, US 40 crosses Wheeling Creek on a huge, concrete four-arch bridge, identified on its historical plaque as the "Arches of Memory Bridge," built in 1932. The bridge's name recalls the experiences of thousands of unknown Road travelers who struggled up the steep slope of Ohio's eastern bluff. Directly adjacent but below the US 40 bridge is the first of several surviving S-bridges along our route. There can hardly be a more stunning site than this one anywhere along the route of the National Road which portrays so forcefully the changes in the means of transportation and corresponding highway technology. This is a required stop. Turn right on Belmont County Route 10 at the east end of the US 40 bridge, and follow it one block to the site, which is clearly visible. Here you should pause and walk across the S-bridge and imagine Conestoga wagons and carriages making their way through the dust churned up by a drove of cattle and sheep herded toward some eastern market. The three-arch S-bridge dates from 1826 and was rebuilt in 1916.

Between Blaine and St. Clairsville, a distance of three miles, US 40 climbs quickly from about 730 feet elevation to 1,280 feet. Only Morristown, a little farther west, lies higher than St. Clairsville. Henry Howe described St. Clairsville as "situated on an elevated and romantic site, in a rich agricultural region, on the line of the National Road."[5] Today, the only evidence of agriculture is Ebert's Fruit Farm on the Road's south side and only a short distance east of St. Clairsville. The farmhouse is stately Victorian with Italianate styling. The Old Pike passed directly in front of the house. Stop here

St. Clairsville Water Towers

Positioned at the highest point in central St. Clairsville, a new fluted column watertower stands in to replace an old truss-legged, double-ellipsoidal tank. Although intended to store water and supply hydraulic pressure, the watertower is also a landmark, and since their successful debut around the turn of the nineteenth century have provided a skyline for small towns all across America.

and walk back to the sales barn. Besides the purchase of some fruit or jelly, the site also permits an excellent view toward I-70 and the surrounding landscape. The rolling uplands of the Flushing Escarpment, because they escape the late spring frosts of nearby deep valleys, are ideal for fruit farming. In fact, a few orchards remain in the area, which, however, is dominated by strip mining of coal and livestock grazing.

St. Clairsville (population 5,162)[6] derives much of its economic livelihood from the regional mall directly east of town and, fortuitously, next to US 40 on the north and I-70 on the south. The town has made a valiant attempt to cash in on its history, so the old downtown storefronts, courthouse, and sidewalks are in excellent condition. In fact, the entire town's presentation is very clean and neat. Two of the town's best-known citizens were the Quaker Josiah Fox, builder of the frigate *Constitution* (now in Boston Harbor), and Benjamin Lundy, who started an abolitionist society in St. Clairsville in 1815 and began publishing in 1821 his abolitionist paper *The Genius of Universal Emancipation*. Lundy's house stands along Main Street.[7]

St. Clairsville's street pattern is typical of other National Road towns. Its development probably relates to the nature of the traffic on the Road and the evolution of a Main Street and so might be compared to Morristown, another typical Road town. The Road town plan centered upon two or, quite often, three parallel streets. Main Street developed over time as people built new businesses and private homes. The other streets, back of Main Street, and in some of the Road towns named North and South Streets, continued to be used by the Road's heavy traffic, freight carriers and drovers.[8] Carriages and their more affluent, acceptable passengers used Main Street, where the inns were located. Today, an old US 40 hotel, the Clarendon, still operates on Main Street. As heavy traffic declined on the National Road and, later on, became motorized, North and South Streets were used less. Instead, they became the site for public places, such as schools, churches, and town halls. Certainly, both the place and the idea of "Main Street," such an integral part of American culture, must have been greatly influenced by the spread of the National Road and its roadside settlements.

ST. CLAIRSVILLE TO MIDDLEBOURNE: OHIO'S EASTERN COAL COUNTRY

West of St. Clairsville, US 40 and the National Road coincide fairly well. Pay attention to the line of heavy telephone cable paralleling Route 40. It

HUBERT G. H. WILHELM AND ARTIMUS KEIFFER

follows an easement that coincides with the Old Pike and can be of help understanding the location of both the National Road and US 40.

About three miles from St. Clairsville and just west of East Richland is the Belmont branch campus of Ohio University. One cannot miss its site on a treeless rise, probably an old pasture, and main building's Neoclassical facade. The school occupies a topographic island within a sea of strip-mined coal land. Much of the area here, particularly the underground or mineral parts, is owned by major utility companies such as American Electric Power or one of its subsidiaries. Because the plateau surface varies from gently rolling to hilly, and because coal seams are close to the surface, strip mining was a logical mining technique as equipment technology improved. In fact, over 60 percent of Ohio's declining annual coal production is stripped by surface mining. Belmont County remains the state's principal coal producer, which at present hovers around 33 million tons annually, a far cry from the glory days of Ohio coal production in the early 1900s and in the two decades following World War II.[9] Strip mining's effects are easily recognized in the vast expanses of reclaimed rounded, grassy hills that were formed during reclamation efforts, processes that accelerated after the state of Ohio passed strong strip-mine legislation in 1971, six years before a weaker federal law was enacted.

The treeless lands of reclaimed strip mines, interspersed with the pasture areas of a few surviving farmers and isolated tree stands, are in stark contrast to the days when the National Road was built through this region of eastern Ohio. This was a land of dense stands of deciduous trees, the Appalachian Forest, whose dominant species consisted of various oaks, especially white oak, hickory, and chestnut. But the forest was known for its great variety of trees and shrubs, a profusion of species. It was both a boon and an obstacle to early settlers. Zane's Trace was the immediate predecessor to the National Road in this area, and was notorious as a narrow, stump-covered route through the forest primeval. It is a paradox that Belmont County, literally turned over by mining, would include only a short distance from US 40, Dysart Woods, the state's only surviving area of virgin timber. The fifty-one-acre tract of oaks, tulip poplar, white ash, black gum, beech, sugar maple, hickory, and so on, was designated a National Natural Landmark in 1967. It stands west of the small town of Centerville (about five miles south of the National Road) and is administered as a field laboratory by Ohio University.[10]

Proceeding westward again, about a mile and a half from East Richland is a major cut in US 40. It is easily recognizable from a distance and is a good example of the newer road bypassing natural obstacles—slopes and depressions. The cut is outlined by two brick buildings, one on the Road's north side and one on the south. Both are examples of the Federal-inspired symmetrical architecture of the East Coast. The National Road is on the right or north side of Route 40 and may have passed slightly closer to the house on the right. According to one informant, that house was an inn on the pike.[11] Judging from the size of the other house, it may have performed a similar function, as a competitor catching the eastward-moving traffic.

A short distance east of the cut and the two Federal-style houses is Great Western School. The small brick building stands on the Old Pike's north side below the fill that carries Route 40. The schoolhouse was built in 1870 and replaced an earlier log school that stood directly across the Old Pike from the present brick building.[12] There is room here to pull off the highway. Stop and look around. A historical marker on the school indicates restoration of the school during Ohio's celebration of the bicentennial of the Northwest Ordinance of 1787.

A short distance from the above locations is a turnoff for Lloydsville. Don't miss the straight stone bridge on the east side of this modest National Road settlement. Also, keep a lookout for the old wooden posts and steel cables along stretches of the old bypassed road. These were early guard rails when the National Road began carrying motor vehicles.

At Lloydsville's west end, rejoin US 40 and continue basically on the course of the National Road. Pass the Jamboree in the Hills site, an annual

Morristown, Ohio

A model plat of a National Road town

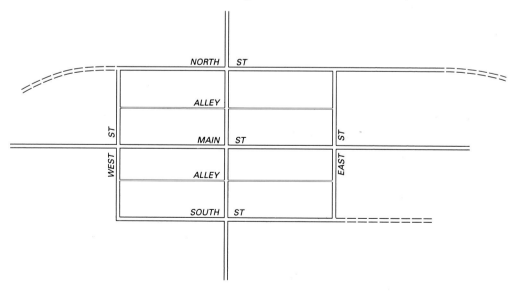

HUBERT G. H. WILHELM AND ARTIMUS KEIFFER

East Ohio Settlers: Principal Places of Origin, 1850

Ohio County	American Migrants		European Immigrants	
	State	Number	Country	Number
Belmont	Pennsylvania	3,252	Germany	303
	Virginia	2,661	Ireland	716
Franklin	Pennsylvania	2,261	Germany	909
	Virginia	1,384	Ireland	588
Guernsey	Pennsylvania	4,322	England	135
	Virginia	1,792	Ireland	982
Licking	Pennsylvania	2,967	England	399
	Virginia	3,154	Wales	761
Muskingum	Pennsylvania	5,385	Germany	1,574
	Virginia	3,563	Ireland	1,283

Source: Hubert G. H. Wilhelm, *The Origin and Distribution of Settlement Groups: Ohio 1850* (Athens, Ohio: Cutler Printing, 1982).

event that fills the air with country music and the fields with cars and campers. By this point, you have passed several original mile markers that were placed along the Old Pike. Although they regularly appear along US 40, they do not necessarily indicate the path of the National Road. They were moved from their original locations after construction of US 40 to lend an aura of history to the new road. When legible, they give the mileage to Cumberland, Maryland, and to Columbus, Ohio.

After a little over three miles, the Old Pike veers toward the north, leaving US 40, and brings us into one of the best preserved towns along the National Road, Morristown. It also stands at the highest point along this segment, over 1,300 feet. Morristown incorporates the road town plan. It stretches for nearly a mile, consisting of a wonderfully preserved main street and a back (or drovers') street with three churches. The following description from the National Register nomination reveals the early relationship of main street and backstreet: "Main Street runs along the base of the hill, and above Main and parallel to it is Church Street, the original main thoroughfare, Wheeling Road."[13] Morristown and Old Washington to the west are the only two towns along the National Road between Bridgeport and Columbus on the National Register of Historic Places. Stop here for a while and walk up and down Main Street to take a closer look at the buildings and appreciate the community's commitment to preservation. In 1991, the Ohio Historical Society honored the Morristown Historic Association with an award for its efforts.[14]

At the height of its development, during the early 1850s, Morristown had a large number of businesses that served the National Road. It included "many blacksmiths, saddlers, wagon makers, grocers, clothiers, and hotels. There was a cigar factory, glove factory and a woolen mill."[15] None is left today. The Black Horse Inn, established in 1807, is presently undergoing renovation. The residences along present-day Main Street included businesses from days gone by. There are a number of rowhouses, one room deep and two stories high with L additions in the rear. Most are brick construction. These houses may have functioned as apartments for families who worked for local merchants and craft shops. Most towns along the National Road include several rowhouses typical in Baltimore, Philadelphia, and other eastern cities.

Before leaving Morristown, walk a block north to Church Street. Here was the original location of Zane's Trace, locally known as Wheeling Road. It would continue to carry the heavy traffic as Main Street evolved on the National Road. Don't forget to read some of the gravestones at the cemetery beyond Church Street and at the Pioneer Cemetery on Main Street. They tell much about the people and the history of this place. Belmont County was settled primarily by American migrants from Pennsylvania and Virginia. The majority of the immigrants were from Ireland who labored on the Road, bought land, and stayed.

Highway Relationships

I-70 and "new" US 40 in relation to the National Road and "old" 40 between Hendrysburg and Fairview, Ohio.

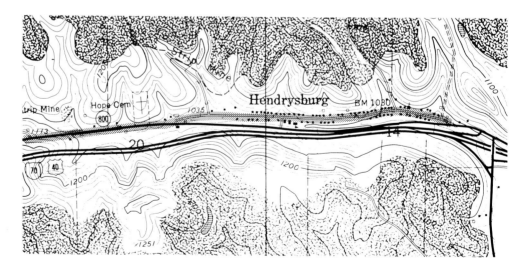

HUBERT G. H. WILHELM AND ARTIMUS KEIFFER

Heading westward from Morristown, we encounter another major US 40 cut. A farmstead stands on the north side of the road. The driveway is the Old Pike, which has a brick surface here. It terminates in a red barn that sits directly on the original right-of-way. About a mile and a half from the barn, US 40 and the National Road end abruptly against the fill of I-70. Here, one is forced to get on the ramp for I-70, which also becomes US 40. After a few miles, however, there is a chance to get back on old 40 and the National Road by way of the Hendrysburg exit. Follow Ohio 800 through Hendrysburg until its intersection with Alternate 40, locally also called the Old National Road. One will also find the following local names between Wheeling and Columbus: National Trail Road, Bridgewater Road, the Old Pike, Zane Road, and Brick Road.

Hendrysburg is a long Road town that occupies a narrow valley and is surrounded by strip-mined (coal) hills. During the National Road's heyday, Hendrysburg had two stagecoach inns.[16] Today the town is strongly residential. From Hendrysburg, at approximately 1,000 feet elevation, the Road climbs, within a mile, to 1,300 feet and then descends gently into Fairview at 1,238 feet. This countryside is typical of the unglaciated part of the Allegheny Plateau in Ohio. The landscape includes old strip-mine benches and highwalls, several woodlots, and baled hay and cattle in reclaimed areas now in pasture.

Fairview is a neat, old town prime for designation as a historic district with the caveat that it not become an antiques mecca as in New Market, Maryland. It is the first of several Road towns in Guernsey County, and it exem-

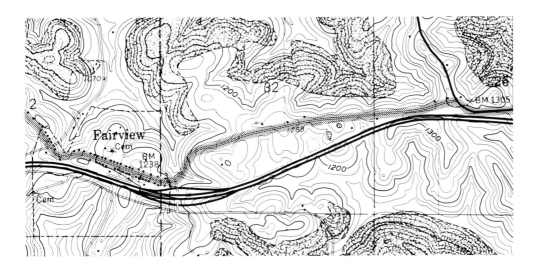

Fairview, Ohio

Grass tufts, saplings, and an electrical pole mark an active coal strip mine's original surface.

plifies how this section of eastern Ohio and southwestern Pennsylvania collected migrants from the three major culture areas along the eastern seaboard during the early nineteenth century. The fusion of habits and ideas from New England, southeastern Pennsylvania, and Virginia's Tidewater are still manifest here in subtle ways—surnames and origins in church records or on gravestones, and in the plans and designs of the houses. Fairview occupies a north-south ridge and the main street ascends from either end of town toward the center. There are some great old houses of many architectural styles and periods, including the ubiquitous I-rowhouse with several variations. For example, an Eastern Shore (Maryland) clapboard I-house with a stepped roof line appears on the left at 200 Fair Avenue, the main street. Adjacent to it on the west at 210 is a brick Pennsylvania one-and-one-half Federal-style, and next, at 240, stands a Greek Revival with a slate roof. Two churches and the cemetery align Oxford Street, the back (or drovers') road along the north edge of town. Fairview is yet another example of a National Road town with its contrasting main street business strip and the back

HUBERT G. H. WILHELM AND ARTIMUS KEIFFER

The rounded hills near exit 202 off I-70 are the signatures of a reclaimed surface mine; the standing water is courtesy of the local beavers. Soil and rock set aside during the mining process are replaced and recontoured and the new surface is often used as pasture by landowners. Since surface mining over broad areas destroys the natural drainage network, undrained pockets will trap rainwater and small marshes may form, with or without the help of castor.

road residential and churchyards. Strip mining continues on County Road 114 at the I-70 interchange; Fairview Cemetery (1808) is on the same county road to the west. A new residential community is planned for reclaimed land on Oxford Street northeast of town.

After Fairview there are two options to continue west. The less interesting is to return to I-70 and present-day 40 until the exit for Ohio 513. Turn north, and at the intersection with old US 40 and the National Road turn and follow these west into Middlebourne. The other option is to take old 40 west out of Fairview, which quickly terminates and becomes a county road, also known as Waymore Road. It loops around toward the north, then back south, and eventually rejoins old US 40.

MIDDLEBOURNE TO GRATIOT: EASTERN OHIO'S MUSKINGUM VALLEY CONSERVANCY REGION

Middlebourne is one of the smaller remnant towns along our route. Here was Hayes Tavern, built in the 1820s or 1830s by Greenberry Penn, a descendant of William Penn, founder of Philadelphia. (Note that Quaker City is six miles to the south.) The tavern was a popular stopping point and included Henry Clay among its many guests. Later owners changed the name to Locust Lodge.[17] Middlebourne's location coincides with the transition from strip-mined coal lands to areas that are under the jurisdiction of the Muskingum Watershed Conservancy District. Ohio conservancy districts date from the early 1900s. Their implementation was closely related to the disastrous floods of 1913 and followed state legislation that led directly to the creation of the first district in 1915, the Miami Valley Conservancy District.[18] The objective of the conservancy districts was to prevent downstream flooding through the construction of earthen dams and "retarding" basins on the tributaries of major streams. One of the principal culprits contributing to floods in the Ohio Valley was the Muskingum River. It forms one of the largest drainage basins of the state and among its tributaries are the Tuscarawas River from the north, the Kokosing-Mohican-Killbuck-Walhonding drainage from the northwest, the Licking River from the west, and the Conotton, Stillwater, Wills Creeks' drainage off the high-plateau portion toward the east. Forest clearance by farmers and lumber companies and strip mining greatly accelerated runoff, thereby contributing enormously to regular and serious floods.

The Muskingum Watershed Conservancy District was formed June 3, 1933. Construction of the first flood control structure, Tappan Dam, on Stillwater Creek in Harrison County, about 20 miles north of the National Road, began on January 3, 1935.[19] Since then many other dams and lakes have been added and the Muskingum Watershed has become one of the all-important recreation areas in Ohio, and offers camping, hiking, boating, fishing, and hunting. One of the most accessible park and lake areas, including a superb lodge, is Salt Fork State Park. The park area can be reached from Old Washington by way of Ohio 285 and Lake Ridge Road or by taking I-77 north to US 22, and then following the latter east for a little over six miles to the park entrance. From Middlebourne west, at the Quaker City exit, old US 40 becomes Bridgewater Road. It dips west into Salt Fork Valley and its broad alluvial plain. There is some evidence of agricultural activity on the bottom lands, while the surrounding slopes are in pastures and woodlots. About two miles out of Middlebourne is Carlisle Cemetery, with large old cedars, on the north side of the Road. The gravestones suggest that the local inhabitants are largely of Irish and English background. Just ahead,

The Salt Fork runs nearly parallel to the National Road west of Middlebourne and illustrates why the S-bridge was a pragmatic design for crossing streams at a time when stone was expensive to quarry and move to a construction site. The run-in ramps and this bridge could be shortened if the bridge turned to cross the stream at a 90-degree angle. More important, stonemasons could quickly cut the arch stones as right-angled cubes.

about half a mile, Bridgewater Road crosses Salt Fork on not only one of the best preserved S-bridges (c. 1828), but also the clearest example of why the S shape was, for the time, the most practical way engineers could find to cross a river. Immediately adjacent to the bridge is a white I-house with slate roof, a barn, and a rusted iron post along the road that once supported a basketball hoop. When the old Road was resurfaced during the early twentieth century and traffic was minimal, residents converted the level and solid road surface to a basketball court.

S-bridges were one of the unique features on the National Road, especially in the hilly sections of eastern Ohio. Stories abound as to why S-bridges were built. One suggests that it forced drivers to rein in their horses as they crossed the bridge, thus preventing possible accidents. Another offers that the bridges were built around huge trees. Still another holds that two bridge builders challenged each other over several beers to construct S-shaped bridges.[20] The most likely explanation, however, is that the Road and creeks or rivers were rarely in a direct-angle alignment. In order for the bridge to be constructed, as it should be, in 90-degree relationship with the stream bed, with entrances to the bridge conforming with the road location, an S-shaped structure was selected to solve this engineering puzzle.

The stone guard rails flared at the outer entrances to the bridge, as if to invite travelers to cross. The flare no doubt permitted drovers to get their animals more successfully onto and across these bridges. At one time, there were numerous S-bridges on the National Road of eastern Ohio. Today only a few remain as Old Pike artifacts.

Immediately west of the S-bridge, the old Road ends against a hillside and the adjacent fill of I-70. To the north of this abandoned link is a farmstead with a handsome brick I-house. This site offers a fine panoramic view of the Salt Fork Valley. An even better viewpoint is from the other side of I-70. From Bridgewater Road, cross the I-70 underpass and make an immediate right turn onto a county road that parallels I-70 and US 40 and takes you past two tiny settlements, Elizabethtown and Easton, into Old Washington. For those traveling on US 40 and I-70, 40 leaves I-70 here at the Shenandoah Inn and truckstop (1972), and rejoins its old course on the south side of Old Washington, where it forms the intersection with Ohio 285.

Before heading into Old Washington, stop at the town's cemetery on the south side of the Road on a prominent hill. The gravestones are old and speak of Scots heritage. The billboard—face to the interstate, back to the cemetery—offers another reminder of the interstate's commercial presence, even here among the evergreens where killdeer have nests in the open grass.

Old Washington is the second town on this section of the Old Pike with

Interstate 70, Exit 186, Old Washington, Ohio

Megalithic concrete blocks segregate a vintage Freightliner at the Shenandoah Inn and Truck Stop, built in the early 1970s. The panoramic windows provide a grand view of the parking lot, fuel pumps, and interchange.

HUBERT G. H. WILHELM AND ARTIMUS KEIFFER

a historic district. Founded in 1805 as New Washington, it became an important stop on Zane's Trace and then the National Road. For years, it competed with Cambridge for the Guernsey County's seat. But the railroad brought decline to the National Road towns and Old Washington, as it became known, was bypassed by the railroad and left to stagnate. Perhaps to soothe the angry citizens for the loss of the county seat, Old Washington received the county fairgrounds, which stand at the east end of town.

Because railroads monopolized the region's commercial traffic by the 1850s, Old Washington, along with other National Road towns, was culturally and economically isolated, caught in an architectural time warp. Since few new buildings were erected, those still standing date from pre-Victorian times and include examples of Federal and Greek Revival architecture. Thus, though the town is small, its buildings retain a purity of design. Preservation efforts in Old Washington have concentrated on this lack in diversity of styles as a central planning element, thereby assuring the survival of the simple historic dignity of the town's appearance and image.

Most of the houses on Old Washington's main street were built between 1830 and 1850. They are largely I-house variety in form, built in frame or brick. There are several rowhouses, and one of the most stylish buildings is the Albert Lawrence House. Built in Italianate style around 1857, it became known as the Colonial Inn. Across the road, but also on the south side of Main Street, was the American Inn, a two-story, row-type structure. Several other gable-front buildings, most originally including businesses and shops, represent a shift in fashion toward Greek Revival forms. Today, the majority are converted to residences, and a few are empty and some dilapidated, the trademark of bypassed towns. As in other Road towns, public buildings (in Old Washington it's the school) occupy land on the back road. The town has a small grocery store but no restaurant. These services are concentrated next to I-70 just south of Old Washington. On July 24, 1863, Morgan's Confederate raiders were overtaken and defeated in Old Washington by Union cavalry.

From Old Washington, Cambridge, its one-time competitor for urban dominance in Guernsey County, lies six miles to the west. The terrain is choppy here, dipping into narrow valleys or hollows to 940 feet or so, then quickly ascending to similarly narrow ridges that extend to almost 1,100 feet elevation. US 40 follows a straight course across cuts and fills. The National Road, in contrast, here known as Zane Road (the path of Zane's Trace), bends

Old Washington, Ohio

I-houses in row-form present a clean if exaggerated Federal-inspired symmetry.

northward about half a mile west of Old Washington and follows a ridge, thereby missing the numerous dips and rises. Peacock Road (also Center Township Road 650) is on the National Register of Historic Places and represents one of the few extant examples of the brick and asphalt road surfaces used to improve the Old Pike. In 1918, and in response to urgent requests to improve the National Road for transporting war-related products, the segment of road from Cambridge to Old Washington received a layer of brick. The task involved leveling the old macadam surface, which then was covered with a four- to six-inch layer of crushed stone or slag. The crushed stone was compressed and topped by an inch or so of sand as a foundation for the brick, which was laid by prison labor. Sometime between 1933 and 1950 the bricked-over sections received an asphalt cover. The latter has been worn away over the years, but is still quite apparent along Peacock Road, especially on the Road's outer edges next to the sandstone curb stones.[21] The improvements of the National Road in Ohio began in 1914 and are memorialized on a huge slab of granite that stands on US 40's north side at a place called Eagle Nest, only a short distance west of Brownsville. The inscription on the slab reads:

Old National Road
Built 1825 Rebuilt 1914
through the efforts of
James McCoy
Governor of Ohio

Also chiseled in the granite are pictures of a Conestoga wagon and an early automobile, as well as the distances to Columbus (32 miles) and Cumberland (220 miles). The white clapboard building near the top of the hill has voting booths on the west end.

Immediately after reentering US 40 from Peacock Road, the National Road again leaves 40 to the north and, following more or less the same contour level, passes the small settlement of Craig. The old National Road and US 40 rejoin where a weathered board-and-batten bank barn serves as a

HUBERT G. H. WILHELM AND ARTIMUS KEIFFER

landmark, about a mile east of the interchange of US 40 with I-77. A small commercial strip lies just beyond the interchange. It ascends the bluff on which Cambridge is located, overlooking the Wills Creek Valley. Cambridge, the county seat, was founded in 1806 and was named after Cambridge, Maryland, because several early settlers had come from that historic town on the Eastern Shore.[22] A branch of the Old Pike very likely passed a block south of present Main Street (on Turner Avenue) with its 1870s business structures, several churches, the restored Beckwith Hotel, and the old courthouse set back from the street and fronted by a small, well-shaded park. Both the Baltimore & Ohio and Pennsylvania Central railroads serviced Cambridge in days past and contributed greatly to the town's manufacturing function. There was a glass factory, several potteries, and a steel plant. Most are gone today, but the history of glassmaking survives in the Cambridge Glass Museum. Hopalong Cassidy spent part of his childhood here and those days are commemorated by an annual festival.

Upon leaving Cambridge, cross the Cambridge Viaduct (a depot stands below on the flood plain). At the Frisbee Hotel, US 40 makes a sharp turn northwest around some steep sandstone bluffs that are part of the

Old Washington, Ohio
Ohio's version of the National Road mile marker in sandstone. This one appears to be a reproduction. It locates the Buckeye Trail Middle School and Old Washington Elementary thirty-two miles east of Zanesville and forty-two miles west of Wheeling. A stagecoach of the National Road Stage Company, whose nineteenth-century headquarters were in Uniontown, Pennsylvania, could have made the trip to Zanesville in just over three hours in the 1840s.

Near Pecock Road, west of Old Washington, Ohio

US 40 follows a cut through black shale, bypassing a remnant of the brick-surfaced old National Road nearby.

southern flank of the Wills Creek Valley. In contrast, Dewey Avenue follows the Old Trail, here called Manilla Road (Guernsey County 430). The old National Road skirts the bluff before crossing Crooked Creek. The crossing here is by way of a great straight stone bridge. Soon the road connects with US 40 at Fairdale. This old road today travels through an extended auto junkyard, but the grade and brick surface provide a glimpse into the past when road travel was by horse and carriage and ox and wagon.

Fairdale is a strung-out road village with Cambridge Tool and Die and a late 1940s truckstop (notice the two concrete-block buildings in the rear once used as truckers' sleeping rooms). On the south side of the highway is a Champion Spark Plug manufacturing plant employing about 250 people. This is the only ceramic spark-plug insulator plant in the United States. Raw materials for ceramic manufacturing are shipped here via train from suppliers in Arkansas and elsewhere. The twenty-one-acre site was developed in

HUBERT G. H. WILHELM AND ARTIMUS KEIFFER

the early 1950s and production began in 1955. Just beyond is the 1960s Chals drive-in restaurant. The exaggerated large windows on the semicircular frame were intended to create an image of modernity, and the bold sign could be seen above the roof of the auto in front of you, even if you were traveling at 55 miles per hour. A mile and a half farther west, a row of houses and power lines on the north side announce the old brick-surfaced Pike. The next jog in the road comes up quickly and leads into Cassel. At the east end of this tiny settlement is a very well preserved S-bridge. The small park here is an ideal location for a panoramic view of the Old Pike and adjacent US 40. The S-bridge is over a small, unnamed tributary of Crooked Creek.

The next settlement west of Cassel is New Concord, in Muskingum County and just across the county line from Guernsey. The Pike-related parts of New Concord follow the classic pattern of a National Road town with a main street and adjacent backstreets. The town's location coincides with the valley of North Crooked Creek. Initially called Concord, the town was founded in 1827, after the National Road had been constructed at the site. By 1836, the town's citizens had established Muskingum College, which continues to thrive as a small liberal arts college with attractive buildings and grounds. Even the new architecture is accomplished. Besides the college, New Concord is known for two of its native sons. One, William Rainey Harper (1856–1906), became president of the University of Chicago. His log-cabin birthplace has been preserved.[23] The other, John Glenn, was America's

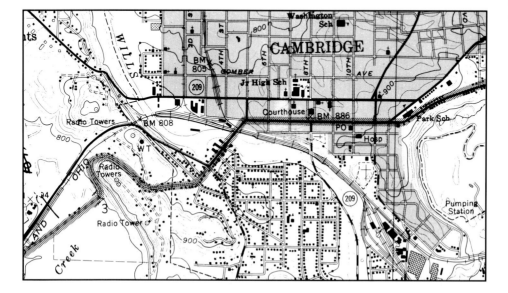

Cambridge, Ohio

Cambridge, Ohio

As important as being a repository of county records and legal documents, and venue for the application of law, the courthouse and its square were the favored place to declare symbolically to the passing public that the land is fertile, the merchants are wealthy, and the residents are patriotic.

first astronaut to orbit the Earth; after leaving NASA he entered politics and in 1992 won his fourth term in the U.S. Senate. At New Concord, Ohio 83 offers north-south linkage between Coshocton and Beverly near the Ohio River. Main Street still hints at National Road ambiance with its architecture, scale, and parallel drovers' streets. A number of great old houses with long brick facades are symbolic of the important interrelationship of house and Road. On the west side of town and on the Road's north side another well-preserved S-bridge crosses Fox Creek.

Two miles west of New Concord, US 40 veers southwest, while the Old Pike cuts north across higher terrain before entering Norwich (pronounced "Norwick"), dropping into town along a tight S curve. Immediately on the right or the north side of the Road stands a historical marker that commemorates the death of Christopher Baldwin, librarian of the American Antiquarian Society, Worcester, Massachusetts. The tablet reads that Baldwin was "killed on this curve, 20 August 1835, by the overturning of a stage coach. This being the first traffic accident on record in the state." He is buried in the small cemetery at the town's west end. The village school and meetinghouse front on Norwich's public green. On the north side of Main Street and west of uptown is the Ralph Hardesty house, a good example of vernacular stone construction. It is, in fact, one of the few stone houses along the Old Road between Bridgeport and Columbus. Norwich is a pleasant hamlet, with dramatic views from west and east out of town.

After the National Road reconnects with US 40 west of Norwich, it is another mile to the National Road Museum, a contemporary structure. The museum stands south of 40 and across from Baker's Motel, a typical 1950s-genre structure with a huge "space port"–type sign. The motel is a drab-looking place that seems to stretch interminably along the highway. It continues to function, although some parts serve as rental units. Here, in the vicinity of Zanesville, old motels are more numerous. Some try to survive as motels; others are abandoned or have changed to other pursuits, including antique and "junque" shops, retirement homes, apartments, sales barns,

HUBERT G. H. WILHELM AND ARTIMUS KEIFFER

and, in one case, a church. *C'est la vie* on contemporary US 40. The Baker's Motel owners are fortunate because interstate planners decided to build an I-70 interchange here. Now commercial traffic pours off the interstate and onto old 40 so even the old motels endure the change. In fact, the museum has led to a parasitic strip of antique shops west of the interchange.

The museum was constructed under the auspices of the Ohio Historical Society beside the National Road, which followed a path just south of US 40. It opened in June of 1973 and the exhibits portray the sequential changes of the Road, from Zane's Trace to National Road to National Trail to US 40. A diorama shows the progress of the National Road to US 40. Artifacts include a huge Conestoga wagon, some vintage automobiles, and the usual paraphernalia that goes with travel. There is also a sizable collection of books dealing with the Road, as well as numerous copies of tales of the West by that local Zanesville boy, Zane Grey, a direct descendant of Ebenezer Zane, the builder of Ohio's first interior road. The museum is open from April through September.

West of the museum, US 40 and the National Road dip underneath I-70 and continue across the low swells and swales characteristic of this part of the Appalachian Plateau. Here, on the outskirts of Zanesville, the Road is aligned by a strip of residential and small commercial properties. There is

Cambridge, Ohio

West of Cambridge, the design—and menu—of Chals Drive-In restaurant reverberates with signals that US 40 has just plunged back into the 1960s.

New Concord, Ohio

Saplings and hardwoods encroach on an impressive 1826 S-bridge near New Concord.

New Concord, Ohio

Rusticated stones show little sign of age, the bridge still competent to carry the bricked-over National Road.

HUBERT G. H. WILHELM AND ARTIMUS KEIFFER

one small Road town before Zanesville, Bridgeville. It is easy to miss, but includes a well-hidden S-bridge, the last one remaining on the route to Columbus. The telephone-line easement is the clue to the Old Pike's actual location.

Before entering Zanesville, US 40 passes the Pleasant Grove interchange with I-70. A small cluster of food, fuel, and lodging services are accumulating here in the shadow of an old US 40–oriented store that sells locally produced pottery. Beyond the interchange, US 40 descends into the narrow valley of a tributary to Mill Run which, in turn, flows into the Muskingum River. On the valley's east side is a truck distribution center and a large machinery dealer and, at the top of the hill, a 1950s-style circular drive-in restaurant. With some imagination, one can still hear early rock-and-roll tunes and the clatter of carhops moving between the gaily colored Chevys, Fords, and Plymouths of the era. It's called Juanita's today and still serves local customers and some long-distance travelers.

From the bottom of the small valley, the roads, which now also includes US 22, climb the sharp hill into east Zanesville, then twist down a last hill into the center of town. The town is a major transportation node where I-70 and US 40 meet US 22, and Ohio Routes 60, 93, 146, 555, and 666.

Pleasant Grove interchange, east of Zanesville, Ohio

Read the changes in fortune and focus on the old, square building beside US 40: the second-floor apartment's stairway has been pulled down. "Local & Area Pottery"—the sign on the building's front is four times as large and meant to be read by interstate travelers—"Olde Towne Antiques 28 Dealers . . . Main Downtown." The stilt signs at the new gas stations are not intended for US 40 traffic.

Zanesville used to be an important manufacturing center with numerous clay-products plants, and glass and steel production. Some of these activities remain, but the town is also a major distribution center for truck-borne goods, capitalizing on its highway connections to supply Appalachian Ohio.

Downtown Zanesville—a boomtown before the Civil War when the canal was king—stands at the confluence of the Licking and Muskingum Rivers. From the top of the east bluff, the old roads descend rapidly from a gritty neighborhood into downtown Zanesville and Main Street. The approach to downtown is curvy and passes the imposing basilica-like (à la Florentine domes) St. Nicholas Catholic Church edifice. Outside of the courthouse-related businesses, little commercial activity remains downtown. Much of that is redistributed along the principal access routes, especially US 22 south of Zanesville, and Ohio 60 to the north.

Main Street crosses the Muskingum River on the famous Y-bridge. The present bridge is the fifth one; a covered bridge was among its predecessors. Zanesville's regional centrality was greatly enhanced when the National Road was built through town in 1830. This was followed by improvements

HUBERT G. H. WILHELM AND ARTIMUS KEIFFER

in the Muskingum River for navigation, linking Zanesville with the Ohio River at Marietta and the Ohio & Erie Canal at Dresden. The canal brought Zanesville into Cleveland's economic orbit. The locks on the Muskingum River remain in operation today. They are rare technological survivors and a nostalgic ingredient of the Muskingum River Recreational Waterway between Marietta and Zanesville.

After crossing the Muskingum and Licking Rivers, the National Road and US 40 hug the Licking River's steep southern bank. This western part of Zanesville has been torn up by numerous cuts and fills for I-70. US 40 once more crosses I-70 via an underpass and at this point is just south of the Old Pike. Again, a row of houses and electric lines give visual clues to the National Road's original alignment. Approximately 2.3 miles west of the interchange, two imposing stone buildings on the highway's north side come into view. The first is the Smith House and its neighbor, the Headley Inn. The Smith House dates from 1830 and the sign on the Headley Inn places its origin circa 1802. The Old Pike passed directly in front and a small creek flows between them and stone bridge remnants. The stone was quarried from a nearby cliff, and so the Smith House has often been called the Cliff Rock House. Both of the houses were operated as inns and taverns and re-

The view of Putnam Hill Park, Zanesville, Ohio

East Ohio's north-south main transport routes followed the Muskingum River valley. The truss bridge used by the Pennsylvania and B&O Railroads crosses the river; warehouses back up to the canal. The courthouse (*left center*) anchors one end of Main Street, St. Nicholas Church (*far right*) the other.

Zanesville, Ohio

Downhill into Zanesville.

Zanesville, Ohio

Genteel English-style and robust American "trail" bikes share a Main Street store window below St. Nicholas Church.

HUBERT G. H. WILHELM AND ARTIMUS KEIFFER

mained in business until the 1860s when wagon and carriage traffic on the National Road declined. The Headley Inn was revived after 1922 and meals were served to auto travelers on US 40. The Smith House, however, became a private residence. The two buildings are on the National Register of Historic Places and remain privately owned.[24]

The Headleys, as so many others along the Old Pike, built their inn initially to provide shelter and a place to eat for the road-building crews.[25] Property owners, fronting on the Road, quickly learned to "make a buck" from the traffic and travelers using the new highway, and America's first strip development was born. Although inns or taverns were licensed, anyone living along the Road could put out a shingle advertising food, drink, and lodging. These "public" houses ranged from the most primitive log huts to grandiose establishments. Columbus taverns included the Colonial Inn, White Horse, Swan, Red Lion, Black Bear, and, perhaps best known, Neil House. The latter survived until the 1980s when it was razed to clear space for a highrise state office tower. In Ohio, "between Zanesville and Colum-

Zanesville, Ohio

The Muskingum County economy must have been booming in 1874 when the elaborately symbolized courthouse was erected. The Main Street facade seems an eclectic collection of Greek Revival and Second Empire styles. Adjacent, an unlikely business building trio. A 1930s Art Deco facade on the four-story building contrasts with 1970s metal sheathing on the right. A narrow vestige of the nineteenth century peeks onto the street through vacant windows. Old or new, the facades have not succeeded in retaining businesses at this location.

Zanesville, Ohio

Y-Bridge, the early 1980s version, at the junction of the Licking and Muskingum Rivers and the National Road. It has since been replaced with a modern, less elegant, version, though retaining the Y.

bus, taverns marked every section of the pike. . . . Public houses were spaced with almost mathematical regularity, one to every seven to ten miles."[26] The small Road towns would have at least two, but often three, four, or more public houses. The better ones stood along Main Street, while less elaborate drovers' houses were on the back streets. These latter ones, especially, were the forerunners to the American motel, located on the periphery of towns and cities and serving all those dependent on the highway for a living.

From the Headley Inn westward, US 40 keeps slightly to the south of the Old Pike as both follow Timber Run Valley. Typically, the National Road hugs the "break of the slope" between the narrow floodplain and the adjacent hills. It was a safe location, above the high water in Timber Run. As the valley narrows, the roads climb toward the ridge, which here lies at a little over 1,000 feet. Signs indicate the approaching turnoff for Mount Sterling, another Road town bypassed by US 40. In fact, 40 bypasses the majority of National Road towns between Bridgeport and Zanesville. From Zanesville westward, the situation reverses as 40 continued through most towns. The reason, in part, was related to the nature of the terrain. In the unglaciated, hillier parts of eastern Ohio, the National Road often switched back and forth from a straight path because it could not span some of the deeper ravines or overcome the higher knobs. US 40 construction employed large cuts and fills to stay a straighter course. In the process, 40 was laid around many old Road towns. West from Zanesville, the terrain is less rugged and both the National Road and US 40 follow a relatively straight corridor. Of course, the town's importance also influenced whether or not US 40 was directed through or to a bypass.

Mount Sterling lies across two hills and a small valley. The latter is still known as Congress Hollow because in 1836 the stagecoach carrying Henry Clay and some congressmen overturned, spilling the passengers.[27] The Mount Sterling cutoff reconnects with US 40 at the small settlement of Hopewell. The National Road continues south of 40 and is well marked by the location of two barns and a farmhouse. It probably passed between the house to the north of the Road and the barns on the south side. It then proceeds

HUBERT G. H. WILHELM AND ARTIMUS KEIFFER

Bypassed Settlements	Settlements without Bypass	Bypassed Settlements	Settlements without Bypass
Bridgeport to Zanesville		*Zanesville to Columbus*	
Brookside	Bridgeport	Mt. Sterling	Brownsville
Wolfhurst	St. Clairsville	Gratiot	Linnville
Lansing	East Richland	Amsterdam	Jacksontown
Lloydsville	Cambridge	Etna	Hebron
Morristown	New Concord	Luray	
Hendrysburg	Zanesville	Kirkersville	
Fairview		Wagram	
Middlebourne		Reynoldsburg	
Elizabethtown		Columbus	
Easton			
Old Washington			
Craig			
Fairdale			
Norwich			
Bridgeville			

Note: In building US 40, highway engineers choose to bypass some settlements but allowed the new highway to follow the old National Road's alignment through others.

East of Hopewell, Ohio

A "double-barreled" bank barn carries the traditional message found on old barns all across the eastern states. The man responsible for painting more than 20,000 such signs on the American landscape since 1946 is Harley Warrick, who retired in 1991. He resides in Belmont, Ohio.

past Hopewell School, cuts across US 40, and enters the turnoff for Gratiot. At this location, the Old Pike passes from the unglaciated Alleghenies into the glaciated hills.

GRATIOT TO JACKSONTOWN: ILLINOISAN AND WISCONSIN TERMINAL MORAINE COUNTRY

Gratiot, named for Brig. Gen. Charles Gratiot, U.S. Army Corps of Engineers, an early Road administrator, stands on a small rise that coincides with the farthest advance of the Illinoisan continental glacier in Ohio. Of the four glacial stages that affected large parts of the United States—the Nebraskan, Kansan, Illinoisan, and Wisconsin—the last two were especially important for Ohio. The last ice advance, the Wisconsin, has been responsible for much of the state's surface detail, especially in western Ohio. It reshaped and covered most of the glacial features produced by the Illinoisan, which preceded it.[28] In east-central and southwestern Ohio, however, the Wisconsin glaciers did not reach the limits of Illinoisan ice. At Gratiot (pronounced Gradeot), the National Road crosses a narrow strip of Illinoisan glaciation about eight miles in east-west extent. The ancient glacial topographic features have been modified by subsequent surface runoff and stream erosion, so the casual observer will notice few differences between the glaciated landscape and the unglaciated areas immediately east. Further complicating the glacial frontier is the underlying Appalachian Plateau, Ohio's Allegheny Hills, which continue for some distance west of Gratiot.

Gratiot again follows the Road town model—its main street is flanked by two parallel streets. Several well-kept I-houses, including the ubiquitous rowhouse and a large L-shaped structure, stand beside the Road. The large building housed an International Order of Odd Fellows (IOOF) Lodge, but probably was an inn in earlier days. At Gratiot, the National Road, US 40, and I-70 track along a corridor barely a quarter mile wide. Just west of town, the Old Pike crosses Valley Run on a well-preserved straight stone bridge. Several restored log structures line the Road's south side. At this point, the National Road, which crossed into Licking County just east of Gratiot, enters the old Refugee Lands of Ohio, a small and unique land subdivision that extends to Columbus. The Refugee Lands area was set aside by the Continental Congress in the Land Ordinance of 1785 as a haven for sixty-seven Canadian refugees "who had assisted the colonies during the Revolution and therefore could not return to their country after the war."[29] Refugee

Road, running east out of Columbus and past the large Eastland Mall, is a well-recognized local highway. Many people travel it daily, but few know its historical and geographical importance.

For the next few miles, US 40 and the National Road coincide. Two miles west of Gratiot and below a small rise is Brownsville. The Old Coach Inn stands in the center of town—a two-story, red-brick survivor, which, according to the large sign over its entrance, was built in 1826. The inn antedates the National Road and most likely served travelers on an earlier road through town. A Union 76 station across the street serves as an informal community center. Ohio 668 forms the principal intersection with US 40. Four miles north of the intersection in Brownsville is Flint Ridge Memorial and a few miles further the Black Hand Gorge of the Licking River. The town's cemetery is on an elevated site immediately off the south back road in Brownsville. West of Brownsville, the Road dips into Berry Run Valley where an old mill stands on the Road's north side.

Brownsville, Ohio

Gasoline is dispensed from roadside pumps as it has been since the 1910s. For sale: a roll of old woven wire, once used across the Middle West to fence hog pens and pastures.

After Berry Run, the roads ascend the next ridge and less than a mile out of Brownsville pass Eagle Nest and a granite marker commemorating improvements to the National Road. From here, the Road continues the slow climb across the Wisconsin-age terminal moraine. The countryside is irregular; a thin veneer of glacial till blankets the remnant hills, while in the valleys the deposits are much deeper. Since the end of the Wisconsin glacial period, about 8,000 to 10,000 years ago, stream erosion has greatly altered the land surface. The two roads diverge frequently in this rough terrain: US 40 makes its way via cuts and fills, whereas the National Road follows the topography, although the alignment deviations are minor.

At Linnville, the landscape begins to open as the amount of timberland decreases. Farms have more pastureland and, here and there, land is tilled and planted, mostly in corn. At Amsterdam, just a few miles west of Linnville, the transition between the less and more intensively farmed areas is apparent to even the casual observer. Although the terrain is still irregular, the soils are more fertile—derived from glacial deposits from the last two ice ages (Wisconsinan and Illinoisan), including differing quantities of lime, incorporated into the glacial till as the ice scraped across the limestone and dolomite bedrock of western and central Ohio. Ohio's soil map identifies this area as having "Soils in Low Lime Glacial Drift of Wisconsin Age." These soils are subdivided into a number of local soil associations which, in general, were formed from sandstone and shale and small amounts of limestone. The roads cut across the Bennington-Cardington-Pewamo Association area, soils, which evolved from "limy clay loam glacial till" and will return good crop yields, provided they are well drained.[30] Although these soils are very acidic and not very fertile, they are more productive than those in the eastern unglaciated sections. Because the unglaciated country is often rugged and stream-dissected, once settlers cleared the forest, soil erosion became a very serious problem, and valley bottoms filled with hillside sediments. Across broad areas in southeastern Ohio, topsoil is thin or totally absent. Ironically, valley farming is severely handicapped by frequent flooding.[31]

Amsterdam is a small settlement set high on a remnant hill of resistant bedrock, elevation 1,180 feet. The site was barely skimmed by a thin sheet of Wisconsin-age ice and buried under a few feet of terminal moraine. US 40 bypasses the village along a ten- to twenty-foot deep road cut. Immediately after passing the sign for Amsterdam, make a sharp right onto the small road that enters the highway from the north side. This is the Old Pike.

HUBERT G. H. WILHELM AND ARTIMUS KEIFFER

It parallels 40 for a few hundred yards before crossing a deep ravine on a great old stone bridge. The bridge has one surviving and well-shaped principal corner stone on its south side wall. It is the only one of its kind found on the surviving bridges between Bridgeport and Columbus. An ideal place to pause and consider the Road's context is on Amsterdam's east side, along a small stretch of the abandoned Pike. Here stands a restored brick I-house, a short distance back from the Road. It dominates today, as it did years ago, the view toward the southeast.

From Amsterdam, both roads follow a straight path into an open basin locally known as Quarry Run and within a mile drop almost 200 feet in elevation. This is a kettle-like feature and is part of the terminal moraine landscape. Stone and gravel from the quarry probably were used to build the Old Pike or make later improvements. West of Amsterdam, and on the north side of the Road on one of the area's great promontories, is Fairmount Cemetery and Fairmount Presbyterian Church. The latter was founded in 1833, the same year the National Road was constructed through this area, and rebuilt in 1883. The site is located directly next to an Indian mound, which most likely functioned as a signal hill. Mounds such as this one were built on a series of elevated places from where smoke signals could be transmitted and received. This mound forms a single, small element in

Presbyterian Church west of Amsterdam, Ohio

A Hopewell Culture mound stood sentinel in the Ohio woodland for almost two millennia before white settlers and the National Road brought different cultural attributes. Some scholars believe the mounds were signal points.

the complex of burial, effigy, and ceremonial mounds that make up the Newark Earth Works, constructed nearly two thousand years ago by the Hopewell group of pre-European native Americans.

West of Quarry Run Valley, the roads climb quickly another terminal moraine slope, passing two farmsteads. After another mile or so, the route enters Jacksontown, a crossroad settlement. Ohio 13 runs north from Athens, Ohio, and served the well-known Hocking Valley Coal Field. It continues northward through Mount Vernon, Mansfield, and Norwalk to Huron on Lake Erie. About two miles north of the intersection in Jacksontown is Dawes Arboretum. Jacksontown is a small place, but had a stagecoach inn that served National Road travelers from the intersection's northwest corner. The inn featured a dining room, bar, billiard hall, barbershop, and thirteen sleeping rooms. In 1918, it was purchased by ancestors of the present owner and operated as Clark's Hotel. It remained in use until Labor Day 1954, when it burned to the ground. A restaurant was constructed on the site, which remains a popular place. Stop to sample some of the best coconut-cream pie in Ohio.[32]

JACKSONTOWN TO COLUMBUS: OUT OF THE HILLS AND INTO THE FLAT COUNTRY

West of Jacksontown, the roads, coinciding almost perfectly, enter the transition area between the subdued foothills of the Alleghenies and the Central Plains. This area was well worked by both Illinoisan and Wisconsin glaciers and little remains of the heights, while lower-lying areas were choked with glacial sediment. Unless affected by subdivision expansion around some of the larger towns and cities, most of the land is in agriculture. Farmers here raise corn, soybeans, and wheat; a few produce beef cattle (look for black angus and mixed breeds, such as a Hereford cross). The small woodlots in the distance are remnants of the original hardwood forest that once covered much of the eastern states—woodland cut down by settlers, primarily from the Middle Atlantic states, and by European immigrants. Just two miles south of US 40 is Buckeye Lake, one of the state's premier recreational areas. It was built from an area of glacial bogs (Cranberry Bog) and in earlier days served to supply water to the Ohio & Erie Canal, whose course intersected with the western end of the lake at the site of Millersport. The area to the south of the lake in Perry and Fairfield Counties was settled primarily by Pennsylvania-German folk. It is a landscape of

well-tended farms and small brick-built country churches. Lancaster, the county seat of Fairfield County, forms the center of this settlement area and is named for Lancaster, Pennsylvania.

A mile west of Jacksontown, the roads dramatically drop off the terminal moraine and enter the valley of the South Fork of the Licking River. Lakewood High School and football field, home of the Lancers, stand along the highway's south side. Immediately across the roads is the National Road Railroad Museum. Both private and commercial investors are capitalizing upon the proximity to Reynoldsburg and Columbus, and the availability of cheap land along US 40; it is possible that in another generation a ribbon of strip development will overwhelm much of the Road between Reynoldsburg and Columbus, given present-day trends.

At Hebron, the National Road crosses the Ohio & Erie Canal just south of the intersection of US 40 and Ohio 79. The canal was the state's principal south-north link during the nineteenth century's early decades. At Hebron (pronounced "*Hee*-bron") near the Licking River summit, workers turned the first spadeful of earth on July 4, 1825, beginning canal construction. Anyone who believes that Americans of that era did not appreciate the symbolic gesture need only look to Hebron. The canal opened for traffic here in 1828.[33] The Road makes a distinct kink where it crosses the canal bed and "clicks" into another small grid of streets on the canal's west side. Here, also, is the intersection with Ohio 79 and a Conrail spur. Ohio 79 comes north from Buck-

Hebron, Ohio

A vernacular roadside reminder that ice cream delights await those who enter the "new" County Fair Foods and Pizza Barn, where the owners still dispense Cummins Flavors, including Bear Claw and Superman.

Luray, Ohio

Autoracing followed
horseracing as a male-dom-
inated entertainment that
employed the tools of
transportation. At the
National Trail Raceway on
a Sunday afternoon, smoke
pours from the tires as a
driver launches a drag-racer
along the one-quarter mile
track in search of maxi-
mum speed in minimum
time. Specially prepared
dragsters now attain speeds
of over 300 miles per hour
by the time they reach the
end of the 1,320-foot track
in an elapsed time of less
than five seconds.

eye Lake and continues toward Newark, the county seat. Hebron's position astride both the canal and the National Road gave it extraordinary accessibility, an advantage that faded when the canal era ended and the railroad began to dominate cross-country travel and freight hauling. I-70 brought Hebron a different kind of accessibility—an interchange is only two miles south—and potential commuters from Newark, Lancaster, and Columbus are all close enough to make the old settlement an attractive place to rehabilitate an old house or for developers to plat new residential subdivisions. The town retains many traditional businesses, including the old Cummins Ice Cream factory, now the County Fair Foods and Pizza Barn.

From Hebron, the National Road and US 40 proceed across a small ridge, still covered with woodlots, and then drop back into the South Fork Valley. Luray, a small crossroads village, stands at the base of the rise and the intersection with Ohio 37. Two farmsteads with Italianate-style houses occupy the intersection's southern corners, a small church the northwest corner. A large lumber store on the northeast corner is a recent strip-development product. Ohio 37 connects northward into Granville.

North of 40 and immediately west of Luray are the Buckeye Valley Airport and the National Trail Raceway (on the Winston drag-racing circuit). Airfields and racetracks require many acres for construction and many more to buffer sensitive neighbors from noise and traffic. Since this place is still about twenty-five miles from downtown Columbus, and land is relatively cheap, developers have blessed Luray with these two institutions that benefit from direct access to US 40 and advantages in low real estate taxes and favorable—or no—rural zoning laws.

Farmsteads along the roads quite often indicate the Old Pike's alignment, as do the telephone lines. The roads now lie on terrain where cuts and fills are less important, and from here to Reynoldsburg follow essentially the same track. Three small towns remain between Luray and Reynoldsburg: Kirkersville, Etna, and Wagram. Kirkersville stands on a bluff adjacent to a small South Fork tributary. The village is close enough to Columbus to be an attractive place to establish a landscaping nursery and raise trees and shrubs for the urban market. Although the village expanded northward

HUBERT G. H. WILHELM AND ARTIMUS KEIFFER

along Ohio 158, its layout suggests the road town model with main street and backstreets. The broad main street suggests that early residents were not as anxious as were people in other towns to encroach upon the National Road's right-of-way by placing their buildings at the very edge of the road. One of the few stone or brick buildings in town is the bank, and it is the only structure whose facade employs a pretense toward a formal "high style" in its arched second-story windows. Most of the other main-street buildings are vernacular clapboarded structures. And they are

Kirkersville, Ohio

A nursery's balled and burlaped trees await a short truck ride to the Columbus suburbs.

noticeably free-standing on their own lots rather than adhering to the rowhouse form with common end walls that dominated the Road towns just a few dozen miles back. Side yards between the oldest buildings begin to emerge as one moves west along the Road. In a further separation with eastern influence, several merchants extended the second floors of their buildings out over the sidewalks as raised porches.

About two miles west of Kirkersville, on the north side of the highway, is the Parkinson-Babcock Cemetery. The National Road here ran inside the cemetery and just north of US 40. The earliest grave is dated 1811.

A half mile west of the cemetery, on the south side, stands another old US 40 motel, the Shamrock, built in brick and Tudor Revival style. Rooms now rent as apartments. The restaurant next to it has been closed for several years. A half mile from the motel and also on the south side is a farmstead with an unusual Pennsylvania-German barn. The overhang or forebay is on the gable end rather than the barn's long side.

Etna is one of the few towns along the glaciated stretch of the National Road which was bypassed by US 40. The town was obviously considered an obstacle to smooth traffic flow, so engineers laid 40 around its north side. Etna again typifies the road town layout but includes a central green.

It was here, near Etna, in 1801 that a young fellow appeared leading a packhorse loaded with burlap bags. For nearly three decades, John Chapman, better known as Johnny Appleseed, crisscrossed Ohio planting apple seeds. In the late 1830s, when Ohio became too crowded for him, he moved on to Indiana. There, near Fort Wayne in 1845, Ohio's best-known folk character died and is buried.[34] The gravestones in the cemetery on the west end of

Kirkersville, Ohio

A small side yard, but enough space for a large maple tree.

Kirkersville, Ohio

Kirkersville portrait: porches down, and up (*below left*) and the neighborly peek (*below right*).

HUBERT G. H. WILHELM AND ARTIMUS KEIFFER

town, across from mile marker 241, indicate that most early settlers here were English and Irish. New suburban development sprawls west of town and on Tollgate Road in the southern part of the township. The commuting drive to downtown Columbus at rush hour requires at least thirty minutes.

Beyond Etna, US 40 turns into an urbanized strip. Several small residential subdivisions border the highway. Wagram, the final road settlement before Reynoldsburg, has been overwhelmed and absorbed into this post–World War II commercial landscape. The village is still in Licking County and on the edge of central Ohio's Appalachian Plateau. About two-and-a-half miles farther west, the roads leave the Licking River drainage basin and enter the Scioto (pronounced "See-oto") River drainage. Several north-south trending rivers are tributaries to the Scioto, including (from east to west) Blacklick Creek, Big Walnut Creek, Alum Creek, and the Olentangy River. The boundary between the Appalachians and the Central Plains lies just inside Franklin County. Reynoldsburg straddles the boundary and shares land of both regions. This one-time Road town is directly west of Blacklick Creek. Little in Reynoldsburg now suggests its National Road past, other than its typical Road town plat—Main Street and two parallel backstreets. A few old houses survive on Main. Otherwise, the town has been engulfed by post–World War II expansion and development from Columbus. In addition, the Outer Belt

Kirkersville, Ohio
Main Street vernacular

Etna, Ohio

An uncommon resource in the Middle West, the village green is the New England town's quintessential feature.

(I-270) around Columbus is immediately ahead, west of Reynoldsburg, and has contributed immensely to residential and commercial growth in the area. In fact, from Reynoldsburg to near downtown Columbus the National Road landscape has been submerged under the architectural "helter-skelter" so typical of the contemporary American roadside. Few old (or new) motels stand along the Reynoldsburg strip. They reappear beyond Hamilton Road (Ohio 317) between the suburbs of Whitehall and Bexley. Prior to World War II, Reynoldsburg was both too far from and too close to Columbus—too far for travelers who wanted to stay downtown or nearby, too close for others who chose lodging in Newark or Zanesville. Just ahead, at Whitehall and Bexley, however, old motels stand closely spaced. Businesses here, including some motels and new restaurants, often include the names "National Road" or "Pike," but the names are the only suggestion that this was once the Road.

The National Road and, later, US 40 entered Columbus on Main Street. Today, that street begins in Reynoldsburg. It crosses Big Walnut Creek west of Reynoldsburg and enters Whitehall, an incorporated subdivision. After passing through a small segment of Columbus, it arrives in Bexley, another incorporated place. Bexley is a high-income, beautifully rendered residential town that includes Capital University and a Lutheran seminary. In Bexley, 40 leaves Main Street and its National Road cousin and turns north on Drexel Avenue and joins Broad Street in a few blocks. Main Street continues westward and upon crossing Alum Creek, immediately west of Bexley, enters an earlier, near-downtown residential and commercial area. Its one-time occupants have long departed this section of Columbus for the suburbs. Today, the area is occupied by a low-income population composed of post–World War II urban migrants.

In Bexley, Main Street was joined by US 33, one of the principal cross-city highways. It connects Columbus with southeastern Ohio and continues northwestward through Marysville, Bellefontaine, Wapakoneta, and eventually enters Indiana. Ahead, at Third and Fourth Streets in downtown Columbus, US 23 crosses the National Road. In linking Mackinaw City, Michigan, and Jacksonville, Florida, US 23 passes through the heart of Appalachia. From

HUBERT G. H. WILHELM AND ARTIMUS KEIFFER

Bexley, Ohio

Bookstores and buildings called "Professional" are defining elements in upper-middle-class neighborhoods. The sign on Graeter's Soda Shop across Drexel reads "Since 1870." McDonald's unsuccessfully tried to enter the neighborhood. Residents like the place just the way it is.

Bexley, Ohio

Bexley's Art Deco Drexel Theater.

1940 to about 1960, millions of people left the central Appalachian region (southern West Virginia, eastern Kentucky, western Virginia) to seek jobs in Northern industrial cities. This era is still referred to within Appalachia as the "great migration." US 23 is one of the few north-south highways through eastern Kentucky coal country and provided a direct exit to Northern industrial cities such as Columbus, Toledo, Detroit, and Flint. Many migrants have remained in Columbus, so the city's current population is about 30 percent first- and second-generation Appalachian. Country-music writer and singer Dwight Yoakam's song, *Readin', Ritin', Rt. 23*, recalls the heartbreak experienced by people who left loved ones behind in the mountains to get assembly-line jobs in the North.

Once Main Street passes the inner-city beltways, I-70 and I-71, it crosses from an underdeveloped area into the city's central high-invest-

Bexley, Ohio

A handsome Bexley residence in bosky Tudor Revival, with manicured grounds to match.

ment zone. Just as the railroads did in earlier times, the interstate highways provide a demarcation line between the "haves" and "have-nots." At this point, Main Street veers slightly off-course toward the southwest as it adjusts to the downtown grid. Central Columbus was platted in relation to the Scioto River crossing point. Thus, the city's two principal avenues, Broad and High Streets, and the surrounding blocks, are slightly askew a cardinal north-south and east-west orientation. As the city grew, its grid was adjusted to the federal rectangular survey system with attention to true north-south and east-west headings. That survey system was in place east of the Scioto River. On the west lay the Virginia Military District, settled and surveyed by "metes and bounds," an informal land survey method found in the original thirteen colonies. This survey relied on physical reference points such as trees (metes), rather than geometric survey lines, and produced highly irregular land-parcel shapes and road patterns. A detailed Columbus city map reflects these contrasting surveys—on the Scioto's east and west banks—in the varied street patterns from one side to the other.

At the Main Street and High Street intersection, beside the Great Southern Hotel, the National Road left Main Street and followed High Street north to its intersection with Broad Street. Here it made a sharp turn west at the Ohio state capitol square, crossed the Scioto River, and left the city following Broad Street's course. The National Road would have passed sev-

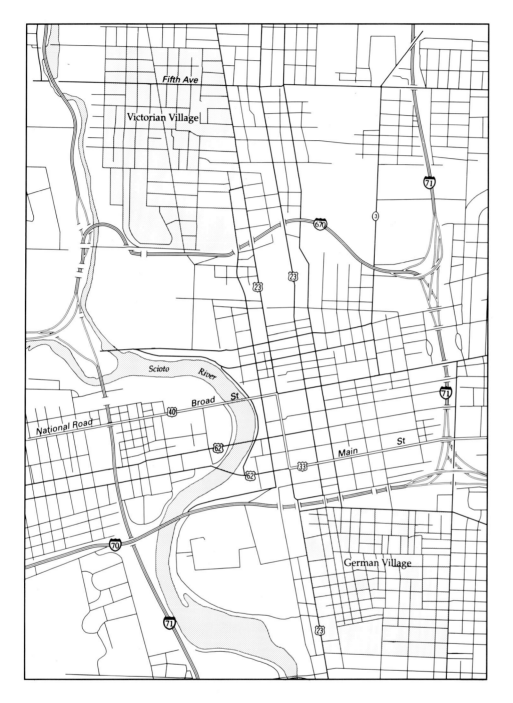

Columbus, Ohio, street patterns

The street patterns east and west of the Scioto River reflect old survey systems, the historical sequence of settlement, and the whim of developers.

Columbus, Ohio

A High Street "skyway" bridges between a traditional department store and the new downtown shopping mall.

Columbus, Ohio

Ohio's state capitol (1861) reflects in a department-store window at a High Street bus stop near the city's most important intersection, Broad Street and High.

HUBERT G. H. WILHELM AND ARTIMUS KEIFFER

Columbus, Ohio

Chain-link fence separates the state capitol building at Broad and High Streets from the remainder of its ten-acre square during renovation. The 47-story American Insurance Union Citadel building (1927) (*upper right*) incorporates a large theater and hotel in wings at the base. At sunset, in summer, the tower casts a shadow across the monument on the square. Roman matron Cornelia standing atop the granite shaft declares "These are my jewels." Below in bronze are seven of Ohio's politicians and soldiers; Ulysses S. Grant, William T. Sherman, Philip H. Sheridan, Edwin M. Stanton, James A. Garfield, Salmon P. Chase, and Rutherford B. Hayes.

Columbus, Ohio

Office buildings line Broad Street (US 40) on the State Capitol's north side.

Columbus, Ohio

One block east of the Scioto River, new office buildings face north-to-south Front Street for nearly a mile.

Columbus, Ohio

Geometry in stone and steel; 100 East Broad Street.

HUBERT G. H. WILHELM AND ARTIMUS KEIFFER

eral of the great old inns here in the downtown area, including the Neil House. Today, only the recently refurbished Great Southern Hotel remains as a reminder of earlier highway travel. During the twentieth century, High Street became the focus of retail department stores.

Columbus is Ohio's largest city and one of the most rapidly growing in the country. It has a well-diversified manufacturing base, a great variety of service industries, including major insurance firms, is home to one of the country's largest state universities, functions as state capital and Franklin County seat, and is at the intersection of two important interstates, I-70 and I-71. It is striving hard to overcome its nickname of "Cowtown." While it is true that it lacks the cosmopolitan flavor of Cincinnati or Cleveland, its skyline reflects the city's financial ascendancy.

Immediately off the National Road route stands the state capitol, which, even sans dome, is one of the finest examples of Greek Revival architecture in the country. Directly adjacent is one of the city's newer hotels and the City Center Mall, as well as the restored Ohio and Palace Theaters. Several of the Capitol Square highrise buildings are state offices that feature restaurants and observation platforms. North of downtown, and along either side of High Street, is the Short North area. This is the city's Historic Preservation District, well known for Victorian Village and upscale shops, restaurants, and galleries. South on High Street and just a short walk from Main Street is the city's outstanding tourist attraction, German Village. It was saved from the wrecking ball during the days of "urban renewal" and is a privately administered preservation area. The Village is now fully gentrified, and only those with a relatively high income can afford to live here. Its nineteenth-century occupants were largely blue-collar and small-business people, the descendants of German immigrants. The Germans helped drain this land and made it ready for urban expansion. In the process, they discovered the clays that became the raw material for the brick houses that give the Village its character. Shops and restaurants dot the Village, including one that specializes in bratwurst, potato salad, and sauerkraut, and a variety of fantastic desserts. The most recent restoration, preservation, and development area in near-downtown Columbus is the Old Brewery District directly west of German Village along High and Front Streets.

A block west of the High Street–Broad Street intersection stands the LaVeque-Lincoln Tower, a monument to early highrise architecture. Also known as the American Insurance Union Citadel building, it was built in

Columbus, Ohio

Germantown, clad in brick.

Columbus, Ohio

A Germantown cottage on City Park Street; copies of this building can be found in small towns along the National Road as far west as Pocahontas, Illinois, where a red-brick version stands at Leaverton and Kavanaugh Streets.

HUBERT G. H. WILHELM AND ARTIMUS KEIFFER

1927 and rises forty-seven stories. For a long time it was the town's only sky-scraper.

Just beyond, and also on the street's north side, is City Hall, featuring a huge statue of Christopher Columbus. Next, the new Memorial Bridge crosses the Scioto River. Completed in 1991, it is part of the greater Scioto River park district. The downtown skyline ends abruptly at the river above a replica of Columbus's flag ship, the *Santa Maria,* anchored here on the Scioto River's east bank since 1992, directly north of Memorial Bridge. This chapter ends here at the bridge. Beyond, US 40 is flanked by commercial strip development and residential areas. The National Road's legacy will not reemerge until the highway reaches the Outer Belt (I-270).

Columbus, Ohio

Skyline looking east across the Scioto.

Columbus to Springfield

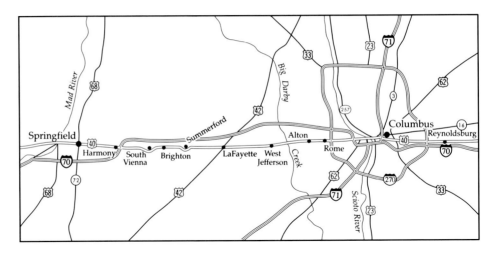

Springfield to Richmond, Indiana

From Columbus to Richmond, Indiana

KARL RAITZ

It is not until we reach Columbus that limestone again makes its appearance in any quantity; this found in abundance on the Scioto River. . . . An interval of nine miles occurs without furnishing any material for [McAdamizing], with the exception of a single gravel bank, already exhausted. At the Darbys an inferior quality of limestone is found; from thence to Springfield, a distance of twenty-nine miles, no quarry stone of any description has been discovered. Gravel . . . is the only material that can be relied on for making and keeping up this portion of the road.

HENRY BREWERTON
Report to General Charles Gratiot

BEGINNING AT THE SCIOTO RIVER BRIDGE IN COLUMBUS, THIS SECTION of the National Road ends 105 miles west at the Whitewater River bridge in Richmond, Indiana. Both rivers, and all other streams the Road crosses between those points, flow south to the Ohio River. Not long ago—if time is accounted against a geological clock—the streams that drained this region flowed north toward another large river, the Teays. The ancient Teays River valley has disappeared beneath glacially deposited gravel, sand, clay, and silt that is dozens, and in some places hundreds, of feet deep. To understand why streams that once flowed one direction now flow another is to also understand why the land crossed by this National Road section is some of the world's most fertile and productive; why National Road construction engineer Henry Brewerton found gravel instead of limestone for roadbed macadam; and why the countryside's gentle roll provokes many naive travelers to revile it as "boring, flat land." This land is Wisconsin-age till plain and moraine laid down by continental glaciers. It is young topography, 15,000 years more or less. In the geologic manner of reckoning time, that is less than required to blink an eye if one tried to offer a corollary that approximates human time measurement.

By adding the human landscape atop the glacial surface, we find that this Road section naturally divides into three related, yet distinctive parts. The first extends from Columbus to Springfield, Ohio. The Road here was the first section built, and it crossed the Virginia Military District, which, as the name implies, was settled by Southern migrants. The second section runs from Springfield to Brandt, Ohio, a fertile moraine and till plain countryside of small farms that was beyond the Military District, in the "Between the Miami Rivers" survey area. The third section extends from Brandt to Richmond. This Road segment was surveyed but not surfaced and maintained, and so was orphaned soon after construction. Travelers preferred to bypass this stretch by following the Dayton Cutoff. When the federal road-numbering system went into effect in 1927, the cutoff became US 35, and one finds along that highway the roadside landscape that never developed along this National Road segment. This third section is also defined by two deep glacial meltwater valleys and a rolling till plain that gradually blends into a hummocky moraine just east of Richmond. This fertile country attracted nineteenth-century migrant farmers who appreciated both the fine soil and the cities—Dayton, Middletown, Hamilton, Cincinnati—in the Miami Valley to the south where they would sell their crops and stock.

SETTLEMENT CONTEXT

The National Road intersected only one county seat between Columbus and Richmond, at Springfield, Clark County. That towns well removed from the Road became important local market and administrative centers suggests early settlement, well before the Road reached western Ohio. Pioneers looked to frontier forts, springs, stream forks, fording points, and Amerindian trails along stream divides for places they could site villages and open farms from forest and from their efforts a new middlewestern landscape began to emerge. A few "tracks of the Ohio frontier" remain across this section's western end between Englewood, Ohio, and Richmond. A treaty between a confederation of Miami, Wyandot, Shawnee, and Delaware Indian tribes and Gen. Anthony Wayne in 1795—the Treaty of Greenville—

divided the Northwest Territory into two parts, Indian land to the north, and lands open to white settlement to the south. The treaty line ran northeast to southwest, passing between present-day Greenville and Fort Recovery, and then south to the Ohio River. Tangent to this line, American forces built a series of forts and cantonments in the 1790s that ran from Fort Wayne in the north to Fort Washington (Cincinnati) on the Ohio River. From these forts sprang a series of frontier settlements: Fort Wayne (Indiana), Fort Recovery (in southwest Mercer County, Ohio), Fort Greenville (now Greenville, seat of Darke County, Ohio), Fort Jefferson (no settlement), Fort St. Clair (now Eaton, seat of Preble County), Fort Hamilton (Hamilton), and Fort Finney (at the junction of the Miami and Ohio Rivers).

The lands south of the treaty line were divided into three distinct parcels through federal deeds to state governments or purchases by land-development speculators. From the Scioto River at Columbus to the Little Miami River lay the Virginia Military District. Congress ceded this land to Virginia in the 1780s so that Virginia could honor a pledge to its Revolutionary War army and navy veterans to provide land in return for military service. Surveyors laid out district land in metes and bounds, producing odd-sized and -shaped properties with no relation to cardinal direction.[1]

The second section begins at the Little Miami (or a survey line that extended from the headwaters of that stream to the Greenville Treaty line) east of Springfield, extends west to the Great Miami River, and became known as the "Between the Miami Rivers" survey. This "Mesopotamian" neck of land extended north from the John Cleves Symmes Purchase that began at the Ohio River and included the site where Cincinnati would develop.[2] Symmes followed the directives contained in the Land Ordinance of 1785, surveying his land into townships six miles square, divided into square-mile sections. He reversed the Township and Range line designa-

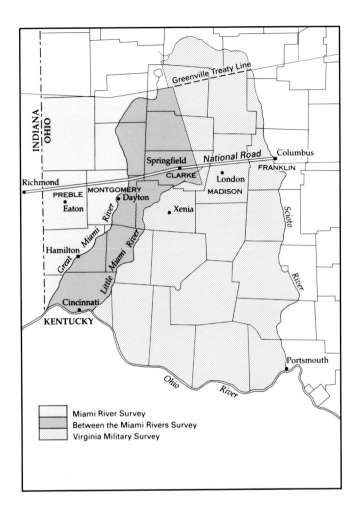

Southwestern Ohio land surveys

tions so that the range lines ran east-west every six miles, and numbered the sections from south to north, beginning with section 1 in each township's southeast corner. While this was a systematic survey compared to the Military District, the township lines canted toward magnetic north so the entire survey is cocked slightly northeast of true or cardinal north.[3]

The Congressional Lands, or Miami River Survey, begins at the Great Miami River and extends west to the Indiana border, which was also the forty-first parallel of longitude and the first principal meridian used in the Land Ordinance's Township and Range survey system. Here surveyors ran township lines east-west and range lines north-south, numbering the sections in sequence beginning with 1 in the northeast corner. For Road-bound travelers on US 40 or Interstate 70, survey lines might seem esoteric, but each survey is the organizational skeleton upon which settlement is laid down, and each survey's trace can be seen in country road alignments, property and field boundaries, grove shapes or outlines, and even odd-angled intersections where US 40 and survey-oriented state highways or country roads cross. From the air, the effect is stunning. Property boundaries in the Military District splinter the countryside in angled confusion, like random cracks in a broken window. Yet cross a line marked only by a road or stream and the survey instantly changes to a regimented grid that, with minor variations, will dictate road and property boundaries all the way to the Rocky Mountains.[4]

INTO THE MIDDLE WEST: COLUMBUS TO SPRINGFIELD

The National Road's corridor—defined here as the roadbed proper and the lands on either side that extend to the visual horizon—has the dialectical quality of being a linear zone along which local residents can watch people and their vehicles pass, on the one hand, and a cross-sectional vantage point from which a traveler can observe place and regional context on the other. Travelers in Maryland and southwestern Pennsylvania follow the Road across a series of topographic regions that are part of a larger section commonly known as "the East." In the nineteenth century, the East was perceived as urban and increasingly industrial, an economic and political power. On crossing into Ohio, the Road began a transition into a different place, the Middle West, a region that Henry Nash Smith called the "Garden of the World." Different from the East, it "embraced a cluster of metaphors expressing fecundity, growth, increase, and blissful labor in the earth, all centering about the heroic figure of the idealized frontier farmer armed with that supreme agrarian weapon, the sacred plow."[5]

Across Ohio, Indiana, and Illinois, the National Road roughly follows a topographic and cultural divide. Lands north are largely fertile glacial tills and moraines. Lands south either lay beyond glacial reach or are sliced into choppy hill and bluff lands by southward-flowing Ohio River tributaries. New Englanders and New Yorkers settled northern reserves and counties, Southerners crossed the river into Ohio's Virginia Military District and southern Indiana and Illinois. Middle Atlantic migrants—especially Pennsylvania-Germans—and European immigrants moved west along the Road and parallel routes spreading both north and south. Yet given such diversity, we acknowledge that these three states are not only different from the East, they are the flank of a new region often acknowledged as the nation's heartland; Middle American–moral and egalitarian; conservative and pragmatic. For the century between 1850 and 1950, the middlewestern countryside was awash in agrarian prosperity and its blue-collar cities places of clever mechanical invention and clanking industrial plants. Where, then, does the National Road leave the East and intersect this next region? Where does the heart, the core of Henry Nash Smith's Middle West begin? James Shortridge gives an answer: approximately here, at the beginning of this highway segment that runs from Columbus to Richmond. Eastern Ohio's people have been in place since before the National Road arrived, and cultural differences north to south remain vivid. Industrial cities—Youngstown, Akron, Canton, Steubenville—responded to corporate control from Pittsburgh or East Coast cities. But west of Columbus, the qualities that Smith identified predominate, and the residents increasingly identify themselves as middlewesterners.[6]

West Columbus: Transition to the Countryside and "West Jeff"

Symbolic acknowledgment that West Broad Street is also the National Road appears immediately at the new Scioto River bridge's west end. The Franklin County Veterans Memorial Park on the north side, overlooking the river and a now-landlocked simulacrum of Christopher Columbus's ship *Santa Maria,* was constructed in 1992. The county engineers' office designed and installed a remnant railing with balustrade from the old bridge, recalling that structure. Central in this vest-pocket park stands an oversized replica of an Ohio National Road mile marker. A kind of Rosetta for travelers, the code carved in stone reads "Cumberland 258" across the cylindrical top, and on the lower face angled for view by westbound travelers, "Springfield 43," and "West Jeff 14." This $10,000 mile marker is cut from the same stone used in the state capitol restoration underway a few blocks east and was donated by the construction company.

From the bridge, the Road crosses the city's west-end industrial district. Time has toyed with context here. A century ago, the riverfront was an unrepentant slum. Breweries drew water from the polluted river, and brothels, shacks, ironworks, abattoirs, tanneries, and bone and rag factories lined both sides of the river and adjoining streets. Remember that Columbus was a river, canal, and roadway town long before the railroads arrived, and since steamtrains excelled at hauling bulky cargo—like lumber, minerals, grain, or other things shipped in quantity—the tracks attracted industry as though the rails were magnetic. Being latecomers to Columbus meant that the railroads had to route their tracks to the city's edge where they would probe and encircle like graceless fingers into the waistcoat of working-class neighborhoods. The highway ahead passes through such a place. The Chesapeake & Ohio Railroad tracks (now CSX) cross the highway a few blocks

The Scioto River, looking at Columbus, Ohio, from the west bank

The riverside is industrial no longer; the Scioto has been remade into an aesthetic resource.

KARL RAITZ

west of the Scioto, and beyond Sandusky Avenue the Baltimore & Ohio Railroad also crosses.

Sometime after 1885, the Toledo & Ohio Central Railroad, a new line that served the eastern Ohio coal fields, entered the city from the south along the Ohio Feeder Canal. In 1895, the company built a station that still stands at 379 West Broad Street on the Road's south side. Although an odd amalgam of Orientalesque towers and pagoda roof lines, the interior is richly finished in Italian marble and mahogany. The station stands beside a railroad viaduct, built to reduce traffic congestion on the National Road, and the passenger loading platform is, of necessity, on the second floor. Through a series of company mergers, the New York Central Railroad obtained the land and used the station until 1930. The Volunteers of America now occupy the property.

The Road's frontage makes a transition from late-nineteenth-century industrial buildings along railroad tracks to an early auto-era commercial strip, exemplified by the Ogden Avenue area where turn-of-the-century Prairie-style rectangular houses and bungalows line the side streets back from US 40. The highway, by turns, passes residential neighborhoods, then linear business-office and retail shopping strips, as near Chase and West Broad where doctors' offices, auto-paint shops, and 1960s supermarkets mimic a small-town main street. Farther out, at Coolidge and US 40, the two-story brick L-shaped 40 Motel stands at the south side. Its heroic-sized arrow sign is an icon to the auto-age US 40, not the National Road. Across the highway from the motel is the appropriately named Consumers Square Plaza in postmodern guise, and alongside a K-Mart store stands the National Road Plaza, followed by a 1960s-era automobile row, where Chevrolet and Dodge dealers cast their advertising hooks to the highway for customers, using primary colors as bait. The old Road may not be forgotten, but the roadside's use has been converted to a consumer's strip. A General Motors Fisher Guide plant stands off the Road's south side. Built in 1937, the factory manufactures door hinges for the General's automobiles.

An appliance store and the Westland Mall stand near the junction of I-270

West Columbus, Ohio

Founded in New Jersey in 1933, the Big Bear supermarket chain motto was "Big Bear, the price crusher." By 1937, Wayne Brown had opened four Big Bears in Columbus. Low prices—one 1930s promotion sold a pound of coffee for 37 cents—attracted shoppers from as far as fifty miles away. The 1930s Big Bear supermarket—the Wal-Mart of its day—sold in carload quantities. By the 1950s, the exteriors were an exaggerated Moderne design incorporating steel, porcelain, brick, and a sign that could be mistaken for no other.

West Columbus, Ohio

In the 1960s, the 40 Motel represented urbane modernity on the western gateway into Columbus. Now it stands as a fresh reminder of Americana amid sterile fast-food restaurants and impersonal strip shopping centers.

and US 40, announcing their wares from stilt signs tall enough to be seen from the freeway. Given the conglomeration of recent commercial activity on Columbus's east side (see chapter 3), where these same two highways cross, one would have expected more modern development here. Although a Bob Evans Restaurant and two or three fast-food restaurants crouch near this exit ramp, few other food, fuel, or lodging franchises have found this intersection a compelling place to build. Evidence abounds that commercial development here is tempered by proximity to industry and the blue-collar neighborhoods on either side of the highway. On the east side, at this distance from the central city, most blocks along US 40 are a matrix of extant older houses and new businesses inserted where homes have been removed so lots could be given over to auto-oriented business. Here, most Road frontage remains as originally built, same-age houses for several blocks followed by commercial blocks and businesses set back from the street to allow parking space. This west-side US 40 strip is distinctive, molded by its context.

New Rome and Alton

The US 40 commercial strip extends six miles west from the capitol to the village of New Rome. Dating from 1836, this settlement was surveyed and laid out after the National Road arrived. Speculative towns were common on the American frontier, and founding dates are popular historic benchmarks from which one might infer entrepreneurial intent. New Rome's boosters intended the settlement to rival Alton, another speculative village laid out the same year two miles farther west. Competition flourished for a few years, but soon New Rome peaked at a population of fifty and then faded while Alton continued to prosper. At Buena Vista Avenue, the 1960s New Rome Motel marks the city's corporate limit. The density of cabin camps and motels along US 40, many now refit to other uses or closed, suggests that traffic along this highway was once sufficient to support them all. They may be good bellwethers for the rigor of the local and regional economy, but they most certainly reflect the original builder's wisdom in selecting an appropriate site and whether any advantages that site might have enjoyed have been mitigated by subsequent highway bypasses or interstate construction. A 1950s arrow sign that once announced the Manor Motel on the street's north side now points to the vacant lot and declares in peeling paint: "For Sale 458' Frontage 2–18 acres All or Part." The motel was torn down in 1982. US 40 frontage here is no longer prime commercial space. Among the commercial strip buildings in New Rome, a 1860s-era white-brick two-story house remains. In 1970, New Rome's population was 104; by 1990, 111.

Two decades after Thomas Graham founded Alton in 1836, the village hosted a post office, church, school, drugstore, grocery, and tavern.[7] Little from the nineteenth century remains in Alton. One passes a sequence of public buildings along the Road's south side. First, a 1915–20 red-brick school built when school consolidation swept Ohio in the 1910s. The school is boarded up; rusty used cars clot the yard; a volunteer tree nearly obscures the faded "used cars" sign. Next is the original frame, one-room school building. The fishscale slate roof shades broken windows; overgrown honeysuckle camouflages the walls. The clapboard school is followed by the sandblasted red-brick Christian Life Church. A line of Victorian-age homes near the church now house automotive machine and tool and die shops.

West of Alton, the highway finally enters open countryside, a good road now just as it was in 1924 when Howard Hobbs recorded that the road surface from the west edge of Columbus to Springfield was "Good Macadam: A fast road through a rich, intensively cultivated region."[8]

About ten miles west of Columbus, US 40 crosses the Big Darby Creek bridge and enters Madison County. On the south side, white plank fences—fifty-six miles of them—announce Darby Dan Farm, a 4,280-acre suburban gentlemen farm established here in 1935 by John Wilmer Galbreath. Until his death in 1988, Mr. Galbreath headed one of Columbus's largest real-estate sales and development firms. His speciality was building and managing city office buildings and constructing housing projects. In Hong Kong, he built 100 fifteen-story apartment buildings on land reclaimed from the sea. For a time he owned Hialeah Race Course in Florida and was principal owner of the Pittsburgh Pirates baseball team (with Bing Crosby and other investors).

The farm is really several farming operations and includes a thoroughbred horse farm; cattle farm; a corn, soybean, and wheat farm; a game preserve with bison, elk, deer, and African antelope; a nine-hole golf course; and a 6,000-foot airstrip. In 1946, Mr. Galbreath purchased a second horse farm, also called Darby Dan Farm, in Kentucky's Bluegrass region near Lexington. At the Kentucky farm, Mr. Galbreath bred his thoroughbred mares to Kentucky stallions and shipped the yearlings to this farm for breaking and training on the one-and-one-sixteenth-mile track. The farm's most memorable horses include 1963 and 1967 Kentucky Derby winners Chateaugay and Proud Clarion, 1972 English Derby winner Roberto, and 1974 Preakness and Belmont Stakes winner Little Current.[9]

West of Darby Creek, past a trailer park and scattered "farmsteads," the 1950s B&B Motel stands near the corner where Ohio 142 intersects US 40. Just outside West Jefferson, the highway crosses the second bridge in Madison County, this one over Little Darby Creek, the west fork of Big Darby Creek. The two streams join four miles southeast at Georgesville, a tiny rail crossing that now stands in the center of Battelle–Darby Creek Metropolitan Park. Blatters Truck Patch operates from an old farmstead at the east side of the bridge, on the Road's north side, growing fresh vegetables in large plots of Little Darby Creek bottom land for drive-in customers. An abandoned Kokoline gas station stands across the highway, boarded up amid its crumbling asphalt lot.

West Jefferson

The business district in West Jefferson—often called "West Jeff"—is two blocks of early 1900s-era commercial buildings facing the highway. Saints Simon and Jude Catholic Church stands in Gothic Revival splendor amid rectory, convent, and school, the ensemble facing US 40. The masons who built the 1893 city hall were artists as much as craftsmen; the brick and stonework dazzle, especially the handsome entrance arch and its surround. The off-center tower suggests the building also housed the fire station. One block south stands the 1895 Jefferson Township Hall. Because Madison County lies within the Virginia Military District, its townships, which serve as the smallest government units, are odd-shaped and do not conform to the rectilinear directives of the 1785 Land Ordinance. Each township usually has a township hall for meetings and elections.

Across the street is a Methodist church, built in 1922, and a reminder that the National Road corridor followed a rough cultural divide across the state. New England Congregational churches and Catholic and Brethren churches tend to be more numerous in northern Ohio; Baptist and Pentecostal churches can be found in many small communities across the state's southern counties; Methodists and Friends tend to predominate along a band across the state's midsection.[10] Many other religious groups, Mennonites, for example, embed this generalized religious landscape with important, often very localized, concentrations. Their presence is often the product of place-directed migration or energetic clergy.

West Jefferson's streets are a patchwork of small grids, not a simple linear strip along the National Road. About 1806, a state road ran between Franklinton (now in West Columbus) and Springfield. In 1822, Samuel Jones and Samuel Sexton platted the village of New Hampton along that road, and the settlement progressed modestly until the new National Road bypassed to the north. Isaac Jones incorporated a new town, Jefferson, a short distance north but along the National Road in 1834, and New Hampton residents promptly moved, houses and all, north to the roadside. The new town prospered and Road traffic kept five hotels busy.[11] For a time, residents considered West Jefferson the county's primary business community, but the village eventually lost leadership to London, the county seat, a few miles southwest. Only a cemetery and historic plaque mark New Hampton's site. With a few exceptions, Main Street businesses are still active. Patterson's Red

& White at the corner of Center and Main has been in the family for three generations, and retains the name and the classic signs from the now-extinct grocery-store chain of which it was once a part; the owners still deliver groceries to local customers three times each week. In the next block west, a bank building now entertains karate students—a common reuse of small-town main street business buildings almost anywhere in the United States.

The Conrail railroad line (formerly the Pennsylvania Railroad) from Cincinnati to Cleveland crosses the National Road at an angle in West Jefferson. And about one-half mile west, an Egyptian Revival mausoleum dated 1917 stands in Pleasant Hill Cemetery near the intersection of US 40 and Ohio 142. A nearly identical mausoleum sets along 142 about seven miles southwest in London, the county seat. Former residents buried in the adjacent cemetery were of English and Irish origin: Bidwell, Byerly, Coe, Golen, Kerr, McCoy, and Wright. Across from the cemetery, the Ranch makes no pretense about still being a traveler's motel; it now rents rooms by the week.

In open country at the town's west edge, the Jefferson Local School District converted the beautiful 1920s rectangular brick school into administrative offices. The new high school, built within the past twenty years, stands closer to town. In the open countryside west of town, a 1980s subdivision of small pastel-colored houses stands about 500 feet south and may be the product of West Jefferson's recent growth; population in 1970 was 3,664 and by 1990 4,505.

The reason for the growth may be at the US 40–Ohio 29 intersection, where three industrial plants cluster, here perhaps because 29 intersects with I-70 about two miles north. The newest of the three, Krazy Glue Company, opened here in 1994. This plant is a joint venture between Borden, a firm with offices at Third Street and US 40 in Columbus, and a Japanese chemical firm. This plant imports adhesives from northern Japan and packages them for reshipment to South, Middle, and North America. The sixty employees, most local people, supply Krazy Glue needs of the entire Western Hemisphere. To the right on 29, Jefferson Industries is a metal-stamping plant employing about 250 people who make parts for Honda and Subaru automobiles. And along US 40 at the intersection with 29 is Capitol Manufacturing Company. This plant opened in 1967 to make steel fittings for plumbing and electrical construction using pipe stock supplied by steel tubing mills in Pennsylvania. Capitol's headquarters is in nearby Columbus, and, like the glue packager across the road, this plant serves customers across North and Middle America via the Interstate Highway System. Capitol ships about 2.5 million pounds of steel fittings each month. US 40 opens to a 50-MPH four-lane with a twenty-foot-wide depressed-grass median here, but the trucks that serve these factories head north to the interstate.

Beyond West Jefferson, the prospect opens to prosperous cash grain farms producing corn and soybeans; the tree stands in the distance are second- and third-growth remnants of the region's original hardwood forest. Although most roadside farmsteads have barns and other outbuildings, few livestock remain. Farmers here raise crops for sale rather than feed them to dairy or feeder cattle, hogs, or poultry.

Henry's Restaurant, a 1950s concrete-block building, and the Royal Motel, with gabled roof, picture windows, and permastone facade, stand beside the Road's south side. The motel still has a roadside sign, but it now caters to people seeking apartments they can rent by the week or month. The Traveler's Motel, still guarded by overgrown mugho pines and junipers, announces a "nonfarm" farmstead on the right. A well-tended yard surrounds the old farmhouse, but the side-entry gabled-roofed barn stands empty, as do the other outbuildings. The largest machine is a lawn tractor. No farm livestock scent the air; no heavy tractors cut tire lug marks into the driveway; no hammermill fills the air with corncob dust. This former farmstead is like many others along the Road that were left empty when farmers retired or sold out, their land consolidated into neighborhing farms. Surplus farmsteads are often torn down, the sites converted to field, or, as here, sold or rented to people who commute to jobs in nearby towns. Looking north from here in the summer, trucks almost two miles away on I-70 seem to sail on a sea of corn leaves.

Lafayette

East of Lafayette, US 42 intersects US 40 at an angle with an elaborate overpass intersection, rare for noninterstate highways. At the intersection stands the thirty-two-unit R and R Motel, a fine example of the large post–World War II motels found along US 40. Built in a broad, open V shape, the structure's two wings hinge at a central office and living-quarters building. The owner recently reshingled the roof and maintains the grounds immaculately. About one and one-half miles north, US 42 intersects with I-70 at an interchange. Two truckstops, gas stations, restaurants, and a large motel at the interchange siphon trade from the R and R. The owner thought

East of Lafayette, Ohio

An abandoned grain bin on an abandoned farmstead site in Madison County. If the great concrete grain elevators of Illinois are "Cathedrals of the Prairie," this might have been the "Chapel of the Back 40." Built during the era when gasoline tractors were beginning to replace draft horses and hybrid corn was debuted, these 1930s steel-sided bins could hold several hundred bushels of grain—the yield from forty acres of corn. Now the harvest from ten acres would fill such a bin.

a small advertisement on the "official" interstate sign that announces interchange services would help rescue his trade. The sign costs $1,500 per year in Ohio. Motel guests are about half overnight travelers, half weekly rentals.

Two other roads, Ohio 38 and the Lafayette-Plain City Road, pass through Lafayette and cross I-70 but have no interchanges. Therefore the traffic on these roads is local and modest, and there is no need for stoplights where they intersect US 40 in Lafayette. The old National Road—street signs in town identify the Road as Cumberland Street—is still the dominant road in this village.

Job Postle platted Lafayette in Deer Creek Township in 1832, and the village was named for the famous French general La Fayette, as were many other settlements across the eastern states.[12] The Georgian-style Red Brick Tavern opened here at 1700 Cumberland Road in 1837 when the completed National Road reached the settlement. Twin chimney stacks at each gable end, Flemish-bond brickwork, and subtle Classical Revival detailing distinguish the structure, the second oldest operating hostelry in Ohio. An old milepost stands in the yard. When US 40 was widened to four lanes in the 1940s, most Lafayette businesses lost their frontyards, having encroached upon the Road's eighty-foot right-of-way in the early years.[13] The concrete road surface now laps at the tavern's doorstep, and a block east a small abandoned filling station's pumps now stand at the curb, its approach and service drive given back to the Road. Lafayette struggles to maintain its institutions with a small and declining population; a loss of thirty-seven people in the two decades after 1970 brings the 1990 population to 449.

A 1908 school building stands across the street from the tavern but no nineteenth-century stores remain standing, nor any old churches. Down the street, a large Georgian-style four-over-four red-brick house, also circa 1830, crowds the roadside. Its ornate doorways, gable-end chimneys, and six-over-six windows make it a kindred structure to buildings erected in southeastern Pennsylvania a generation earlier. Other suggestions of a connection with Pennsylvania can be found eighteen miles north of Lafayette on US 42 at Plain City, a German Mennonite settlement. But don't visit Plain City expecting to see streets lined by horses and carriages or farmers working their fields with horses. These Mennonites drive cars and use tractors. Along 42 on the south side of town, one can find three large "family-style" restaurants that capitalize on an "Amish" motif to fill their parking lots with tour buses, but the downtown antique dealers are from Columbus.

About one mile west of Lafayette, at the intersection of Ohio 38 and US 40, the Ohio State University Molly Caren Agricultural Center exhibits new farm machinery and equipment during special summer expositions. Another mile ahead, past the Madison County Airport, is Summerford, the first village surveyed in Somerford Township (spelled differently, pronounced the same). Joseph Christman, tavern- and storeowner, selected the site and laid off the home lots. Since the village is within the Virginia Military District, he would have recorded the property descriptions in metes and bounds terms. In 1871, residents built a brick township hall; the Independent Order of Odd Fellows met upstairs as suggested by the gable-end date stone.[14] A Methodist church stands one block west along the old Road. The 1920 Somerford Grade School, just north of the intersection of Routes 40 and Ohio 56, is still used. When engineers widened US 40, they chose to bypass Summerford, although the village has access to I-70 by way of an interchange about one mile north. The L-shaped Madison Motel hugs the road just west of town where the bypass and the old highway join.

Brighton

Just east of Brighton, US 40 crosses from Madison into Clark County. Brighton, being a small village bypassed by US 40, bears a strong resem-

Lafayette, Ohio

Built in Georgian style, the 1837 Red Brick Tavern closed during the railroad era but reopened to welcome the automobile-borne traveler.

blance to Summerford. Early Brighton residents were from New England and from the time of founding in 1835, when David Ripley and Marvin Gager platted the site, until 1848, the town enjoyed relative prosperity as a stagecoach stop.[15] Then the railroad arrived, and as happened in many National Road towns, the train brought a quick end to any boom-town visions locals might have entertained.

A simple gable-roofed, frame-and-clapboard Methodist church with pointed "Gothic" windows stands beside the Road in Brighton. The front steps have been removed and the sidewalk sloped up to floor level, suggesting that some congregation members might be wheelchair-bound. At the Houston Pike intersection near the village's west end stands a stoutly built brick building between the old Road and the US 40 bypass. This is the old Brighton power house, built about 1902 to provide electrical power to the Columbus-Springfield interurban rail line that passed just south of the building. Part of the first floor was a waiting room for passengers. The basement still contains a large brick cistern and a steel-reinforced bench where electric dynamos once sat in a line. The building's west wall is marked by three round portholes under the eve on each end where the electrical cables entered the building. The power house was converted to a home in the 1930s. Two I-houses mark the town's west edge; the one on the north side at Houston Pike is in prime condition, the other across the road appears abandoned, although a past resident arranged a collection of wrecked cars around the yard. The traveler should not be deceived by these small US 40 villages. Functionally they are part of the extended city. Residentially, most residents love the small town as a safe and wholesome place to raise their children or to retire. Many commute to Springfield, Columbus, or other nearby towns to work or shop. And the sense of community is palpable, as on a warm summer evening when people gather around the fire station to plan a village festival or children ride bicycles up and down the bypassed highway.

The countryside around Brighton is choppy, almost rough, a glacial moraine that serves as a drainage divide. To the east, creeks flow off Markley Hill (marked by Markley Hill Lodging, a recycled 1950s motel) south and east into the Scioto watershed; to the west streams head west and southwest into the Little Miami River and Mad River drainages. Between Brighton and South Vienna, about three miles ahead, the Road crosses another major divide. This is Israel Ludlow's survey line, circa 1800, that marked the Virginia Military District's western boundary and the eastern boundary of the old Between the Miami Rivers survey. The line is visible on any state highway map because it aligns with the angled section of Ohio 54 north of South Vienna, and extends northwest where Ohio 814 follows it all the way to Bellefontaine, seat of Logan County. Across the line, here just east of South Vienna, property lines and country roads largely follow geometric survey lines.[16] The survey line corresponds to the first secondary road, a driveway, to intersect the highway west of the point where the US 40 bypass swings south past the town. A tennis court stands at the corner. A small marker declares the names of those who contributed the tennis court. The road beside it, one of the most important survey lines in the state, is anonymous.

South Vienna

South Vienna was platted in 1833, four years before the National Road was completed. The site is about one mile south of the old Columbus Road that ran from Columbus to Springfield before the National Road was built. After a post office was established here in 1838, four-horse stagecoaches carried the Great Western mail through South Vienna along the National Road for two decades.[17] Like Brighton, US 40 has bypassed the town center. Old 40 still runs through town, past a gray-painted brick school with a gabled doorway and docked roof gables, now a private home, on the south side. A new United church is next. Johnson's Lamp Shop and Antiques, established in 1963, occupies a brick two-over-two I-house west of town at Buena Vista Road. Glass greenhouses, now shattered, a smokeless steam-plant chimney, and a field of overgrow yews mark the site of an abandoned horticultural nursery across the road. The village gained population modestly through the 1970s and '80s, putting the 1990 count at 550. West of town, rural nonfarm residential density increases as farm fields give way to houses on narrow piano-keyed lots, each with direct access onto the highway.

West of South Vienna, Crawford's Farm Market and Campground specializes in firewood, garden mulch, and concrete yard ornaments. A red sign for a fax service glows in a window. On this converted farmstead, the tin machine shed also serves as the base for a large sign that declares "CAMPING" in six-foot letters. But the sign faces north, its back

South Vienna, Ohio

South Vienna celebrates harvest with a Corn Festival each September. Angie Dooley and Shane Lusk paint the festival logo in the middle of the old National Road.

East of Harmony, Ohio

US 40 travelers read the small signs. The largest sign (seen behind the telephone pole) faces away from the highway; its message is intended for I-70 traffic three-fourths mile north.

to US 40, the owner intending the message for interstate travelers three-fourths mile away.

Harmony

Just east of Harmony, and about three miles from Springfield's eastern suburbs, I-70 crosses from the north to the south side of US 40, bypassing the city through open farmland on the south side. Two more large campgrounds lie east of the I-70 and US 40 interchange. Laybourn Newlove platted Harmony in 1832. Soon after, Irishman Henry Martin built a store and became the town's first merchant; Joseph Newlove and Robert Black became early innkeepers. Residents built a schoolhouse in 1835 and later added a separate school for African-American students. In 1852, many town residents died of cholera, and most businesses failed after the railroad bypassed the town about a mile south.[18] Laybourn Newlove's dream languished after the railroad's arrival, but it is now renascent thanks to its proximity to an interstate interchange. Two brick houses, circa 1840 and 1860—the older structure now refitted as apartments—share the site with a drive-in, a motel, and a new service station. The 1950s motel has been refurbished and fills every night. The owner has recently bought two other old motels and is reopening them as overnight or weekly rentals. A small room rents for $85 a week, a larger one for $90. Weekly tenants are often "in between"; they are going through a divorce, construction workers from out of town, or people from southeastern Ohio who commute here to work in a factory during the week. Knight's Antiques occupies an old general store along the highway.

Just over two miles ahead, two motels announce the city just over the hill. The one on the north side is the newly refurbished Springfield Motel. The old sign read "Sp i gfield Motel" because the *r* and *n* had fallen off, and passersby wondered if the *S* would also fall off and what that might suggest about the owner's fastidiousness. On the Road's south side, the Melody Drive-In (subtitled "Cruise in Theater") is still in fine condition and shows first-run films during the summer months. Its marquee is classic 1950s design that lights the night with a large arrow of sequentially blinking yellow bulbs, and the word "Melody" and six music notes in neon. In 1950, Ohio had 135 drive-in theaters.[19] Popular during the 1950s and '60s before television became America's evening entertainment, drive-ins required at least five acres of open space. To find that much cheap land near a town or city, the owner would have to build a few miles from the edge of town. Each drive-in theater along US 40 shares this locational trait. A second drive-in theater, the Show Boat, stood in the field on the Road's north side. All that remains is the ticket booth atop a low rise to the right and the marquee sign that declares that an archery club meets here. Archers, too, require lots of open space.

At the intersection of Bird Road and US 40, the beige-and-red painted Silver Swan Motel is an example, perhaps the best anywhere along this highway section, of how roadside businesses grow in response to increased highway traffic, and decline when traffic wanes, metamorphosing into something new. Howard Hobbs, in his 1924 *Grade and Surface Guide,* recorded a "Pay camp in grove; 50¢ a car [water and comfort stations], gas station," near this place.[20] Tiny board-and-batten cabins stand at the back edge of the Silver Swan's asphalt parking lot, vestiges, perhaps, of the original cabins that succeeded the pay camp. Additional units were added and connected by a common roof. When I-70 bypassed Springfield in the 1960s, this motel lost its potential clientele. Now, rusty and battered 1970s cars up on blocks punctuate the lot, and charcoal grills, pets, and children's toys idle before the room-sized units. The Silver Swan's last incarnation is apartments that rent by the week or month.

Springfield, Ohio

Towed on its own trailer to stand at roadside in front of home or business and declare birthday greetings, the Rent-A-Cake is a triumph of vernacular business ingenuity. This "senior cake" is now officially retired along US 40; four new ones have replaced it.

A short distance beyond this theater and motel cluster, the gateway into town is marked by the Nursery Outlet at Larchmont Drive, which purveys concrete yard ornaments and demonstrates their application by use in a miniature golf course next door. More notable, though, is what may be America's only rent-a-birthday-cake-on-a-trailer business. Built of sheet metal and mounted atop small trailers, the "cakes" are cheerfully decorated with colored paper, fringes, and painted wooden candles. Clients rent them for display in front of a home or business to announce a friend's or relative's birthday.

Springfield

To enter Springfield, one must cross another swath of choppy topography. These low hills are the remnants of a pair of glacial moraines, one east of town, the other west, which form an inverted U and mark the edges of two parallel Wisconsin-age glacial ice lobes that extended well south from here. These low hill ranges mark the west and east boundaries of those lobes and provide Springfield's elevated site. Buck Creek cut a valley through the hills and had sufficient gradient and flow to turn mill wheels, making the site a prime place for settlement. John Humphreys and Simon Kenton, with six families from Kentucky, founded the first white-occupied village nearby on the Mad River in 1799. Their fort near the Buck Creek–Mad River confluence, west of present-day Springfield, became a "jumping-off-place into the wilderness." Kenton built grist- and sawmills along Buck Creek.[21]

In 1801, John Daughtery platted a settlement site here, and by 1830, the town's population was just over 1,000. The finished National Road bed reached Springfield in 1838. Within a short time the Pennsylvania House tavern at 1311 West Main Street became the terminal for the Ohio Stage Company, and passenger and commodity traffic through the city increased perceptibly. The new Road stimulated business which, in turn, drew more residents, and by 1850 over 5,100 people lived in Springfield. German immigrants arrived in sufficient numbers to assist in founding Wittenberg Lutheran College on forty acres in northwest Springfield in 1845. German immigration continued to the eve of the Civil War. Between 1880 and 1900, when the migration stream from Europe shifted from Northern Europe to the north Mediterranean rim, Italians and Greeks arrived.[22]

Farmers in the surrounding countryside found markets for their products in Springfield, Columbus, and points east along the road, and used their

Some of Springfield's old, closed industrial plants are almost elegant in their lethargy.

profits to improve stock and upgrade farms. Springfield became a logical place to build farm machinery, initiated by the Warder and Brokaw Company in 1850. Five years later, William Whiteley invented a grain binder, founded the Champion Binder Company, and his East Street shops became the largest farm machinery factory in the country by the early 1880s. Another machinery manufacturer, P. P. Mast, built cultivators and advertised them in *Farm and Fireside,* a journal that he printed in the plant. The Champion Company failed in 1886, its business acquired by McCormick, and then International Harvester, but Mast's little publication grew into the Crowell-Collier firm that published four national magazines—with combined circulation of 20 million copies each month—by the 1940s. The farm-machinery business moved west to the heart of the Corn Belt—Chicago, Minneapolis, Peoria, and Davenport–Rock Island–Moline—and Springfield's skilled labor force turned to metal fabrication industries, such as trucks, boilers, and engines.[23]

One can visit the old reaper plant site by turning right on Belmont Street (beside the Story Hypes United Methodist Church) and driving north about half a mile. Belmont heads downhill into the Buck Creek valley. At the intersection of Lagonda and Belmont, turn right and proceed one block to

Decorative "stacks" front Building 1, a new glass and steel office tower on Main Street. Perhaps an architect's acknowledgment of Springfield's smoke stack skyline, the stacks also announce square-blocks of renewal at the city's heart.

Lagonda and Reaper Streets, where stands the Navistar Plant that manufactures International trucks. Buildings from at least three different manufacturing eras are tied together by conveyors into a modern facility employing about 5,700. Return to US 40 by way of Belmont Street and pass a spectacular 1930s Pure Oil gas station at the Belmont-Lagonda corner, now refurbished as a fresh-produce market.

Nineteenth-century Springfield manufacturers and merchants prospered and their success was soon mirrored in the business district. Some clues to that prosperity are as small as the brass compass rose and street names embedded in the sidewalk at the northwest corner of Main and Fountain Streets. Others create a grand skyline of public, commercial, and industrial buildings. From the late nineteenth century until the Depression, large brick and stone buildings replaced frame and clapboard structures in downtown Springfield. Perhaps the grandest of all presides over Fountain Avenue—formerly Market Street—between High and Washington. With an eye toward H. H. Richardson's Romanesque Revival style, Springfield architect Charles Cregar designed a red-brick and gray-stone city building to fit a 465-by-50-foot lot near the railroad tracks. Completed in 1890, the four-story structure is awash in Gilded Age architectural gewgaws; towers, finials, dormers, chimneys, and gables. A forty-foot clock tower rises from the east end above the old Market Square; a shorter tower punctuates the west end. Designed to also serve as a city market, this is a rare and wonderful reminder that this city's commercial district was once a dynamic and vital place, frequented by folk of all social stations. A new hotel, the Kuss Auditorium, and a post-modern public library nearby suggest that community leaders would like to reinvent those days. The library's architect clearly references the city's industrial skyline in the choice of two-tone red-orange brick and the raised shed roof design which is best appreciated from Jefferson Street south of the railroad tracks.

Further reminders of Springfield's late entrepreneurial successes align High Street, which parallels US 40, about two blocks south on the east side of town. Of special interest here is Frank Lloyd Wright's 1905 Prairie-style house built for Burton S. Westcott at 1340 High at the intersection with Greenmount. Typical of a number of Wright's early houses, the Westcott House has tan stucco walls that reach up to low-pitched hip roofs that seem heaped together when viewed from the cemetery on the east side. The home's High Street (or south) side is really a side yard with a lily pool; one enters the front off Greenmount. A long-walled loggia connects the four-bedroom home to a garage that has direct access to the back alley. Although now in need of rehabilitation, the home is only one example of the richly varied landscape elements one finds in Springfield, a place where city and country, class and ethnicity, and historic transport and industrial technologies blend in fascinating ways. The city warrants a traveler's undivided attention for a full day or more. Like many industrial cities in Ohio, Springfield has been losing population since the 1970s when 81,941 people lived here. By 1990, only 70,487 remained.

After passing a mile-long auto-strip gauntlet past the "Hilltop" watertower, US 40 enters downtown Springfield and splits to follow two one-way streets: West 40 on North Street, East 40 on East Main. I-70 skirts the city's south side. A few motels remain along the old US 40 strip through town. To engage fast food and a modern

Springfield, Ohio

Across Main Street from Building 1, Block's Department Store, a kind of Richardsonian Romanesque Revival–style structure, stands shuttered by sheets of plywood. The next intersection is Fountain and Main. The majestic 1924 Crowell-Collier plant, also closed, looms in the distance.

The Hartland Motel on West Columbia was a 1960s Travelodge; the TL logo still resides in the steel, second-floor balcony railings. Rooms rent by the night, or by the week to retirees. The Crowell-Collier plant provides locational reference.

franchise motel, one must return to the east-end strip or take Ohio 72 south to the I-70 interchange.

West of Springfield, US 40 passes a Madonna of the Trail statue in a small park near the Mad River. The National Road crossed the river here through a two-lane "double-barreled" covered bridge. Up the hill to the west, the Ohio State Masonic Home stands near the remnants of tiny Sugar Grove Hill—a roadside community that once had a garage and stores—and two 1950s motels, the Sandman and the Adobe.

FROM SPRINGFIELD TO BRANDT: ACROSS THE MAD RIVER

That Springfield is the only city of size on this National Road section from Columbus to Richmond is the result of geographic coincidence, it being one of only a few existing settlements that the Road would intersect. Yet, a few miles southwest lay Dayton, and southward along the Miami Valley Middletown, Hamilton, and Cincinnati, a cluster of rapidly growing industrial cities that spawned heavy commercial traffic. Dayton was a powerful attraction for the Road's builders and could be ignored by National Road surveyors such as Jonathan Knight only if they strictly interpreted the federal directives that required that the Road follow a straight-line transect from Columbus to Indianapolis. Dayton began with a late-eighteenth-century plat by frontiersman Israel Ludlow, and by 1805 had incorporated as the Montgomery County seat.

The Dayton Cutoff

By the time the National Road reached central Ohio, even the dimmest town official could see that it offered a spectacular advantage in providing a direct link to eastern markets, especially since the new canals across the state ran north and south, connecting the Ohio River to Lake Erie. Little surprise, then, that when boosters of Newark and Granville—established towns east of Columbus—found that their town sites lay well north of the Road's intended alignment, they exhorted the surveyors to divert the Road toward their towns. Their attempts and their failure would not be unique. When Road surveyors reached Springfield, Dayton, and Eaton—county seat of Preble County, directly west of Montgomery County—officials proposed a short diversion through their cities. This southern route, they argued, would intersect the new Mad River & Erie Railroad line, and would provide access to riverside industry. A route directly west from Springfield, on the other hand, would traverse open and little-improved farmland. When state legislators presented their appeal for a diversion to Washington, Pres. Andrew Jackson decided, on legal grounds, that the Road would follow the prescribed Springfield-to-Richmond route. Although Dayton and Eaton backers failed to change the Road's alignment, cutoff roads into Dayton siphoned nearly all traffic from the National Road for the next eight decades. Old milestones unearthed in downtown Dayton on Third Street suggest that the cutoff was more than a simple side road.[24]

Just west of downtown Springfield, the Dayton-Springfield Road intersects US 40. This was one of several roads—Ohio 4, Lower Valley Pike, New Carlisle Pike, and Brandt Pike were others—that would link the National Road–US 40 to Dayton. Therefore, this short Road section between Springfield and Brandt is distinguished not by its roadside, or the qualities of the land that the highway traverses, but by the large urban area a few miles south and west that siphoned traffic from the National Road and diverted roadside investment to a parallel highway.

In 1925, an Ohio transportation survey reported that the National Road from Brandt to the Indiana border remained an "unimproved" gravel, stone, or cinder-covered road, and that most through traffic still detoured through

Enon, Ohio

From glacial gravels come interstate pavements. The Hilltop Basic Resources gravel pit unexpectedly showcases modern efficiency and sublime beauty.

Dayton and Eaton. Only 240 vehicles used that section of the Road each day in 1925, compared to 3,400 on the section from Brandt to Springfield.[25] And the road surface was not in poor condition because materials were scarce or technology for highway construction lagged. Several innovative road-surfacing experiments had been conducted across Ohio, and were used on other Road sections. In 1893, for example, laborers laid the state's first brick surface on four miles of Wooster Pike in Cuyahoga County. That same year four Bellefontaine streets received the first Portland cement-concrete pavement after a two-year-old test strip proved durable. When Congress appropriated $500,000 in 1912 for the improvement of mail routes, the appropriation included $120,000 to construct a sixteen-foot-wide concrete experimental pavement on the National Road from Zanesville westward twenty-four miles to Hebron.

In open country about two miles east of Donnelsville, watch for the Ohio 369–Tecumseh Road intersection. A short side trip south will pass two important Native American landmarks. The first is the George Rogers Clark Park and Pickaway Settlements Battle site, which occupies till plain upland and Mad River bottom land. This was the site of Piqua, an important Shawnee town until it was destroyed by Clark's army of Kentucky volunteers in 1780. The militia's victory contributed to the eventual forced removal of the region's Native Americans and opened the Northwest Territory to white settlement. South of the park, turn southwest onto Lower Valley Road, passing a large limestone quarry on the north side that furnished stone for many Springfield buildings.

At the intersection of Lower Valley and Enon Roads, turn left or south toward Enon. After crossing the Mad River bridge, the road passes an extensive gravel pit on the right, operated by Hilltop Basic Resources. A glacial meltwater stream deposited the sand and gravel here during the Pleistocene era, and today the site is covered by a few feet of Mad River–deposited silt. The sand and gravel are of exceptional quality, very resistant to breakup by freezing and thawing, and are the preferred constituent in concrete used for airport runway and freeway construction. The village of Enon stands above the Mad River floodplain about a mile south of the gravel pit. South of the Dayton-Springfield Road, near the library, stands the Enon Mound, an Adena Culture earth mound that is about 40 feet high, 574 feet in base circumference, and contains an estimated 12,800 cubic yards of top soil. It is the second highest Adena earth structure in the state. The Adena peoples lived in the Ohio and Mississippi River valleys from about 1000 B.C. to about A.D. 100 and, in addition to cultivating sunflowers and other domesticated plants, built thousands of earth mounds and effigy earth works across Ohio. A local landowner deeded the mound to the city in 1953 and today it is surrounded by a subdivision called Indian Mound Estates. Return to US 40 by driving north on Enon Road. Turn west on 40 to resume your route.

Donnelsville

Continuing west seven miles from Springfield, through a dense strip of Road-frontaged Cape Cod and ranch-style houses, one arrives in Donnelsville, a town laid out along Donnels Creek in 1832 by Abram Smith. The town's First Lutheran Church was founded in 1828 and so predates the town plat; its new freestanding belltower incorporates a commemorative date stone. Fifty years later, the settlement had managed to attract 232 residents, and had a dry-goods store, two grocery stores, two shoe shops, and a black-

Donnelsville, Ohio

Small towns do not get new gas stations unless a nearby interstate is interchanged or large city suburbs encroach. Instead, local business people recycle and upgrade old stations.

smith.[26] Venerable frame and brick I-houses stand close together, roof peaks parallel to the highway, recalling similar buildings in eastern Ohio Road towns, and reflecting Middle Atlantic cultural connections. A canopied 1920s gas station, with attached 1950s cement-block two-bay garage, sits at the main intersection, cocked at a 45-degree angle to US 40. The new free-standing gas pumps stand fifty feet away at roadside. The station has been refitted as Ronnie's Donnelsville Mall. Across the street from the "Mall," Hillards Auto Sales, circa 1930s, features a fine collection of 1960s and '70s automobiles, mostly Pontiacs. The two-story grade school dates to 1928. The gas station and the school suggest that traffic on the National Old Trails Road (1912–25 era) and US 40 (post-1926) was sufficient to foster optimism in Donnelsville's future. The village clings to its people, and benefits from proximity to nearby employment centers in Dayton and Springfield. The population in 1990 was 276, essentially unchanged since 1970.

KARL RAITZ

From Springfield west to Richmond, US 40 is two lanes wide, much of the traffic tapped off by the cutoffs that lead into Dayton. Several Road sections here lay atop an older roadbed; the land surface was not shaved down by heavy machinery into a leveled sequence of cuts and fills. This is an "organic" road; its narrow-shouldered asphalted surface undulates from one swell to another by diving through swales deep enough to hide a four-door sedan from oncoming traffic. West of Donnelsville, beginning near the Glen Haven Memorial Cemetery, the swells pitch up and down in rotund amplitudes that approximate overfed speed bumps that will "unload" a car's springs should one exceed the speed limit. It is cheaper to paint double yellow lines down a lightly traveled road than regrade.

Driving across country on badly marked public roads in the 1920s was an adventure. Although wealthy travelers patronized city hotels, most travelers strapped tents, folding cots, blankets, and food baskets on their car's running

Forgy, Ohio

Two old auto-camp cabins stand on a circular gravel driveway in front of a 1970s ranch house. Rooms now rent by the week or month. The grounds resemble a wooded park.

East of Brandt, Ohio

The roadside red strawberry at Denlingers Strawberry Farm. The function of the field and stand are clear, no additional signs are required.

boards. They camped at night in schoolyards or in farmers' groves near the highway. In 1924, at Forgy, near the intersection of Tillie Road and US 40, Howard Hobbs found a pay camp in a grove with water and comfort stations on the Road's south side. A cluster of six 1928 tourist cabins still stands in the grove. Evenly spaced around a circular gravel driveway, the clapboard and shingle cabins are painted white or have white trim. Hobbs also recorded the road surface from Donnelsville to Brandt as "Fine Concrete."[27]

About one-half mile beyond the camp, on the north side, a white-painted nineteenth-century four-over-four brick farmhouse stands back from the highway amid other farmstead buildings, including a Pennsylvania forebay barn. Another half mile brings another forebay barn, this one beside the Road and recently refurbished, painted red and white and surrounded by a white plank fence. The barn now shelters riding horses, another nonfarm farmstead. About a mile west of the Ohio 235–US 40 intersection a farmer plants an acre or two of strawberries beside the highway each year. The landmark for this U-Pickum patch is a tiny white market stand topped by a outsized red-fiberglass strawberry icon that belongs to the same family of roadside signs and symbols as the rent-a-birthday-cake in east Springfield.

BRANDT TO RICHMOND: THE GREAT MIAMI COUNTRY

Just past the Ohio 571–US 40 junction stands another grand four-over-four brick house with a banked Pennsylvania forebay barn in back. This barn has been neglected for many years, although the stone foundation and superstructure seem sound. The Road enters Montgomery County just past the Ohio 235 intersection, and about two miles west Ohio 201 intersects US 40. Both 235 and 201 lead south into Dayton, although 201 functioned as the main Dayton cutoff road. Howard Hobbs, for example, routed travelers south from Brandt into Dayton, and then west to Eaton along the cutoff road that would later be designated US 35. At Eaton, 35 cut back north to intersect US 40 in Indiana, just east of Richmond. Hobbs recorded that sections of US 35 were surfaced with macadam, brick, asphalt, and concrete. We do not know the National Road's condition, but that bypassed section was reputedly an evil stretch of road at the time. By contrast, US 35, Hobbs said, was "a pleasant ride," and the scenery "typical Ohio landscape."[28]

The U.S. Congress made its last appropriation to support National Road administration and maintenance in 1838, although the government had begun relegating control to the states earlier in the decade. The Road was in such poor condition across most of its length that some states required extensive repairs be made before they would accept ownership. To pay for repairs Ohio built toll houses, about ten miles apart, and began collecting tolls. The $1.25 million in tolls collected from 1831 to 1877 was insufficient to maintain roads adequately. Although Congress granted some states the right to make the Road free as early as 1879, tolls remained in force in some areas until 1910.[29]

Brandt and Phoneton

One of Ohio's tollgates stood at Brandt's east edge at the intersection of US 40 and Ohio 201. A sign here commemorates the gate. Brandt, established in 1839, became a favorite resting spot for Road travelers, and an important point to turn off the National Road and head for Dayton along the cutoff. Two farm plow manufacturers were among the first residents, and they were soon turning out 1,500 plows each year. By 1868, Brandt had sufficient population to warrant construction of a two-story brick school, and by 1880 250 people lived here.[30] Brandt remains a tiny hamlet. At roadside, a solid-looking brick four-over-four house with rear ell stands next to a nifty little craftsman-style cottage, and the Methodist and Lutheran churches appear well attended and well maintained. Several machine tool and metal fabrication plants in nondescript concrete-block or metal-sided buildings stand at the highway's edge or along side roads from Brandt to Vandalia. These factories are often integrated into the regional metal fabrication industry as parts or tool suppliers to larger firms across Ohio, but especially here in the Miami Valley from Cincinnati north to Richmond, Indiana, or east to Columbus.

Phoneton, originally named Phonetown, began as a junction of three long-line telephone and telegraph wires at the intersection of the National Road and the Old Troy Pike (Ohio 202). The American Telephone and Telegraph Company founded the settlement in 1893, started operations in here in 1901, and soon employed forty people. The company built a twenty-six-room hotel to house employees and started a bus service to carry others the five miles from Tippecanoe (Tipp City) and back. In 1928, the company moved most of its operation into Dayton, and after 1936 the station here was no longer used.[31] The old telephone building is now occupied by a different business. Phoneton is a true crossroads settlement—no side or cross streets.

One mile west of Phoneton, just past the stucco National Trail Apartments on the left and an old roadside dancehall or hotel on the right, US 40 makes an abrupt left turn and heads south along the lip of the Great Miami River valley. About one and one-half miles south, the highway drops into the valley bottom and crosses Taylorsville Dam. Travelers may park at the roadside stop at the dam's east end, read the historic marker, and view the Great Miami Valley, eroded deep into the till plain by glacial meltwater. The river's floodplain is now the Miami Conservancy District's Taylorsville Reserve. To understand why the National Road and US 40 have been diverted south to cross the valley at this point—instead of following a direct line as the Road had originally been surveyed and laid out—one needs to appreciate the influence that Wisconsin-age glaciation had upon this landscape.

From Columbus to Richmond, the National Road cuts across the countryside's topographic grain. Wisconsin-age glaciers moved south, then melted back north, leaving behind looping moraines and several meltwater streams that cut steep-sided north-south channels into the till plain.[32] The Mad, Stillwater, and Great Miami Rivers now flow along the meltwater bottoms, the three streams joining in downtown Dayton to the south. Below Dayton, the Great Miami Valley cut a low-gradient ramp down to the Ohio River floodplain, providing an easy route for travelers to move north out of the Ohio's steep-sided valley. This route became a logical path for canal construction, and in 1845 the Miami & Erie Canal, linking Cincinnati to Fort Wayne and Lake Erie, opened along this corridor.

Southwest Ohio has a long (since the Pleistocene) history of flooding. The Great Miami River drainage basin covers about 4,000 square miles and extends some seventy-seven miles north of Dayton. These northern tributaries cut down into heavy clay soils that shed rain or melting snow water like a firefighter's rubberized coat. Stream gradients of 10 to 100 feet per mile accelerate the flow. Such conditions assure that runoff from the upstream tributaries will be copious and quick. These small streams then feed into the Stillwater, the Great Miami, and the Mad, and their deeply entrenched meltwater channels focus runoff water as though it flowed through a conduit. Wolf Creek joins the grand stream a short distance south of Dayton. This elaborate drainage network is tree-shaped or dendritic, a pattern that, because the branching tributaries are roughly equal length, has the predictable effect of delivering storm runoff into the main trunk steam, the Great Miami in downtown Dayton, at about the same time. Below Dayton, the Great Miami channel gradient is not nearly as steep as the upstream tributaries, three feet per mile or so; consequently, the flow there slows somewhat.

Although the Native Americans who lived here warned the first settlers from Cincinnati that the site selected by frontiersman Jonathan Dayton and others was a hazardous place to build a blockhouse—never mind a large city—the transportation advantages offered by the Great Miami River were too attractive to resist. The first major flood occurred the year that officials declared Dayton's incorporation in 1805, and for a century thereafter the city had a long and regrettable flood history (1814, 1828, 1832, 1847, 1866, 1883, 1884, 1897, 1898, 1913). Valley residents should have understood practical hydrology after the first few floods but they remained complacent until March of 1913 when water reached the second-floor windows in downtown business buildings and over 8,800 people had to be plucked from trees and rooftops by boat-borne rescuers. Dayton's 1913 flood became a catastrophe, an event that would change stream-water management not only here but across the nation.

> All communication lines were dead. Bridges were washed out, fires broke out everywhere, and explosions inflamed the sky. Houses were lifted from their foundations and carried down the river. Flood water climbed to second-story windows marooning thousands of people on house tops. On Thursday night [two days after the river overflowed the levees] the wind changed, blowing the fires back over the burned areas. Then the waters began to recede, and by Friday morning citizens were able to get down on the streets again. The flood had taken 361 lives and destroyed property worth more than $100,000,000.[33]

The solution to the Miami Valley flood problem came in 1914 when the state legislature passed the Conservancy Act of Ohio that enabled community and business leaders in the Dayton area to form a public corporation that would plan, finance, and oversee construction of a comprehensive river-control system. Engineers straightened stream channels, built levees, redesigned bridges, relocated railroad beds and highways, and built five dry dams and retarding basins. Two dry dams, Englewood and Taylorsville, would require rerouting the National Road. Engineers built the 3,000-foot-long Taylorsville Dam across the Great Miami Valley about one and one-half miles south of the point at which the National Road had bridged the river. The dam's purpose was to impound runoff long enough for the danger of flood to pass, and then release water at a controlled rate. This design required a 9,600-acre retarding basin above the dam that extended about eleven miles north along the channel to Troy. Given the dam's seventy-five-foot height, the National Road would have been under several dozen feet of water any time the dam spillway had to be closed to retain flood water. The solution was to reroute the Road south across the top of Taylorsville Dam. Engineers employed the same strategy five miles west where the Road crossed the Stillwater River. Here they diverted the Road south to cross atop the Englewood Dam.[34]

In addition to relocating the Road and railroad beds, clearing the floodplain in each dam's retarding basin required the removal of farmsteads and other settlements, including the village of Tadmore, which once stood on the Great Miami floodplain west of Phoneton. Tadmore's site lay at the conjunction of the region's major transport routes, an admirable location in the mid-nineteenth century. The Miami & Erie Canal ran along the west side of the Great Miami floodplain, and next to it the Dayton & Michigan Railroad. The National Road passed through the settlement to cross the river on a covered bridge. Today, the Taylorsville basin is managed as a recreational reserve with hiking trails—a section of the state's 1,200-mile Buckeye Trail passes through—camping, and nature interpretation.

Vandalia

Across Taylorsville Dam, the Road crosses the old Dixie Highway, or US 25, and enters Vandalia, named for the Road's intended destination at Vandalia, Illinois. Benjamin Wilhelm, the first merchant and postmaster in town, laid out Vandalia in 1838.[35] The Dayton and Troy interurban came through town about the turn of the century, allowing people to commute into Dayton to work, and giving Vandalia a commuting suburb character. When I-75 was built to parallel US 25 in the 1960s, US 40 and the interstate were linked by an interchange. Now Dayton's suburbs extend to Vandalia's south side, and commuters travel either the interstate or North Dixie Drive, the old Dixie Highway. Although Dayton has lost population recently (243,023 in 1970; 182,044 in 1990), Vandalia has gained by one-fifth during that same period, its 1990 population having risen to 13,882.

Between the I-75 interchange and Dixie Drive, developers have turned the US 40 roadside into a garish, modern, auto-oriented strip with fast-food restaurants, gas stations, and linear shopping centers, although industry lurks nearby. Just four blocks north on Dixie Drive is a Delco Chassis manufacturing plant, which turns out automobile parts. This strip is the first en-

Vandalia, Ohio

Beneath these pollarded silver maples 100,000 trap-shooters and spectators gather during August every year for America's largest trapshooting event. During the meet, over a half million clay targets will be thrown each day from the 100 traps that line the one and one-half mile long firing line. On the right, beyond the traps is the Cox-Dayton International Airport runway.

counter with such an agglomeration since leaving Columbus, and a stark contrast to the traditional US 40 roadside. On the right, west of Dixie Drive, the Amateur Trapshooting Association maintains the Trapshooting Hall of Fame and the grounds where they conduct an annual national trapshooting tournament. The Cox-Dayton International Airport lies just north of the highway. From the 1850s on, Dayton was a dynamo of mechanical invention and manufacture—farm machinery and railroad rolling stock, cash registers and automobiles. And of course the city was the home of Orville and Wilbur Wright, who conducted aircraft experiments here, and their factory later built the de Havilland airplane. Across the highway from the new airport a postmodern Howard Johnson's motel recalls the barnstorming era in their Waldo Pepper Club, an example of national corporate image blended with "local color."

Two miles west from the airport entrance road, US 40 again turns south for about one-half mile where it crosses the Stillwater River on the 4,700-foot-long Englewood Dam. This is the largest dam in the Miami Conservancy system. The floodplain on the dam's upstream side is the Englewood Reserve controlled-inundation area, closed to private or commercial development but used for recreation and agriculture. The Aullwood Audubon Center and Farm can be accessed at the dam's east end.

Englewood

Travelers now enter Englewood from the south after crossing the dam to reach the top of the Stillwater River's steep west bank. US 40 turns right at Ohio 48 and, after passing a shopping center on the left and recreational vehicle sales lots, turns left onto the original US 40 alignment. At this corner stands a 1930s-era cottage-type gas station, refurbished and refitted as a real estate office. (Two similar stations can also be found in Richmond, Indiana, one on Ninth and South A Street [US 40 East], the other on Eighth and North A Streets.) Englewood got its start in 1841 under the name of Harrisburg and became a center for Mennonites and Dunkards migrating west from southeastern Pennsylvania. US 40 here is lined with strip shopping centers, fast-food restaurants, and parking lots. Several old Road-oriented structures remain, especially near the 40/48 intersection. Ohio 48 leads south into Dayton and has become a commuter road lined with subdivisions. And, like Vandalia, Englewood has benefited from its access to Dayton. The town grew by 30 percent from 1970 to 1990; its current population is 11,432.

Englewood, Ohio

The Stillwater River spillway below the Englewood Dam provides a focus for fishing.

KARL RAITZ

Proceeding west from Englewood, US 40 leaves the entrenched river valleys behind to again cross a farm-dominated countryside. German Baptists, Mennonites, and United Brethren migrated to the lands west and northwest of here during the first years after the National Road opened. Their presence is recorded in place names: Swanktown, Swisher's Mill, Warnke Bridge, Holtzmuller Road. Their descendants still farm the land. The Baptists' simple white churches can be found in rural neighborhoods, often with separate front doors for women and men.

The traveler will find fewer roadside artifacts here; business people built their taverns and other road-fronting commercial and residential structures on the Dayton-to-Eaton road, now US 35, which parallels this highway section about eight miles south. The vistas are noticeably open and invite glances across a mile or more of gently rolling till plain. Farmsteads here generally have few trees, perhaps a quick-growing silver maple for summer shade and an unpruned apple tree or two, but most have preserved a tree lot. The lots or groves are the second-growth remnants from the presettlement beech and maple forest that screen the distant horizon in several places. A century ago, the tree lots provided fenceposts, firewood, and building material. Now they mark land that is poorly drained or is on the property's "back side."

The farm country west of the Stillwater River is deceptively common—farm buildings stand in tight clusters and crops thrive in rectangular fields. Nothing striking or startling. But this is the upper Miami Valley and a plaque should be erected here to commemorate one of the places that contributed farming practices that led to the formation of one of America's most important regions, the Corn Belt. Companion Corn Belt cradles north of the Ohio lay to the east along the Scioto River on the Pickaway Plains south of Circleville, and the west along the Wabash River alluvial terraces up- and downstream from Vincennes, Indiana. Although these corn- and livestock-producing areas were initially dependent upon southward-flowing rivers, or riverine bottoms, for transport or routeways, the National Road would link each district east-west and provide alternative routes to both eastern and middlewestern markets. Growing crops in rotation, feeding hay and corn to livestock to fatten them for market, and saving manure to enrich the soil were common practices among Pennsylvania and Maryland Piedmont farmers—many of them German pietist immigrants—in the mid-eighteenth century. They also built huge multipurpose barns to house

stock, store hay and grain, and provide a sheltered place for threshing. Some
migrated here via the National Road, others took flatboats down the Ohio
River to Cincinnati where they followed the river valleys north to this countryside west of Dayton. In addition, migrants from the Kentucky Bluegrass,
just south of the Ohio River, who also raised corn and fed it to swine and
cattle, settled here early on.[36]

The agriculture transferred here by migrants was not subsistence farming intended to feed the family and little more; it was commercial from the
first decades of settlement. Most farms raised clover as a hay crop, a small
grain such as oats or wheat for stock feed or milling, and corn. Farmers ro-
tated these crops systematically and manured their fields. Some farmers
sold corn to brewers and distillers, but most fed it to their livestock. By 1839,
this region's farmers led Ohio in corn production. Hogs thrived on the
clover and corn, and farmers drove so many south to Cincinnati abattoirs
that the city became known as "Porkopolis."

The Pennsylvania Germans built scaled-down versions of the great Pennsylvania barn with ramps to second-level threshing floors on one side and
forebay extensions on the stockyard side. The Upland Southerners from
central Kentucky brought with them a tradition of fattening cattle on corn
and a large feeder barn in which to store hay and corn. Their barn was

Concrete posts, eighteen inches on a side or larger, still stand at many Miami Valley quarter section corners where they anchored the woven-wire fences that farmers strung to separate fields and pastures and contain cattle and hogs. The conversion to cash grain farming has turned thousands of miles of fences into historical artifacts. US 40 runs across the till plain past the houses on the horizon, one mile to the south.

shaped like a flattened *A* when viewed from the end, and had a central passage between cribs or bins and flanking lean-tos that covered alleyways where implements might be stored. A few migrants from New England also moved into the Miami Valley. They often built simple English-style barns with gable roofs and a large door in the side wall. The crop and animal husbandry ideas put in place in the Miami Valley spread west and north across the Middle West where it became known as Corn Belt farming.

Migrant farmers also introduced cigar tobacco into the Miami Valley. In the early 1800s, cigars were a popular tobacco product—the "stogie" was a medium-sized cigar favored by National Road Cone*stoga* wagon drivers. Manufacturers used three different tobacco types to make cigars. Filler tobacco formed the core, a binder tobacco leaf held the filler together, and a high-quality wrapper leaf provided the outside cover. In 1838, Thomas Pomeroy of Suffield, Connecticut, migrated to the Miami Valley and began farming and raising tobacco in Montgomery County near Miamisburg. Within two decades, air-cured cigar filler tobacco production had spread from the Pomeroy neighborhood into the Pennsylvania-German communities, and southwestern Ohio had become an important tobacco-producing area.

After the Civil War, the demand for lighter-smoking tobacco products, especially blended cigarettes made from air-cured Burley and flue-cured Carolina tobaccos, increased while cigars fell from favor. Consequently, Ohio cigar tobacco production fell steadily, and by the mid-1960s acreage was only a fraction of what it had been a century earlier. Nevertheless, the link between tobacco and Germans remained, and by the early 1970s most growers were still German or had mixed-German parentage.[37]

The Ohio cigar tobacco barn, or "shed" as it is usually termed, does not resemble livestock barns or other farm buildings. The classic Ohio cigar tobacco barn, found in Montgomery and Preble Counties along the National Road, is a simple gable-roofed shed. Large outside-mounted sliding doors along both sides give access to interior cross driveways, and a small shed, where cured tobacco leaves are stripped from the stalk in preparation for marketing, attaches on one side. The likely model for this barn form is the old Connecticut tobacco barn, which is, in turn, a simple variation of the old English side-entry barn. Miami Valley tobacco barns retained the Connecticut barn's form but were often much longer, some over 100 feet, resembling several Connecticut barns spliced together. Some barns may have as many as ten outside-mounted doors on each side.[38]

About a mile west of Englewood, bordered by a white picket fence, a white-and-green-trimmed Italianate farmhouse fronts the highway; a spectacular Pennsylvania forebay barn, louvered windows still intact, abides the backyard. Painted on the barn's gable end is the name L. Schroeder and the date 1875. By taking a side trip north to Wengerlawn Road (one mile), or Sweet Potato Ridge Road (two miles), the traveler will discover more Germanic-looking farm structures. Thick concrete posts appear along the roadside at periodic intervals. Until the 1950s, this countryside was laced by woven wire fences and the concrete posts anchored corners to keep the wire tight. The fence networks were used in the old crop rotation system where a farmer would allow a field to lay fallow as pasture for a few years. Or farmers would turn hogs or cattle into the cornfields to "hog down" the field or clean up the corn missed by mechanical pickers. Today, many farms here have converted to cash grain production, the livestock are gone, and the fences are no longer needed.

Arlington and Bachman

About two and one-half miles west of the Ohio 49–US 40 intersection is the hamlet of Arlington, laid out along the Road in 1838, with a United

Methodist church that dates from the nineteenth century. A stone mausoleum built in 1917 stands at the settlement's west edge next to a cemetery whose markers carry English names: Lees, Williamson, Weller, Black.

An optimistic investor platted Bachman, one and one-half miles west of Arlington, in 1842 where the Dayton & Union Railroad crossed the National Road. The railroad tracks have since been removed and only a few small modest homes remain to mark the site.

Lewisburg

About halfway between Vandalia and Richmond, Lewisburg stands near the intersection of Ohio 503 and US 40. Henry Horn platted Lewisburg(h) in 1818 on high ground just west of Twin Creek, so the settlement predates the National Road. Horn's plat included "One street running north, five degrees east, namely: Greenville street; with three streets running parallel with each other and crossing Greenville street at right angles, namely Dayton street, Twin street and Water street . . . with alleys extending around the town."[39]

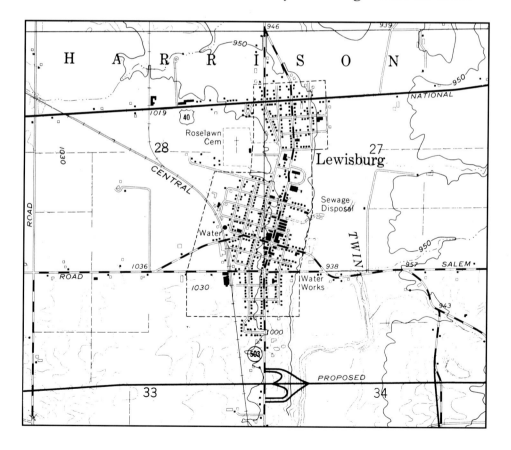

Lewisburg, Ohio

Lewisburg street grids reflect distinct eras of town expansion.

Lewisburg, Ohio

Modest Victorian ginger-
bread detail adds a touch of
grace on this roadside
house's side porch. A new
subdivision of brick ranch
houses expands along Twin
Creek in the distance.

The village had a hotel and a full complement of businesses serving the local farm community. A large tannery processed livestock hides.

Lewisburg had neither highway nor railroad connections until the National Road passed one-half mile to the north. Seizing the opportunity, entrepreneur John Muma laid out a second street grid along the highway, here called Cumberland Road, oriented not to Lewisburg's canted grid, or to the Township and Range survey lines, but to the National Road that angles south from west. Muma named the place Euphemia, and business people opened dry goods and grocery stores at roadside and built enough homes to house about 250 people. The two settlements grew together and became known as Lewisburg. Eventually, a spur of the New York Central Railroad passed just west of town. The town once had four cigar tobacco warehouses, two beside the railroad between Singer and Clay Streets, which have been demolished. The other two remain; one on Clay Street is still used as a warehouse by a container company, the other on Dayton Street is now an apartment building.[40] Businesses in Henry Horn's original town center still serve the village and surrounding neighborhoods. Few road-oriented businesses remain on US 40 in old Euphemia; the exception is Herschel's Auto Service, a tiny single-bay garage on the right that dates from the Model-T era. Most stores here now sell antiques and gifts to city residents who prowl the Road on weekend shopping excursions.

At the town's south end, a third addition to Lewisburg's street grid aligns with the cardinal survey grid and Ohio 503. In the 1960s, I-70 passed just south of town and engineers placed a diamond-shaped interchange where the freeway intersects 503, and a few freeway-oriented services have opened here, giving Lewisburg a fourth-generation building cluster. Perhaps the interstate has helped Lewisburg maintain its population, even gaining modestly since the freeway interchange opened: 1,553, in 1970, 1,584 in 1990. The traveler can visit two covered bridges at Lewisburg. The Warnke Bridge spans Swamp Creek on Wengerlawn Road northeast of town, and the Geeting Bridge takes the Lewisburg-Western Road across Price Creek three miles west.

Lewisburg, Ohio

An old gasoline station from the 1930s, built to resemble a cottage, still operates along the highway as an auto-repair shop.

Lewisburg, Ohio

Step into this motel lobby and enter the 1960s, a refreshing departure. Or is it the '50s?

Intersection of US 40 and US 127, Ohio

The US 40 roadside is quickly adding a new generation of abandoned and bypassed structures; the cement-block truckstop predates the interstate two miles south. The east window mirrors a 1960s motel.

Intersection of US 40 and US 127, Ohio

Across US 40 from the relict Sinclair truck stop, a new Marathon station incorporates a convenient store and gas pumps sheltered by a tall canopy. A Prairie-style cube house, a style popular around the turn of the twentieth century, stands opposite.

West of Lewisburg, US 40 intersects US 127. This modern north-south highway links Lansing, Michigan, and Chattanooga, Tennessee, and here follows the survey's cardinal directions. But a short distance south of Eaton, 127 abandons the survey alignment and follows the topography approximating a much older Native American road, the Wabash Trail. The junction of two important highways suggests that a large town should occupy this place. Instead, 1920s-era tourist cabins stand in a small cluster on the Road's north side behind a new Marathon gas station and food mart across from the 1950s Sandman Motel on the south. Both have been renovated into apartments that rent by the week or month. The massive two-story concrete-block Hines Sinclair truckstop on the southeast corner is closed; faded gas pumps still stand in unmatched pairs on the five service islands, the asphalt-covered lot has oxidized to white, and tall weeds grow from weathering cracks.

Gettysburg

The hamlet of Gettysburg resides five miles west of the US 127 intersection. Pennsylvanian John Curry platted the place—originally named Harrisburg—in 1832, optimistically intending that it be the largest town on the road.[41] Within fifty years (1881), Gettysburg's population had soared to 117. At one time, Gettysburg had both a sawmill—the hardwood forest throughout the area had to be cleared to open land for farming—and a tile factory. Today, Gettysburg is little more than a cluster of small houses surrounded by corn and hog farms, and announced by a hog market that stands a mile east along the Road's south side.

THE INDIANA BORDER AND RICHMOND

The Indiana-Ohio state border is five miles ahead. There US 40 will climb a low moraine and again intersect I-70 as the interstate crosses to parallel the Road on the north side, where it will remain from Richmond to Indianapolis. The National Road was graded to this point by 1840. A short section of the old US 40 bed survives—about one mile from the US 40 and I-70 interchange—to the right, or north side of modern, realigned, and widened US 40. The old surface is crumbling where exposed, although much of what remains is now covered by grass and weeds.

At the state border, two large truckstops stand on the east side of the I-70 interchange. The I-70 Truck Plaza on the south side closed in 1992, although the adjacent 40-70 Truck Wash still operates. The Petro truckstop on the north—

Richmond, Indiana

Signs on stilts sprout around the US 40–I-70 interchange on Richmond's east side. The intent is obvious: to impede the traveler's progress with a barrier of information and irresistible deals.

a large, multibay truck service garage, truck wash, restaurant, and echeloned fuel pumps—thrives island-like amid several acres of asphalt parking lot. Automobiles are not welcome here; the truck yard is segregated behind a chainlink and barbed-wire fence, and guarded gate. "Civilian" car drivers do have access via a second entrance to separate gas pumps and the restaurant. This interchange, and the two others north of town, have not helped Richmond maintain its population. The city has lost over 5,000 people since 1970, bringing its 1990 total to 38,705.

US 40 crosses under the interchange and abruptly enters an extended automobile-oriented suburban shopping strip. Franchise motels and fast-food restaurants cluster on the interchange's west side—the side nearest downtown Richmond. Within a quarter mile, these roadside services give way to strip shopping centers, Wal-Mart, K-Mart, and other commercial structures.

Richmond predates the National Road. Soldiers from George Rogers Clark's militia founded Richmond in 1805, and the settlement soon attracted Quakers and Germans who moved to the Indiana frontier by way of Cincinnati and the Great Miami River valley. The Quakers founded Earlham College on the town's west side. Both groups became active in the abolitionist movement before the Civil War.

The Road enters downtown Richmond along East Main Street and from 23rd Street to 10th passes a line of large old homes, Victorian and Queen Anne giving way to Craftsman, Stick, Italianate, and Greek Revival styles as the road approaches the town's center. The original business district ran north-south, but business people relocated when the Road came through town. In the business district, US 40 diverts into one-way streets, North A and South A, two blocks apart. To see the original Main Street, turn south and park. Several business blocks are closed to vehicles and the street is now a "pedestrian mall" with planting boxes, benches, and metal shades on pedestals that resemble pastel-colored mushrooms. The city rerouted US 40 and installed the promenade in 1972 in response to a catastrophic natural gas explosion here in 1968 which incinerated two city blocks. The remaining businesses attract few customers. The refurbished 1928 Leland Hotel

Main Street: The pedestrian mall

Richmond, Indiana

stands at Ninth and South A Street, its 200-car parking garage for hotel guests' vehicles an early attempt to adapt the central-city hotel to automobile-borne travelers. As with most grand city hotels, the Leland was Richmond's social hub for thirty years after construction.

Beyond the Romanesque Wayne County Courthouse on Richmond's west side is the Whitewater River valley. This chapter ends at the Whitewater bridge. The present bridge parallels the original National Road crossing, which one can still see about two blocks to the left or south. West bank quarries supplied the stone that German stonecutters cut and laid as abutments for a long covered bridge completed in the 1830s. The National Road crossed the river on that wooden bridge until 1896 when it was torn down and a new steel-girder bridge erected in its place.[42]

From Richmond to Terre Haute, Indiana

ROBERT W. BASTIAN

Franklin suddenly approached me and said, quite apropos of nothing: "How would you like to go out to Indiana in my car?"

THEODORE DREISER
A Hoosier Holiday (1916)

US 40 EXTENDS FOR NEARLY 140 MILES BETWEEN RICHMOND AND TERRE Haute, Indiana, with Indianapolis occupying an almost exact middle position between these smaller cities. For most of its distance between Richmond and Indianapolis the Road's bearing is a few degrees south of due west. Beyond Indiana's capital city the highway assumes a west-by-south alignment that continues as far as Putnam County. Here it crosses a Pleistocene boundary separating recent Wisconsin glacial drift from older, and more highly dissected, Illinoisan till. The Road makes this transition in a series of curves of a magnitude not encountered along US 40 in eastern Indiana. As the highway crosses into Clay County, it resumes a diagonal orientation, which it follows with little deviation to Terre Haute. Where stream erosion is less advanced, as between Centerville and Greenfield and westward from Plainfield to Put-

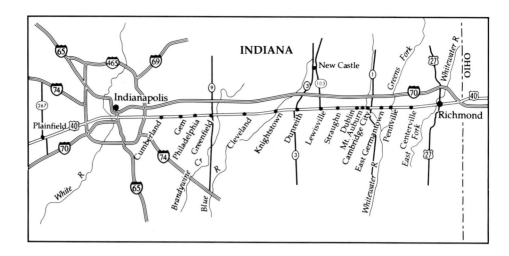

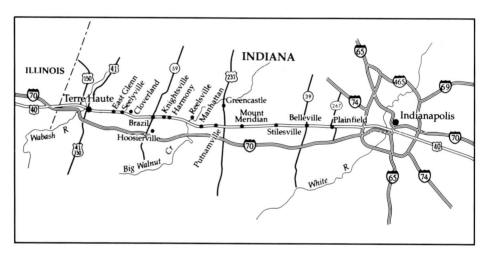

namville, an open landscape of corn and soybean fields prevails. In hilly terrain the countryside panorama closes in to the roadside, the view obscured
by stands of locust, maple, and walnut. Sycamores grow in valley bottoms
and redbuds line upland roadsides. Residential and commercial buildings in
bands along the Road between closely spaced communities limit visual reference to the countryside. Roadside development along this stretch of US 40
began in the early days of the electric interurban railway. An interurban line
ran beside US 40 for most of its length across Indiana, providing the first re-
liable means of all-weather access to rural building sites.

Four communities traversed by the Hoosier segment of US 40 were established before surveyors laid out the route in 1827. The main streets in
downtown Richmond, Centerville, Indianapolis, and Terre Haute betray

ROBERT W. BASTIAN

their age through their east-west orientation instead of aligning with the diagonal Road. With the exception of older main street blocks, many structures along US 40, sited according to the federal rectangular land survey, appear to have been erected askew to the highway. An absence of school buildings in smaller towns is another attribute of the Indiana roadside. This reflects the popularity of countywide school districts in the Hoosier state. Recently constructed buildings house consolidated schools in rural locations that can be seen near the highway. The most common structures facing US 40 between Richmond and Terre Haute are vintage motels and aging gasoline stations. With few exceptions these buildings no longer serve their original purpose, owing to competition from newer facilities gathered around Interstate 70 interchanges. Many old motels survive as apartment complexes for low-income residents. And many former gas stations now function as automobile repair shops or offices for used car businesses.

RICHMOND TO CENTERVILLE

Prior to leaving downtown Richmond the curious traveler ought to turn north on US 27 (Ninth Street) and proceed to E Street. Standing on the north side of E, between Ninth and Tenth, is the old Pennsylvania Railroad Depot (1902) designed by Daniel H. Burnham, a prominent Chicago architect and city planner. (Buildings designed by Burnham also stand in Indiana's other two US 40 cities, the seventeen-floor Merchants National Bank Building [1909] in Indianapolis and the impeccable one-story Terminal Arcade Building [1911] in Terre Haute.) For many years this two-story brick structure, of Classical Revival design, welcomed the public through a tall portico. Two tracks on which passenger trains stopped are in a state of disrepair similar to the depot's condition. Freight trains still pass frequently on a well-maintained adjacent track. Westward this line leads to New Castle but there is no longer a direct rail connection, adjacent to US 40, running to Indianapolis and Terre Haute. The empty railroad station is still imposing and is best viewed from the pedestrian walk on the viaduct that carries US 27 across the tracks. As the third depot to occupy this site, Burnham's portal to Richmond symbolized competition between the railroad and successive versions of the National Road and US 40. The contest for freight and passenger traffic began in the 1850s when steam locomotives first pulled trains between Richmond, Indianapolis, and Terre Haute. As the depot's condition attests, the Road won.

Before crossing the Whitewater River in Richmond the highway passes

Richmond, Indiana

The Sundowner Tavern (*above*) stands across E Street from Daniel Burnham's Pennsylvania Railroad Depot (*facing page*). E Street and the depot were once the center of town for the traveler, but the elegant building is now a candidate for preservation.

the Wayne County Courthouse (1893). This imposing Romanesque structure was designed by Cincinnati architect James W. McLaughlin. The depot and the courthouse illustrate that in Richmond US 40 has made an important transition into the Middle West, marked here by an acceptance of regional architects for important structures rather than contracting exclusively with architects from New York City, Philadelphia, or other prestigious East Coast design firms. Numerous late-nineteenth-century buildings in Indianapolis and Terre Haute were also designed by middlewestern architects. The Whitewater River bridge parallels the original National Road, which crossed the river one block to the south on one of the many covered bridges that carried the Road over the larger streams.

On the Whitewater River's west side, US 40 again follows the original survey's diagonal alignment. Tall shade trees line the roadway past Earlham College's park-like campus. This Quaker liberal arts school opened in 1847 along the Road's south side. The adjacent Earlham Cemetery grounds (1861) occupy both slopes of Clear Creek valley. Although the site of this picturesque cemetery was originally rural, its intended residents have al-

ROBERT W. BASTIAN

ways come primarily from the city. This elegant cemetery shares with the more extensive Crown Hill burial ground in Indianapolis, and Highland Lawn in Terre Haute, an initially peripheral site and a mode of landscape design originally used at Pere Lachaise in Paris (1804). That novel approach to a landscape for the dead was first imitated in this country at Mount Auburn in Boston (1831). In Philadelphia and Baltimore, cities with direct overland connections to the National Road, cemeteries following this same plan opened in the 1830s. Several large and well-maintained homes built before and during the early twentieth century face the Earlham campus, but near the cemetery entrance give way to a conveniently situated monument dealer and a florist. Here begins the first of many suburban commercial strips that align US 40 between Richmond and Terre Haute.

The undivided highway that serves the business strip on Richmond's west side continues without a median all the way to Centerville. Road-fronting businesses enforce an uncomfortable congestion here, as do many other auto-oriented strips along this highway. The age of many roadside buildings reminds us that business encroachment upon the Road's right-of-way and

Richmond, Indiana

Sharing E Street are the Perfection Manufacturing building and the Richmond Hardware store. A billboard reminds the visitor that Putt-Putt Golf with batting cages and family arcade can be found at the new "center" of town, the I-70/US 40 interchange.

the traveler's sight lines has been problematic here for seventy years. By the mid-1920s, the density of roadside business along the National Road's Indiana section was so great that the State Highway Commission announced a plan to extend the Road's right-of-way to eighty feet. Travel along the "main street of America," the commission said, should not be endangered by encroaching "barbecue and other refreshment stands, filling stations, or other obstructions [which] will be barred." A 1928 *Terre Haute Star* editorial suggested that the highway required wider pavements and that "the National Road . . . should be twice as broad through its entire length across the state of Indiana as it is today. Traffic thus could be handled without congestion and with little of the danger now involved in attempting to pass the slow-moving automobiles."[1]

Few agricultural fields front directly on this Road segment. A narrow band of mixed residential, commercial, and industrial buildings on piano-keyed lots borders both sides. On reaching Centerville one encounters a typical small-town rural-to-urban transition zone. Contemporary house styles grade into those of earlier eras, and immature trees planted within deep frontyards give way to venerable streetside specimens that form a partial canopy over the wide pavement. An unusual early-twentieth-century dwelling stands at the northwest corner of Fourth and Main. To the untrained eye it has the same boxy appearance of any other house built in the form of

228   ROBERT W. BASTIAN

a cube and capped by a steeply pitched roof. Structures of this sort are found on farms and in towns across a wide area, including the Middle West, parts of Pennsylvania, and Virginia's Shenandoah Valley.

To someone familiar with Frank Lloyd Wright's Prairie-style houses this is no ordinary cube-shaped building. It displays the kind of detail he employed to create a horizontal image conformal with the region's flat terrain. Several techniques attributed to Wright accent the horizontal: individual stories made to appear as separate layers by using different facing materials, a porch with low pitched roof, and paired windows intended to resemble longer ribbons of casement windows. This dwelling includes unmistakable Prairie-style details on porch columns, and typical geometric glass panes. Nevertheless, it constitutes an awkward example of the Prairie approach as opposed to one planned by an architect well versed in this idiom. Like Daniel Burnham, Wright was a son of the Middle West. The Centerville house, which borrowed selected traits from those he designed, helps confirm the role of Chicago as arbiter of middlewestern architectural taste at the beginning of this century.

Along its central Main Street blocks, Centerville loses its Middlewest flavor; here the town's early National Road heritage becomes apparent. Front-yards and trees disappear altogether and what were residential and commercial structures abut the sidewalks. These two-story buildings have party walls except where separated on the ground floor by open archways. Most are brick with end gable roofs, and floor plans that are one or two rooms deep. Right-angle ells and later appendages add considerable depth to some structures. These building details represent ideas carried here by National Road migrants, and give today's Centerville a quaint appearance. The quaint and the historic attract tourists and the community is cashing in on its image. Main Street merchants no longer serve the surrounding farm population but have converted stores into antique shops and other businesses catering to travelers. Marketing a real or imagined past has helped reverse local population decline. After losing close to 100 residents in the 1970s, Centerville gained more new citizens during the following decade. Nearly 2,400 people lived here in 1990.

CENTERVILLE TO DUBLIN

Centerville's commercial strip is focused predominantly eastward toward Richmond. Only a few businesses align the roadside on the town's west end.

To Pennville the Road passes into open countryside. One of the few live-stock-feeding operations found along US 40 in Indiana fronts the highway's south side. The Pennsylvania Railroad's vacated bed crosses the right-of-way, and from here to Pennville it parallels the Road on the south, its grade a low straight ridge covered with wild grasses and volunteer trees. Occasionally it is more clearly marked by surviving telegraph poles.

From Pennville to Dublin, US 40 continues as an undivided four-lane road through a row of closely spaced towns and villages: East Germantown (or "Pershing" as announced on road signs at either end of town), Cambridge City, and Mount Auburn. Pennville (established in 1836), a small village, functions almost exclusively as a residential community today. For many years its eye-catching restaurant, built to resemble a coffeepot, was a popular stop for travelers. Although some might think such structures preposterous now, during the 1920s roadside merchants and other business people often turned their buildings into signs in an attempt to attract customers. Unfortunately, this example of the genre burned recently and has not been replaced. As in other small settlements along US 40, Pennville has few commercial and service businesses. What survives most often are convenience stores with gas pumps, small churches, and modest post offices. These establishments and the occasional funeral home or elderly health-care facility reflect economic decline and aging populations. West of Pennville rural dwellings front the Road's south side until it reaches East Germantown.

Another small community with only a few hundred residents, few businesses remain in East Germantown and none occupy the oldest commercial structures on Main Street. The scene is more promising across the abandoned railroad bed where the grain-elevator operator has added new storage sheds to an existing facility. As in many other modest-sized settlements, East Germantown demonstrates the breakdown of the traditional linkage between local retail merchants and nearby farmers. Only businesses that handle products related to farm output, seed and fertilizer for example, maintain the connection. Farmers travel to larger towns now for their retail needs. A sand, gravel, and paving materials operation survives at the village's west end. This firm mines sediments on the floor of the Wisconsin-age glacial meltwater channel across which Martindale Creek now meanders. Glaciation left behind numerous sand and gravel deposits, some occurring as shallow lenses in the till or moraines, others along stream floodplains. These sites are called gravel pits ("borrow pits" in the regional

ROBERT W. BASTIAN

dialect), and are often surface-mined to supply material for road construction and concrete manufacture.

On the creek's west side the highway enters Cambridge City (established c. 1835). This community more or less qualifies for the generic part of its name. With some 2,000 inhabitants it is the largest place among the towns between Pennville and Dublin. Approaching the business district, one passes a genuine historic landmark on the Road's south side: a two-story, double-pile, brick dwelling at the southeast corner of Main and Lincoln. Its design and architectural detail proclaim this house a descendent of fine homes common to the East Coast's Middle Atlantic region, its plan carried here along the National Road.

The business district begins in earnest two blocks beyond the Whitewater River—West Fork—bridge. A number of old three-story commercial structures display nineteenth-century decorative details on their upper floors. Vacant stores are a problem along Main Street, and the opaque material covering most upstairs windows suggests that these traditional office spaces are either now used for storage or stand empty. West of the downtown, commercial intrusions spot the residential blocks, among them a Chevrolet dealer on the street's south side. This is the first authorized new car agency seen since the highway left Richmond. Turn south on Foote Street and drive through the "mouse hole" underpass beneath the old Pennsylvania Railroad bridge (1910). The rail bed has been removed from the bridge's west end, leaving a level lot upon which a trucking company parks its vehicles. Nearby, at East Church and South Center Streets, stands the Bertschland Family Practice Clinic. Dating from 1853, the building was clearly built for purposes other than the practice of medicine. During the middle nineteenth century, it served as a warehouse and canal-boat repair center. The Whitewater Canal ran along the building's southwest corner, then west for one-half block where it turned north to cross the National Road. One can still follow the old canal bed through the north side of town where it disappears in a line of trees. In 1879, John and Charles Bertsch bought the building and turned it into the Cambridge City Agricultural Machine Works. In the 1890s, the Bertsch family turned the building into a foundry and began to manufacture heavy equipment here. Needing more room for expansion during World War I, the foundry moved across the street and the old building became a Ford motor car dealership. In 1927, the 12,000,000th Ford car was sold at this dealership and Henry Ford came from

Detroit to celebrate the occasion. By World War II, the foundry again required more room for expansion so the Ford dealership moved uptown. In the mid-1970s the Bertsch family sold the operation and the building remained a warehouse until refurbished as a clinic in 1989.

West of town, on the approach to Mount Auburn, the old Huddleston Farm's main structures are standing close to the highway's south side. The three-story, single-pile, brick dwelling served as both a farmhouse and an inn shortly after the National Road opened. Both the house and adjacent barn are in good repair, maintained and operated as a museum by Historic Landmarks Foundation of Indiana. Although diminutive in size, Mount Auburn (established in 1840) offers tourists another attraction: a large family restaurant serving good food and a good view. It stands on the Road's north side, in Springs Run Valley, where a low dam has impounded a small artificial lake. The large parking lot and presence of signs informing trucks where to park suggest that the owner has succeeded in making the restaurant a tour-bus destination. Although a small-town restaurant might attract weekend customers from a broad area, the profit margin can be greatly enhanced if one can make arrangements with tour companies to become an eating stop. Several other large motels and restaurants along US 40 maintain their solvency though such arrangements.

Across Springs Run the highway enters Dublin; a tavern stood here as early as 1825. Although larger than all the other settlements along this stretch of US 40, except Cambridge City, its economy has not been sufficiently dynamic to avoid a quaint, down-at-the-heels appearance. Its early connections eastward across the National Road show in two sets of nineteenth-century single-pile rowhouses built against the south side of Main Street. The older row is brick and little altered, although it suffers from peeling paint and aluminum siding. The more recent frame buildings are far from pristine although some have been re-sided. No one here has followed Centerville's example and taken advantage of the town's historic context. Only a few essential but low-overhead enterprises still function. The community's name does not refer to Irish immigrants who may have helped build the original Road or an early canal passing through nearby Cambridge City. Dublin is a corruption of the word "doubling," and referred to the teamster habit of hitching a wagon with double teams to negotiate a rise in the old Road, which was in wretched condition at this point.

DUBLIN TO KNIGHTSTOWN

As US 40 departs Dublin, its four lanes separated by a grass-covered median, it begins to look more like a modern highway. Only scattered dwellings line the road, but after crossing the county line large wholesale nurseries extend for some distance along both sides of the highway. Tight rows of young trees and shrubs screen the banked, and now overgrown, Pennsylvania Railroad grade, which here comes clearly into view for the first time since being obscured near East Germantown. The highway median disappears just outside the community of Straughn, a small settlement established during the railroad era. With only a few hundred inhabitants Straughn is exclusively residential today. Its few business structures stand vacant.

Along the three- to four-mile distance between Straughn and Lewisville the almost-level road surface grades into an open landscape of productive farmland. The Pickering Seed Company, a producer of hybrid corn seed, occupies a small acreage along the north side. Ahead lies Lewisville, which is a National Road town (established in 1829) and a somewhat larger community than Straughn. A business district has a few historic brick structures,

Lewisville, Indiana

US 40 necks down from four lanes with a median to two lanes upon entering Lewisville.

Dunreith, Indiana

Traffic-signal lights swing from cables above the intersection of US 40 and the road that links Dunreith to I-70 about four miles north. Before the interstate was completed, neither sign nor signal stopped US 40 traffic here. In recognition of the old Road's subservience, an antique store and gun shop have nailed directional arrow signs to a tree at the top of the intersection (*above*). A steel and plastic "arrow sign" directs shoppers to the Olde National Trail Antiques and Gun Shop (*right*).

ROBERT W. BASTIAN

and continues to function after a fashion. But vacant buildings and nontraditional business establishments offer more evidence that small towns are in economic decline, and occupied by aging populations.

Immediately west of Lewisville, US 40 crosses the Flatrock River. The wide floodplain appears out of proportion with the narrow stream channel that has been engineered to resemble a ditch. The river runs in a straight line rather than being allowed to meander as a natural water course. On the river's west side the highway lanes again divide. This road, designed for heavier traffic than it carries today, continues through open farmland for nearly five miles before arriving at Dunreith on Buck Creek's inconspicuous west bank. Like many other small places along the way, this quiet community dates to the National Road's arrival (1828). Its only apparent connection to present-day highway travel is a gas station at the northwest corner of Indiana 3, which leads north to an I-70 interchange. On the eastern edge of town is a classic "disconnected" or nonfarm farm; the buildings remain intact but the family no longer works the land for a living. Known as the Henshaw House, a clapboard I-house painted white stands behind mature shrubbery. The house was set back sixty feet when US 40 was widened to four lanes. An attractive Southern barn, characterized by a gable-end entry door, stables on the ground floor with a hayloft above, and shed additions on both sides, stands back from the house about 200 feet. In 1883 the Henshaws and several other families moved here from Stokes County, North Carolina, on the Virginia border.

From Dunreith, one can reach Knightstown via alternative routes. Most obvious is the approach on new US 40, which changes orientation at this

Dunreith, Indiana

A field (*left*) east of Dunreith is newly planted in corn. The concrete disk is the base of an old wire-sided corn crib that once contained ear corn. The pole-and-wire crib near the white barn (*right*) was also used to store ear corn, its long, narrow shape promoted rapid drying. Corn is no longer harvested "on the ear," but is picked and shelled in a single operation by the same combine that harvests grain and soybeans. Today, farmers store their corn as they would other grains, in steel-walled bins, and dry it with forced air and natural gas-fired heaters. The barn has large numbers of architectural relatives across the Upland South.

Ogden, Indiana

Locusts bloom to incredible luminescence and aromatic delight behind the Huddleston Lodge.

point; it follows a direct east-to-west alignment for more than two miles. Thereafter the highway curves into Buck Creek valley by way of cut-and-fill, which has reduced its grade of descent to the floor of an old glacial meltwater spillway occupied by the Big Blue River. The Road follows a raised bed allowing safe approach to the bridge that spans a flood-prone water course. Knightstown stands atop the spillway's steep west bank.

Before engineers relocated and widened US 40 in the 1940s, motorists leaving Dunreith had to drive through Ogden and Raysville to reach Knightstown. Old 40 angles southward away from the new Road as it departs from Dunreith at the corner of South Water and East Washington Streets. This is the old Conestoga wagon road; it and its roadside landscape relate at one of the sweetest scales on the old Road in Indiana. Its older surface is capped by asphalt oxidized almost white, and where the Road has shoulders, they are narrow and grassy. Closely spaced dwellings front the old highway for a mile or so across stream-dissected land on the way to Ogden. The only substantial structure in Ogden is a brick I-house (currently the Bryket place; originally the Huddleston Lodge) that was reputed to be a stop in the Un-

ROBERT W. BASTIAN

derground Railroad. This village's street grid is cocked to align with the National Road, betraying its heritage. Perched against Buck Creek's east bank, Ogden is a pleasant, if not prosperous-looking place with many mature shade trees, but no public sidewalks.

Across Buck Creek, one gets a sense of what the rural roadside looked like in Indiana before US 40 was widened almost fifty years ago. Farm fields on both sides almost touch the old highway and lines of utility poles run close by either edge. Along the south side stand remnants of a once-continuous row of stately maples. Shade trees, planted beside the highway, gave low-speed motoring an aesthetic quality. That experience is hard to appreciate when driving at high velocity on the widely separated lanes of today's interstates with their broad shoulders and deep right-of-ways. This once-treelined stretch ends abruptly as the Road drops into a steep-sided ravine cut by Raysville Run. Once into the narrow valley engineers directed Old 40 on an east-west course, adjusting its alignment to Raysville's cardinal compass point street grid. Upon entering this village, which extends downslope onto the Big Blue River floodplain, the old highway passes beneath a derelict Pennsylvania Railroad trestle. Trains formerly crossed this low-lying, flood-threatened community well above grade on what resembles an earthen fortress wall. The orientations of town streets and elevated track are incongruous and indicate that community platting took place prior to railroad construction. The manner in which engineers aligned the old highway with the town's grid also suggests that Raysville predates the National Road, and its streets were laid out to conform with the federal Township and Range survey. What survives today is a bypassed residential community with an appearance of casual maintenance.

Across the river in Knightstown streets align to the angle of the original National Road. This community is an early settlement (established in 1828) named for the engineer, surveyor, and Road commissioner responsible for the National Road's alignment across Indiana. The current volume of trade carried by US 40 and state highways, coming in from the north and south, is insufficient to keep Knightstown merchants prosperous, and the local population has declined at a rate of 5 to 10 percent during the past two decades. About 2,000 people lived here in 1990. The decline is evident in the empty stores and vacant lots in the three-block-long business district, but the town's historic architecture (sans 1960 storefront embellishments) and Constitution Square provide building blocks for a spirit of revival.

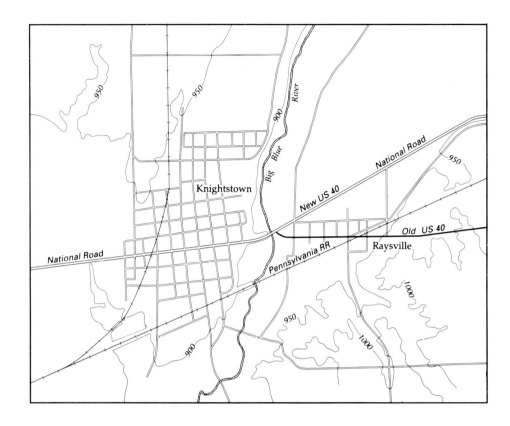

KNIGHTSTOWN TO GREENFIELD

West of Knightstown, across Montgomery Creek where highway lanes divide, a commercial strip of sorts aligns the Road. The most prominent structure here belongs to a Dodge and Chrysler dealer. A short distance beyond, a two-story brick I-house faces US 40 from the north. Dwellings of this type, and streams designated as "runs" rather than "creeks," remind one that the National Road originated in the Middle Atlantic culture area. As the highway passes through open farm country the familiar abandoned railroad grade comes back into view to the south. Just over the boundary in Hancock County stands Charlottesville, an unincorporated place. This residential community has a definite north-south axis aligned with medium-duty roads that intersect the highway here. Just west of Charlottesville on the north side is a small bank barn, outpost of Pennsylvania influence; across the street is a modest English barn with a side-wall door entry.

After another brief excursion through corn and soybean fields the highway enters Cleveland, a village smaller than Charlottesville. A historic church-meeting camp stands north of the Road at the entrance to this place. A longer run across an agricultural landscape leads to a small dwelling cluster called Stringtown. One mile to the east, at a section road crossing, the aging Hoosier Poet Motel remains open for business. Its name signals proximity to the birthplace of James Whitcomb Riley. Stringtown could easily be mistaken for part of exurban Greenfield with which it merges today.

Greenfield is not only a county seat but also the largest town between Richmond and Indianapolis. Established in 1828 beside the newly surveyed National Road, it grew to a place with over 11,000 residents by 1980. Greenfield now functions as a bedroom community for nearby Indianapolis and has considerable suburban development beyond its corporate boundary. A few blocks inside town, US 40 crosses Brandywine Creek, whose valley is used as a municipal park. This water-course name also reflects early influence from the Middle Atlantic region. (A creek by the same name enters the Delaware River at Wilmington close to the site where Swedish colonists settled in 1638.)

Greenfield's historic downtown borders US 40 for three and one-half blocks and exhibits signs of prosperity not seen since Centerville. The old business district survives even though there are commercial strips on the

Charlottesville, Indiana

Modern Indiana hog farms have several distinguishing units or parts. This one boasts a 1970s ranch house, a steel machine shed, and round steel grain bins and grain driers connected by an upright system of elevators and delivery pipes called a "leg." A concrete pig in the front yard welcomes visitors.

Greenfield, Indiana

Poet James Whitcomb
Riley's home is now
defended by vinyl-clad
fencing.

town's east and west sides and a newer, more vigorous one extending northward along Indiana 9 to link with I-70. Two-story business buildings line old
Main Street. Standing out from this backdrop are two taller limestone-faced
edifices displaying Romanesque details: the Hancock County Courthouse
(1898) and the old Masonic Lodge. A few blocks west is a frame I-house of
modest proportions, birthplace of James Whitcomb Riley. It is operated as
a museum and survives in good condition.

I-70 has had a visible impact upon Greenfield. By comparing a 1952 map
with one completed in 1981, one can see new curvilinear subdivisions between North Broadway and East Road, and a commercial strip developing
between the interstate and Park Avenue. This two-square-mile area was
farmland and farmsteads in 1952. New development begins at the interchange with two chain motels, a franchised restaurant, and the local newspaper's postmodern headquarters facing Indiana 9 from the west. The *Daily
Reporter*'s presence here dramatically proclaims the new highway's drawing
power. Across the road, commercial activity is limited to an off-brand gas

ROBERT W. BASTIAN

station and an independent eatery, but signs advertising corn and soybean fields as available commercial properties forecast more change. An incipient industrial park is taking form behind the newspaper building. The park is a sure sign that local developers are convinced that prospective tenants will seek building sites proximate to the interstate and not US 40. South of New Road two strip shopping centers, numerous fast-food businesses, and several gas stations line the state highway. At the strip's city end stands a community hospital with an original International-style unit and a recently constructed postmodern addition. From this point into Greenfield's old

Greenfield, Indiana
1952, (*left*); 1982 (*right*).

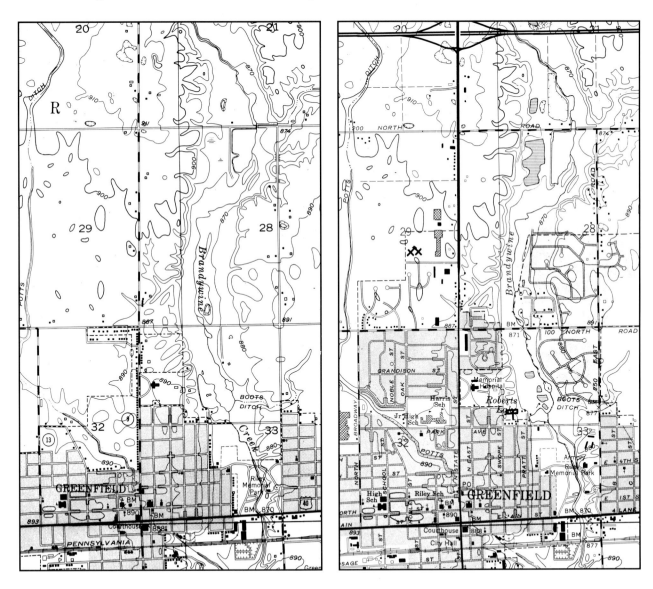

business district entrepreneurs are converting vintage residences into commercial uses.

GREENFIELD TO CUMBERLAND

An extensive industrial facility, dating to the early automobile era, is the most notable feature on Greenfield's west-end strip. The Indianapolis-based Eli Lilly Company's pharmaceutical laboratory stands back from the highway's south side on campus-like grounds. Spanish Mission–style buildings in the older section reveal its vintage (1913). These fanciful structures contrast sharply with a more recent International-style unit.

From Greenfield through Indianapolis and on to Plainfield, US 40's opposing lanes are side by side, no median here. A few open fields align with the Road for a short distance out of town. Mixed exurban land use is more evident on the highway's south side where one can still glimpse the abandoned Pennsylvania Railroad grade. On the north side linear suburban development follows section line roads and newer roads running along half-section and quarter-section lines. This landscape continues to Philadelphia, an unincorporated village, and reappears on that community's west side. Philadelphia's commercial establishments reveal that the village is now awash in Indianapolis suburban sprawl: a cash-and-carry lumberyard, a one-way truck and trailer rental agency, and two pet clinics.

Beyond Philadelphia a fragmented commercial strip includes several old motels (many put to other uses), aging restaurants, and occasional nursery and landscaping businesses. These enterprises mingle with small farmland patches as the highway approaches Gem, a tiny village. Converted roadside land and building spaces continue into Cumberland—named for Cumberland, Maryland, the National Road's origin point. Situated just inside Marion County, this hamlet has become part of Indianapolis.

INDIANAPOLIS

Cumberland's absorption by Indianapolis brought substantial growth to this small community. In 1970 it had fewer than 1,500 residents. The population increased threefold by 1990. And from this point to the other side of Marion County, the old highway is named Washington Street, another indicator of amalgamation. The original mile-square survey of Indianapolis, carried out by Alexander Ralston and Elias Fordham in the early 1820s, included a main east-west thoroughfare thirty feet wider than other streets. The name

Indianapolis, Indiana

In the 1960s, Al Green's Drive-in on east Washington Street was a haven for young people. One could place an order for a Jumbo Cheeseburger on a speaker phone from your car: convenient and fun, but impractical. More important, although this place stood at the edge of town, it was a central point on teenage social maps. Here one took dates or made new acquaintances on the pretense that the drive to get there had a purpose and a destination. Parents were reluctant to let their children borrow the family car simply to cruise around. But going to Al's was different. The remaining signs and speaker posts offer small hints at the importance that this place once had as a social institution.

they selected for this future traffic artery was Washington Street. A small residual business district survives at Cumberland's center. German Church Road follows a section line, forming the town's western boundary. There begins a classic urban commercial strip lined by all sorts of business establishments operating at diverse scales. These range in size from Washington Square, a large shopping mall at the northeast corner of Mitthoefer Road, to small enterprises contained within former single-family dwellings. Motorists approaching from the east first glimpse the downtown Indianapolis skyline at Shortridge Road. Across Shadeland Avenue residential land use reappears on the highway's north edge, and on the south side, beyond Arlington Avenue in Irvington. By giving careful attention to building-facade design, one can judge how the strip ages as you approach the central city.

Irvington, established in 1870, is a railroad-era suburb, as indicated by its curvilinear streets and the styles of older dwellings. Named for Washington Irving, this neighborhood became the preferred address for literary as well as business and professional people disillusioned with city life. Its appeal lasted until the 1920s when the city's north side became more attractive. Butler College (Butler University today) was also lured to Irvington from the inner city and occupied grounds in the neighborhood between 1875 and 1928. During the early twentieth century, Pleasant Run Parkway, connecting Ellenberg Park (1909) with Christian Park (1921), formed a protective green space that symbolically checked the city's advance. But by the 1920s, construction of a one-story commercial row on Washington Street's north side signaled capitulation to urban sprawl. Recent revival can be seen in a high level of private property upkeep and the neighborhood's listing on the National Register of Historic Places.

Across Pleasant Run, a reasonable level of residential maintenance continues for half a dozen blocks, but west of Euclid deterioration sets in. Beyond a vintage railroad trestle (now belonging to Conrail), old industrial sites are more frequent and impoverish all that surrounds them. Trees no longer line the street or stand in frontyards and building upkeep fails. Vacant lots are common. Closer to downtown is a nearly empty redevelopment zone typical of many American cities. One does not encounter new construction until crossing a north-south leg of I-70. Here investment is still attracted to office, convention, and entertainment functions that survive in the old central business district. Indicative of this area's contemporary fo-

Indianapolis, Indiana

Sam Wolf's Washington Street car lot sign announces six decades of automobile sales. The dignity associated with longevity recedes across the street where a rented car might include a fiberglass pig or chicken on the roof.

ROBERT W. BASTIAN

cus are recently built skyscrapers, sports arenas, and hotels; old theaters have also been renovated for use by the performing arts.

New skyscrapers (four of them taller than 500 feet) obscure traditional landmarks on the city's skyline. These include the domed Indiana Capitol Building (1888), the old Union Depot and clock tower (1888), the 284-foot Soldiers and Sailors Monument (1889–1902) at Meridian and Market, and the tallest office building in Indianapolis for half a century. The state capitol building at Washington and Capitol dates from 1888 and was built of Indiana limestone—as were so many other capitol buildings and courthouses across the nation. The Soldiers and Sailors Monument marks the center of the city's street grid and was completed in 1902. The seventeen-story Merchants Bank Building (1909) still stands at the southeast corner of Washington and Meridian. A zoning ordinance limiting new buildings to a 200-foot height prevented the bank, and subsequently erected commercial structures, from blocking the view of the city's chief public monuments. This restriction remained in force until the 1960s. The Merchants Bank was Chicago architect Daniel Burnham's early-twentieth-century contribution to downtown Indianapolis. And Pittsburgh architect Thomas Rodd designed the magnificent Union Depot.

Before proceeding west from downtown Indianapolis take an excursion north along Meridian Street. The suggested destination is the North Meridian Historic District between Fortieth Street and Westfield Boulevard. Here, well-preserved residential blocks are legally protected against intrusion from conflicting land uses. In the 1920s, North Meridian became a new res-

Indianapolis, Indiana

Eastward (*left*): if building heights correspond to land values, the transition to expensive real estate downtown requires only two blocks once Washington Street passes under I-65/70. New buildings house banks, insurance companies, and corporate offices. Westward (*right*): Buildings completed in the 1890s reflect in a 1990s polished-stone facade.

idential retreat for the city's upper-middle class. Most of the mansions display Revival designs popular between the two world wars. Their pretentious scale attracted some buyers, but privacy, insured by deep setbacks on spacious lots, was also appealing. Comfortable incomes from business, various professions, and even the arts supported the families who lived here. The well-known Hoosier writer Booth Tarkington bought a home on upper Meridian in the twenties. Access to this linear neighborhood was by automobile. Among the homeowners were the Duesenberg and Stutz automobile manufacturing company presidents. Today, this neighborhood includes the Indiana Governor's Mansion.

Indianapolis, Indiana

Beneath bronze Victory's gaze, carved stone and gold-leaf lettering suggest a prime business address, but Monument Circle is first and foremost a place to honor soldiers and sailors.

Indianapolis, Indiana

Nineteenth-century city buildings often stood on narrow lots with a dozen or more different structures to a single block. Late-twentieth-century architects conceive buildings on a grand scale that often occupies entire blocks. Only the thin stone facade of a demolished building remains as a reminder of the scale of change.

ROBERT W. BASTIAN

On the downtown's west side, an extensive new state government complex fronts Washington Street. Beyond this point the highway becomes a divided parkway and curves toward the White River. This roadway provides a fitting approach to the Eiteljorg Museum of the American Indian and Western Art, the recently opened White River State Park, and the relocated city zoo across the bridge. The museum, situated at the northwest corner of Washington and West Streets, was designed to evoke a southwestern or Mexican image. It opened in 1989 with sufficient space to house coal-company executive Harrison Eiteljorg's entire collection of Western and Native American art and artifacts that he began to assemble in the 1940s. The city's attempt to create a new image extends only a few blocks beyond the river. No west-side neighborhood is comparable to Irvington. A turmoil of auto-oriented businesses in varied states of conversion and repair—a gritty landscape—follows US 40 all the way to the Marion and Hendricks County boundary.

Indianapolis, Indiana

Capitol reflections upon the Art Deco National Old Trails building on West Washington Street. This facade is singularly one-of-a-kind on the entire National Road.

Established in 1821, Indianapolis has prospered from its central point within the state's transportation network, and as capital city. Effective leadership has helped ward off population decline, common to so many large American cities. Through a political merger between Marion County and the corporate city, the area was able to claim a population of more than 735,000 in 1970. A decade of decline followed, but revitalization in the 1980s brought the number of residents back to the 1970s level. Alternating periods of growth and decline can be traced out along this Washington Street transect. And the city's once-important role as an automobile manufacturing center is represented by the Indianapolis Motor Speedway's annual 500-mile race. A less glamorous echo of this history can be seen and smelled while passing a Chrysler Corporation foundry on the south side of I-70, west of downtown.

INDIANAPOLIS TO BELLEVILLE

A commercial strip that originates in Indianapolis follows the north side of US 40 all the way to Plainfield. To the south business buildings intersperse with open fields, but stop short of the new Wal-Mart Plaza, which marks

Only a few miles away the Indianapolis strip begins, yet Stacey's stays in business.

the edge of a business ribbon advancing eastward from Indiana 267. This state highway provides a link, southward from Plainfield, to I-70 and is becoming another commercial axis. West of the home office of an electrical utility firm (PSI Energy), whose service area extends to Terre Haute, one encounters well-kept residential properties. Situated on the eastern edge of Plainfield's old business district on an attractive bosque is the Friends Church (or Western Yearly Meetinghouse) for Quakers residing in western Indiana and eastern Illinois (first yearly meeting in 1858, present brick structure erected in 1914). Congregations of this religious denomination moved westward across the National Road, settling in Richmond, Plainfield, and at points between and beyond.

Although easy access to employment opportunities in the adjacent metropolis underwrites Plainfield's growth—about 10,000 people in 1990—few signs of commercial vitality remain at the town's historic center (established in the 1830s). Business here has withered in the face of strong competition from the strip on the town's east side and the large retail malls in nearby Indianapolis. Just outside the community, across White Lick Creek, stands the State Boys School. This reformatory, established in 1867, has served as a historic source of employment for local residents.

West of White Lick Creek, US 40 becomes a divided highway for the first time since entering Greenfield, fifteen miles east of Indianapolis. Here the Road is bordered by open country with only limited intrusions from residential, commercial, or recreational land use. A few miles out of Plainfield paired bridges carry opposing lanes across White Lick Creek's West Fork. Immediately upstream stands a narrow two-lane bridge used by old 40. From here corn and soybean fields follow the highway to Belleville where it crosses Indiana 39. On a rise beyond this small community eastbound travelers first see the Indianapolis skyline. Belleville (established in 1829) is a National Road town lacking notable historic structures. Only small-scale businesses function at the village center, but new firms at the west end reflect the presence of a growing number of commuters who work in greater Indianapolis. Enterprises that have located here in response to suburban development include a construction machinery dealer, a custom-home builder, and an electrical contractor.

Kenworthy's west of Plainfield, Indiana

A simple handpainted sign sells watermelons by the roadside. Folk art and summertime eating at their best.

BELLEVILLE TO PLEASANT GARDENS

Each small town from Belleville to Harmony is a stagnant community with an aging population. Westward along US 40 land gradually becomes hillier and less productive. Nor are the communities here conveniently situated to serve as places of residence for members of either the Indianapolis or Terre Haute labor force. Between Belleville and Stilesville the divided highway plows along through open Corn Belt countryside. Only occasionally is roadside land used for some purpose other than cash grain farming. Examples of isolated intrusion include a nursery/lawn ornament business and recently built Cascade High School on the north side. Down the Road, on its south edge, a thirty-six-acre tract is occupied by the Stilesville Implement Auction. Here used farm machinery is sold on the first and third Wednesdays and Thursdays of each month. Customers who cultivate less productive land elsewhere and cannot afford to buy new implements acquire used tractors and combines here. They come from as far as Canada and the American South, and from New York State to Kansas.

Stilesville (established in 1828) is a small village that shows no evidence of being engulfed by Indianapolis suburban sprawl. Nineteenth-century dwellings line both sides of Main Street and only a few essential businesses survive.

Beyond town an open rural landscape faces the Road. No-till farming is practiced here. Despite its simplicity, the term "no-till" is descriptive of a

Near Stilesville, Indiana

A seemingly simple country scene can tell a complex story. The barns are empty; the overgrown feed lot contains no livestock. This means that crops in adjoining fields were not fertilized with manure but with chemical fertilizers. The midsummer corn crop will be harvested with a combine and the corn crib will remain empty. Corn will be stored elsewhere or sold. If a farmer ignores the farm buildings one suspects that a major transition to cash grain farming has taken place.

radical, even revolutionary change in how Corn Belt farmers manage their crop lands. Traditional practice included plowing a field after harvest to bury the stalks or straw. This enhanced rapid decomposition of plant residues and helped prepare the seed bed for the next season. In the spring, the field would be disked and harrowed to kill weeds and level the surface for planting. Corn and soybeans were usually planted in rows and after the plants reached three or four inches in height the farmer would cultivate the crop every two or three weeks to control weeds. By early July the plants were usually too tall to cultivate but they cast enough shade to discourage further weed growth. After harvest, the tilling cycle was repeated. No-till means that the weeds must be controlled with chemical herbicides. Because the no-till field is not plowed in the fall, the field becomes weedy and plant stalks and stubble remain on the surface. Farm-implement companies developed a new type of planter that will slice through the surface accumulation of plant residue and place seed at the appropriate depth for germination. The only field preparation required is to spray the spring weed growth to allow planting, and spray for weeds, and perhaps disease and insects, during the growing season. The no-till field looks unkempt, even messy. Brown weeds seem scorched by herbicide and stalks cover the surface. But thin lines of new plants emerge from the litter and thrive.

ROBERT W. BASTIAN

Stilesville, Indiana

An early two-room motel, freshly painted, still stands in a side yard along US 40 in Stilesville. The sidewalk and maple hearken back to an earlier day.

Stilesville, Indiana

Johnsons Corner gas station ("since 1903") remains, still attached to the house on this corner lot. Another antique mall.

Near the intersection of US 40 and US 231, Putnam County, Indiana

All that remains of the Cinema 40 Drive-In Theater is a grove of white pines and the weathered marquee.

West of Mount Meridian, Indiana

As the land surface becomes rougher, and the glacial till and loess soils thinner, pastures and hayfields reappear. A rare white plank fence merges with woven wire to contain a hay field. Corn Belt farmers do not, as a rule, build plank fences or paint their fences white. People who raise horses seem to prefer this kind of fence.

Near the Hendricks-Putnam County line, on the south side of the highway, stand spacious brick Italianate buildings of a fashionable nineteenth-century farm (1870 dwelling). This carefully restored complex is being used as a rural retirement residence. A mile beyond, a more traditional brick I-house with unusually tall windows continues in use on a working farm. Chandler's apple orchard is beyond.

As the terrain becomes hillier US 40 enters Mount Meridian, an unincorporated village. This place has no posted speed limit, no businesses, and no public sidewalks. From this point topography becomes progressively rougher and cultivated fields fade into pasture and woodland. The highway's intersection with US 231 serves as a gathering point for recently built dwellings, a few small businesses, and another consolidated high school. These structures reflect the intersecting highway's role as connector between nearby Greencastle, a county seat five miles to the north, and I-70 three miles to the south.

Irregular terrain indicates that US 40 is no longer traversing a surface deposited by relatively recent Wisconsin-age glaciation. Here the Road crosses an older and more heavily eroded area left by an earlier advance of Pleistocene ice. Shallow road cuts reveal only a thin veneer of soil resting on limestone bedrock. While still on high ground both sides of the highway

ROBERT W. BASTIAN

are bordered by short concrete drives that mark the site of a weigh station removed after I-70 opened. Immediately beyond, off the Road's north edge, a 1950s-vintage motel stands in a grove of mature trees, facing US 40 where it begins a graded descent into the steep-sided valley occupied by Deer Creek. Its builder positioned this motel to take advantage of the Road's re-alignment. The old blacktop-covered highway runs behind the motel, down a precipitous ravine to a slender concrete bridge. Across the creek asphalt disappears and the old highway's cement ribbon leads through a densely wooded valley bottom and back to the modern Road. Not far from this junction is the small community of Putnamville, established in 1830. This village has lost most of its commercial functions, but every Saturday night during the summer one can see sprint-car racing at Lincoln Park Speedway.

On ascending the next ridge US 40 runs past the 3,500-acre Indiana State Prison, which includes a maximum-security unit. The old Road is visible on the right, below the existing four-lane, but don't attempt to turn off the highway here to investigate or you will invite the attention of a security guard. Prisoners operate a farm, where they once made brick and tile, samples of which are displayed on the exterior walls of older penal structures and vintage dwellings that house institution employees. Beyond the prison the roadside is bordered by pasture, woodland, and scattered dwellings. The unincorporated village of Manhattan was established as a National Road settlement in 1829, but shows no signs of ever having prospered.

On approaching the next community the Road rises and falls, conforming to dissected topography. Steep hills are mainly wooded, but they support occasional apple orchards. Small cultivated fields lie in narrow valley bottoms in this marginal farming area. Pleasant Gardens, at the top of a ridge, is a bypassed hamlet. What is left of this place faces the old highway's narrow pavement for a short distance. Across the highway is C. C. Cook & Son Lumber. Established in the 1930s, this sawmill employs forty people to process red and white oak, walnut, and poplar into high-grade furniture wood and pallet stock. The finished dimensional wood is kiln-dried before shipping. The mill supplies customers all across the United States and as far north as Calgary, Alberta, and containers carry the wood to Chicago for re-shipment to the West Coast and to foreign buyers on the Pacific Rim. Current prices paid to landowners for standing timber: a twelve-foot-long, sixteen-inch-diameter walnut log will fetch $86. The sawdust is sold for live-stock bedding and the bark goes to landscaping firms.

Near the intersection of US 40 and US 231, Putnam County, Indiana

Jean Stallcop is the proprietor of "Raintree Garden" on US 40.

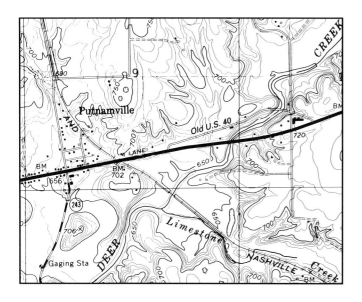

Putnamville, Indiana,
1970

PLEASANT GARDENS TO TERRE HAUTE

Where US 40 begins its descent into Big Walnut Creek valley, a turnoff on the north side leads to another segment of the old Road. Next to the creek's bank stand remnants of a rustic tourist court. A long narrow cement bridge and a stretch of old concrete pavement survive. Toward Harmony roadside scenery remains the same, but the old Pennsylvania Railroad grade crosses back to the highway's south side. Harmony was formerly a coal-mining town with a few thousand residents. Today, with a reduced population, it is a residential extension of Brazil, three miles to the west. Roadside structures here suggest that Harmony and Brazil are on the way to becoming the same place. Brazil's clearly labeled water-treatment plant stands north of US 40. Across the pavement two industrial plants draw employees from a broad area, but especially from Brazil. One manufactures plastic drain pipes and the other makes Great Dane–brand truck trailers. The in-town commerce at Harmony is conducted at comparatively small establishments. Two of these businesses occupy remodeled early-twentieth-century gasoline stations. Some houses in Harmony are oriented to the Road, others to the Township and Range grid. Without any noticeable landscape change the highway leaves Harmony and proceeds along the northern residential fringe of Knightsville, another village in decline.

From Brazil's eastern boundary on through town a commercial strip faces one side of the highway or the other. North of National Avenue streetside businesses first appear in the vicinity of a recently opened Wal-Mart plaza. Old two-story commercial buildings extend as far east as Alabama Street across which stands the Clay County Courthouse. This commercial expansion beyond the town center was made possible by a former electric interurban railway. It ran through the community to Harmony beginning in 1893. With fewer than 8,000 residents today, Brazil has lost population slowly over the last two decades. Downtown, this loss is evident in a material form; many older store buildings stand empty, others are now "antique malls." The businesses that serve the surrounding farms seem active and vibrant, the grain elevators and machinery dealers, for example. Vacant lots

ROBERT W. BASTIAN

and new quick-stop businesses suggest that the local economy has pitched into decline from which recovery may be slow at best.

Brazil was established later than many National Road towns (1844). The site lies atop clay deposits and the shallow outer (eastern) seams of the Illinois basin's high-sulfur coal beds. Numerous brick and tile manufacturers formerly mined the clay. The coal formation dips west and must be mined by labor-intensive deep shafts in southcentral Illinois. Here the seams lie close enough to the surface that shaft mines have been replaced by large-scale drag lines, which strip off soil and bedrock to expose the coal. Before natural-gas pipelines reached western Indiana, the coal was used for domestic heating and as fuel for local steam-powered factories. Strip mines move, and today mining has shifted south and west from Brazil where it can

East of Brazil, Indiana

A grand 1871 Italianate house stands alone beside the Great Dane truck trailer factory along US 40, its yard now a field. The Italianate style blended classical symmetry and romantic details in a manner that nineteenth-century landscape architect Andrew Jackson Downing praised as expressing elegance and accomplishment.

Brazil, Indiana

A room in the Clay County Courthouse, where symbolic space and functional space are interchangeable (*below*).

In keeping with the unspoken rule that courthouse squares are appropriate places to erect symbolic structures, a Korean War–vintage jet fighter (*right*) sits among the trees on the Clay County courthouse lawn, an icon for military veterans and a suggestion of which social groups are dominant in local affairs.

be seen from I-70. Unit trains haul the coal to nearby thermal electric generating plants that are equipped with devices to reduce sulfur and fly-ash emissions. Being a county seat has not compensated for the loss of mining employment and related factory jobs. Native son James Riddle Hoffa was born to a local coal-mining family here early in this century. He would become a union organizer and preside over the International Brotherhood of Teamsters. If pastoral Greenfield produced James Whitcomb Riley and gritty Brazil fostered Jimmy Hoffa, what can be said for the role of environment in shaping personality?

A typical commercial strip trails out of Brazil on a divided segment of US 40 as it curves to the south. Over the years this highway has been an attractive place for businesses to relocate from

Brazil, Indiana

National Avenue's business district is anchored on the east by the Clay County Courthouse. Nineteenth-century storefronts, some disguised by new mansard roofs, stand in a row with a few plain brick structures from the 1920s or '30s. Shoppers here can purchase insurance, antiques, tropical fish, Chinese food, or liquor. The second-floor windows—narrow and arched Italianate—admit daylight to vacant spaces.

Brazil, Indiana

From National Avenue a one-way street leads two blocks south to the grain elevators beside the railroad tracks. The square, tin-covered central elevator was built of dimensional lumber laid flat to produce a thick wall able to hold thousands of bushels of grain. When area farmers sold their livestock and produced grain for sale instead of feed, the need for grain storage space increased rapidly and the concrete and steel cylindrical bins were added after World War II. The bins now dominate the town's skyline. They stimulate questions about whether or not the structures people erect come to possess meanings greater than the basic forms that engineers derive from applied physics.

downtown. These include three authorized automobile agencies using spacious roadside properties as display lots.

On the way to Seelyville varied topography borders the Road. Tree cover prevails on the hills and along the old Pennsylvania Railroad grade. Farm fields occupy level land to the north, but rural dwellings are also common. A more interesting way to exit Brazil is to follow the old Road, here labeled Indiana 340. Beyond town, this narrow two-lane route is accompanied by an early residential extension of the community. Eventually one passes a new consolidated high school building and enters open country. Here, inside Terre Haute's commuting zone, farmers are gradually selling roadside lots from their corn and soybean fields to individuals seeking homes in the country. The old highway crosses several small creeks as it approaches Seelyville. Against stream banks on the pavement's south side narrow abutments remain at points where interurban railway bridges once stood. At Seelyville's east edge, 340 and US 40 merge.

Seelyville is the first community inside Vigo County. This place is another former coal-mining town, but has little employment base remaining. As a densely built residential appendage of Terre Haute it has a stable population of more than 1,000. Recycled motels became a common feature here after I-70 bypassed the town. What businesses survive are mainly quick-stop customer enterprises. Another kind of landscape transition is visible along this segment of US 40. Crossroads are labeled "Stop 18" or "Stop 19." These signs refer to interurban railway stops, the only remaining evidence that a line ran along this highway.

ROBERT W. BASTIAN

Seelyville, Indiana

Pollarded trees mark a 1930s roadside autocourt where the cabins now rent as long-term lease apartments (*above*). The vine-covered cement-block garage, its doors blocked by saplings, seems forlorn, relegated to storage (*left*). Pollarding does great harm to trees, but its practice is pervasive throughout most of America.

Rows of closely built houses face each other across the Road as it enters East Glen, an unincorporated community. The only active business, a gasoline station, stands at the traffic light. A short distance west US 40 crosses the old Pennsylvania Railroad bed for the last time. After climbing the next hill westbound motorists encounter the eastern edge of Terre Haute, with its impressive new suburban developments and more established homes.

TERRE HAUTE

Although not mirror images, the roadside exiting Richmond and the entrance to Terre Haute strongly resemble one another. Reminders of Richmond include the Rose Hulman Institute of Technology's spacious wooded campus (on this site since 1922), and a picturesquely landscaped cemetery, Highland Lawn, with its 1894 Romanesque portal. Interred in elegant mausoleums are the dead of many leading business families from the nineteenth and early twentieth centuries. A less pretentious monument marks the burial site of widely remembered native Eugene V. Debs, labor organizer, World War I pacifist, and five-time presidential candidate on the Socialist ticket. The home occupied by Debs and his wife is preserved as a local museum open on selected days. Situated at 451 North Eighth Street, this vintage dwelling stands as an island surrounded by the campus of Indiana State University.

At the entrance to town US 40 becomes Wabash Avenue and is bordered

Terre Haute, Indiana

The central city is still a node for information management. A microwave tower rises above the Indiana Theater, and the Swope Art Museum faces the *Tribune Star* newspaper loading dock.

ROBERT W. BASTIAN

by green space on both sides. Indiana State University's football stadium, a former venue for minor-league baseball, stands to the north. South of the pavement is Edgewood Grove, a modest early-automobile-era suburb with tall trees, winding streets, and dwellings displaying diverse architectural styles. A commercial strip begins at Brown Avenue and continues, with few interruptions, to the old downtown. From Fourteenth Street to the original business district a nearly continuous line of vintage commercial structures reflects a once-vibrant economy and the impact of electric streetcars and interurban railway coaches. Ahead, between Eighth and Ninth Streets, a shift in alignment of taller buildings indicates a change in highway orientation. Terre Haute (established in 1816) is the third oldest community along US 40 in Indiana. Here, the original section of Wabash Avenue predates the National Road survey and conforms to the federal Township and Range survey grid.

At the corner of Ninth and Wabash, US 40 turns north and passes a five-story Romanesque structure occupied by Hulman and Company since its construction 100 years ago. This firm distributes wholesale groceries and manufactures Clabber Girl brand baking powder. The building was designed by the same Cincinnati architect, Sammuel Hannaford and Sons, who planned the Vigo County Courthouse (1888). One block north the highway moves west on Cherry Street until it crosses the Wabash River. Along the north side of Cherry is the Indiana State University campus.

Eastbound traffic, entering Terre Haute on Ohio Street, passes the oldest commercial building in the city. A small Greek Revival structure erected (1834–36) to house a branch of Indiana's Second State Bank faces the courthouse. Today it is preserved as a law office. At Seventh and Ohio the recently restored Indiana Theater (1922), an example of Spanish Baroque Revival design, continues showing motion pictures and is also used for occasional stage performances. At Twelfth Street the highway turns back to Wabash Avenue and resumes its original course.

For nearly a century and a half the National Road followed Wabash Avenue all the way to the river after which it is named. The old main street bears scars of urban renewal, but two surviving structures relate directly to earlier eras of travel. Less imposing is the single-story Terminal Building, with Beaux Arts facade, standing between Eighth and Ninth. Erected in 1911 as an interurban railway depot and shopping arcade, this is Terre Haute's only structure designed by Daniel Burnham. The presence of a

Terre Haute, Indiana

Daniel Burnham's Terminal Arcade building, draped in wreaths and garlands, is a classical stack of blazing white limestone. It seems a vest pocket–sized version of structures built for the 1893 Columbian Exposition in Chicago, and stands in jarring juxtaposition to the empty lot and brick wall palimpsest where signs still read, in part, "Greenback Tobacco" (the trademark is a frog) and "Chew Mail Pouch." Scale and style are out of sync here, though the beauty is undeniable.

Burnham building gives the city something in common with Indianapolis and Richmond, and further demonstrates the influence Chicago once exerted on three US 40 communities in the Hoosier state.

Occupying the northeast corner of Seventh and Wabash is the ten-story Terre Haute House, third hotel on this site. It opened in 1928 during the automobile era and provided a parking garage and other conveniences that guests of better hotels had come to expect. The closing of this facility in 1972 was symbolic of downtown decline. A less-than-successful urban-renewal program, rapid retail expansion at the US 41–I-70 interchange, and residential flight to the suburbs all worked to the old business district's disadvantage. Between 1970 and 1990 the corporate city (about 70,000 people in 1970) lost more than 10,000 residents.

In the minds of many outsiders, Indiana is imagined to be a predominantly rural state. Yet US 40 actually traverses the Corn Belt's southern margin. As the highway passes through numerous closely spaced towns and several cities, considerable stretches of the Road are bordered by urban land uses, and frequent suburban and exurban extensions into the countryside. Large-scale Corn Belt farming takes place, but often at a distance from the Road's edge. And one must give careful thought to deciding whether or not a roadside farmstead is still part of a real farm, or has been converted into

ROBERT W. BASTIAN

a commuter's residence. US 40, having surrendered heavy through traffic to I-70, is now traversed by increasing numbers of commuters who will tolerate ever longer journeys to work in order to maintain their preference for rural and suburban home and business sites. The sprawl they create extends and intensifies along the Road. Ongoing farm consolidation and mechanization favors abandoning less-productive land and allowing it to revert to woodland. The railroads have also consolidated and vacated selected lines—including the old Pennsylvania track beside the Road—producing other changes. In this case old rail beds become linear colonies of wild grasses and fast growing trees.

When I-70 opened, it substantially reduced long-distance traffic on US 40 and lured business away from the old highway. Evidence of this transition can be seen from Richmond to Terre Haute in the form of recycled or vacant roadside cafes, motels, and gasoline stations. Farm consolidation and interstate construction has also affected small towns, and is reflected in decaying main streets. Vibrant commercial strips persist only in larger urban centers, and the newest business developments grow up beside roads connecting cities and towns with interstate highway interchanges. The architectural evolution of urban America is mirrored in successive building-design fashions diffused from different source areas. From the early nineteenth to the early twentieth centuries new Middle West building forms and styles first came from major cities in the Middle Atlantic area, then from others along the Ohio River, and finally from Chicago. Motorists driving any segment of US 40 between Richmond and Terre Haute will confront a dynamic landscape, one that has been undergoing continuous change from the start.

Terre Haute, Indiana

The historic plaque in front of the Terre Haute House (*left*) reminds passersby that the corner of Wabash and Seventh Street was also the intersection of the National Road and US 41, one of the nation's primary north-south routes. Thus, "Their intersection . . . became the 'Crossroads of America.'" Indeed.

Terre Haute to Livingston

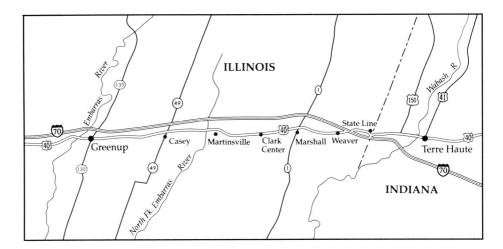

Livingston to Vandalia

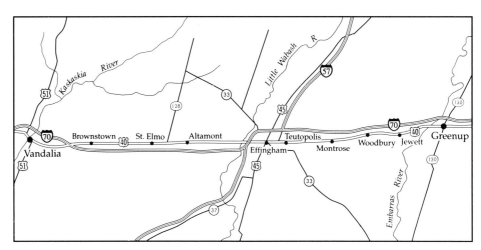

From Terre Haute to Vandalia, Illinois

KEITH A. SCULLE AND JOHN A. JAKLE

*This road is one of the greatest evidences of the enterprise of
Americans I have ever seen.*

HENRY B. WHIPPLE
Bishop Whipple's Southern Diary, 1843–1844

ONE HUNDRED AND FIVE MILES STRETCH VIRTUALLY STRAIGHT ALONG
US 40 and parallel Interstate 70 between Terre Haute, Indiana, and Vandalia, Illinois. Four major watersheds in low relief and all but one in gentle
slope dissect the glacial till plain throughout. Cash grain farms claim forest
and prairie soils, opening the land to easy view and permitting the contemporary traveler long vistas from windshield to horizon. At intervals
the way is punctuated by small towns. Effingham alone contrasts by size
and the volume of commerce energized primarily by interstates intersecting on its western edge. Arrival in Vandalia delivers the traveler to the
largest concentration of the route's oldest historic buildings, although
evocative historic landscape ensembles and recent automobile landmarks
can be ferreted out all along the way. Here is middle America at its unpre-
tentious best.

TERRE HAUTE TO THE ILLINOIS LINE

The courthouse is the logical point of departure westward from Terre Haute. A French Second Empire building of the post–Civil war era, the structure once stood in the middle of a square surrounded by brick commercial blocks housing the city's leading banks and merchants. Down Wabash Avenue, which once carried the National Road along the north side of this square, it was but three short blocks to the ferry where later a succession of bridges gave immediate access to open country across the Wabash River. The courthouse today stands marooned in a kind of traffic island between recently engineered one-way streets accessing the residual of Terre Haute's downtown. Three decades of "urban renewal" have eliminated all semblance of a traditional city center here. The tall business buildings have been replaced by low, squat gasoline stations, fast-food restaurants, and other small structures in parking-lot surrounds. Few travelers will even guess that here was once a public plaza, a grand pedestrian space of much character and grace.

Terre Haute (or "Terry Hut" as the place is still often affectionately called) was a railroad, iron foundry, brewery, glass factory, and coal-mine town through the decades of the late nineteenth and early twentieth centuries. It had all of the virtues and vices of a blue-collar workingman's town. Gone also at Terre Haute's center is the "levee" comprised of houses of prostitution, saloons, and gambling halls that once stretched several blocks north of the square along the river. It was this area, more than any other, that inspired songwriter Paul Dresser's "On the Banks of the Wabash Far Away."

Today the smell of gaslight, the taste of beer, the sound of raucous laughter lingers only in memory. Reformers never fully came to grips with prostitution in the city until urban renewal reduced the area's frame houses and brick storefronts to the vacant lots one sees largely today. The campus of Indiana State University encroaches from the east in the form of parking lots and athletic fields.

Cross the bridge (where two new replace-

Terre Haute, Indiana

Two miles north of I-70, Third Street's four lanes have lopped off the Vigo County Courthouse square, placing the bronze Civil War soldier's toe at the sidewalk. A Korean War–vintage F-84 defends the south lawn from further encroachment. Traffic light standards at the intersection of US 40 East mount fifty-five highway information and directional signs to enhance traffic flow through the city.

KEITH A. SCULLE AND JOHN A. JAKLE

Terre Haute, Indiana

Visitors to the Vigo County Courthouse are treated to unexpected elegance in iron and marble (*above*). The courthouse has new neighbors (*left*). So this is what zoning is all about?

Terre Haute, Indiana

A view to the east from the Wabash River's west bank reveals the terraces that confirm Terre Haute's French name meaning "high ground." Paul Dresser's sycamores give way to cottonwoods and silver maples.

Terre Haute, Indiana

Once a corridor for French fur traders, the Wabash invites a leisurely afternoon of fishing, with two rods.

West of Taylorsville, Indiana

Riverine trees thrive on the Wabash floodplain. One billboard exclaims "Expressions in Style." The other informs passersby that Miss Softball America will appear at the "MSA Stadium on Old 63 Across from the Prison." In the distance West Terre Haute awaits.

KEITH A. SCULLE AND JOHN A. JAKLE

ment spans are rising at this writing) and the traveler is on the Wabash flood-plain. Look back and Terre Haute rises to the eastward on a series of terraces—the "high ground" of the city's French naming. South of the embanked highway is an attempt at park-making dedicated to Paul Dresser's memory, Terre Haute's favorite son early in the twentieth century. Dresser's younger brother, Theodore Dreiser, has only recently been remembered in the naming of a dormitory on the Indiana State University campus. Tiny Taylorsville, a Depression-era "Hooverville," occupies the river's bank south of the park. Here is a frequently flooded neighborhood of very modest houses and mobile homes, most with cars and pickup trucks lodged on postage-stamp frontyards. Another mile across the wooded and backwatered floodplain is an intersection where US 150 bears right and US 40 tips toward the southwest. Here is West Terre Haute, still resembling a coal town of the 1910s and 1920s except for US 40, which carries the clear imprint of subsequent commercial strip–making. Of interest is the old diner fabricated in the 1930s from a Pullman car. It sits beneath the shadow of a vintage watertower. The traveler's eye is attracted by the jumble of such structures that line the highway.

Beyond Toad Hop (one can still chuckle at the humor long poked at Terre Haute through this named place) the traveler's attention can focus more

West Terre Haute, Indiana

Election signs in front of the Street Car Diner. A candidate for sheriff (Watts) displays a purple heart on his sign. Traffic past the VFW Post is light. No parking meters are required.

West Terre Haute,
Indiana

Roadside business; self
service; visual clutter

completely on the Road itself. It is not so much the highway margins that
attract attention as the highway as an unfolding ribbon of concrete and asphalt. Here is a relic stretch of the oldest road paralleling closely on the
south the more modern divided highway of the 1940s. In succession, the
old road is submerged by this four-lane pavement which, in turn, is submerged by today's I-70. Here the traveler can be jerked forward and backward in time as by the iterations of a time machine. One's journey across
Illinois commences at the relic hamlet of State Line, with the old Road visible on the north side.

CROSSING INTO ILLINOIS

Past Terre Haute, the diesels pound,
Eastward, westward, and under the highway slab the ground,
Like jello, shakes. Deep
In the infatuate and foetal dark, beneath
The unspecifiable weight of the great
Mid-America loam-sheet, the impacted
Particular particles of loam, blind,
Minutely grind . . .

ROBERT PENN WARREN
"Homage to Theodore Dreiser on the Centennial of His Birth"

KEITH A. SCULLE AND JOHN A. JAKLE

Terre Haute to Vandalia was the original "last" segment of the National Road. In 1820 when the federal government ordered completion of the road, Terre Haute was the portal of Illinois and Vandalia was its primitive capital and the Road's western destination. By the account of the Road's first historian, Thomas Searight, the Old Pike "was practically lost amid the primitive prairies of Illinois." The prairie was stigmatized as green desolation, nearly a wasteland. Today, Illinois is the western end of a corridor much like that near the National Road's eastern starting point between Hagerstown and Cumberland, Maryland, in its passage through open farmland and along occasional town corridors lined mostly with houses and a few businesses. The greater magnitude of these features in the East does not substantially alter the look of the Road, however. Searight's vantage point was bustling Uniontown, Pennsylvania, a century ago. Any vantage point along the segment from Terre Haute to Vandalia at the end of the twentieth century presents a hustle and bustle not unlike that of Searight's report about the East.

Statistics and impressions corroborate this opinion about the nature of the traffic. Even the least-traveled segment of this link, that west of Greenup, witnessed an annual daily average of 950 vehicles in 1989. At the same time, most of the distance between Marshall and Vandalia averaged roughly 1,500 vehicles. The highest annual average of daily vehicles in 1989 was 3,500 and 3,450, respectively, west of Effingham and east of Marshall. This made US 40 as busy as any busy highway in eastern Illinois; and this did not include the immense traffic volume on I-70, roughly 13,000 vehicles. US 40 carries primarily local traffic, whereas that on I-70 is long-distance commerce and tourism. Collectively, the two roads along the National Road corridor in eastern Illinois convey a large volume of traffic. Poet Agnes Irene Smith, whose *The National Road and Other Verse* (1964) acquisition by the Marshall library is one of the few signs of local awareness of the Road, distinquished it as the "proletarian road," and personifying it she wrote, "I carry the world on my shoulders." This is true in Illinois.

Inside the Illinois portal the traveler may notice a contrast in the relationship between the Road and the natural landforms that it crosses. On the other hand, the National Road engineers aligned the Road as the straightest possible path to Vandalia in keeping with the pragmatic value of time-saving to travelers by providing the shortest route. Hence, the Road is not wound along ridges as were many early wagon roads. A map clearly illustrates the Road's direct southwestward track from Terre Haute to Vandalia.

Hawk's Creek, Illinois, about one mile west of the Indiana state line

About 1922 the National Road's concrete ribbon from Marshall to Terre Haute was widened with a new apron on each side. Contractors hired local men to excavate and pour concrete. Bricklayers then laid seven-pound bricks between the aprons to create a new driving surface.

The straight road contrasts with the topographic relief in the five miles west of the Indiana line: the undulation of the Road down the valleys and up the ridges formed by crossing the Wabash River's successive tributaries, Hawk's Creek, Crooked Creek, Ashmore Creek, and East Little Creek. The Road is gently graded. But the relief of fifty to sixty feet, depending on the tributary, is noteworthy in an area commonly perceived as flat. The entire distance between Terre Haute and Vandalia is of the Illinoisan till plain with its characteristically fertile soil and shallow drainage. Furthermore, when this section of the National Road was surveyed it followed a borderland between the Grand Prairie to the north and forests to the south. Although the National Road alignment to Vandalia lies roughly at the southern edge of this borderland, there is no more striking place in this segment between Terre Haute and Vandalia to sense the merger of the two ecosystems than in the first five miles inside the Illinois portal.

KEITH A. SCULLE AND JOHN A. JAKLE

A mile inside the portal is the eastern end of an important artifact of the Terre Haute–Vandalia roadside, the earliest surviving automobile pavement, the National Road's successor. The pavement begins on the south side of the point where the road from State Line intersects US 40. The old road was a fifteen-foot width of brick set in common bond on a concrete bed forming a thirty-one-inch curb on either side, and it survives throughout most of the seven miles inside Illinois. Although lack of materials slowed construction east of Marshall in 1920, this federal-aid road was pressed to quick completion by the end of 1921. In western Clark County and Cumberland County to the west, this earliest automobile pavement continued in concrete and is unrivaled for its extent and integrity along the entire National Road. Only in Ohio's several hundred feet of uncovered brick pavement about one-half mile east of the National Road Museum in Muskingham County, and nearly a mile of similar pavement in Guernsey County, east of Cambridge, are these automobile landmarks present in the National Road. Illinois's most arresting view of this old road is westward from the eastern end of the brick pavement looking to the horizon where US 40 passes over I-70. Here the old brick pavement winds through Hawk Creek's valley in a fashion more compatible with the natural landscape than its modern successors to the north and south. Yet, inspection of an automobile bridge abutment over Hawk's Creek (the bridge has been removed) reveals that early automobile pavements were not compliant with natural slopes but were graded by cuts and fills, a practice that has become more pronounced as vehicle speed has increased.

The early automobile pavement is interrupted in Clark County where the interstate transects the alignment and newer pavements have covered or dictated removal, namely, in Marshall, Clark Center, and Martinsville. Nonetheless, the old pavement's periodic reappearance along the current roadside functions as a kind of technologic ruin that should remind the traveler of larger historic and geographic continuities.

LIVINGSTON

The first settlement inside the Illinois portal is Livingston, which lies seven miles west of State Line on the eastern bluff of Big Creek. Unlike State Line and Weaver, which are mere names on the map, this is a hamlet, population about 50 in 1990. Bifurcated by US 40, Livingston's residential area to the north is separated from the church and cemetery to the south. The

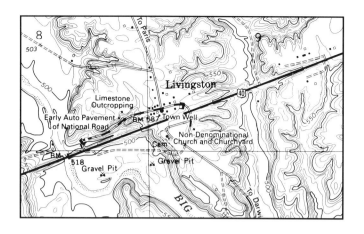

Livingston, Illinois

old brick highway forms a half-mile loop out of US 40 into the hamlet.

Livingston was platted in 1830 by a man drawn from Indiana by the National Road's construction. The hamlet flourished at the National Road's junction with the Darwin Road, which ran between Paris, fifteen miles to the north, and Darwin, on the Wabash River nine miles to the southeast, until a more aggressive speculator in nearby Marshall, William B. Archer, won the county seat in 1837. Before then, "Livingston became quite a business point, and was the center of a large trade," in the words of Clark County's first historian. The drinking trade flourished in the two taverns at the main intersection and eventually houses were built on both sides of the National Road.

The "town pump" (on a concrete slab) still marks Livingston's center at the roads' axes and is accompanied by a one-story frame store with faded advertising graphics (reading Chas. Kirchner's Lumber Yards) on the east wall. West of the hamlet, the National Road descends to Big Creek. Here, the Road is sunken between Pennsylvanian limestone outcroppings. South of US 40, the barely maintained brick and stucco (nondenominational) church and large attendant cemetery contained by an iron fence suggest that the community had once been larger and vibrant. The earliest legible gravestones date from the 1840s and 1850s, the heyday of the National Road in Illinois, before it was challenged in succession by railroads and automobiles.

MARSHALL

Immediately west of East Big Creek, Marshall serves the farms that occupy the cleared forest lands. Marshall's founder, William B. Archer, planned on economic hegemony over the rural countryside. He platted Marshall in 1835 at the junction of the National Road, just cleared and graded through the area, and the Vincennes and Chicago State Road. Six years later, a two-story brick inn anchored the southwest corner of the two roads; it still stands in the center of Marshall and is called the Archer House today.

Marshall and its roadside business were good bets to prosper if only because of their location. Archer's entrepreneurial energy, however, drove him to improve the bet. He convinced Joseph Duncan, a prominent politi-

KEITH A. SCULLE AND JOHN A. JAKLE

cian, to add his name to the plat as a cofounder shortly before Duncan was elected governor. Archer also convinced bricklayers and blacksmiths to locate in Marshall. His financial backing of development in the northwestern part of the county helped make Marshall the county seat two years after it was platted. Eventually, Marshall eclipsed three other speculative towns platted along an eight-mile span of the National Road.

The axis of Archer's plat tilted to the National Road's northeast-southwest direction and only recent plats are set to the cardinal compass points on the north and south edge of town. The town's busiest intersection is still Archer Avenue, the original National Road, and the Vincennes and Chicago Road, now Illinois 1. The county seat Archer won for Marshall has its courthouse square two blocks west and is faced on four sides by stores and offices. Most prominent of these is on the north, the three-story brick business block that George Stewart called "an architectural gem." To be sure, it was an architectural expression of the grandiose dreams that captivated Marshall for several decades after the St. Louis, Vandalia & Terre Haute Railroad was laid in 1870. Because it came through one mile north of town, however, the railroad lacked the anticipated potential to augment dramatically Marshall's economy. The city founders, who missed the opportunity

Marshall, Illinois

The National Road's historic and preserved Archer House (*left*) as seen from Jerry's Cafe. Clayton Rhoads established his garage (*center*) in the 1930s when he bought it as a Chrysler-Dodge dealership. To encourage shopping in Archer Avenue stores the town has removed the parking meters, leaving a line of beheaded red pipes along both sides of the street.

Marshall, Illinois

Billboard space on the US 40 Bypass is not as valued as it was when it opened in the 1950s. An I-70 interchange lurks only one mile north and is now the center of new highway service and retail business.

to pay the railroad's surveyor for trackage closer to town, were clearly not of Archer's caliber.

Neither did the automobile-borne trade bring strong and lasting economic vitality. "Now that the paved road is completed from Terre Haute to Marshall and not from Marshall to Terre Haute, the merchants of Terre Haute, who have had a monopoly on the trade of the Wabash Valley for several years, had better watch out, or they will lose it," boasted the editor of Marshall's *Clark County Democrat* when the pavement was opened on the last day of 1921. Instead, successive efforts to speed travelers ever more quickly along the National Road have accumulated in a corridor of bypasses and new highways on the north, which effectively dealt Marshall out of the economic scramble. Population stood at 2,222 when the highway was opened and rose only slightly by 1950 to 2,960. When Bypass 40 was opened in 1953, the *Clark County Democrat* lamented that "Archer Avenue through Marshall has become alarmingly quiet, and traffic over the street has thinned considerably." Today, no Grabenheimer, the store name boldly displayed in

George Stewart's photograph of the courthouse square, lives in Marshall. Local people shop for clothes in Terre Haute, acknowledged the young retailer of children's wear in Grabenheimer's once-key location. The most recent blow to Marshall's indigenous retail businesses is the interstate, opened eastward in 1969 and westward in 1971. It has been so profound as to cause one merchant to periodize Marshall's previous economy as "Pre-Wal-Mart," a reference to the pervasiveness of the all-purpose discount store on Route 1, north toward I-70.

Marshall's residents, however, benefit from the quiet of commerce deflected off the National Road. Small bungalows and hall and parlor houses occasionally interspersed with buildings adapted from earlier highway businesses—hints of a southern landscape—stand along the east end of Archer Avenue. Their subdued air joins them imperceptibly with the modest businesses that surround Marshall's core. Along West Archer is an assemblage of attractive homes with large frontyards, the product of deep setbacks from the street, and tree-lined parkways. Marshall survives as a service center for the agricultural hinterland. Marshall numbered 3,555 in 1990.

Two landmarks survive at opposite ends of the National Road in Marshall. One is a stone-arch culvert on the west side of town. It was built in the late 1830s of limestone probably quarried near Marshall. (A slightly larger stone-arch culvert exists a few miles west on the original alignment but is inaccessible from the surrounding private land.) Although not as dramatic as the S-bridges or as large as the multispanned stone bridges of the East, the stone of Marshall's culvert is distinctive in the glacial till–covered prairie and woodland of Clark County and it is a survivor from the period of federal construction. Three miles east, where Bypass 40 is pinched back into the National Road, two motels remain as testimony to the automobile highway's impact. The neatest of these is the East Marshall Motel (opened 1950), green-roofed and white-walled cabins in a semicircle around an office of the same colors, that has become a mix of long-term residence apartments and motel. Its disheveled tarpaper neighbor immediately west (opened 1946) has been adapted as a bazaar for second-hand goods.

Marshall, Illinois

West Archer houses retreat into deep shade on a warm spring morning. Landscape architectural historians can't help but draw comparisons here to Frederick Law Olmsted's pioneering work at Riverside, Illinois, where he brought house placement off the street, introduced a wide parkway and sophisticated tree design, to establish a new standard for suburban and residential development.

MARSHALL TO MARTINSVILLE

Seven miles of slightly rolling countryside predominate between the US 40 bypasses of Marshall and Martinsville to the west. Here the traveler will pass corn and soybean fields and occasionally be permitted views from seven to nine miles uninterrupted except by farmsteads, woodlots, and fence lines, usually overgrown. Unlike the hillier region eastward, where the old automobile pavement survives as many short accesses to farmhouse lanes, long stretches of the old highway have been appropriated for private farm roads in this open terrain. Might the state have originally planned a wider highway here? About halfway to Martinsville and several hundred feet south of US 40, Clark Center subsists as a National Road stringtown, its few houses aligned along either side. A private home built in 1850, which also lodged and fed National Road travelers, stands north of Clark Center after two relocations. Consolidated Rail Corporation tracks (once the Vandalia and then part of the mighty Pennsylvania) have meanwhile sliced from north of Marshall to within several hundred feet of the National Road–US 40 corridor east of Martinsville. They will not diverge again more than a half-mile from the corridor for the forty-six miles to Vandalia.

MARTINSVILLE

Martinsville is another creation of the National Road. It was platted in 1833 on the Road's axis and also honors its nativity in the name of its main street, Cumberland, a National Road alias. Although reprehensible to the first county historian because of the "floating class of people . . . chiefly characterized by their dissolute habits and general lack of thrift" who first populated Martinsville, this third-largest town in Clark County (1,161 in 1990) is similar to Marshall in its residential configuration. Entrance westward is along US 40 paved atop the National Road along a residential roadside where the absence of storm sewers and curbs symptomizes stagnation since traffic was diverted by Bypass 40. Commerce downtown includes the Rowe Foundry; nearly every storefront is also occupied, though there are signs of decline. The canyon-like effect of Cumberland Street's relatively narrow width in proportion to its tall buildings adds to the busy feeling. Main street remains essentially like it was in its turn-of-the-century heyday, similar in function although many architectural details have been lost. In contrast, the historic John Chancellor Home (built c. 1860) stands in pris-

KEITH A. SCULLE AND JOHN A. JAKLE

Martinsville, Illinois

School consolidation in the 1920s eliminated many one-room country schools. In their place communities built new, multistoried brick school buildings. The setting is pristine and park-like.

tine condition on the road west out of town. It is the last home of Martinsville Township's first white settler.

BYPASS 40

Martinsville is linked to the next town west, Casey, a thriving agricultural community, by two major strands of the National Road corridor which parallel each other for six miles. This is unique in Illinois. The two strands are US 40 atop the old road and Bypass 40. These routes bypass two other Illinois towns in the corridor, Marshall and Greenup, but only for comparatively short loops that are merged with the older alignments immediately outside of each town. The unique six-mile Casey-to-Martinsville link affords an opportunity to study the influence of Bypass 40 development.

From Martinsville, the new road follows a swathe cut for automobiles from farms that face the section roads marking the Township and Range. Farmsteads, turned away from the bypass, although distantly visible, help impart the strange, unpeopled look to the bypass. As one approaches Casey, there is little sense of approaching a town. For example, the Casey Motel is set about 100 feet south of the bypass and seems remote. Even upon arrival

A wheel fence west of Martinsville, Illinois

Rubber-tired farm implements were rare before 1940 and rationing during World War II made tires too expensive for many farmers. A steel-wheeled machine had little value when worn out and was seldom traded when a farmer bought a replacement. Farmers simply parked their used-up implements in a grove or a machinery lot. Here salvaged wheels make a fence.

at the bypass intersection with the state's north-south Illinois 49, one must refer to a highway map to confirm that Casey is nearby. Local services—Bottle House Liquors, Casey Feed, Casey Implement Company, LeRoy Staley Tire Service, Nebergall Appliance Store, Fork Lift Sales, Service and Repair, and a Cafe / Mobil Gas (abandoned) sign—seem carelessly strewn about the intersection because of the wide gaps separating each. North along 49 usual traveler services congregate at the interstate interchange, and south along 49 the strip has joined to old Casey downtown. Only two businesses face the bypass that loops southwestward into US 40: Tri-County Clinic and a Case and International Harvester dealer. A sign on a farm-supply store wall advises potential customers to "Enter Old Rt. 40."

CASEY

The activity along US 40 between Casey and Martinsville contrasts with the pall along the bypass. Bulk plants, propane tanks, prefab and pole buildings fill the space between US 40 and the railroad at Casey's west entrance. These are natural gas and oil industry facilities, a prime source of Casey's income since the great deposits of the Eastern Illinois Field were tapped at the start of the twentieth century. Many homes with synthetic siding further east of the gas and oil facilities suggest that their owners are commit-

KEITH A. SCULLE AND JOHN A. JAKLE

Casey, Illinois

Three large nineteenth-century buildings and a new drive-in bank front US 40 in downtown Casey. The tall front doors on two suggest that they were once liverys, garages, or fire stations. The massive side wall now provides space for nearly as many auto-parts advertisements as an Indianapolis racecar.

Casey, Illinois

A weigh building in tile beside the railroad tracks in Casey: vernacular architecture at its best.

ted to permanent residence here. This residential zone blends into the downtown, Clark County's busiest on the National Road. Casey, one of several towns on the Road begun by those who both built the Road and then settled along it, was originally platted in 1854 on the Road's diagonal axis. Casey (locally pronounced "Kay-zee"), numbered 2,914 in 1990, down from 3,026 a decade earlier.

CASEY TO GREENUP

Two and three-fourths miles east of Casey, the Blackburn Cemetery survives on a twenty-foot elevation overlooking Turkey Run and the National Road. A cemetery of thirty-one local settlers, its first burial was in 1850 and its last in 1904. No cemetery exists on the bypass; the relationship of the dead to the old Road and US 40 illustrates that though the bypass functions in a mechanical way to ease congestion and speed traffic around the town it has not found a comparable niche in the community culture.

Casey's productive hinterland is suggested by the collection of more than a dozen large concrete grain elevators owned by the Huisinga Company

West of Casey, Illinois

From an immaculate farm at the Clark-Cumberland County line, the Huisinga grain elevators create Casey's skyline.

KEITH A. SCULLE AND JOHN A. JAKLE

which stand in a tight cluster on the town's west side. This railside grain-storage capacity is supplemented by steel grain bins on farms across the county, many visible from the highway.

West of Casey, US 40 is unflinchingly straight and encourages little pause along the eight and one-half miles into Greenup. Exit from Casey is also an imperceptible entrance, save for a generic state sign, into Cumberland County and resumption of the now-familiar old concrete highway, here beyond 40's north shoulder. Two miles along, however, a huge two-story frame building looms abandoned and weathered of its paint on a fragment of the old highway. It is a store and the last easily seen remnant of Vevay Park (locally pronounced "*Vee*-vee"). The store was originally oriented to the railroad, and Vevay Park grew from a railroad watering station at the end of the nineteenth century into a small trading center and school by the early 1900s. US 40 tracks to the north side of the old pavement for the remaining distance into Greenup, traverses the valley of Ranger Creek (supply for the former watering station), and passes the Vevay Park cemetery, whose gateway fronts on the old pavement. Two miles beyond, down the apparently featureless highway to Greenup, stand two inactive motels, one on either side of US 40 and once a constellation of three begun in the post–World War II revival of the highway trade.

West of Casey, Illinois
Stripped of its companion outbuildings, an empty clapboard house and summer kitchen seem discomforted by the new steel grain storage bins and elevator leg that punctuate a old Clark County farmstead, but what a roadside sight!

GREENUP

Legendary in the historical record for its languor, Greenup's structures are the product of several economic jolts injected by successive new transportation modes. The coincidence of the Embarras River (locally pronounced *Am*-braw), one of four important drainages between Terre Haute and Vandalia, and the National Road gave it life. A gristmill was built just north of the Road on the river and prospered quickly from the influx of people along the Road; about 1828, settlers formed Rossville. William C. Greenup, a political insider since Illinois's territorial period, was appointed in 1830 to oversee Road construction in the state. Always alert to personal gain from development along the alignment, he helped start several of its

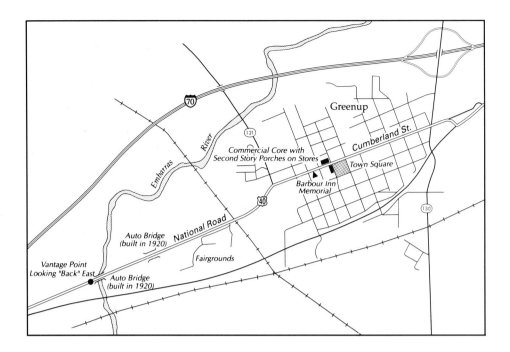

towns. One of these he named for himself and construction began after he quit as superintendent of the Road. He platted Greenup in 1834 with one of his business associates, Joseph Barbour, astride the Road's northeast-southwest axis, south of the busy gristmill and east of Rossville. The partners also won the contract to supply lumber for two bridges west of their plat. One bridge spanned a slough and another immediately west of it crossed the Embarras River. The population grew and economic activity surged. Barbour profited from an inn he had built beside the National Road near the center of the town three years before it was platted. Greenup became the seat of a new county, Cumberland, in 1843. But activity soon subsided. By 1857, the diffusion of settlers throughout the new county dictated relocation of its seat to the more-central Toledo. Although a railroad was proposed in 1852, none was forthcoming until 1868–69 when the St. Louis, Vandalia, & Terre Haute was built parallel to the National Road. As a result, one historian wrote,

> It was a proud era in the history of Greenup, and the anticipations of many of Greenup's citizens knew no bounds. New additions were made to town, new lots laid off, large increases of population, buildings went up daily, and Greenup for once was aroused from her long, deep slumber, and to a newness of life and activity.

KEITH A. SCULLE AND JOHN A. JAKLE

The prospect arose that Greenup would wrest the county seat back from nearby Toledo to the north, and in anticipation residents left the public square undeveloped in the hope that it would be the site of a new courthouse. It did not. The economic boom spawned by the railroad lapsed into gradual growth. Greenup's commercial district was built while the railroad was still the most advanced transportation, and many buildings were two-story with second-floor porches that sheltered passersby. When an automobile pavement was scheduled to be laid atop the National Road about 1920, local entrepreneurs hoped for an economic revival but, again, hopes proved excessive. Greenup was home for 1,230 at the time and for 1,616 in 1990. The automobile has not clinched Greenup's fortune. Nonetheless, the latest financial ambitions have focused at the busiest traffic nodes, at the east end of Greenup where passage of Illinois 130 over the interstate has generated the usual collection of franchised traveler services: Unocal; 500 Plato-lene convenience store; Amoco; Gateway Inn; and Dairy Queen. Local businesses are intermingled: Colonial Liquor and Dutch Pan Restaurant. Above

Greenup, Illinois

From the fine old wooden grandstand, visitors to the Cumberland County Fair can watch sulky horse races in comfort. The welcome sign on the stage declares that the fair has been held since 1888. US 40 bypasses in the distance.

them all soars a watertower ironically screaming the observer should "Try Greenup First." Three-fourths of a mile south, at the state road's intersection with US 40, local merchants have situated a bank, auto dealership, and a convenience store to snare the usual mix of local and area customers. An earlier generation of roadside businesses, three gas stations and a restaurant, crowded the corner beginning in the 1940s.

Starting at the corner of US 40 and Illinois 130 is Greenup's business core on Cumberland Street, known first as the National Road, then as US 40. At its southwest intersection with Delaware, the nondescript post office (1956) and village hall (1961) occupy the relocated town square instead of the courthouse dreamed of in headier times. Greenup's porched stores and canopied sidewalks dating from the turn of the century—now unique along the National Road in Illinois—survive one block west, at the town's heart, the corners of Cumberland and Kentucky Streets. One block west is a 1915 memorial to the Barbour Inn, razed in 1972 for a used car lot that stands virtually empty.

Two blocks beyond the inn marker, the National Road begins a winding descent out of town and into the shallow Embarras Valley. This is another stretch of well-preserved early automobile pavement, unusual here for its regular use as the town's backroad access. A half-mile beyond stands the county fairgrounds. Although the fairgrounds in each of Illinois's four National Road counties still stand by the Road, this fairground at Greenup is the best preserved. West of the fairgrounds down the old pavement is the now-drained slough, earlier negotiated by timber bridges provided by Greenup and Barbour. Beyond stand two early (1920) concrete automobile bridges, one an eighth mile and the second one-half mile away. Arrival at the bridge permits a view to the east during the period of defoliation along a transect that includes the Road, bridges, slough, fairgrounds, town, bypass, and railroad, in an especially dramatic landscape summary of Greenup's history.

GREENUP TO THE EFFINGHAM COUNTY LINE

Beyond Greenup the highway emerges again onto the open countryside. Thornton A. Ward's house, a two-story brick Italianate (built c. 1855), stands on the north side. Surrounded by a crescent of trees and yard dotted in summer with volunteered flowers, Ward's house, although unoccupied, is the most charming old mansion along the Illinois corridor. At Jewett (194 people in 1990), the traveler can turn off US 40 to follow the old automobile

Jewett, Illinois

Lee Myers built his tile house by himself. A house trailer with a permastone foundation stands at the back.

Jewett, Illinois

While some trailer homes in Jewett do not have permastone foundations, they do have well-trimmed yards. Because the riding lawnmower closely simulates a tractor, mowing astride this miniature implement has become a favored pastime for retired men.

Jewett, Illinois

Closed for the day; the post office flag has been taken down.

Jewett, Illinois

Euris Roberts lives on Cumberland Road where his garden thrives in the good south Illinois soil.

pavement into town. Main street buildings face south, testifying to Jewett's keener orientation to the railroad laid three decades after the National Road. Postmaster Frances Roberts has hung a sign, "National Road," a rare public awareness in Illinois, on the tiny office. No significant evidence remains, however, of the old highway's once-vibrant life despite Roberts's memory of it. Instead, traffic drones, both on the interstate and on nearby US 40. A mile and one-half west of the old Road's reconvergence with US 40 at the west edge of Jewett is the unincorporated hamlet of Woodbury. Platted (1835) as one of William C. Greenup's grand speculations, Woodbury today is a collection of modest houses that straggle along the north side of the early automobile pavement that was poured atop the National Road. North of Woodbury's access road the railroad, old Road, and interstate lie bundled within a quarter-mile corridor. (Between the latter two, US 40 stands on a lower alignment.) Four miles west through open countryside the routes cross into Effingham County.

MONTROSE

The name "Effingham" suggests a place of English origins, or Eve Effingham from James Fenimore Cooper's classic American novel *The Pioneers; or The Sources of the Susquehanna*. But for Illinois the county of that name carries strong German connotation by association. At Montrose evidences of things German-American begin to appear. Roman Catholics from Westphalia and Oldenburg (as well as southern Germany) settled in the eastern portion of the county following the aborted 1848 revolution in the old country. Lutherans from Saxony and other parts of northern Germany settled the western townships at the same time. Both groups mixed in the county seat with settlers from the American Upper South, especially Kentucky and Tennessee.

In 1970, construction of a connector, temporarily linking US 40 to a then–partially completed I-70 east of the village, revealed the blackened logs of an old corduroy road. Here was originally a marsh at the headwaters of

KEITH A. SCULLE AND JOHN A. JAKLE

Little Salt Creek. Although never glaciated, the local terrain felt the impact of meltwater from the ice of the last (or Wisconsin-age) glacier, which advanced to a point some twenty miles to the north. Outwash deposition was substantially reworked by the wind, leaving extensive areas overlain with loess. Geologically immature (the terrain was poorly dissected by stream courses before modern ditching), it was predominantly marshland of the long grass prairie that pioneer farmers first encountered here.

Today's freeway interchange sits north of the village. Montrose is really a creature of the railroad, which closely parallels US 40 on the south. Around the railroad station, only recently demolished, grew a small commercial district, remnants of which face the railroad tracks from the north side of the highway. The first clear architectural hint of Germania is the former Meislin grocery store. Here from the 1890s to the 1970s a family worked and lived in a two-story edifice, half store and half house, faced in stone as in their native Germany. Next door stood the family's hardware store in a single-story, tin-sided structure (1906), the product more of American building tastes. Although a tavern and the post office are relatively new, the derelict bank and adjacent garage dominates visually. As a place of business the town is an anachronism (306 people in 1990). Only the grain elevator, a nearly ubiquitous sight in all of the towns along US 40 in Illinois, suggests commercial prosperity, although an improved tavern in the old gas station is new to the landscape.

MONTROSE TO TEUTOPOLIS

In the eight miles to Teutopolis, the Road and railroad run parallel on straight diagonals, intersecting the Township and Range section roads at oblique angles at approximately mile intervals. Rectangular fields are planted most summers either in corn or in soybeans. The farms are large, with farmsteads widely scattered, since operating units of at least 600 acres are necessary today for families to survive in modern grain farming. Soils in this area are among the most fertile in the Middle West, having developed

Montrose, Illinois

Across US 40 from the town grain elevator, a former bank keeps company with an early gas station now serving as an "air-conditioned" tavern.

KEITH A. SCULLE AND JOHN A. JAKLE

Montrose, Illinois

Fire department geometry in formed concrete block, pressed metal, and false front. The date stone reveals that this building also performed other functions.

primarily from loess in the uplands and from alluvium along the tributaries of the Little Wabash River. Most of the farmsteads have grain storage bins, but only a few still possess the barns and silos reminiscent of a previous time when farmers milked dairy cows and grew hay along with the corn. Houses, cribs, and other buildings tend to stand out boldly in greenswards of carefully mowed lawns and carefully tended fields. There is an aesthetic valuing of isolated objects sharply defined in horizontal space which gives to the landscape an overt simplicity. Only on the margins of the railroad or in the occasional woodlot is vegetation given license to be wild. Only here does a kind of rusticity set in.

TEUTOPOLIS

On the horizon a tall church spire announces that this is no ordinary region, at least as defined by the places previously encountered along the National Road eastward. Although it is generally conceded in rural Illinois that grain elevators constitute the "Cathedrals of the Prairie," as Le Corbusier wrote, here is an actual cathedral-like church, its tower dominating the horizon. It is to the base of this spire that the motorist is instinctively drawn down the line of the highway.

Teutopolis (affectionately called "T-town" locally) dates from the late

Teutopolis, Illinois

Four-square brick houses, like many along eastern sections of the National Road in Maryland and Pennsylvania, and the grand spire of the dominant Catholic church convey an essence of "covenanted community."

1830s, when a colony of several hundred Germans settled here by way of a short sojourn in Cincinnati. Other emigrants followed more directly from Germany, coming up the Mississippi River from New Orleans and overland from St. Louis. Although it offered great promise for future commerce, the National Road was originally little more than a furrow plowed through the blue stem, buffalo, and other grasses. Franciscans arrived just prior to the Civil War to establish schools and eventually a college. A convent was also built. Most important was the establishment of Saint Francis Parish, whose Gothic Revival church dominates the town even today. From the late nineteenth into the mid-twentieth century, Teutopolis carried a very distinctive European look. First, the substantive brick buildings of Roman Catholicism stood cloistered behind massive masonry walls, their towers and turrets visible to travelers hurrying past by road and rail. On the main street, commercial buildings were likewise of brick, many with distinctive front gables typical of German towns. Brick was used predominantly on houses—even on the small two-room cottages, forms reminiscent of the old country.

Through the 1950s, streets were lined by rows of mature shade trees, many pollarded. Today, only the church remains of the various church buildings that once stood and only a tiny remnant of wall survives. The old

KEITH A. SCULLE AND JOHN A. JAKLE

trees are gone, having reached old age, replaced on some streets by new plantings of maple. Surviving commercial buildings carry layers of facade alteration. Nonetheless, the Germanic image carries through in the orderliness of both public and private spaces. Maintenance levels are extremely high; sidewalks are repaired, buildings painted, lawns cut, gardens tended. Many gardens display religious statuary in the flowerbeds.

Although clearly under the trade shadow of the City of Effingham only three miles west, Teutopolis still contains a wide array of retail functions. Clothing, jewelry, furniture, hardware, beer and liquor, and grocery stores stand as separate establishments along with a bank, many taverns, a cafe, a mortuary, several gasoline stations, several garages, and several implement dealers. A large grain mill along the railroad and assorted small industrial plants out toward Effingham on US 40 (beyond the high school where the "Wooden Shoes" play basketball and other sports), suggest a viable employment base beyond that of retailing. Local money, much of it generated in farming, has been invested in homegrown small-scale industry. The town numbered 1,417 inhabitants in 1990.

Teutopolis stands as a "covenanted" community. Families intermarried and otherwise related through the church display a rootedness in this community that is rare for American society generally. Within farm families each generation strives to develop and pass to its successors a legacy of land and know-how. They patronize relatives and other parishioners in town who provide retail services. Here are traditional small-town retailers who appear to prosper. In places such as Marshall, Greenup, and Martinsville the attractions of shopping centers in large cities and/or the appeal of recently arrived corporate franchises have captured the trade of farm and town dweller alike. Most of the other towns on the National Road in Illinois originated purely as commercial speculations rather than as communities of "colonists." Consequently, the sense of community appears to be much less developed in those places today.

EFFINGHAM

Effingham dates from the arrival of the railroad. Originally called Broughton when platted in 1853, its name was soon changed to honor an investor in the Illinois Central Railroad. Effingham was located on a branch line that quickly became the north-south mainline connecting Chicago with Memphis and New Orleans. After the Civil War, what is now the east-west

Conrail line was built connecting Indianapolis and St. Louis, and another Illinois Central branch was built accessing Evansville to the southeast. What railroads promised for Effingham—a central location in a system of intercity connectivity—the modern interstate highways provide today. I-57 (Chicago to Memphis) and I-70 (Indianapolis to St. Louis) now merge as a single traffic artery for some ten miles in a sweep around Effingham's north and west sides. Large truckstops and numerous motels, gasoline stations, and fast-food restaurants cluster at each of the town's three interchanges. US 40 does not enjoy an interchange. And nowhere on the freeway is US 40 identified as a possible alternative or connecting route.

South of US 40, one can still follow a remnant of the old National Road through Effingham on National Avenue between Second Street on the east and Banker Street on the west. Here one will see the railroad station and old railroad hotel (now a furniture store). North of US 40, one can reach the downtown shopping district by following Jefferson Street, which runs from the cemetery on the town's east side, to the courthouse square. Downtown suffered a business decline during the 1960s and 1970s as local retailers relocated to peripheral shopping centers and national retailers arrived to siphon

Effingham, Illinois

One of southern Illinois's largest concentrations of truck terminals and service stations strings from Exit 160 to Exit 163 along the I-70/I-57 bypass northwest of Effingham. A wash and a weigh is available at the Truck-O-Mat, even at night.

KEITH A. SCULLE AND JOHN A. JAKLE

more trade into peripheral shopping locations. But the 1980s brought partial renewal through the construction of several public parking lots, the timely renovation of old buildings (for example, the 1920s hotel into a courthouse annex), and the judicious locating of new offices (for example, the new post office and a new bank). Careful attention to tree planting and street furnishings has produced a visually pleasing business location. There is a reawakened interest in the neatness and orderliness of this reconstituted place. New and remodeled houses along residential streets east of the square suggest gentrification—the renewed strengthening of the town's traditional prestige neighborhood by the community's more affluent.

US 40 was rerouted in the 1930s several blocks to the south. Now lined by the residual of some five decades of commercial-strip development, the formerly residential Fayette Street is now lined by vintage motels, gasoline stations, and automobile showrooms in most blocks. The venerable Coach and Four Restaurant, formerly the Greyhound Lines Post House, is still operated at this writing in the traditional manner as a bus station. Opened in 1940, the pine-paneled cafeteria serves bus passengers in obligatory half-hour layovers, the calls of the loudspeaker hurrying diners along.

Effingham has always been a manufacturing center. The making of church furnishings and butcher blocks goes back well into the nineteenth century.

Effingham, Illinois

Billboard Theater, an apt, if inverted, metaphor here. The billboards and their messages are on stage, yet they are rigid, unmoving. The people in trucks and cars, the intended audience, move past at speed, at a distance. Sized and angled to be read at 65 miles per hour by interstate traffic, the sponsors of these billboards have abandoned the audience on US 40.

The manufacture of home appliances and prefabricated houses dates from after World War II. The printing industry is more recent. The new interstate freeways have strengthened Effingham's hand in the bidding for new employers. Physical access to markets has been enhanced and the commuter field enlarged, increasing the number of workers available. Effingham with its 31,704 people (in 1990) has become a regional center, no longer one among equals in the array of towns along US 40 in Illinois.

EFFINGHAM TO EWINGTON AND FUNKHOUSER

Effingham is very much a forward-looking small city with relatively little energy lost in nostalgic concerns. History, to be relevant, must serve the progressive thrust of the moment. Nowhere in the city is the National Road celebrated as a part of the town's past. US 40 on Fayette Street does carry the "Three-Star Highway" designation established as a memorial to those killed in World War II. Only at the reststop on I-70 ten miles west of Effingham is the National Road remembered. Named the National Trail Plaza, plaques outside the restrooms (on both the eastbound and westbound sides) supply travelers with degrees of misinformation. Not only is the National Road misnamed, but the reader is told that it terminated in St. Louis, reaching Vandalia not in the 1840s but in 1830. The main message is that nearby ran the "first interstate road to be built with federal funds"—a celebration

KEITH A. SCULLE AND JOHN A. JAKLE

useful to highway interests past, present, and future. All around stands the fulfillment of the motorist's heritage. Trucks idle in parking lots out front. Families jettisoned from station wagons and vans picnic out back. Here passes a restless America in review. Seemingly, only the errant waster-of-time would seek out the paralleling old Road two miles to the north, hardly remembered either in fact or in fiction.

EWINGTON AND FUNKHOUSER

Back on the old highway heading west one comes to Ewington, once the county seat of Effingham County. "But," in the words of one of the county's early chroniclers, "like everything human, it had its time to die." Settled in the 1830s, it initially formed around a tavern near the crossing of the Little Wabash River, the third major drainage traveling west from Terre Haute to Vandalia. Little remains of Ewington. The 1950s highway grade disrupts the site, leaving scattered pieces of old right-of-way visible. More remains of the hamlet of Funkhouser (fifty people in 1980), two miles farther west, since the Road's original alignment stands unchanged there. But Funkhouser appears to be more the relic of the railroad as opposed to the highway since burials in the cemetery date only to the late 1860s. In this stretch of road the black locust, maple, oak, and hickory close in again and one loses the sense of being on the open prairie. Distant views are limited largely to the highway's trajectory. There is more nonfarm occupancy of the land with modest cabins and small houses strung out in stringtowns, suggesting more the Upper South than German or other origins. At Funkhouser Creek, the 1950s highway crosses on a high embankment to obscure below an old concrete highway bridge with a remnant quarter-mile ribbon concrete lined by six-inch curbs. The plaque here reads: "Built 1919 by State of Illinois with Federal Aid." Here is history accurately recorded, but, in its isolation, summarily ignored.

KEPTOWN

At Keptown, another of the stringtowns on the Pike, the Freemanton Cemetery features a sign with a quote from Longfellow setting the tone:

Lives of great men remind us
We can make our lives sublime,
And, departing, leave behind us
Footprints on the sands of time.

Altamont, Illinois

A Lutheran cemetery. Most markers carry German names, the oldest German text. Cemeteries are useful indicators of a community's ethnic heritage.

A depression through the center of the cemetery is possibly the right-of-way of the original Road. Westward from this place the prairie economy reemerges.

Cash grain agriculture fully reasserts itself—Germania regained. For those who doubt the change, the prevalence of German names in the cemetery at Altamont's eastern edge will prove the point. Here are represented mostly Lutheran rather than Roman Catholic families, but, again, covenanted community is clearly evident.

ALTAMONT

Altamont has literally turned its back on the National Road. It is to the railroad, which parallels the Road one mile to the north, that the town has been oriented. Uptown is located an even wider range of retail activities than at Teutopolis, no doubt reflecting Altamont's greater separation from Effingham. Here is a full-scale supermarket, a drugstore, and a clinic as well as a barbershop, appliance store, and insurance and realty offices, among other businesses. Everywhere the telltale neatness of high maintenance suggests prosperity. Several Lutheran churches serve the town, one positioned to intercept farm families coming to church from the west along the National Road. Formal tree plantings, largely maples, line many streets. Gardens are numerous and well tended, but lack religious statuary. The county fairgrounds are here, rather than at Effingham, the county seat. Whereas the Teutopolis street grid is oriented to the National Road and railroad, Altamont's is aligned to the cardinal directions, the National Road representing a diagonal tangent bounding the grid to the south. In recent decades this part of town was filled with new ranch houses, although the highway itself does reflect a half-century of limited commercial development largely automobile-oriented. A total of 2,296 lived in Altamont in 1990, down from 1980's 2,389.

ENTER FAYETTE COUNTY

The land continues open in long vistas westward the five miles to the Fayette County line. The Road cuts across a gently rolling plain comprised

KEITH A. SCULLE AND JOHN A. JAKLE

substantially of loess-derived soils formed under prairie grass. US 40 sits directly on the old Road here and there are no vestiges of relic roadway accordingly. The railroad parallels to the north, but is seldom visible, especially in the season of tall corn. At the Blue Mound Tavern (where more liberal Effingham County liquor laws have traditionally attracted Fayette County drinkers) the Blue Mound northwest of Altamont is not visible. Only I-70's overpasses to the south provide topographic relief. At each overpass there is a flooded borrow pit from which dirt for embanking has been dug. Here on the interfluve between the Little Wabash and Kaskaskia Rivers, the land appears totally flat. It is drained by large ditches dug to follow straight surveyor's lines rather than topographical relief. Fields are underlain by drainage tiles that, along with the ditches, characterize Middle Western prairie land generally.

ST. ELMO AND BROWNSTOWN

US 40 crosses into Fayette County without notice, save for a generic state highway sign. This is the last county on Illinois's original Road segment. Its first two towns illustrate the railroad's priority. Both St. Elmo (1,473 inhab-

St. Elmo, Illinois

An oilfield service company stores spare parts beside a warehouse along US 40. Steel grain bins provide a passive backdrop. Modest oilfields are scattered in this area where cash grain farming dominates the rural landscape.

St. Elmo, Illinois

Larry Stolte's Barbershop
with his amazing collection
of "gimme" caps. A cus-
tomer owns the lone straw
Stetson. Grady Clay, the
renowned writer, appears
in the reflecting mirror.

itants in 1990; 1,611 in 1980), two and one-half miles west of the county line,
and Brownstown (668 inhabitants in 1990), six miles beyond, were platted
(1871) on the "Vandalia" rail line, the local nickname for the St. Louis, Vandalia & Terre Haute. Both towns literally turned their back to the National
Road. Commerce developed along the roadside but downtowns lie to the
north. There, several tree-lined streets of sound middle-class houses from
the end of the last century enclose small business districts. But the similar-
ity ends here. St. Elmo has not survived the drain of dollars to larger markets, but its Main Street is remarkable for its brick buildings from the 1930s.
A dazzling blue and red and yellow marquee accents the Elmo Theater
(1941) where the northeast end of Main Street intersects the rail line. Cat-
tycornered at the southwest tip of Main Street, an antique store that thrives
on out-of-town trade sits behind two freshly painted stone fronts. Antique
stores are one of the most common businesses that mark the most recent

KEITH A. SCULLE AND JOHN A. JAKLE

St. Elmo, Illinois

The Richardson Brothers Nursery, a large regional enterprise, wraps around Maplewood Cemetery, an ongoing enterprise. The delivery truck fleet stands staged in readiness.

East of Brownsville, Illinois

Surrounded by eighty acres of soybeans, a primordial-looking pump draws oil from deep primordial rock at a languid, but unrelenting pace. The U.S. Forest Service might refer to this as a land of many uses.

stage in the succession of Main Street businesses as traditional merchants abandon their stores. "Olde National Trail Antiques" brochures for the taking portray an effort at common marketing by thirty-six dealers along the road (Terre Haute to St. Louis) and a heretofore-unimagined profit possible from historical association with the corridor. The barber shop in the old hardware store opposite the beautiful Monarch Gas Company building (1939, and formerly Atwood Men's Clothing store) boasts an incredible collection of baseball caps. The remains of a nine-room motel and nearby ice cream shop stand at the west edge of town on the south side of US 40. Their condition is a liability to the eighteen-room motel (opened c. 1955) immediately north across the highway, which thrives because its industrious owner has placed two signs on the interstate, cut losses by closing the restaurant, and invested heavily in remodeling. The interstate cannot sap all small-scale commerce from US 40, for there are special places where advantages can be pressed. Confirmation exists in the extensive Richardson Brothers plant nursery complex on the highway's south side behind the Maplewood

KEITH A. SCULLE AND JOHN A. JAKLE

Cemetery. Ninety-eight glass greenhouses, each about 5,000 square feet, and numerous large cold frames spread across 300 acres. Herman and Ole Richardson were barbers in St. Elmo in 1936 when they built a greenhouse and began selling setting plants—geraniums, impatiens, begonias, marigolds, petunias—locally. Today the business is operated by their children who employ about 150 people, and supply bedding plants to wholesale and retail outlets across twenty-two states each growing season.

In Brownstown a new post office, bank building, and grocery stand on the business block that parallels the railroad, where the grain elevators are of noticeably smaller capacity than those in the eastern part of the state. But along the highway both towns exhibit strips of recently used and abandoned roadside structures. Sun bleaches the paint and weeds overgrow the driveways of two former motels that remain on either side of East Cumberland Street, west of Third, in Brownstown.

BROWNSTOWN TO THE KASKASKIA FLOODPLAIN

After passing the Fayette County line, travel on US 40 is proverbial free sailing along ten miles of straight highway. The right-of-way is narrow and devoid of trees. The old roads lie beneath. The railroad is north. The interstate is south. They parallel. Speeding is easy here. Corn, soybeans, and oil pumps intermingle on the till plain on either side of the road.

One and one-half miles west of Brownstown, the Griffith Cemetery is indicated a half mile south of US 40 by a small sign more noticeable from the west than the east. Here, on a wooded knoll beyond a gently curving fork of Sandy Creek, is a recent memorial to the "gypsy girl" who died (1860) at the "twin pumps" on the National Road. Her burial started the cemetery. Today the interstate passes about 100 feet to the south.

Back on US 40 and west, the Road crosses over the interstate. Here, on the left, a temporary sign proclaims a coming event: "Road Angels Truck Centre." The groundskeeper at the sixteen acres of former campgrounds assures any who stop that it will be reborn as the site of a local ministry for the National Association of Christian Truckers—a wayside haven for those whose homes are really the miniature living rooms attached to the back of their Kenworths and Peterbilts. On the right side is a most confusing scene: US 40's interruptions by I-70. Fragments of old concrete pavements are snarled like tossed yarn at the northwest foot of new US 40's embankment over the interstate. Close inspection of the pavement, however, proves it to be a divided highway comprised of one older lane separated from a second lane more recently laid. The old two-lane now provides access to campgrounds. Across the interstate some of the same chaos occurs where the old alignment splits from the new and Illinois 185 splits from them both.

THE KASKASKIA FLOODPLAIN

A half-mile west is a two-story, white-painted-brick house on the south side of US 40. Local legend holds that it was a former National Road inn. Bluff City, three-fourths of a mile further west and another stringtown along the Road, had 320 people in 1980. Thereafter the Road descends rapidly for twenty-five to thirty feet onto the broad and infamous floodplain of the Kaskaskia River. It is one of the four prominent drainages in the Terre Haute–Vandalia segment. Today a drainage ditch empties what to early travelers was a chronically forbidding quagmire.

Beyond the drainage ditch, US 40 meets Illinois 51 at a right angle. About 100 feet north the old concrete automobile pavement rests abandoned exactly atop the original National Road, the only place in eastern Fayette County where the three roads are not one. The old highway fragment rides a high embankment safe from the troublesome floodplain. Its construction in 1923 took nearly four years.

VANDALIA

Up the steep western Kaskaskia River bank, US 40 climbs into Vandalia, the National Road's terminus and Illinois's second capital (1820–39). Yet, neither sign nor landscape announces Vandalia's historic prominence. Just beyond the Kaskaskia bridge is an empty lot on the north side of US 40. Here a National Road toll house survived until 1974. Ironically, a campaign was launched only seven years later to attempt to revitalize downtown commerce by highlighting historic architecture. Past three blocks of mundane roadside convenience stores and garages lies Vandalia's oldest glory, Illinois's third statehouse (1836–39), a bona fide contemporary of the National Road, which ran in front of the statehouse, and rightfully an official historic site. A Madonna of the Trail statue stands at the west end of the block. A fitting self-tribute and expression of America's tribal pride in the myth of a nation forged from wilderness, the statue has become a focal fixation for periodic commentators. The information proudly incised on one side of its base boasts of Abraham Lincoln's time in the legislature at Vandalia as if to

KEITH A. SCULLE AND JOHN A. JAKLE

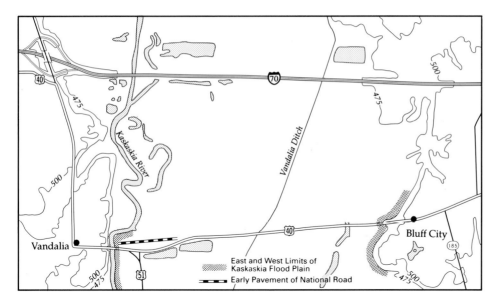

Bluff City to Vandalia, Illinois, Kaskaskia floodplain

East of Vandalia

The Vandalia Ditch flows south, hastening drainage on the formerly infamous crossing on the National Road of the Kaskaskia River floodplain. The river lies one mile farther west.

sanctify the town as the highest order of tourist site in the state that advertises itself as the "Land of Lincoln." West is Gallatin Street, named for the secretary of the treasury who conceived the National Road, with a gentle descent for three blocks along a traditional main street and a rise beyond accentuated by the steeple atop St. James Lutheran Church. Here the main street seems dispirited.

Vandalia means swells and dales, too. To the south, down another gently descending street to another rise, is the Old State Cemetery, authorized in 1823 by the legislature in Vandalia, and a resting place for several early state officials. Included is William C. Greenup (1785–1853) who coplatted Vandalia in 1819. Politician, surveyor, and speculator: in a way Greenup is the father of the National Road in Illinois. After moving a third of the way across the new nation west from his Maryland birthplace, he made a fortune in frontier Illinois along the National Road, and he symbolizes how and why the National Road came to be in his adopted state. Greenup's memory rings through the traditional lament of a Vandalian who settled in the town in the early 1960s:

> People are very proud of their history here, of Abe Lincoln, and I think we have a very good historical society, but we don't always bring our history up-to-date by practicing the kind of things we did in the past. I don't think there is the energy here that perhaps made this town a little more progressive in the days when it was founded.

Actually Vandalians have created a heritage of progress measured in terms of material gain, one in which regular bursts of individual business sense have been modulated occasionally by civic booster programs dependent on history. Hence, no one can reasonably expect a quaint landscape preserved from the capital era; for it was, in fact, a village of many perishable log buildings. Sidewalk plaques on Gallatin Street may poignantly memorialize lost buildings but they also imply the business ambitions of those whose buildings replaced primitive antecedents. Today, Vandalia is "expending a great deal of effort to attract new industry to this area, along with tourists" as is declared with some gusto in the recent "Fayette County Tourism Guide." Clearly Vandalia has not been a stagnant town; its 1990 population was 6,114. Change has been more common in Vandalia than might be expected of small towns generally. It is the slow pace that deludes.

The traveler across Illinois between Terre Haute and Vandalia encounters scenes strongly commonplace across the whole of Middle America. There is little pretension here other than to being quintessentially rural and American. The evidences of recent farm consolidation and related population loss play out on the land and in the look of most small-town main streets that no longer provide the central place functions available formerly. Here is rural America in profound transition, if not decline. Only where the infrastructure of recent interstate highways focuses movement at Effingham is growth of the urban kind truly expansive. Displayed is a landscape of continuities, not contrasts. The traveler's attention is drawn to the relics of pastness which speak of history, both recent and distant. The traveler's attention is drawn to the relic roads, the relics of the roadside, and layers of accumulation generally that comprise landscapes traversed in this, a linear slice of traditional Americana.

Vandalia to Alton and
St. Louis

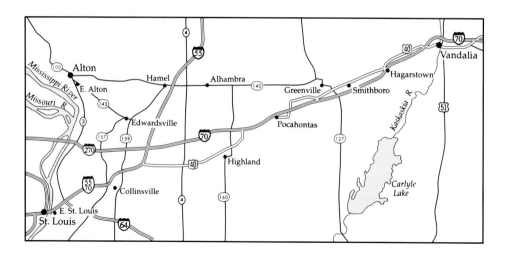

From Vandalia to East St. Louis and Alton, Illinois

DOUGLAS K. MEYER

From Vandalia, westward, the road is not yet located, but the legislature of Illinois with great unanimity have consented to its passage through the state, only on the contingency it shall pass Alton and cross the Mississippi, above the mouth of the Missouri.

JOHN M. PECK
A Gazetteer of Illinois, 1837

US 40 AND INTERSTATE 70 RUN PARALLEL FROM VANDALIA TO ST. LOUIS, their objective, some seventy miles away. East of Vandalia the National Road, US 40, I-70, and Conrail—formerly the Penn Central main-line railroad—overlap in the movement corridor. Although the National Road arrived in Vandalia in 1839, it never reached the Mississippi River at either St. Louis or Alton. By the late 1830s, four trunk highways entered Illinois at Shawneetown, Golconda, Vincennes, and Terre Haute. Converging on St. Louis, these roads traversed a growing German enclave east of the Mississippi River. Political leaders in Missouri and Illinois debated whether the National Road's exit point from Illinois would be at St. Louis or Alton. The disagreement, together with federal and state financial problems, a competing Illinois & Michigan Canal from Chicago, and a growing railroad network, conspired to end the Road at Vandalia. This final highway segment to East

St. Louis and Alton provides a historical and geographical context for the debate as to where the Road should terminate.

The countryside west of Vandalia is the gently dissected Illinoisan-age Springfield glacial till plain. Hurricane, Shoal, and Silver Creeks, tributaries of the Kaskaskia River, proffer minor undulations. Near the Mississippi River, loess-covered limestone bluffs present a distinctive profile and abrupt change in relief, contrasting with the flat Mississippi floodplain. Landscapes along the corridor from Vandalia to the Mississippi at St. Louis are diverse and rich in meaning: cash grain and dairy farms; tiny hamlets, villages, and towns; bedroom suburbs; prehistoric Cahokia Mounds; derelict buildings; and economic blight. Linear villages, street grid towns, and curvilinear subdivisions reveal change in urban form over time. Main-street business districts include quiescent linear strips, open squares, and courthouse squares. These places contrast with commercially vital contemporary communities that center on businesses clustered along bypasses and at freeway interchanges. Here is modern roadside America, replicating standardized conveniences, services, fast-food restaurants, and other businesses which increasingly results in abandonment or adaptive reuse of old main streets.

VANDALIA TO ALTON AND ST. LOUIS

Boosters and vested interests in Alton and St. Louis, rival riverside towns, competed to become the National Road's Mississippi River crossing point. In the early 1820s, roads connected each river town with Vandalia, the second state capital (1820–39). The county seats of Greenville, in Bond County, and Edwardsville, in Madison County, were astride the Vandalia-Alton Road. Alton proposed its westward route extension from Vandalia as the shortest distance and most direct line to the river. The corridor would have extended across the Missouri and Mississippi River confluence area to St. Charles and then to Jefferson City, the capital of Missouri. Illinois 140, built between the world wars, parallels the earlier 1820s road between Alton and Vandalia, but lies south of the route.

A southwesterly National Road extension was proposed to terminate at St. Louis. As the mercantile linchpin of the middle Mississippi Valley basin, St. Louis functioned as the gateway to the upper Mississippi Valley and the trans-Mississippi west via the Missouri River and the Santa Fe, California, and Oregon Trails. Because of changes in the upriver channel, St. Louis served as the break-in-bulk point for the transfer of goods—upstream and

DOUGLAS K. MEYER

downstream—from large New Orleans–type steamboats to smaller upriver steamboats. But wagon and water routes connected the old French fur-trading posts at St. Louis and St. Charles, weakening Alton's counterpoint argument that it provided the best road-to-river route. The St. Louis terminus route had the advantage of overlaying the earlier 1820s Vandalia-Illinoistown Road. Illinoistown on the Mississippi River was the ferry portal for St. Louis. This route linked the market centers of Vandalia, Greenville, Highland, Troy, Collinsville, and Illinoistown. These communities recognized the advantages of an upgraded federal route traversing their settlements. It would improve their access to St. Louis, downstream plantations, and New Orleans markets for their grain and livestock products.

In 1839, when the National Road reached Vandalia, Springfield in Sangamon County, with its more central location, became the state's third and final capital. After World War I, the original US 40 concrete ribbon followed a southwest path paralleling the earlier 1820s corridor to cross the Mississippi at St. Louis. US 40 was upgraded between Vandalia and St. Louis after World War II, bypassing villages and towns but offering a straighter road. When the federal interstate system connected American cities in the 1960s and '70s, I-70 overlaid this corridor with cloverleaf interchanges that provided access for many bypassed small towns.

Searching for old US 40 as it disappears and reappears along this corridor between Vandalia and St. Louis can be frustrating. Travelers not accustomed to interpreting past roadside landscapes will find that their notions of roadway logic usually fail. While post–World War II US 40 may furnish helpful clues to old 40's path, sometimes travelers become lost as new 40 merges with I-70 and old 40 vanishes in poorly maintained county roads. And current highway maps contribute little to one's understanding of old roadways and roadsides. Clues to roadside history and geography can be found along the corridor if one knows where to look. The key to following this road segment is its relationship to the St. Louis, Vandalia, & Terre Haute Railroad (Penn Central), which, after the Civil War, linked St. Louis on the Mississippi and Terre Haute on the Wabash. The railroad was intended to follow the exact line that the National Road was supposed to take between St. Louis and Vandalia, and would have overlaid the earlier 1820s road connection. The original US 40 runs parallel to the Penn Central tracks. Whether one drives a designated highway or an unnumbered county road, the main-line rails are either just north or south of the roadway.

VANDALIA TO MULBERRY GROVE

Historic-cultural landmarks, quaint places, and abandoned landscapes unravel astride the alternative routes available to the traveler. Our journey projects both pleasing and disturbing roadside images of a changing America. Three alternative routes along this corridor stretch the first nine miles southwestward from Vandalia to Mulberry Grove. The departure point is the historic Greek Revival state capitol built in 1838 at the intersection of Third Street (now Kennedy Boulevard or Bypass 40 and US 51) and Gallatin Street (old 40) in Vandalia.

The quickest route to Mulberry Grove heads north on Kennedy Boulevard (Bypass 40) for one mile to the interstate interchange. Large Italianate- and Queen Anne–style houses line the first two blocks of Third Street, suggesting that this place was once a residential showcase, which is understandable given its proximity to the old state capitol. The next blocks display smaller dwellings, bungalows among them, whose construction was tied to popular national building traditions. The remainder of Third Street represents the replacement of a residential street by one lined by auto-related services. A block before the interchange, Bypass 40 heads west to Mulberry Grove paralleling I-70 on the south, while US 51 crosses the interstate and heads north to Decatur. The space between the three highways displays corporate and entrepreneurial investment strategies, and travelers' consumption preferences: food, fuel, and lodging.

On the interchange's south side a Marathon Pump-N-Pantry and a Shell Self-Serve Station compete as convenient points for weary travelers to pause. On the interchange's north side a boarded-up gas station and a defrocked Holiday Inn stand as reminders that someone in the early 1970s interstate era anticipated that a large investment here would lead to prosperity. The motel sought to capitalize on interstate travel and tourism associated with the old state capitol and Lincoln history. The motel followed the classic two-story L-shaped Holiday Inn form that included a detached reception and dining-room building. A swimming pool occupied the U-shaped landscaped courtyard. Travelers increasingly sought their bedroom-for-a-night one hour away at St. Louis, mandating motel business consolidation and rapid ownership changes in the 1980s, so this structure became the Vandalia Inn in 1984, a Comfort Inn in 1985, and a Markham Inn in 1991. Other roadside businesses in the immediate vicinity are a Long John Silver's, isolated from the Bypass 40 roadside commercial strip on the south side of the interstate, and an adapted Phillips 66 station that now sells chainsaws, lawnmowers, and tillers. In addition, the small Chuckwagon 76 truckstop employs a pseudo-Western motif to attract business, but still cannot compete with the huge truckstops at Effingham, thirty-five miles east at the intersection of I-70 and I-57.

For the hurried traveler I-70 provides 65-MPH views of a narrow strip from the Kaskaskia River bluffs at Vandalia to the bluffs above Hurricane Creek at Mulberry Grove. In nine minutes the traveler traverses a typical Illinois interstate scene. The only vertical dimension on the horizontal landscape for the first three miles is the parallel line of high-voltage electrical poles in the median between I-70 and new US 40 to the north. Uniform corn and soybean fields align the corridor on both sides. Given the low interstate gradient, truckers and auto travelers barely notice their ascent of Hurricane Creek's bluffs, and at interstate speeds Hurricane Creek receives little more than a passing glance. Yet Hurricane Creek played an important role in the early-nineteenth-century development of western Fayette and eastern Bond Counties. In spring, frontiersmen frequently floated their flatboats downstream on Hurricane Creek's high water to the Kaskaskia River. The first state capital (1818), Kaskaskia served also as a market center at the confluence of the Mississippi and Kaskaskia Rivers. More important, it functioned as the regional exit point for downstream trade with New Orleans.

On Vandalia's north side, Bypass 40 provides this town (6,200 people) with two interstate interchanges. Construction on Bypass 40 began before World War II. The bypass was intended to remove the increasing vehicle traffic from Gallatin Street, old US 40. Bypass 40, and the new straight stretch of US 40 (generally one to one-and-one-half miles north of serpentine, old 40) between Vandalia and Mulberry Grove, were finished around 1950. When Vandalia's first I-70 interchange was built, engineers shifted US 51 eastward from Fourth Street to Third Street or Bypass 40 (now Kennedy Boulevard), thus providing both the east-west and south-north highways with direct interstate access. The two-mile bypass strip between the two interchanges is a diverse collection of changing roadside businesses.

Three distinctive strip zones have evolved here. The first segment focuses on the intersection of Bypass 40 and Fourth Street (old US 51). West of Third Street stands a Kentucky Fried Chicken restaurant and a Travelodge Motel with an arch sign similar to Jefferson Memorial Arch in St. Louis. On the northeast corner stand an Amoco gas station, a Hardees, and a Pizza Hut restaurant. Built in 1951, the Robbins Motel on the northwest corner, a classic linear one-story motel, was recently leveled because it could not compete with the newer motels. Its restaurant was noted for its weekend buffets. All that remains of the structure is the reception area and family living quarters, which now is a gift shop. Two other bypass-era motels, Jays Inn and Mabry Motel, remain on the southeast corner. A McDonald's restaurant stands on the southwest corner in proximity to the town's north-end post–World War II high school.

The bypass strip's second section harbors a roadside relic, the Witte Hardware plant, and Vandalia's tie to agribusiness. The Bypass 40 and Illinois 185 (the highway to Hillsboro, county seat of Montgomery County) intersection serves as a farm business hub: Rural King, Purina Mills, and Ford New Holland and John Deere equipment dealers all cluster here. Bunyard's Cafe on the southwest corner is an archetype 1950s roadside restaurant and auto/truckstop. The gas and diesel pumps and repair facilities are gone, but local people still enjoy "Home Cooked Meals! Ho-Made Pies!" The final sector of Bypass 40 links with Vandalia's second 1980s interstate interchange. Represented here is contemporary roadside America: a postmodern-style Days Inn, a Ponderosa Steakhouse, and a Wal-Mart. A new lumberyard stands across from Wal-Mart. Bypass 40 is a 1950s roadside strip reinvigorated with modern roadside commercial activity.

Bypass 40 extends north over the second interchange where US 40 stretches southwest straight as an arrow to the distant horizon. At the interchange, the mileage sign announces that Mulberry Grove is eight miles away. US 40 contrasts sharply with parallel I-70, here only about 100 feet to the south. Two-lane 40 is out of proportion with the limited-access divided interstate. US 40's shoulders have deteriorated and are unsafe. The roadside offers little of interest. The north side opens to large corn and soybean fields, but the countryside is void of houses and barns. This is a cash grain agribusiness landscape of large-scale mechanized farms and dwindling farm populations. Only the riparian woods along Hurricane Creek's tributaries offer visual breaks between stretches of open fields.

Four north-south county roads in eight miles cross US 40 and I-70. From the Hagarstown Road overpass one can view the contrasting rhythms of trunk-line routes: US 40 (1950s–60s) and I-70 (1970s–90s). Each roadway serves a different population; each has a different traffic pace, volume, and

DOUGLAS K. MEYER

The Hagarstown Overpass offers a perspective on two different worlds, one centered here in Bear Grove Township, the other in transit across south Illinois. US 40 is to the left; I-70 is center and right.

character. I-70 is the modern corollary to the railroad, a lifeline along which "eighteen-wheelers" move regional, national, and international commerce across America's midsection. Increased local commuter and agricultural traffic prompted construction of three replacement bridges on US 40. The grade is steeper on US 40 than on I-70, but the curve is still graceful and automobiles can easily climb the Hurricane Creek bluffs. Intersecting in the bluffs with Illinois 140, US 40 bypasses upland Mulberry Grove a half mile to the north.

Back in central Vandalia, one also can elect to follow old US 40 to glimpse a roadside that dates from the era when American federal and state highway networks became interconnected in the 1920s and 1930s. Proceed westward on Gallatin Street past the Madonna of the Trail on the state capitol ground's southwest corner along the original US 40. Today the route is designated as Illinois 140 and links with Alton. Along Gallatin, historic commercial facades dominate the foreground, the Illinois Central Railroad in the valley forms a middleground, and St. James Lutheran Church and the Italianate Fayette County Courthouse a background. The three-block strip of historic main-street facades depicts Vandalia's late-nineteenth-century prosperity underwritten by the arrival of two railroads. Crossing east-west

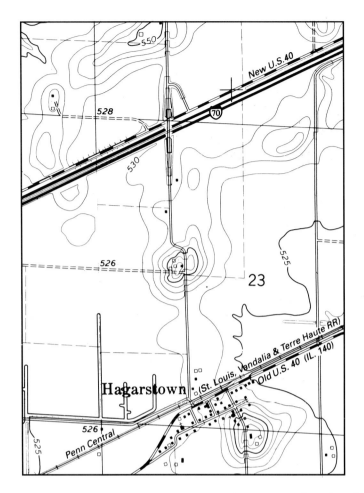

Hagarstown, Illinois

This map from 1974 illustrates parallel routes at Hagarstown, New US 40, Old US 40 (Illinois 140), I-70, the railroad.

(St. Louis, Vandalia, & Terre Haute, later Penn Central) and north-south (Illinois Central) mainline railroads improved the town's accessibility and interconnections to regional and national marketplaces. At Seventh Street, old US 40–Illinois 140 turns south for three blocks before turning west on St. Louis Street. The highway follows a historic 1820s road that connected the state capital with the "Gateway to the West." This road exits Vandalia through a varied residential area of a few large houses, bungalows, and small cottages.

The trip to Mulberry Grove will be almost two miles longer this way than it was following I-70 and new US 40. The narrow, shoulderless road alternately winds through undulating swells and runs straight across nearly level topography. This old road's graceful S-shaped curves invite a leisurely pace that it rewards with pleasing views. About one mile north America speeds by on I-70, where time is money. Adjacent new US 40 is lost in the blur of trucks-passing-trucks on the interstate.

The Bunyard Elevator's steel bins announce Hagarstown, a dilapidated stringtown railroad market center that lies four miles southwest of the old state capitol. Near town, the Penn Central Railroad tracks parallel the highway's north side. Next to the grain elevator is a farmstead with a three-bay English barn, a New England cultural signature. Central Illinois is a culturally diverse area. Hagarstown has a Middle Atlantic cultural namesake in Maryland (spelled Hagerstown). When the St. Louis, Vandalia & Terre Haute Railroad was built after the Civil War, William Henninger, a prominent landowner from Virginia, laid out Hagarstown in 1869. The tiny hamlet's two parallel streets yield a simple grid of unpaved streets that converge after four blocks as the highway exits. With two churches (Baptist and Methodist), a grain elevator, and a post office, the community has fewer functions today than at the turn of the century. Missing are the old grain- and sawmills, commercial structures, and even the gas station. Hagarstown (population about 150) is now a node of rural poverty as the burned-out houses, trashed environment of

DOUGLAS K. MEYER

auto-related debris, derelict cars and trailers, low level of housing maintenance, and the smell of wood-burning stoves all attest. Old 40 beckons.

Within one-half mile a two-story farmhouse stands on a slight rise on the road's south side. The house is two rooms wide and one room deep, a narrow rectangle or hall-and-parlor house. The front facade suggests a large structure, but the narrow, windowless gable ends reveal that it is a small house of four rooms with a rear kitchen appendage or ell. The first floor has six openings or bays: a window, a door, two windows, a door, a window. The second story has four window openings that align over the first-floor windows. Some cultural geographers identify this as a Cumberland House, a Middle Atlantic cultural imprint. Others call it a Pennsylvanian I-house. This simple house is another reminder that America's first national pike was not a segregator, but an integrator along which cultural traditions fused.

Past the Cumberland House, summer travelers may encounter large sorghum fields along the highway. Cash grain farmers have integrated sorghum, grown for livestock feed, into their operations here in recent years. As the roadway curves to descend and cross Raccoon Creek, a tributary of Hurricane Creek, a relic US 40 concrete bridge and small stretch of old highway appear on the south side. Less than a mile west of the old bridge, McInturff Cemetery lies along the road's north side. The family cemetery served the dispersed pioneer homesteads across this Hurricane Creek countryside. No country church stands adjacent; the cemetery alone marks the center of a dispersed settlement established by Upland Southerners. A chainlink fence separates the cemetery from the road, but a wrought-iron entrance gate announces the McInturff family name, and family gravestones stand just beyond. Modern commercial tombstones and an entrance road suggest continued use and expansion. The hilltop position, the uniform, simple gravestone decorations, and Scots-Irish, Irish, and English surnames on the gravestones define this as an Upland South cemetery. A few German names represent a small contingent of nineteenth-century migrants that moved into this border area of Fayette and Bond Counties.

About one and one-half miles west of McInturff Cemetery, the road descends about fifty feet through the Hurricane Creek bluffs. A sign at the bridge announces the creek while tractor-trailers speed past on I-70. Old US 40–Illinois 140 passes under the interstate, intersects with new US 40, and continues to climb the eighty-foot bluffs. Hurricane Creek is about two miles from the center of Mulberry Grove (about 700 people). Settlers from the Upland South settled the Mulberry Grove vicinity in the early 1820s, and a post office was established in 1831. Originally named Houston, the village was laid out in 1841. The post office's name was changed in acknowledgment of the large number of mulberry trees nearby.

This place, like Hagarstown, manifests economic malaise and rural poverty—abandoned fields and untended woodlots, abandoned houses and town lots, abandoned school and commercial buildings, and low levels of maintenance. Small cottages and houses align old US 40–Illinois 140 that traverses the town along a S-shaped route. The houses include examples of folk and vernacular building traditions from the late nineteenth and early twentieth centuries.

The First National Bank (1929) stands where the intersection of Maple (old US 40–Illinois 140) and Wall Streets (Illinois 140) forms the community's center. Commercial activity developed primarily on Maple Street's west side. Whether it was the early 1820s road that connected Vandalia and Alton (Illinois 140), the postbellum railroad, old-new US 40, or I-70, Mulberry Grove's economy has been muted and unsustainable. The modest decorative trim on the remaining business facades and the dominance of one-story buildings suggest minimal economic prosperity during the railroad's heyday. During the interwar and post–World War II eras, when increasing vehicle traffic brought merchants more customers, the business facades were upgraded. Today, the main street is a place of abandoned lots and derelict building shells; only four viable businesses remain. Another Bunyard Elevator with steel grain bins stands along the main-line Penn Central tracks, but the older railroad station and freight buildings are gone. Another quarter mile south at the Keyesport Road (Maple Street) and Bypass 40 intersection stands Feher's Restaurant and Kerr McGee Gas Station, positioned to serve Mulberry Grove and the traffic on the three highways. I-70 lies another quarter mile south.

A SIDE TRIP ON ILLINOIS 140: MULBERRY GROVE TO ALTON

Before continuing on US 40 to St. Louis, we offer a side trip to Alton via Illinois 140 that overlays the old 1820s Vandalia-to-Alton road. The National Road extension that Alton boosters proposed as a connection between Vandalia and Alton would have passed two miles north of Mulberry Grove and almost three and one-half miles north of Greenville. Greenville, the Bond County seat, lies nine miles southwest of Mulberry Grove. Heading west

DOUGLAS K. MEYER

into the country on Wall Street, the road passes housing wedged between Illinois 140 and the Penn Central tracks. At the village's edge on the road's north side stands the 1950s school complex. Ahead, a broad horizontal panorama of corn and soybean fields seems to straddle the highway.

For about four and one-half miles, Illinois 140 runs southwest true as an arrow, north of and paralleling the Penn Central tracks. A right-angle turn south for a half mile and then another right-angle jog west breaks the straight highway's monotony, a reminder that roads here often follow Township and Range survey lines, not the most direct route or the topography's most gentle gradients. Illinois 140 ascends a railroad overpass of the Burlington Northern tracks. To the south, Smithboro, a railroad hamlet, stands at the Penn Central and Burlington Northern track crossing. One-half mile further, the road ascends a hill passing an old gravel pit on the south side. Hilltops are rare vantage points on this countryside and this one offers the amenity of prospect. Golf-course designers seek hills in flat country, and the Greenville Country Club course lies here in rolling topography on Illinois 140's north side. The wealthy often seek housing sites near golf courses. Across the road from the country club, a recent upscale exurban housing development with large ranch houses, immaculate lawns, and open landscaping offers residents attractive sunset and town vistas. Near Bypass 140 on Greenville's north end stand new secondary and junior high schools and a hospital. Old Illinois 140 becomes Beaumont Avenue, a showcase of large homes, which leads to the courthouse square. Greenville will be discussed below with US 40.

Greenville to Hamel

Leaving the Greenville bypass, Illinois 140 descends creek bluffs about 100 feet to a broad floodplain where it intersects with Illinois 127. In the past, 127 continued northwest, but the Illinois Department of Transportation straightened the road across the floodplain. The two highways coalesce for one mile and ascend the bluffs before 127 heads north eighteen miles to Hillsboro, the Montgomery County seat. For another serpentine mile the road crosses a rolling countryside dominated by woodlands. In the next two miles corn and soybean fields predominate with considerable woodlands in the flat upland divide that separates the East Fork of Shoal Creek and Shoal Creek. The road traverses Shoal Creek valley farmland. A large auto salvage yard and an abandoned gas station refitted into living quarters stand at the T-intersection of

East of Alhambra, Illinois

Canopied corn. The most prominent buildings on the distant farmstead are a steel-walled machine shed and steel-walled grain bins. Farmers erect few new wooden buildings today, because they are more expensive and less practical.

Illinois 140 and the Pocahontas Road. One mile east of Old Ripley the Pocahontas Road runs south four miles to I-70 and old US 40 at Pocahontas.

Near Bond County's western margin, (Old) Ripley was platted in 1818, five years after Upland Southerners began to settle the Shoal Creek vicinity. Tiny Ripley (population about 150), a Sorento Road stringtown, never prospered. It lies eight and one-half miles west of the Greenville courthouse square and eight miles south of Sorento, coal town and Burlington Northern and Norfolk & Western (also known as the Clover Leaf Railroad) railroad crossing. The only urban functions in Ripley are ephemeral, a Church of Christ building and the volunteer fire department, but kitchen gardens thrive. The town is surrounded by large sorghum fields.

West of Ripley on Illinois 140, large sorghum fields are interspersed with corn, soybeans, and winter wheat. The road runs west from Ripley nine miles to Alhambra in Madison County. The road at the county line realigns east-west on the Township and Range section lines. Without a curve, and

DOUGLAS K. MEYER

Middlewestern geometry
in which the driveway leads
exactly to the front door.
The corn rows (right) run
north-south; the soybean
rows (left) run east-west; all
buildings are set to the cardinal compass. The Town-
ship and Range survey is
rarely invisible. Only the
electric utility dares the
expediency of tangents.

with minor undulations, the highway reaches a high point of almost 600 feet above sea level two miles east of Alhambra. Illinois 160 from Highland on old US 40 ends at 140 three miles east of Alhambra. At the intersection, El Patio Restaurant (formerly Flicks) has horseshoe pits and an impressive new volleyball court in the back; it is a popular watering hole for local folks who drive pickups, four-wheel-drive vehicles, and motorcycles.

Before statehood, Upland Southerners settled the Silver Creek community near Alhambra and Hamel, but German immigrants later outnumbered the Southerners. Alhambra (population about 700) was platted in 1849, but grew slowly, even after the Clover Leaf Railroad arrived in 1883 ("Nickel Plate," Norfolk & Western). One-half mile north, the Illinois Central and Norfolk & Western railroads intersect and parallel each other. Alhambra is a quintessential stringtown with a two-block-wide street grid that stretches almost one and one-quarter miles along Main Street–Illinois 140. Box-shaped, four-room, brick German cottages with neat lawns mingle with other common house forms. The east end includes a newer tract covered with ranch houses built between the 1960s and 1980s. Some residents are retired German farmers who have sold their farms and moved into Alhambra. Others are commuters who take advantage of the village's location six miles east of I-55, well within the East St. Louis and St. Louis metropolitan laborshed. A modern nursing home stands along Main Street, and a newer one is situated in the village's southwest corner. The business district includes a grocery store, volunteer fire department, post office, the Galaxy Restaurant—an upscale eating establishment in the refitted First State Bank—Aviston Lumber Company, and the FS Grain Elevator. Locals attribute the high level of home and yard maintenance—for all housing, new or old—to a Germanic sense of community identity and responsibility.

Railroad tracks interlace across southwest Illinois as transcontinental routes focus at the Mississippi crossing and port at East St. Louis. Every few miles, the highway intersects another track or railroad settlement. Between

Illinois 140 and Illinois 160 intersection, Madison County, Illinois

A tile-walled tavern with a dance floor inside and a volleyball court and horseshoe pits out back; this place becomes the community center on weekends. The sign atop the roof reads "Illinois, Land of Lincoln, El Patio, US 40, Jewett, Il." Of course, Jewett lies about 75 miles east of here.

DOUGLAS K. MEYER

Alhambra and Hamel, Illinois 140 continues to follow the east-west section lines. Hamel (population about 550 people) originated as a tiny Illinois Terminal railroad hamlet in 1895. Three miles north, in the village of Worden, rail lines (Missouri Pacific, Norfolk & Western, Chicago & North Western, and Illinois Terminal) intersect and diverge as they converge on the East St. Louis railyards and the Mississippi River bridges. Although Hamel stood at the intersection of 140 and US 66 (now Illinois 157), the hamlet grew slowly during the 1920s and post–World War II era. Today, Hamel is only one-quarter mile west of an I-55 interchange where a John Deere equipment dealer, a motel, and a gas station now cluster. The

Hamel, Illinois

The Hamel grain elevator exhibits two generations. The tile weigh building and the tin-covered, gable-roofed elevator sufficed until production increases after World War II prompted construction of new storage bins.

junction of Illinois 157 (old US 66) and 140 is a typical highway intersection made secondary by the adjacent interstate, and the cluster of auto-related businesses here reflects the recycling strategies that people employ in such bypassed places. The auto/truckstop and restaurant complex has been refitted as the Institute for Behavioral Insight. The housing near the crossroads intersection is a mix of interwar and post–World War II era housing types. Contemporary ranch houses in suburban-like subdivisions, occupied by I-55 commuters, now fill Hamel's northwest and southeast quadrants. Hamel's recent growth is related to its affordable housing in a country setting.

Hamel to Alton's Fringe

Carpenter, a linear Norfolk & Western Railroad hamlet, stands three miles west of Hamel on Illinois 140. The community formed in 1877 and for six months was known as "Nobody's Switch." The "whistle-stop" community offered traditional late-nineteenth-century goods and services: a general store, grain dealer, blacksmith, wagon shop, harness and saddle shop, shoemaker, and hotel. Today, tiny Carpenter (about 150 people) has an abandoned gas station, a tavern, and an American Legion Hall. Commercial activity focuses at the Hamel Coop Grain Company. The Zion Lutheran Church links to postbellum German farm settlers. A quarter mile west, 140 crosses the Norfolk & Western and Missouri Pacific Railroad tracks. A German cottage with double front doors stands along the road's north side.

North of Edwardsville, Illinois

Greg Reinhardt (*left*) and Kyle Brase discuss baling wheat straw that they will use for livestock bedding. The John Deere baler compresses the straw into small rectangular bales that it pushes into the pipe "hay basket" wagon. The wagon empties by simply tripping the catches on the rear gate; unloading is by gravity. Labor-saving innovations such as this allow one or two people to accomplish the same work that would have required a crew of six in the not-too-distant past.

East of Meadowbrook, Illinois

Shade trees, a slat-sided corn crib, and a livestock barn are all that remain of an old farmstead near the intersection of Illinois 140 and 159.

DOUGLAS K. MEYER

Suburban night spot in
neon.

Between Carpenter and the Illinois 140–Illinois 159 intersection (four
miles distant) the highway crosses the Cahokia Creek valley on the way to
Alton. Open farmland blends into new exurban ranch housing. West of 159,
a grocery store and a Phillips 66 dairy store with video rentals announce unincorporated Meadowbrook (about 1,100 people), a blue-collar bedroom
community. This place is an accretion of interwar-era streets with trailers,
small cottages and bungalows, and newer 1960s and 1970s streets lined with
ranch houses and low-income apartments. Landscape and housing maintenance is minimal, and abandoned vehicles and smoke from wood-burning
stoves produce a distinctive ambiance.

About a mile west of informal, unplanned Meadowbrook stands Bethalto
(pop. 10,000), a traditional middlewestern railroad town that has acquired

1960s through 1980s suburban ranch-house and two-story apartment developments and a commercial strip. The community originated in 1854 on the Indianapolis & St. Louis Railroad (the Penn Central track has been removed). The town was originally called Bethel, but another market center with the same name in Illinois meant a name change; *Beth-alto* is a fusion of *Bethel* and *Alton*. A German proprietor established a grain mill and elevator here in the late nineteenth century for local wheat-growing farmers, many of whom were Germans. Between Bethalto and Cottage Hills, a suburban, commuter residential development a mile west, Illinois 140 unravels into a four-lane, national franchise commercial strip. West of Gordon F. Moore Park on the West Fork of Wood River, Illinois 140, 111, and 3 join, and at Alton's eastern suburban fringe Bypass Illinois 111–Illinois 3 split to head north around Alton.

Alton

Rufus Easton, a Litchfield, Connecticut Yankee, arrived in St. Louis in 1804, appointed by President Jefferson to serve as judge for the Louisiana Territory. Easton served as the first St. Louis postmaster in 1808, and the Missouri attorney general from 1821 to 1826. He laid out Alton (population about 33,000 in 1990), named for his son, in 1817, a year before statehood. Although Easton established a ferry across the Mississippi so that his town might compete with St. Louis, his Missouri rival had the advantage of an early start, already a steamboat port and in hegemonic control of upstream fur and lead trade. St. Louis embraced a pivotal location where upper river commerce stopped and lower river trade commenced. Not only the "Gateway to the West" via the Missouri River and westward wagon trails, the entrepôt emerged as the "Gateway to the Back Country of the North" by way of the upper Mississippi River. By 1840, Alton had lost the regional commercial rivalry to St. Louis.

Although Alton would operate in the mercantile shadow of St. Louis, city merchants maintained vigorous upstream commercial activity and supplied arriving immigrants, whose nearby settlements would stimulate an expanding economy in the late 1820s and 1830s. Manufactured goods arrived at Alton's river landing from the Ohio Valley and eastern seaboard. During the 1830s, upstream commerce with a rapidly developing farming hinterland transformed Alton. John M. Peck, a gazetteer writer, observed: "Seven or eight steamboats are owned here in whole or in part, and arrivals

DOUGLAS K. MEYER

and departures occur every day and at all times in the day during the season. Alton now commands a large proportion of the trade of the Upper Mississippi and Illinois rivers, and of the interior country for one hundred miles."[1] Towns upstream—Beardstown, Peoria, Pekin, and Galena—were also dependent upon Alton's wharf for goods. Alton could not compete with St. Louis for access to western lands, but it emerged as a regional center for commercial, distributive, agricultural processing, pork packing, and manufacturing activities in frontier western Illinois.

Early on, "Bluff City" was comprised of Lower and Upper Alton. Upper Alton was founded by Joseph Meacham, a Vermonter, about the same time as the river port. As it enters old Upper Alton, Illinois 140 becomes College Avenue, and a sign announces Southern Illinois University School of Dental Medicine. Baptist minister John M. Peck, noted Illinois gazetteer writer, founded historic Shurtleff College as Rock Spring Seminary in 1827. The seminary relocated to a 362-acre Upper Alton site in 1832 and became Alton Seminary. In 1835, owing to a substantial donation of $10,000 from Boston medical doctor Benjamin Shurtleff, the college name was changed to honor the benefactor. The original administration and classroom building, Greek Revival–styled Academic Hall (Loomis Hall), still stands on College Avenue's south side. The college closed in 1957. Across the street is Western Military Academy, founded in 1879, on Seminary Street just off College Avenue. English Tudor Revival—with battlements—characterizes the main buildings built to replace those destroyed by fire in 1903. The military academy persisted until 1971.

The old college and academy neighborhood is now the Upper Alton Historic District. Although the number of houses associated with the two campuses is not large, they are a distinctive grouping of large Classical Revival– and Queen Anne–styled houses on spacious lots. The two campuses, with their assemblage of faculty and administrators' houses, preserve an impression of a late-nineteenth-century college town that formed Upper Alton's core, sharply contrasting with the workers' housing and wharf community in Lower Alton.

Three blocks west on College Avenue, Illinois 140 turns left on Washington Avenue toward Lower Alton and the Mississippi River. The Upper Alton business district at the intersection, though altered, remains viable—a collection of gas stations, fast-food restaurants, and a strip mall. The dwellings here are a mix of late-nineteenth- and early-twentieth-century middle-class two-story houses, small cottages, and bungalows. Lower levels of property maintenance here suggest social down-filtering. Washington Avenue follows the Mississippi bluff. From the 1950s through the 1970s, this was a popular place for developers to build apartment buildings with vistas of the industrial Mississippi River Valley. The road descends about 150 feet to Broadway Avenue.

A view of a late-nineteenth-century industrial Lower Alton unfolds: a large industrial glassworks area (Illinois Glass Company and Owen-Illinois), the Penn Central; Gulf, Mobile, and Ohio; and Illinois Terminal railroad tracks, and the Illinois Terminal railyard. This two-mile-long industrial and transportation complex wedged between Broadway Avenue and the river levee epitomizes American deindustrialization. Derelict structures predominate. A new, architecturally impressive, Lewis and Clark Bridge has replaced the old Lewis and Clark Bridge, whose design speaks of a previous aesthetic and engineering technology. To accommodate the new structure,

Alton, Illinois

Old Alton's new Lewis and Clark Bridge rises over the tarpaper roofs like the masts and rigging on a silver sailing ship.

DOUGLAS K. MEYER

an upgraded four-lane highway (Illinois 143) approach has been built between the levee and the old railyard. Interwar and post–World War II structures comprise the Broadway Avenue business strip. Many are abandoned. An auto-parts store, restaurants, a bank, and motel are still functioning. Few national franchises can be found here. The two most popular institutions are local—Fast Eddies, a bar and restaurant with live music, and Mike's Wedge Tavern, named for its flat-iron lot—at the intersection of Fourth and Pearl Streets. To sample the ambiance of a "real" community, take a brief side trip up Pearl Street toward the limestone bluffs.

Alton, Illinois

Competing priorities confuse the old Lincoln-Douglas Debate site. Enough said.

Philip Yakel established Alton's first brewery in 1837 in a bluff ravine here. The abandoned Union–Bluff City Brewery, an intact thirteen-building complex, prospered by serving the rapidly growing immigrant population and through access to upstream and downstream markets. In 1882, another German, William Netzhammer, bought the establishment and renamed it the Bluff City Brewery. Netzhammer had served as a master brewer in two other river towns, Louisville and St. Louis. Over the next 115 years, two families operated the brewery, passing it from one generation to the next. Today, its maximum production capacity of 20,000 barrels a year classifies it as a "boutique" brewery. In 1863, George Yakel built the 2½-story , eight-room, central-passageway brick house, subsequently occupied by the Netzhammer family. Its arched window hoods and cornice blend Classical Revival– and Italianate-styling. Brewery workers lived on the adjacent streets in small, brick Germanic cottages. The underground beer cellars extend under adjacent Alton National Cemetery.

When the main road linking Vandalia to the Mississippi ended in East St. Louis, Alton was bypassed and, consequently, much of the nineteenth-century city remains intact. Travelers should explore the town's two superb historic districts: Middletown and Christian Hill. Middletown Historic District is comprised of two neighborhoods. One is Middletown, a part of the original town along Henry Street that has a compass-orientated street grid. The extant middle- and upper-middle-class housing is a collection of house forms and styles popular during the eight decades between the 1830s and World

Alton, Illinois

When the automobile gained popularity during the 1920s, old downtown railroad hotels struggled to retain their clientele. Some added parking lots and changed their names to Motor Hotel. Casino patrons now patronize the Stratford.

War I. The second Middletown district is Hunterstown, an annexed area abutting Middletown to the east. Here, on a street grid cut through bluffs that parallel the Mississippi River and the industrial valley below, stands a working- or artisan-class neighborhood reminiscent of Germantown in Columbus, Ohio (chapter 3). The homes are small, one- and one-and-one-half-story brick cottages, two rooms deep, on small lots. Many were built by or for German immigrants who came to Alton before the Civil War. Although plain, several have subtle Greek Revival and Gothic trim detail. Both neighborhoods share several common landscape details: deviations in street grid imposed by topography, pleasant tree-lined streets, limestone house foundations and retaining walls.

Christian Hill Historic District lies on the steep slopes and bluff tops west of the Third Street business district. Alton's steepest street is Seventh between State and Belle Streets—perilous if dry, hara-kiri if wet. This is a middle- and upper-middle-class neighborhood with street names like Summit and Prospect that suggest both acquired social status and the potential vistas that this site offered its residents. Most early-nineteenth-century houses were built of brick in Federal and Greek Revival styles, and the neighborhood retains one of the most significant antebellum landscape ensembles of architectural, historical, and cultural character in Illinois. After the Civil War, wood was the building material of choice for the Italianate, Second Empire, and Queen Anne–style homes. Brick streets, yard and street trees, limestone retaining walls, and wrought iron fences are all still intact. Christian Hill remains a fashionable neighborhood and a stronghold of historic preservation.

The Mississippi crossing, as seen from the Summit Street prospect, is a reminder that Alton aspired to be the National Road's exit point from Illinois. Today, highway and rail traffic focuses south at East St. Louis, one of America's most blighted landscapes. Perhaps being bypassed has more merit in the long term than Alton's early-nineteenth-century boosters—many residents of Christian Hill and Middletown, no doubt—believed at the time. Below the city, diesel-powered tows work the river. Old Lock and Dam Number 26, once a bottleneck for tows and their barges, has been removed. A larger lock and dam now manage traffic and water levels downstream. The old Lewis and Clark Toll Bridge (US 67) is to be removed now that the new suspension bridge is complete. The bridge and connecting US 67–Missouri 367 provide Altonites quick linkage to the I-270 Beltway and the access it affords to employment, shopping, restaurants, entertainment, and cheap gasoline across the river in St. Louis.

At Broadway Avenue and Market Street stands a historic marker commemorating the Lincoln-Douglas Debate. Evidence of change and continuity surround the site: the steamboat riverfront has vanished; the Third Street business district is infected with abandoned buildings; antique and craft shops, restaurants, and drinking establishments at Broadway Avenue and Market Street suggest a different clientele and renewed prosperity. The railroad tracks are rapidly disappearing into a series of parking lots, although rails into the Con Agra Elevator and Mill remain in service. The

Alton, Illinois

Con Agra elevators, the Mississippi River, and a visiting Camaro.

Alton, Illinois

Alton's steamboat gambling casino (*above*) shares the riverfront with Con Agra and a windrow of driftwood deposited by the retreating 1993 flood. Barges with party tents, security cameras, and valet parking are all constituents of this new amphibious landscape. Tourists, drawn by riverboat gambling, prompt investors to refit Old Alton's old buildings into shops and apartments (*right*); but the river view still belongs to Con Agra.

DOUGLAS K. MEYER

newly painted Con Agra Elevator sports a huge American flag and welcome sign; a sign on the elevator superimposing the 1973 and 1993 Mississippi flood high-water marks serves as a reminder of this site's hazardous context. In the grain elevator's shadow, below the painted flag, and a block from the historical debate site, the Alton Belle Casino lies docked awaiting patrons seeking to "strike it rich." Illinois's gambling laws are more liberal than those of Missouri, and Alton's "bridge-end" site is ideal for a "parasitic" gambling operation within easy reach of St. Louis wallets and purses. Soon, the Mississippi River downstream will be arrayed with casino "steamboats" as Missouri reconsiders and plays catch-up with Illinois and Iowa, where politicians seek to erase state budget deficits through legalized gambling. Already old Alton is being changed by the increased traffic spawned by its casino. Old buildings in the grain elevator's shadow are being refitted as fancy antique shops, boutiques, and pricey restaurants, and some structures are being torn down for parking space.

This marks the end of the side trip from Mulberry Grove to Alton, the alternative Mississippi River crossing point proposed for the National Road. The route will now return to Mulberry Grove and trace the US 40 route to East St. Louis.

MULBERRY GROVE TO GREENVILLE

At Mulberry Grove, near Vandalia, US 40 exits town on the southwest side past the village cemetery, an abandoned Shell station, and a derelict collection of 1920s roadside cottages. Someone built the original nine units of fake logs in an apparent attempt to invoke a frontier motif, popular in roadside service buildings during that era. The place was refurbished after World War II but failed when I-70 opened. Royal Lake Resort (fewer than 150 people) is a 1960s African-American rural retreat one mile southwest of Mulberry Grove between US 40 and I-70. Comprised of two units, Royal Lake No. 1 and No. 2, developers intended to create a rural, recreational resort with a fishing lake and large lots for African-Americans from middlewestern cities. The streets remain unpaved, many lots remain empty. Housing is a mix of trailers, prefab and ranch houses, interspersed with abandoned homes, trailers, and vehicles. Mostly retired couples, they support three churches; Bibleway House of Prayer Church, Prayer Temple United Holy Church, and First Missionary Baptist Church.

In the seven miles between Mulberry Grove and Greenville, US 40 runs parallel to the old Penn Central Railroad tracks on the north, and I-70 a half mile to one mile south. Farmland either side of the highway is nearly flat. Farmers here often plant winter wheat as a double crop in some corn and soybean fields. Smithboro, four miles southwest of Mulberry Grove, is a tiny railroad hamlet of less than 200. The abandoned school is the result of small school district consolidations. Presidents' names identify north-south streets, numbers the east-west streets. A viable business district never developed, and only Lee's Party Center, the volunteer fire department, and the post office remain. Small cottages, trailers, and a few ranch houses predominate; two-story houses are scarce. US 40 crosses the Burlington Northern tracks on an overpass providing a bird's-eye view into Smithboro. Greenville lies three miles distant.

In southeast Greenville, Carlisle Syntec Systems and Peterson Spring occupy a new industrial park that stands in the wedge created by the curving railroad tracks, US 40 (here running northeast-southwest), and Illinois 127 (running north-south). Commercial road-oriented businesses cluster around the US 40–Illinois 127 intersection, serving both the local community and freeway-borne customers, including franchise restaurants, gas stations, and motels, an abandoned roadside diner (now antique dealer), and the 2 Acres Restaurant and Motel, an old US 40 room-for-the-night. A refitted gas station sells bait and camping supplies. Its customers are no doubt headed for Lake Carlyle, a reservoir on the Kaskaskia River and the largest lake in Illinois, eight to twenty miles south on 127, depending upon point of access.

Greenville (about 5,000 residents) is two miles northwest on Illinois 127, and is a quintessential middlewestern courthouse and college town. Founded in 1821 on the East Fork (Shoal Creek) bluffs, Greenville is the approximate geographical center of Bond County. Illinois 127 leads two miles to the courthouse, crossing the old Penn Central tracks and passing the railyard that served an old industrial area and grain elevators. The railroad depot is now a real estate office. The Helvetia Milk Condensing Company (Pet Milk), the oldest milk condensing plant in America, opened here in 1899. The 1909 Model Glove Company made cotton gloves, and the Coates Steel Products Company, circa 1924, made steel grinding balls. The Pet Milk Company plant has been rehabilitated by Mallinckrodt, a St. Louis chemical company; the glove factory serves as Greenville College's theater and physical plant; the steel plant is derelict. Other manufacturing operations producing spark plugs, and air conditioning and refrigeration equipment

have come and gone. These plant closings represent the end of a deindustrialization cycle—
closed plants, lost jobs, population decline, stagnation—evident in many middlewestern small
towns. The oldest industry still in operation is
DeMoulin Brothers, founded in 1892 to manufacture lodge memorabilia and costumes. Today
this firm makes band uniforms and academic
apparel.

Central to the square stands the Italianate
courthouse, completed in 1884 as a replacement
for the previous temple of justice that burned.
Streets intersect the courthouse square's corners
at right angles, a pattern also found in Shelbyville, Tennessee, and many other middlewestern
county seat towns. The commercial buildings'

one- and two-story facades suggest that Greenville enjoyed post–Civil War
prosperity. Main Street parallels the square's south side; College Street the
north. Baptists founded Almira College, a school for women, in 1855, two
blocks east of the square. In 1892, the Central Illinois Conference of the
Free Methodist Church purchased and incorporated the institution as co-
educational Greenville College. Hogue Hall, or "Old Main," dates from
1855. Cottages and houses near the square and campus belonged to business and factory owners, professionals, artisans, faculty, and administrators.
Although most dwellings are nineteenth- and early-twentieth-century vernacular forms, many are small-town imitations of nationally popular architectural styles.

Greenville, Illinois

A small town's soul often
appears in its shop win-
dows. Here we learn about
a fund-raising dance and
chicken dinner to raise
money for someone's
medical expenses; a Pink
Flamingo Days festival to
cement community rela-
tions; and a white t-shirt
with no commercial mes-
sage on the front. Also,
they're open and very
possibly friendly folk.

GREENVILLE TO POCAHONTAS

From the US 40–Illinois 127 intersection, it is four miles to Greenville's
second I-70 interchange. At the intersection of US 40 and Fourth Street
stands Belfry Antiques, a readapted post–World War II linear motel
building, and an abandoned bowling alley. Across the highway is the largest
building project ever seen in Greenville. The U.S. Department of Justice has
constructed a large, postmodern-styled, federal correctional institution between US 40 and I-70.

From the US 40–I-70 interchange, Pocahontas (about 800 people) lies five miles southwest. The interstate here runs less than 100 feet south of US 40; the railroad tracks parallel about one-third mile beyond the freeway. A few hog farms align the road's north side, which winds through Shoal Creek's wooded western bluffs to Bypass 40, which intersects with I-70 at an interchange northwest of Pocahontas. Old 40 follows State and National Streets through town. Small cottages, trailers, small ranch houses, abandoned dwellings, and vacant lots fill in the street grid. Settlement in the Shoal Creek region predates statehood. Pocahontas was originally called Amity and was platted as a three-block-wide grid paralleling State Street, the old post road. Although National Street forms the square's south side, the National Road never reached Pocahontas. When the St. Louis, Vandalia & Terre Haute Railroad arrived in the late 1860s, the grid was extended south one-third mile to the tracks. Huge bituminous coal deposits underlie much of Illinois and western Indiana, and the beds form a basin, dipping deep below the surface near the state's center. Here, near the basin's rim, the beds are close enough to the surface to be mined. A coal mine operated in Pocahontas between 1906 and the 1930s; to house the miners, the company built cottages on new streets in the Shoal Creek bluffs between the tracks and the coal mine. A relic brick smokestack and mine waste heaps are the only clues to an industry that once shipped coal via the Penn Central Railroad to St. Louis markets.

The village watertower stands in the rectangular town square surrounded by the volunteer fire department, post office, taverns, an abandoned gas station and other abandoned buildings, a funeral home, grocery store, laundromat, churches, and several antique stores. The newest building on the square is the American Bank of Bond County. Nothing here suggests that Pocahontas ever knew prosperity. Antique shops in recycled buildings are the most common businesses. Roadside businesses are all on the north side, near the I-70 interchange, and include an abandoned Nickerson Farms Restaurant and gas station. Three classic US 40–era motels with Amerindian-theme names still operate here: the Tahoe Motel has a tepee logo, the Powhatan Motel and restaurant has an Indian chief sign, and the Wikiup Motel has an Indian mask on its sign.

POCAHONTAS TO HIGHLAND

West on State Street from the square, old US 40 heads west passing a large park. The old highway becomes 470N Bond County Road and runs within 100 feet of I-70. Driving west on old US 40 is hypnotic; the interstate traffic

DOUGLAS K. MEYER

seems to converge upon the traveler at 65 miles per hour, and the corridor of high voltage power and telephone poles passes in a blur. Bauman Road is the first county road to cross I-70, three and one-half miles southwest of Pocahontas, where it forms the county line between Bond and Madison Counties. Old US 40 becomes Schuster Road in Madison County. Both road names are a clue to the region's nineteenth-century German settlers. Black-and-white Holstein cows and blue Harvestore silos indicate that this flat farming country lies within the St. Louis milkshed. German-heritage farmers operate these dairy farms. Some dairy barns are nineteenth-century gambrel-roofed or transverse crib structures, others are new "pole" barns. The number, height, and diameter of silos offer cues to herd size and farm acreage. And, unlike the cash grain farms near Vandalia, farmers here diversify their crops; each farm has land in pasture, corn, soybeans, winter wheat, and hay (clover). The Jack L. Schuster dairy farm on the south has registered Holsteins and a large, new ranch-style house. A new exurban ranch subdivision with large lots and minimal landscaping lies near the intersection of old-new Route 40, Illinois 143, and I-70 at the Highland-Pierron interchange; the location suggests that residents include St. Louis commuters.

Highland lies four miles southwest of the interchange via US 40 and Illinois 143. One-half mile from the interchange, just north of post–World War II US 40, lies an original US 40 concrete road remnant and bridge. The twenty-foot-wide concrete strip is exposed for about one-half mile before it disappears into a field only to reappear for another mile. Where the abandoned road crosses US 40, another original bridge is hidden in the vegetation. The original highway ends at the Church of Christ, a metal rectangular box on US 40's south side. At the Country Club Road–US 40 intersection cluster the nine-hole Highland Country Club golf course, the Highland-Winet Airport—where gliders soar on weekends—and an abandoned, concrete-block, eight-room motel. Where US 40, Illinois 143, and Illinois 160 intersect, Bypass 40–Illinois 143 heads west around Highland's north side. Illinois 160 is old US 40 and becomes Broadway Avenue in town. (If these road numbers and name changes and crossings seem complex in text form, they are no less so on the ground. This is one of the more difficult sections of US 40 to follow.) The Village Motel, now converted to apartments, stands at the eastern approach to Highland (population about 7,500).

Highland's grain elevator punctuates the skyline ahead and a small, red-painted-brick cottage with decorative German-Swiss symbols hints of

Highland's heritage. The ranch homes in the east-end subdivision, older dwellings, and brick Germanic cottages along the town's streets are all well maintained. In town, US 40–Broadway Avenue enters a three-square-block cluster of institutions that announce Highland's ethnic constituency: German Catholic St. Joseph's Hospital, St. Paul's Church (1951), St. Paul's Hall and School (1940), and new St. Paul's School (1956). A new city hall and fire station at Broadway and Zschokkes Streets incorporate "Swiss" motifs. Banners with American and Swiss flags stand in welcome at the Broadway Avenue approach to a classic town square with a gazebo or bandstand, a 1937 fountain (dedicated on the first day of the town's centennial celebration), benches, and a brightly colored 1981 mural. The mural is a special community project every visitor should see. School children created images of important places and events in ceramic tiles that were then mounted together in panels. The center features a tile map of the town square showing individual business buildings.

Dr. Kaspar Koepfli, and his nephew, Joseph Suppiger, from Sursee in the Swiss Canton of Luzerne, purchased about 1,000 acres on the Looking Glass Prairie here for a German-speaking "New Switzerland" colony. German-Swiss and German immigrants began to settle the divide between Silver and Sugar Creeks in Madison County's southeastern townships in the 1830s. This area would become the early "mother area" of Swiss settlements elsewhere in America's midsection. Surveyors laid out Highland as a forty-five-block grid on the Sugar Creek bluffs in 1836. One- and two-story business buildings surround the square, some with "Swiss" motifs added to their facades since 1960. Although the Ben Franklin store failed, despite its Swiss facade, many town merchants still find this downtown square a viable business location. Shoppers can purchase appliances, shoes, bakery goods, tires, jewelry, and furniture (in a beautiful Art Deco building on the square's southwestern corner). Several individuals have converted buildings into craft, antique, and specialty shops, including the Italianate Helvetia Trading Company, now restored and the square's focal point. The craft and antique shops attract shoppers arriving by tour bus and automobile from St. Louis, less than an hour away, repeating a conversion-and-reuse theme found all along the National Road–US 40 (see especially chapter 1). The Swiss settlement's pathfinders are buried in Highland Cemetery on the Silver Creek bluffs west of Illinois 143 and north of Bypass 40.

When the St. Louis, Vandalia & Terre Haute Railroad (Penn Central) arrived, the street grid was extended north to parallel the tracks. The Wicks Organ Company (founded in 1906), and Wicks Aircraft Supply Company, Jefferson Smurfit Corporation, and the Oberbeck Feed Company grain elevator parallel the tracks. Helvetia Milk Condensing Company, producers of evaporated milk, was established here in 1885, and expanded into a new plant along the railroad tracks in 1904. In 1923 the company was reorganized as the Pet Milk Company and moved to St. Louis. The Schott Brewery, once the town's icon, stands abandoned at 13th and Mulberry Streets southwest of the square. Built in the late 1880s with a capacity of 75,000 barrels annually, the large brick brewery's beer vaults extended behind it under the hill. The original German brewery was built in 1843.

HIGHLAND TO TROY

If US 40 travelers find town squares and antique shops overly "quaint," and yearn for modern, roadside America, it awaits on Bypass 40–Illinois 143 around Highland. Here, predictable consumer-oriented America unfolds, ensconced not in "Swiss" motifs but in popular, banal, lowest-bidder-constructed facades. Illinois 143 links Bypass 40 to I-70 four miles away. At the 143–Bypass 40 intersection the roadside is awash with auto dealers, chain food- and drugstores, and garish franchise restaurants purveying Mexican food, steaks, pizza, hamburgers, and submarine sandwiches. Drive-in savings and loans, banks, and a Wal-Mart array 143 for about one-half mile. Two miles west on US 40, the Midway Motel stands abandoned at the roadside.

In the next seven miles between Illinois 143 and Illinois 4, US 40 parallels the north side of the railroad tracks and bypasses St. Jacob. An alternate route west leaves Highland's square via Broadway Avenue, passing Michael's Swiss Inn and Restaurant as old US 40 intersects with new Route 40 one and one-half miles west. Before crossing the railroad tracks and joining new US 40, the old highway passes a white-painted, gable-front farmhouse with German brickwork. A large rectangular barn has entrances in both gable ends, typical for middlewestern German barns built on level ground. The more venturesome road here is old US 40, which becomes a poorly maintained county road paralleling the railroad tracks for one and one-half miles as it approaches St. Jacob.

A tree line, houses, grain elevator, and watertower announce St. Jacob, population about 750. The community dates from 1849 and it enjoyed a brief spurt of growth when the railroad arrived in the late 1860s. Douglas

Street serves as the connector between old US 40 and the railroad district and new US 40, about one-half mile away. All that remains at rail-side is an abandoned grain elevator and the Iron Horse Inn, an old railroad tavern and hotel. St. Jacob lacked a distinct business district; instead, businesses collected along Douglas Street, the railroad track, and old US 40. The village has a small grocery store across from the grade school, but no gas station. Residents occupy vernacular nineteenth-century cottages, including a few brick German cottages, and new ranch houses at the village's eastern and western margins. At Napoleon and East Second Streets, a German barn similar to the one west of Highland has been converted into an auto-repair shop.

Two miles west of St. Jacob old US 40 intersects with Illinois 4 and new US 40; a post–World War II roadside restaurant and truckstop stand at the junction on new US 40. In the two miles between Illinois 4 and Illinois 162 the road crosses the East Fork of Silver Creek and Silver Creek, and old highway remnants remain on US 40's north side. Although the original St. Louis, Vandalia & Terre Haute Railroad grade paralleled the 1820s and Bypass 40 routes, the old Penn Central tracks diverge from US 40 at Silver Creek and head southwest to East St. Louis. Urban sprawl is invading this countryside; the recent population growth is here served by the West Triad High School. Between Illinois 162 (old US 40 that leads to Troy) and Main Street (O'Fallon Road), a two-mile-long stretch of 1960s-1980s subdivisions lie along the road's north side. US 40 merges with I-55 and I-70 two miles west, and sixteen miles away stands the Jefferson Memorial Arch on the St. Louis riverfront. But the interstate is not the adventurous way to enter the city.

Near Troy, on the Madison County uplands east of the Mississippi bluffs, lies a countryside known to early Illinois pioneers as the Land of Goshen. Colonial French settlers were attracted to the floodplains below the bluffs, called the American Bottom. Later, Upland South migrants settled both the floodplains and the uplands, obtaining property deeds at Edwardsville, county seat and U.S. Government Land Office. Settlement spread from here north, east, and south to the Silver, Shoal, and Hurricane Creek watersheds during the ensuing decades. Beginning in the 1830s, large numbers of German immigrants moved into the area in a process of settlement succession duplicated further south in other counties next to the Mississippi River: St. Clair, Monroe, and Randolph.

Old US 40 and Illinois 162 split from Bypass 40 two miles east of Troy. Along old 40, corn, soybean, and winter-wheat fields lie to the north, subdivisions to the south. The Sunset Inn, a 1930s-1940s roadside restaurant, stands abandoned about one mile southeast of town. Old US 40—now Market Street—enters Troy along a corridor of interwar housing that gives way to nineteenth-century dwellings near the business district. When US 40 was upgraded in the 1950s, the community experienced a spurt of population growth that was reinforced when the interstate highway and St. Louis–area beltways (Interstates 55, 64, 70, 255, and 270) were completed. Subsequently, Troy (about 6,000 people) has been surrounded by new "bedroom" subdivisions.

One year after statehood, 1819, Troy was a ten-acre crossroads village. The National Road had been surveyed through town and, by 1843, daily stagecoaches operated on the Vandalia-to-St. Louis Road. Troy was the first coach station east from St. Louis where horses were changed. A coal mine operated in the late nineteenth century near the St. Louis, Vandalia & Terre Haute Railroad depot, supplying coal locally, to villages and towns on the rail line east, and to St. Louis markets.

Troy's muted growth is reflected in its Market and Main Street business district where the buildings are principally one story, and few stores have late-Victorian or early-twentieth-century commercial facades. The skill of German brickmasons is evident in Allen's Rexall Drug Store, particularly in the cornices. Traditional downtown businesses still cluster within a two-block area.

West of Troy, Market Street joins the Interstate 55/70 interchange. The approach is the new "commercial heartbeat" of Troy, a roadside of franchise and chain stores, strip malls for the locals and truckstops for the freeway's eighteen-wheelers. This interchange is the first major truckstop complex between Effingham and St. Louis, and an ideal staging area where truckers can spend the night in their sleeper cabs and arrive at their destinations in St. Louis before morning rush hour begins.

TROY TO ST. LOUIS

Old US 40 runs west from Troy, through Collinsville and East St. Louis, to the Mississippi River waterfront. This route is a cross-section into the heart of a troubled American city, and the roadside is marked with the detritus of a place bypassed and deindustrialized. Many will travel this road reluctantly but its extensive collection of abandoned businesses offers a reprise of a 1920s-to-1960s US highway roadside, and a mirror of national economic and social change not found along the interstate. Old 40 runs southwest from town past ranch houses, a nursery, and wheat fields. The interstate lies on the horizon less than one and one-half miles away. About a mile from Troy Center is pre–depression era roadside America, abandoned-in-ensemble: a gas station and restaurant, motel cottages, a rollerskating rink, and a baseball field. The Moonlight Cottages date from 1923. The Moonlight Roller Rink, also used as a dance hall, was added the next year. In 1925, the lighted baseball field was built. The next year the final single cottage units were completed, creating a crescent pattern around the roller rink. During and after World War II, when traffic increased on old US 40, two four-room motel units were added. The view from the Moonlight Cottages catalogues changing American mobility. Under the old US 40 asphalt, a few feet south of the derelict Skelley gas pumps, is the original 40 paving brick. A half mile south, Bypass 40, completed in the 1950s, continues in use by commuters and local people. Less than a mile west is the interstate interchange that put the Moonlight Cottages out of business in the early 1980s.

Old US 40 deadends at the interstate. To proceed, one must turn south at the frontage road, cross Bypass 40, and immediately turn right on Troy Road, old US 40. The highway serves as one of two frontage roads that parallel Interstates 55/70 for about two and one-half miles. Subdivisions built in the 1960s and 1970s cover the rolling terrain north of the interstate. At the Illinois 159 and interstate interchange, the route turns left where Troy Road intersects 159. Illinois 159 here is also US 40 and where the road enters Collinsville (about 22,500 people) the name changes to Vandalia Road. In about four miles the highway enters the Collinsville business district. Main Street is a one-way street going east. Many business buildings exhibit streamlined Art Deco facades, popular in the early twentieth century when the community prospered. Originally platted in 1837, Collinsville became a coal-mining and manufacturing center on the St. Louis, Vandalia & Terre Haute Railroad.

US 40 leaves town by Clay Street, a one-way street west. At Combs Street the route turns left for one block to Main Street, then right again. At St. Louis Street, the route turns left again. US 40 cuts through the loess-covered Mississippi bluffs and becomes Collinsville Road on the floodplain, running atop the Madison and St. Clair County boundary for about four miles. The road becomes a depressing four-lane commercial strip, lined with abandoned auto-related businesses, where it passes Fairmount Park

horseracing track. Again the parasitic gambling theme—the track stands in Illinois, close to the state line and a Missouri metropolitan area.

Ahead, US 40 bisects Cahokia Mounds State Park. The Interpretive Center (open 9 to 5 daily) offers an exceptional perspective on the great prehistoric Amerindian civilization established at this site. The Mississippian Culture at Cahokia was at its height about 900 to 1200 A.D. when the population of some 20,000 spread over about six square miles. Its many mounds made Cahokia the largest prehistoric city north of Mexico's Aztec culture area. Rising 100 feet above the floodplain, Monks Mound stands across US 40 from the visitor center. From the top of Monks Mound one can view the St. Louis skyline to the southwest; US 40 and the Penn Central and Baltimore & Ohio tracks to the south; Interstates 55/70 north, and Woodhenge, a circular sun calendar of large log posts, to the west.

Collinsville Road (US 40) makes a left turn at the intersection with Illinois 111. Old Mississippi meander scars and oxbow lakes (Horseshoe Lake) lace the floodplain to the right. Four-lane US 40 is an exhibit of roadside Americana from the post–World War II era: the Rainbo Court-Motel, the 1886 Lounge, Indian Motel, Surrey Restaurant, and Nite Spot Cafe. On the left, Fairmont City (about 2,100 people) stands by the Penn Central (Conrail) railyard. Across the road is a nine-hole golf course. Approaching East

Collinsville, Illinois

Friendship and sunshine between races at Fairmount Park.

East St. Louis, Illinois

Two shotgun houses.

St. Louis, the road passes a derelict motel, burned and torn down. A two-block-long stack of discarded automobile tires aligns US 40.

Crossing the East St. Louis corporate boundary (population about 41,000) the highway passes through a landscape in demise. Road quality deteriorates. A burned-out derelict school stands on the east. The housing stock is shotgun houses, southern bungalows, and cross-plan cottages. Abandoned businesses, boarded-up storefronts, and empty lots reflect a depressed community with severe social and economic problems. The revitalized St. Louis skyline looms above the Collinsville Avenue and Martin Luther King Drive intersection, the new skyscrapers there punctuating the differences in culture and economy that occur across the state boundary. In contrast, the four-block-long business district along Collinsville Avenue is a serial of abandoned buildings, empty lots, boarded-up businesses, and broken glass or no-glass storefronts. Building facades witness that East St. Louis prospered in the early twentieth century, but after World War II the business district declined, and then died. Most activity now centers at the State of Illinois ADC Check and Food Stamp Pick-Up Center, although three banks—Union, First National, and First Financial—still operate at the intersection of Collinsville and Missouri Avenues.

344   DOUGLAS K. MEYER

Just outside the business district at the end of Collinsville Avenue, the landscape is empty, forlorn. A small sign says "Make East St. Louis Beautiful—Operation New Spirit." Abandoned and derelict buildings and empty lots comprise the foreground. The middleground is a melange of industrial blight and interstate entry and exit ramps, elevated over the floodplain like a monstrous concentration-camp fence on stilt-legged support piers that angle to align with the Poplar Street Bridge over the Mississippi River. The background is the upper half of the steel and glass St. Louis skyline rising above the concrete interstate. The railroad's decline left an agglomeration of rail tracks and yards that once covered the floodplain here, protected behind the Mississippi levee. The yards have been pulled up, the steel rails salvaged, and the National City stockyards and adjacent packing industry have gone, as have other industries, sucked out by the vacuum of rapid deindustrialization.

East St. Louis, Illinois

A St. Louis Gateway Arch, in miniature, lends grandeur to a small yard, a gateway to home.

The cross-country journey on US 40 ends at the Mississippi riverfront; the way from here is easy to find. Simply follow the signs to the Casino Queen riverboat. The street is well marked and recently paved, at night well lit. Like the gambling boat at Alton, this boat is parasitic, placed here with the intent to drain capital from Missouri across the river. Light-rail trains started operating between downtown East St. Louis and the St. Louis international airport in 1993. The light-rail tracks use the historic Eads Bridge, the first steel bridge across the Mississippi River built in 1874, and the world's first steel truss span. The bridge was a double-decker with a double rail track on the lower level and vehicular traffic on top. Now the light-rail uses the bridge's lower level to reach East St. Louis and its station at the Casino Queen.

Across the river in the Laclede's Landing area, the President Casino operates on a refitted St. Louis river cruise boat, the Admiral. Missouri's legislature was slow to legalize gambling. The casino site is adjacent to Eads Bridge and near the new convention center and new enclosed sports stadium where the St. Louis Rams NFL football team will play as of the fall of 1995.

East St. Louis, Illinois

The city that marks the terminus of the branch that extended the National Road west from Vandalia, a western edge of the old Northwest Territory, now gazes across the Mississippi at a place more favored. St. Louis, too, is an edge marker; the country bought in the Louisiana Purchase began on the river's far bank.

Since the 1950s, planners have proposed many projects intended to initiate a riverfront renaissance for East St. Louis: condos, hotels, marinas, and parks. The plans have failed because private developers lacked capital or nerve. The most recent proposal collapsed because of a multimillion-dollar bond fraud. Now riverfront revitalization has been reinitiated to support the Casino Queen. The casino steamboat is the first major private employer—some 1,000 workers—to come to East St. Louis in decades. Redevelopment may include the creation of a new national park, to mirror Gateway Arch, by the end of the decade.

Up- and downstream from the Casino Queen, the East St. Louis riverfront is ugly and blighted. Weeds choke abandoned lots, and derelict railroad tracks, railyards, and rail-oriented structures (many now removed) stretch along the riverfront. The Continental Grain Elevator, with its paral-

D O U G L A S   K .   M E Y E R

leling railroad tracks and river-barge loading facilities, are the sole symbols of the area's past economic vitality. One can scale the river levee, look across the river, and see a postcard view of the Jefferson Memorial Arch and the "Gateway City" rising from the water's edge. Turn around and see the remnants of East St. Louis, for a time the National Road's intended terminus, now ruined, removed, relict. The responsibility for rejuvenation seems consigned to government-fostered gambling. Converging Interstates 55/64/70 in East St. Louis kindled no major revitalization. Like a host of American towns and cities, East St. Louis was bypassed; it became not a destination but a place in-the-way, a place to pass quickly.

The last National Road segment from Vandalia to East St. Louis was never built, but in the 1920s US 40 connected Baltimore and Cumberland to the Mississippi River and the West. Southwest Illinois landscapes along the highway display as many contrasts as continuities. Bypassed small towns retain vernacular dwellings, while countryside subdivisions follow popular regional or national styles. Interstate interchanges attract national chain or franchised businesses housed in buildings replicated a thousand times across the country. Local people reclaim and revernacularize abandoned US 40 roadside businesses, turning old gas stations and motels into used car dealerships and apartments. The upland highway segment between Vandalia and East St. Louis crosses prosperous farms, bypasses thriving and declining towns, and borders both upper- and lower-class suburbs. Below the Mississippi bluffs the highway corridor is a counterpoint of place images: Cahokia's Monks Mound and a mountainous landfill; freeways on stilts and derelict railroad yards; the stainless-steel Jefferson Memorial Arch and empty brick business buildings dark with grime. Deindustrialized East St. Louis is the antithesis of the renaissance skyline across the Mississippi River in the background where International- and postmodern-style skyscrapers represent a growing postindustrial service economy. It is appropriate that the journey ends here, amid the clutter of four different transportation technologies—river, road, railroad, and interstate. This landscape mirrors the social and economic polarities that accompany America's changing transportation preferences, and the nation's best and worst times. Here, in ensemble, lies America at the end of the Road.

A Path So Bent

KARL RAITZ

In the same way a primitive road of 1900, itself developed from a packhorse trail, has been patched and relocated gradually, but the improvement has always been made on the basis of what was there already. Thus the pavement may have progressed from dirt to macadam to oil to thin concrete, and the route may have been straightened and made less steep, and the right-of-way may have been gradually widened. At length and after lamentable wastage of money, the path may have become a freeway, and yet the freeway may still bend here and there a little, because the path so bent.

GEORGE R. STEWART
U.S. 40: Cross Section of the United States of America

THE ROAD AS ROUTE HAS GREAT RESILIENCE, ALTERING LITTLE OVER generations, as George Stewart reminds us, from the way of a historic path. The road as highway is a different matter entirely. The highway and the wayside that grows up beside it change and evolve. The highway has given Americans mobility and freedom, and their settlements and economies often take new forms that mirror roadway changes: linear, nodal, galactic. Much of what Americans do, much of their life, is either conducted along the road and street, or in the context of access to highways for business and recreation. The highway and motorized transportation for individuals was a new form of freedom that people found irresistible. In adopting this new transport mode they also invented new urban forms that continue to evolve—in the 1930s tightly clustered at crossroads or along roadsides in linear strips, today extruding in great galactic patches of subdivision that distend with postmodern shopping centers and office towers.

East of the Mississippi River, it is difficult to find a place that is more than a few miles from a decent road. Even those "more distant" lands are often farmed, or mined, or timbered, and are not beyond the reach of cultural institutions fostered along the American roadside. A century ago America was largely rural and laced together by railroad tracks. Now it is urban and addictively road-bound. In nineteenth-century America, the river, canal, and railroad created and reinforced focused settlements, and towns and cities grew up around harbors, landings, wharfs, locks, or depots. People's lives likewise focused upon local affairs with almost feudal ties to place and land. To understand American life in 1880 one needed to examine farms and small towns. By 1980, the better vantage point was the highway. Jean Baudrillard exaggerated somewhat when he drew this conclusion about American life, but his observation merits consideration:

> All you need to know about American society can be gleaned from an anthropology of its driving behaviour. That behaviour tells you much more than you could ever learn from its political ideas. Drive ten thousand miles across America and you will know more about the country than all the institutes of sociology and political science put together.[1]

We might add that in addition to driving America, one must learn to "see," read, and interpret America's landscapes—not a straightforward task on a modern interstate where the 65-MPH pace narrows the practical line-of-sight to a visual tunnel along the roadway proper, but more possible at a slower pace along our highways and byways.

As the traveler who has come from Baltimore across America's Middle West, you now leave the extensions of the old National Road either in Alton or East St. Louis. The Mississippi's muddy waters lap at your feet; a western horizon still beckons. Illinois 140, following the bed of the old road to Alton, terminates near the new version of the Lewis and Clark Bridge, a powerful reminder that Pres. Thomas Jefferson had sent this famed expedition team to the far west seeking a routeway to the Pacific at about the same time that Jefferson and his cabinet officers were considering the building of a road that would span the Appalachians and splice the East Coast to the promise of new markets in the Ohio River country. About twenty-five miles south of Alton, before tracking across the continent's western half, US 40— merged at East St. Louis with Interstate 70—crosses the Mississippi River on the Poplar Street Bridge. Just to the right, Eero Saarinen's ageless stainless-steel arch stands within an urban park reserve, towering over other symbolic structures assembled, like the Lewis and Clark Bridge at Alton, to commemorate the nation's expansion west under Jefferson.

Americans are generally not fond of weak or subtle symbolic gestures; we seem to prefer monumental scale and flamboyant facades as exemplified by the Gateway Arch in St. Louis. How better to signify recognition that a coast-to-coast American Empire was one of the predominant objectives of national politics during the eighteenth and early nineteenth centuries than to place at the end of both forks of the National Road's westward extensions from Vandalia two of the country's most spectacular memorial structures.

Following US 40 into the Great Plains and the west one finds great cities linked by the route: Kansas City, Denver, Salt Lake City, Reno, Sacramento, San Francisco. The highway—merged with I-70 along some stretches, with I-80 along others—crosses the prairie, skirts the Rocky Mountains, follows desert-dry valleys in the Basin and Range Country, and overcomes the High Sierras on its way to the Pacific. The way stands marked not by milestones but by places treasured for beauty or historicity: the Santa Fe Trail, the Kansas River valley, the Front Range, Rocky Mountain National Park, Dinosaur National Monument, the Wasatch Oasis, Great Salt Lake Desert, Lake Tahoe, Donner Pass, the Central Valley, the Golden Gate Bridge.

The National Road was intended to be a central lifeline in a vast centrifugal transportation network that bound new territory to established centers. Its extension, US 40, and the interstates, extrapolated that theme across the continent. The western highway awaits.

Notes

Introduction

1. Meinig 1993, 346.
2. Reedy 1993.
3. Atherton 1954, 237.
4. Steinbeck 1939, 121, 125.
5. Codrescu 1993, 4.

Chapter 1. From Baltimore to Cumberland, Maryland

1. Steffen 1979, 103.
2. Searight 1894, 192–93; Bruce 1916, 15–17; Semmes 1953, 6, 14.
3. Orser and Arnold 1989, 11–21, 61, 123.
4. Travers 1990, 67–84; Holland 1970, 1–28.
5. Travers 1990, 72–73, 77.

6. Lewis 1979, 189–92.
7. Garreau 1991, 345.
8. Purvis 1986, 94; Gaustad 1962, map (back pocket).
9. Hooper 1974, 1–67.
10. Purvis 1986, 94.
11. Hollifield 1978, 16.
12. The Washington County Historic Sites Survey has compiled a collection of all the historically significant structures in the rural areas of the county. Photographs and detailed histories accompany many of the entries. The collection is housed in the Western Maryland Room of the Washington County Public Library in Hagerstown. See also Stoner 1977, 512–22.

13. Nesbitt 1860–65, 189–90, 198–99.

14. Rideing 1879, 814.

15. Ibid.

Chapter 2. From Cumberland to Wheeling, West Virginia

1. Meyer 1986, 3.

2. Harvey 1969.

3. Stegmaier et al. 1976, 232.

4. Stewart 1953, 89.

5. Rosenberg, quoted in Lawson-Peebles 1988, 23.

6. Alberts 1976, 17.

7. Baily [1796] 1904, 142; and Flint [1822] 1966, 75.

8. Faux [1823] 1966, 165.

9. Alberts 1976, 6.

10. Cuff et al. 1989, 6.

11. Stone 1932, 167. See also Koegler 1992, 1995.

12. Ellis 1882, 289.

13. Sheppard 1991 [1947], 102.

14. Bissell 1949, 14.

15. Grantz 1985.

16. The hotel had not been built when Howard F. Hobbs traveled the Road for the Mohawk Rubber Company. He described Brownsville as "a purely industrial city" with "limited hotel accommodations."

17. Cuffs et al. 1989, 68, 183.

18. Forrest 1926, 493.

Chapter 3. From Wheeling to Columbus, Ohio

1. Ohio Writer's Project 1940, 488.

2. Williams 1972, 451.

3. Ohio Writer's Project 1940, 488.

4. Ibid., 489.

5. Howe 1847, 57.

6. Vonada 1992, 430.

7. Mary Ann Peters, personal interview by H. G. H. Wilhelm, Athens, Ohio, January 8, 1993.

8. Road town street patterns in eastern Ohio resemble the linear types identified for Pennsylvania by Pillsbury 1970, 433–40.

9. Peacefull 1990, 52.

10. Vonada 1992, 576.

11. Peters, personal interview by Wilhelm, January 8, 1993.

12. Simmons 1978.

13. Andrews 1979.

14. *Barnesville Enterprise* 1991.

15. Andrews 1979.

16. Ohio Writer's Project 1940, 490.

17. Ibid., 491.

18. Jenkins 1976, 8.

19. Ibid., 45, 88.

20. Ohio Writer's Project 1940, 491.

21. Burton 1984.

22. Ohio Writer's Project 1940, 493.

23. Ibid., 494.

24. Taylor 1976.

25. Ibid.

26. Jordan 1948, 272, 257.

27. Ohio Writer's Project 1940, 495.

28. Noble and Korsok 1975, 31–34.

29. Sherman 1925, 116 and 119.

30. Ritchie 1973.

31. Noble and Korsok 1975, 46–53.

32. Staff, Clark's Restaurant, personal interview by H. G. H. Wilhelm, Jacksontown, Ohio, October 23, 1992.

33. Ohio Writer's Project 1940, 497.

34. Ibid., 498.

Chapter 4. From Columbus to Richmond, Indiana

1. Peters 1930, 117–42.

2. Brown 1948, 232.

3. Ibid.; Peters 1930, 279–84; White, n.d., 27.

4. Ibid.; Peters 1930, 276–77.

5. Smith 1950, 123.

6. Shortridge 1989, 99–109, map on 98.

7. Alexander and Alexander 1909, 437–38.

8. Hobbs 1924, 13.

9. Bowen 1988, 10–12; Goetz 1983, H 1; Daniell 1976, 50–53, 75–76, 83.

10. Halvorson and Newman 1987, 34, 36, 54, 59, and 61.

11. *History of Madison Co. Ohio, Illustrated* 1883, 642–43.

12. Ibid., 661–62.

13. Hulbert 1901, 118–19.

14. *History of Madison Co. Ohio, Illustrated* 1883, 822–23.

15. *History of Clark County, Ohio, Illustrated* 1881, 645–46.

16. Peters 1930, 138–39.

17. *History of Clark County, Ohio, Illustrated* 1881, 646–47.

18. Ibid., 647.

19. Durant 1950, 24–25.

20. Hobbs 1924, 13.

21. *History of Clark County, Ohio, Illustrated* 1881, 426–34.

22. Price 1922, 423–24.

23. Ohio Writer's Project 1940, 316–17.

24. Conover 1932, 164.

25. Bureau of Public Roads and the Ohio Department of Highways and Public Works 1927, 107, 115.

26. *History of Clark County, Ohio, Illustrated* 1881, 709.

27. Hobbs 1924, 13.

28. Ibid., 12.

29. Hulbert 1904, 91–118.

30. *History of Miami County, Ohio, Illustrated* 1880, 418; and Toma 1953, 137–38.

31. Toma 1953, 138–39; and Barnhart 1982, 126–31.

32. Goldthwait 1959, 206–10.

33. Ohio Writer's Project 1940, 271.

34. Morgan 1951, 229–74.

35. Conover 1932, 797.

36. Hart 1991, 107–9; Hudson 1994, 3–10.

37. Raitz 1973, 297–98.

38. Ibid., 302–6.

39. *History of Preble Co., Ohio, with Illustrations* 1881, 212.

40. Helen Felton, Lewisburg, Ohio, Interview by Glenn Harper, February, 1994; and Ohio Writer's Project 1940, 503.

41. *History of Preble County, Ohio* 1881, 272.

42. Royer 1989, 36.

Chapter 5. From Richmond to Terre Haute, Indiana

1. *The Terre Haute Star,* December 19, 1928, 4.

Chapter 7. From Vandalia to St. Louis

1. Peck 1837, 149

Coda

1. Baudrillard 1988, 54–55.

Glossary

Acre. An old English land measure. Originally the amount of land a yoke of oxen could plow in one day. Common dimensions were formalized as forty rods (a rod is 16½ feet) in length by four rods wide, equaling an area of 160 square rods or 43,560 square feet. Roughly equivalent to an American football field, minus one end zone. The basic unit of land measurement in the Township and Range survey used across the Middle West, but also used in areas surveyed according to metes and bounds, or other survey systems found along the National Road corridor.

Anticline. A convex upward fold in sedimentary rock layers with older rocks at its core. May form valleys or ridges at the surface, depending upon the positioning of easily erodible or resistant rock layers. Numerous examples in western Maryland, and Chestnut Ridge in southwestern Pennsylvania. See *Syncline*.

Baltimore-Frederick Turnpike. Private toll road, organized in 1805, between Baltimore and Boonsboro, Maryland.

Baltimore National Pike. Local name for US 40 in the Ellicott City, Frederick, and Cumberland, Maryland, areas; and Interstate 70 between Baltimore and Frederick.

Bank Barn. A large wooden frame or post-and-beam structure whose design was brought to Pennsylvania from Switzerland by Pietist immigrants. The ground level shelters livestock. The farmer can reach the grain threshing floor and storage area on the second level by way of a ramp. An upper-level forebay extends out over the ground level.

Bituminous Coal. Soft coal. Formed from peat accumulations in ancient swamps. Compression increases the carbon content to about 90 percent in high-rank bituminous coal. Bituminous fields underlie half of Pennsylvania's counties. The high volatility of southwestern Pennsylvania's bituminous coal makes it ideal for the coking process. Maryland's Georges Creek District coal, extracted from more warped strata, is of low volatility.

Break-in-Bulk Point. A place where a change in transportation mode, change in carrier size (downstream versus upstream), or change in the freight-rate structure occurs. Such places often become urban nodes.

Bungalow. A house style built throughout the United States from 1880 through the 1930s, with California playing the principal role in its diffusion. From the Bengali word *bangla* by way of the British colonial experience with low houses wrapped in porches. Very horizontal silhouette in line with the Prairie School aesthetic of meshing the house with its site. Broad gabled roofs, exposed rafter ends, low open porches, and stout porch posts are also exterior design characteristics. Interiors comprise compact rooms, exposed decorative ceiling beams, built-in shelves and cabinets, and natural or stained woodwork.

Cash Grain Farm. A large, highly mechanized farm specializing in producing corn and soybeans to be sold in the grain market rather than being fed to livestock. The farm may produce secondary crops such as winter wheat, oats, and sorghum.

Coal Measures. High-rank coal beds are sandwiched with other rocks of the Pennsylvanian geologic age. The cyclicity of coal seams separated by sandstones, shales, and limestones reflects the sedimentation that accompanied a shallow inland sea's advances and retreats when Pennsylvania was equatorial. Roadcuts will be colorfully banded: buff and gray sandstones protrude as layers of darker shale and black coal erode.

Coking Coal and Coke. Coke forms when bituminous coal is heated to remove its volatiles. The spongy carbonaceous residue provides a matrix for limestone and iron ore in blast furnaces, leaving molten iron for steel-making in its wake. Over 40,000 beehive ovens operated in the Connellsville coke region of southwestern Pennsylvania where the Pittsburgh seam provided the ideal raw material.

Company Town. To house laborers near (or on) the resource, companies, particularly mining concerns in Appalachia, built communities easily distinguished by their visual order and regularity. Identical multifamily dwellings, larger homes for officials, a company store, a ballfield, and company policing were characteristic of the Appalachian Plateau's soft coal–mining towns. Often called "coal patch towns," they still bear the stamp of corporate design.

Covenanted Community. A community whose members dominate a particular locality linked by kinship and friendship engendered by church and other institutions. The community promotes a sense of rootedness passed from generation to generation. Most were originally colony towns settled by people of a given national or regional origin which, separated from the American mainstream, became inward-focused.

Cumberland House. A rectangular hall-and-parlor house that is two stories high, one room deep, and two rooms wide. A rear ell produces an L- or T-shaped perimeter. The front facade cues its Middle Atlantic cultural heritage. The first floor has six openings or bays—a window, a door, two windows, a door, and a window. The second floor has four windows that align with the first-floor windows.

Cumberland Turnpike. Toll road, financed by Maryland banks, from Conococheague Creek, in Washington County, to Cumberland, Maryland.

Double Pile House Plan. A house in which the space between front and back walls is deep enough to accommodate two full rooms. End walls are commonly far enough apart to provide a two-room width. An urban variation has only one room behind another with a side hallway providing access to both. Variations on the arrangement of internal space were introduced from the British Isles and continental Europe. See *Folk House*.

End Moraine. A long, low, and usually narrow line of hills comprised of glacial debris—clay, silt, sand, gravel, and boulders. The debris accumulated when the ice pack paused in its retreat, or backwasting, from its terminal or southerly-most extension. Clay and stony materials were dumped by melting ice, or pushed into broad arching piles by a brief readvance in the ice front. A sequence of end moraine crescents begins at the National Road corridor in western Ohio and eastern Indiana, with individual moraines marching off to the north at eight- to fifteen-mile intervals. See also *Till*.

Folk House. An architecture without architects. Houses built from mental templates, fusing cultural tradition with natural conditions. Fashioned from locally available materials, surviving examples are more common in rural areas. Described by form (massing, fenestration) rather than style. Such houses—like the I-house, four-over-four, or upright-and-wing—are useful in delimiting culture regions and their diffusion because of their persistence in the landscape.

Forebay. The diagnostic "overhang" or "overshoot" on a bank or Pennsylvania-German barn. Variable in size, this second-level extends balcony-like over the doors into the animal stalls on the ground level.

Frederick Avenue. General route of National Road in Baltimore.

Frederick Road. National Road from Catonsville to Frederick, Maryland.

Gentleman Farmer. Although the term implies that this figure is male, perhaps as many such "farmers" were or are female. These farmers are usually wealthy city residents who buy farmland and "farm" as an avocation. Nineteenth-century gentleman farmers often sought to improve agricultural productivity through practical experimentation with seed or stock importation. Often found beyond the suburban fringe of large metropolitan areas in the East, a rough "belt" of twentieth-century gentleman farms extends along the Maryland and Virginia Piedmont where people from Richmond, Washington, D.C., Philadelphia, and Baltimore have large horse farms and fox-hunting clubs. Such farms usually represent large investments in buildings and land improvement and are often demarcated by white plank fences and formal stone or brick entrance gates.

Glacial Spillway. Melting glacial ice may collect into large streams and rivers and flow down gradient away from the ice front. Since continental glaciers like the Wisconsin-age ice lobes that blanketed the Middle West 10,000 to 14,000 years ago were hundreds of miles across and a thousand or more feet thick, the volume of meltwater was sufficient to carve deep valleys into the till or moraine surface. Today, these valleys are often occupied by small streams that meander across a broad floodplain. Examples include the deep and steep-sided Stillwater and Great Miami River valleys in western Ohio.

Gothic Revival. Popularized by Alexander Jackson Downing and others during the 1840s and 1850s, this architectural style employed the pointed arch, towers, steep gabled roofs, lacy bargeboards, verandas, bay and oriel windows, and leaded stained glass. Gothic was often used in "romantic" country cottages, churches, and other public buildings.

H. H. Richardson Romanesque. Named for the architect that reinterpreted the style, Henry Hobson Richardson, these late-nineteenth-century buildings are usually built of massive, rough-hewn stone with round arches framing deep window and door openings. Windows were often set within stone bands of contrasting color and texture. A favored style for public buildings, structures often included bell or clock towers.

Hagerstown and Boonsboro Turnpike. Connects Hagerstown and Boonsboro in Washington County, Maryland. First macadam road in United States, constructed 1822–23.

Hagerstown and Conococheague Turnpike. Provides link between Hagerstown and beginning of the Cumberland Turnpike at Conococheague Creek, in Washington County, Maryland.

Hall-and-Parlor House. A cultural artifact with American origins in the South, distinguished by a gable end roof and main entrance on the long axis, either an interior vestibule opening to two rooms or main entrance directly into one of the two rooms. An addition frequently results in an L- or T-shaped house perimeter.

Highwall. Residual vertical bluff formed by cutting a surface mine into a hillside and removing the earth and bedrock—called overburden by the mining industry—above a coal seam. Highwalls often remain after the coal is removed, especially if mining activity ended before the federal 1977 surface-mine reclamation law went into effect.

I-House. A symmetrical two-story dwelling with a single pile plan on both floors. It is distinguished from similar-looking houses by a central hallway separating pairs of rooms with identical dimensions. This house form is common in the states of Indiana, Illinois, and Iowa, hence the designation as I-house.

Illinois 140. A two-lane state highway that follows a historic 1820s road connecting Vandalia and Alton. Between Vandalia and Mulberry Grove it corresponds to the National Road and the original 1920s US 40.

Illinoisan-age Glaciation. The Pleistocene glacial advance, about 300,000 years before present, that covered about 90 percent of present-day Illinois under the Lake Michigan and Lake Erie ice lobes. The ice reached the northern slopes of the Shawnee Hills in southern Illinois and in southwestern Ohio extended as far south as the present course of the Ohio River.

Interstate 68. Modern divided limited-access highway between Hancock, Maryland, and Morgantown, West Virginia. Same orientation as National Road and occasionally follows the same general course as the original Road.

Interstate 70. Modern divided limited-access highway between Baltimore and Hancock, Maryland; and between Washington, Pennsylvania, and East St. Louis, Illinois. Same orientation as National Road, but different course.

Interurban. City electric-traction streetcar lines extended into the countryside. Usually built by private investors or traction companies whose concern was to profit from freight and passenger service and real estate development. The interurban often ran from cities to nearby towns and the tracks often paralleled roads or highways. These traction lines provided farmers better access to city markets and services than did the steam railroads. Construction was very active after the turn of the twentieth century. An interurban line ran along the National Road between Indianapolis and Terre Haute, for example.

Italianate Style. Architectural style of early (1860s) Victorian era characterized by cubic two-story houses with low-pitched roofs and projecting bracketed eaves with pronounced bracketing. Rectangular windows topped with elaborately molded hoods. A highly variable style, vernacular middlewestern examples are often square in perimeter and cubic in massing.

Kame. Low hill made up of sand and gravel that accumulated in Wisconsin-age glacial ice crevasses or deposited by glacial meltwater. The soils on kames are shallow and farm crops on kame hills often yield poorly after a summer drought. Kames may be mined as gravel pits to supply road surfacing and material for construction and concrete. Outside of glaciated regions—in southwestern Pennsylvania, for example—rock must be quarried and crushed to supply these same needs or sand must be dredged from stream beds.

Kettle. Small, often water-filled, depressions that formed when large ice chunks broke off the Wisconsin-age glacial front, became partially covered by till and meltwater-borne silt or sand, and eventually melted, producing "holes in the ground" that may range from less than one acre to several acres in size. To utilize this land for crops, farmers often drained kettles by digging drainage ditches and laying drainage tile in shallow, dirt-covered trenches. Much of the Wisconsin-age till across Ohio, Indiana, and Illinois has been drained in this manner.

Loess. Very fine-grained clay and silt particles in glacial outwash material that is blown by the wind to accumulate in homogeneous layers atop existing surfaces. The Mississippi River valley was the major source for the loess that blankets southcentral Illinois and Indiana along the National Road corridor. The deposits are much thicker in the west, nearer the river, than in Indiana, and are generally fertile when cultivated and planted to farm crops.

Macadam. A roadbed built of broken rock, layered in sequence with larger rocks in the bottom layers, smaller in the top where four-ounce pieces formed a solid, interlocking roadbed. A Scottish engineer developed the technique and it was used extensively in National Road construction.

Maryland 144. Maryland designation for roads following general route of original National Road.

Metes and Bounds. An informal unsystematic method of surveying land based upon lines surveyed between found corners. Surveying usually followed instead of preceded settlement. Boundary lines rarely acknowledged cardinal directions and properties were oddly shaped and irregularly sized. Because corners were often imprecise—large trees, rock outcrops, fence posts—and boundaries sometimes followed changeable stream channels, litigation over landownership was common. See *Township and Range Survey.*

National Freeway. Interstate 68 between Hancock and Cumberland, Maryland. US 48 from the mid-1970s to 1992.

National Pike. National Road between Baltimore and Cumberland, Maryland. Composed of four private turnpikes—Baltimore and Frederick Turnpike, Hagerstown and Boonsboro Turnpike, Hagerstown and Conococheague Turnpike, and Cumberland Turnpike—that were upgraded between 1805 and 1823. All the roads were in existence before federal legislation created the National Road.

New US 40. Post–World War II US 40 was straightened and upgraded with a wider pavement, improved shoulders, and bypasses. Interstate 70 replaced new US 40 in the 1970s. See also *US 40.*

Old Frederick Road. Earliest road between Baltimore and Frederick, Maryland; did not become part of National Road system.

Old US 40 (Route 40). The 1920s federal highway conformed to the National Road route between Vandalia and St. Louis. US 40 overlaid a historic 1820s road between the second state capital and "Gateway City." See also *US 40.*

Pennsylvania German Barn. See *Bank Barn*

Pennsylvania Town. Coined by geographer Wilbur Zelinsky in 1977 to describe the density and no-nonsense commercial orientation of small towns, especially those in the southeastern quarter of the state. In the classic Pennsylvania town, the houses are built close to each other and close to the street. The "nearly total anarchy" of functions in the towns indicate that they were built for business. The use of brick, town squares or diamonds, alleys, shade trees, and street naming patterns are also typical.

Pittsburgh Seam. A continuous bed, distinguished by its thickness, extending from Chestnut Ridge under five southwestern Pennsylvania counties. The seam forms the base of the Monongahela group of rocks laid down during the Pennsylvania period of the Paleozoic era. One of several easily accessible and nearly horizontal beds that underpin what came to be known as the Connellsville coking coal district, it was mined with a frenzy in the late nineteenth and early twentieth centuries. The Pittsburgh seam is usually preceded by the word "fabulous" when it appears in print because it is considered the world's most valuable single mineral deposit. Although mined in the Pittsburgh area since 1761, reserves remain in Washington County that could last another 150 years.

Rowhouse. Attached two-story houses either two rooms or one room deep. Contiguous construction was determined by end gable–oriented houses and narrow town lots.

Scenic US 40. Designation of original US 40 in mountainous areas of Washington and Allegany counties, Maryland.

Single Pile House Plan. A British-derived arrangement of interior space whereby the depth of a single room separates front and back walls. Structures of this sort are commonly two rooms wide and many have been deepened by rearward extensions known as ells.

Soil Association. A subdivision of soil regions related to land types, especially slope and bedrock conditions, and containing two or more soil types (i.e. Bennington-Cardington Association). When slope and bedrock or till conditions change, so change soil composition and fertility, and prospects for productive agriculture.

Sorghum. A tropical grass from Africa and Asia grown as a secondary crop by cash grain farmers for livestock feed, grain, syrup, and broom fiber. Milo is a common grain sorghum.

Springfield Till Plain. Distinguished by its flatness, this Illinoian-age till plain occurs south of the Shelbyville Moraine that was formed during the Wisconsin-age glaciation period about 15,000 years before the present and marks its southern-most extent.

Swiss-German Motif. Chalet-like building facades that supposedly evoke Swiss and Bavarian Alps architecture. Brown-stained timber and white stucco are added to old and incorporated into new buildings to obtain a pseudo Old World half-timbered ambiance.

Syncline. A concave downward fold in sedimentary rocks with younger rocks at its core. Numerous examples in the Ridge and Valley section of western Maryland. May form valleys or ridges at the surface. Sideling Hill, near Hancock, is a synclinal ridge and the spectacular cut made for I-68 reveals the downward fold structure. See *Anticline*.

Terminal Moraine. A low, sinuous line of glacial debris material—clay, silt, sand, gravel, and boulders—which accumulated ahead of the ice front and marks its furthest extension. Remains as a crescent- or arc-shaped line of low hills that may be the most noticeable topographic variation on an otherwise gently rolling till plain. Moraines are favored places for golf courses and microwave relay towers, but farmers may find the slopes too steep to cultivate and so moraine land often remains in pasture or trees. See *End Moraine*.

Till. Clay, silt, sand, and gravel deposited by glacial action. Till plains often have gently rolling to nearly level surfaces. Much of the National Road corridor from western Ohio to western Illinois crosses till plain of Wisconsin age, 10,000 to 14,000 years old, approximately. Since these till surfaces are comparatively young, they are often poorly drained—streams have not had sufficient time to erode channels into the surface. Consequently, if farmers wish to cultivate this land they must ditch and tile the low-lying areas to drain marshes and the water that ponds in depressions after a heavy rain.

Tipple. Chute for loading minerals by gravity flow into rail cars and river barges. More complex tipples sort coal by grade and separate culm (waste rock).

Township and Range Survey. Conceived by Thomas Jefferson, adjusted by Congress, and formalized by the Land Ordinance of 1785, this systematic survey was based upon a network of intersecting baselines and meridians that followed cardinal directions. Township lines were surveyed every six miles north and south of a baseline. Range lines fell every six miles east and west of a principal meridian. This grid described a pattern of thirty-six-square-mile townships. Each square mile was a section or 640 acres, and each section within a township was numbered 1 through 36. Each portion of a section was numbered with a standard code. For example, the northeast quarter of section 17 was identified as the NE¼ and was 160 acres. The southwest quarter of this 160 acre parcel was 40 acres and identified as the SW¼. In this way, each land parcel, down to fractions of acres, could be identified by a unique numerical description. Eventually gravel roads were built along section lines and the effect was a checkerboard of section roads that enclosed square or rectangular fields. The National Road corridor intersects some surveys that resemble the Township and Range west of Springfield, Ohio, the Between the Miamis survey, for example, and then crosses the formal Township and Range in Indiana and Illinois.

Upland South and Upland Southerners. The Upland South includes southern Appalachian valleys, plateaus, piedmonts, and mountains. Upland Southerners were hunter-farmer and yeoman farmer pioneers from those areas of Virginia, North Carolina, South Carolina, Kentucky, and Tennessee.

US 40. Federal highway that succeeded the National Road; designed to accommodate early automobile traffic. May or may not follow original course of National Road. See also *Old US 40; New US 40; Scenic US 40.*

US 48. Transition highway between Hancock, Maryland, and Morgantown, West Virginia; the road represented the changes that occurred as old US 40 evolved into I-68 between 1976 and 1992.

Vernacular House. See *Folk House.*

Virginia I-House. A "Southern" version of the I-house usually having a lower pitched roof, raised foundation, a central dormer or full two-story portico.

Western Pike. Designation of original National Road west of Hancock in Washington County, Maryland.

References

Adler, Jeffrey S. 1991. *Yankee Merchants and the Making of the Urban West: The Rise and Fall of Antebellum St. Louis*. Cambridge: Cambridge University Press.

Alberts, R. C. 1976. *Mt. Washington Tavern*. Eastern National Park and Monument Association for Fort Necessity National Battlefield, Pennsylvania.

Alexander, Taylor, and William Alexander. 1909. *Centennial History of Columbus & Franklin Co. Ohio*. Chicago and Columbus: S. J. Clark Publishing.

Andrews, Kathleen. 1979. "Morristown Historic District." *National Register for Historic Places Inventory*. Columbus: Ohio Historic Preservation Office.

Atherton, Lewis. 1954. *Main Street on the Middle Border*. Bloomington: Indiana University Press.

Baily, F. 1904 [1796]. "A Pilgrim on the Pennsylvania Road." In *Pioneer Roads*. Historic Highways of America 11, ed. A. B. Hulbert. Cleveland, Ohio: Arthur H. Clark Co.

Barnesville Enterprise. 1991. "Morristown Group Recognized on State Level for Preservation Activities." Barnesville, Ohio.

Barnhart, Julia R. 1982. "Phoneton." In *History of Miami County, Ohio,* ed. E. Irene Miller. Tipp City, Ohio: Miami County Historical Society.

Baudrillard, Jean. 1988. *America.* London: Verso.

Belloc, Hilaire. 1923. *The Road.* Manchester: Charles W. Hobson.

Bissell, Richard. 1949. *The Monongahela.* Rivers of America 46. New York: Rinehart and Co.

Bowen, Edward L. 1988. "A Mover, a Builder: John W. Galbreath: 1897–1988." *Ohio Thoroughbred.* September/October.

Brown, Ralph H. 1948. *Historical Geography of the United States.* New York: Harcourt, Brace & World.

Bruce, Robert. 1916. *The National Road.* Washington, D.C.: National Highway Association.

Bureau of Public Roads and the Ohio Department of Highways and Public Works. 1927. *Report of a Survey of Transportation on the State Highway System of Ohio.* Washington, D.C.: Government Printing Office.

Burton, Vicki L. 1984. "National Road, Peacock Road." *National Register of Historic Places Inventory.* Columbus: Ohio Historic Preservation Office.

Celnar, Philip. 1972. *Flint Ridge.* Report No. 84. Columbus: Ohio Division of Geological Survey.

Codrescu, Andrei. 1993. *Road Scholar: Coast to Coast Late in the Century.* New York: Hyperion.

Conover, Charlotte R., ed. 1932. *Dayton and Montgomery Counties: Resources and People,* vol. 1. New York: Lewis Historical Publishing.

Cuff, D. J., et al., eds. 1989. *Atlas of Pennsylvania.* Philadelphia: Temple University Press.

Daniell, Linda C. 1976. "Darby Dan's John Galbreath." *The Country Gentleman.* Spring.

"Diary of Otho Nesbitt." 1860–65. *Windmills of Time.* Clear Spring, Md.: Clear Spring Alumni Association.

Dreiser, Theodore. 1916. *A Hoosier Holiday.* New York: John Lane.

Durant, John. 1950. "The Movies Take to the Pastures." *Saturday Evening Post* 223.

Ellis, F. 1882. *History of Fayette County, Pennsylvania.* Philadelphia.

Faux, W. 1966 [1823]. "Memorable Days in America: Being a Journal of a Tour to the United States." In *Early Western Travels, 1748–1846,* vol. 12, ed. R. G. Thwaites. New York: AMS Press.

Felton, Helen. 1994. Interview by Glenn Harper, Lewisburg, Ohio, February.

Flint, J. 1966 [1822]. "Letters from America." In *Early Western Travels, 1748–1846,* vol. 9, ed. R. G. Thwaites. New York: AMS Press.

Forrest, Earle. 1926. *History of Washington County, Pennsylvania,* Vol. 1. Chicago.

Garreau, Joel. 1991. *Edge City: Life on the New Frontier.* New York: Doubleday.

Gaustad, Edwin S. 1962. *Historical Atlas of Religion in America.* New York: Harper and Row.

Goetz, David. 1983. "The Master of Darby Dan Farm." *Louisville Courier-Journal.* April 1.

Goldthwait, Richard P. 1959. "Scenes in Ohio during the Last Ice Age." *Ohio Journal of Science* 59:193–215.

Grantz, Denise. 1985. *National Road Historic Resources Survey.* Harrisburg, Pa.

Halvorson, Peter L., and William M. Newman. 1987. *Atlas of Religious Change in America, 1971–1980.* Atlanta, Ga.: Glenmary Research Center.

Hardin, Thomas L. 1967. "The National Road in Illinois." *Journal of the Illinois State Historical Society* 60:5–22.

Hart, John Fraser. 1991. *The Land That Feeds Us.* New York: Norton.

Harvey, K. A. 1969. *The Best Dressed Miners: Life and Labor in the Maryland Coal Region, 1835–1910.* Ithaca, N.Y.: Cornell University Press.

History of Clark County, Ohio, Illustrated. 1881. Chicago: W. H. Beers Publishers.

History of Madison County, Illinois. 1882. Edwardsville, Ill.: W. R. Brink.

History of Madison County, Ohio, Illustrated. 1883. Chicago: W. H. Beers Publishers.

History of Miami County, Ohio, Illustrated. 1880. Chicago: W. H. Beers Publishers.

History of Preble County, Ohio, with Illustrations. 1881. Cleveland, Ohio: H. Z. Williams Publishers.

Hobbs, Howard F. 1924. *Hobbs Grade and Surface Guide: National Old Trails and Connections.* Akron, Ohio: Mohawk Rubber Company.

Holland, Celia M. 1970. *Ellicott City, Maryland: Mill Town, U.S.A.* Chicago: Adams Press.

Hollifield, William. 1978. *Difficulties Made Easy: History of the Turnpikes of Baltimore City and County.* Towson, Md.: Baltimore County Historical Society.

Hooper, Anne B. 1974. *Braddock Heights: A Glance Backward.* Baltimore: French Bray.

Howe, Henry. 1847. *Historical Collections of Ohio.* Cincinnati: Henry Howe and E. Morgan & Co.

Hudson, John C. 1994. *Making the Corn Belt: A Geographical History of Middle-Western Agriculture.* Bloomington: Indiana University Press.

Hulbert, Archer Butler. 1901. *The Old National Road: A Chapter of American Expansion.* Columbus: F. J. Heer Press.

———. 1904. *The Cumberland Road.* Historic Highways of America 10. Cleveland: Arthur H. Clark Company.

Illinois Nature Preserves Commission. 1973. *Comprehensive Plan for the Illinois Preserves System: Part 2, The Natural Divisions of Illinois.* Springfield: Illinois Nature Preserves Commission.

Jenkins, Hal. 1976. *A Valley Renewed.* Kent, Ohio: Kent State University Press.

Jordan, Philip D. 1948. *The National Road.* New York: Bobbs-Merrill Co.

Koegler, Karen. 1992. "Building in Stone in Southwestern Pennsylvania." Ph.D. dissertation, Department of Geography, University of Kentucky.

———. 1995. "Building in Stone in Southwestern Pennsylvania: Patterns and Process."

In *Gender, Class, and Shelter: Perspectives in Vernacular Architecture V*, ed. Elizabeth C. Cromley and Carter C. Hughes, 195–210. Knoxville: University of Tennessee Press.

Lawson-Peebles, Robert. 1988. *Landscape and Written Expression in Revolutionary America*. Cambridge: Cambridge University Press.

Liebs, Chester. 1985. *Main Street to Miracle Mile*. Boston: New York Graphic Society.

Mahoney, Timothy R. 1990. *River Towns in the Great West: The Structure of Provincial Urbanization in the American Midwest, 1820–1870*. Cambridge: Cambridge University Press.

Meinig, D. W. 1993. *The Shaping of America: A Geographical Perspective on 500 Years of History*, vol. 2, *Continental America 1800–1867*. New Haven: Yale University Press.

Meyer, Eugene. 1986. *Maryland Lost and Found*. Baltimore: Johns Hopkins University Press.

Morgan, Arthur E. 1951. *The Miami Conservancy District*. New York: McGraw-Hill.

Noble, Allen G., and Albert J. Korsok. 1975. *Ohio—An American Heartland*. Bulletin 65. Columbus, Ohio: Division of Geological Survey.

Norton, W. T., ed. 1912. *Centennial History of Madison County, Illinois, and Its People, 1812–1912*. Chicago: Lewis Publishing.

Ohio Writer's Project. 1940. *The Ohio Guide*. Sponsored by the Ohio State Archaeological and Historical Society. New York: Oxford University Press.

Orser, Joseph, and Joseph Arnold. 1989. *Catonsville, 1880–1940: From Village to Suburb*. Norfolk, Va.: Donning Company.

Peacefull, Leonard, ed. 1990. *The Changing Heartland: A Geography of Ohio*. Needham Heights, Mass.: Ginn Press.

Peck, John M. 1837. *A Gazetteer of Illinois*. 2nd ed. Philadelphia: Grigg & Elliot.

Peters, William E. 1930. *Ohio Lands and Their History*. Athens, Ohio: Lawhead Press.

Pillsbury, Richard. 1970. "The Urban Street Pattern as a Culture Indicator, 1682–1815." *Annals of the Association of American Geographers* 60:3.

Price, Benjamin. 1922. *A Standard History of Springfield and Clark County*. Chicago: American Historical Society.

Purvis, Thomas L. 1986. "The Pennsylvania Dutch and the German-American Diaspora in 1790." *Journal of Cultural Geography* 6.

Raitz, Karl. 1973. "Ethnicity and the Diffusion and Distribution of Cigar Tobacco Production in Wisconsin and Ohio." *Tijdschrift voor Economische en sociale Geografie* 64.

Reedy, Ralph. 1993. Interview by Daniel Reedy, Livingston, Ill., June.

Rideing, William H. 1879. "The Old National Pike." *Harper's New Monthly Magazine* 59:354.

Ritchie, A. 1973. *Know Ohio's Soil Regions*. Columbus: Ohio Department of Natural Resources, Division of Lands and Soils.

Royer, Donald M. 1989. *The German-American Contribution to Richmond's Development: 1833–1933*. Indianapolis: Augustin Press.

Searight, Thomas B. 1894. *The Old Pike*. Uniontown, Pa.: By the Author.

Semmes, Raphael. 1953. *Baltimore as Seen by Visitors, 1783–1860*. Baltimore: Maryland Historical Society.

Sheppard, Muriel Earley. 1991 [1947]. *Cloud by Day*. Pittsburgh: University of Pittsburgh Press.

Sherman, C. E. 1925. *Ohio Land Subdivisions,* Vol. 3, Final Report. Columbus: Ohio Topographic Survey.

Shortridge, James. 1989. *The Middle West: Its Meaning in American Culture*. Lawrence: University of Kansas Press.

Simmons, David A. 1978. "Great Western Schoolhouse." *National Register of Historic Places Inventory*. Columbus: Ohio Historic Preservation Office.

Smith, Henry Nash. 1950. *Virgin Land: The American West as Symbol and Myth*. Cambridge: Harvard University Press.

Steffen, Charles G. 1979. "Changes in the Organization of Artisan Production in Baltimore, 1790 to 1820." *William and Mary Quarterly 36*.

Stegmaier, H. Jr., D. Dean, G. Kershaw, and J. Wiseman. 1976. *Allegany County: A History*. Parsons, W.V.: McClain Printing Co.

Steinbeck, John. 1939. *The Grapes of Wrath*. New York: Viking Press.

Stewart, George. 1953. *U.S. 40, Cross Section of the United States of America*. Boston: Houghton Mifflin.

Stone, Ralph. 1932. *Building Stones of Pennsylvania*. Harrisburg: Pennsylvania Geological Survey.

Stoner, Paula. 1977. "Early Folk Architecture of Washington County." *Maryland Historical Magazine 72*.

Taylor, David L. 1976. "Headley Inn, Edward Smith House, and Farm." *National Register of Historic Places Inventory*. Columbus: Ohio Historic Preservation Office.

Toma, J. A. 1953. "One Hundred and Fifty Years of Transportation." In *A History of Miami County, Ohio (1807–1953)*. Columbus, Ohio: F. J. Heer Printing.

Travers, Paul J. 1990. *The Patapsco: Baltimore's River of History*. Centreville, Md.: Tidewater Publications.

Vonada, Damaine, ed. 1992. *The Ohio Almanac*. Wilmington, Ohio: Orange Frazer Press.

Warren, Robert Penn. 1974. "Homage to Theodore Dreiser on the Centennial of His Birth." In *Or Else—Poems 1968–1974*. New York: Random House.

Whipple, Henry B. 1937. *Bishop Whipple's Southern Diary, 1843–1844*. Minneapolis: University of Minnesota Press.

White, C. Albert. N.d. *A History of the Rectangular Survey System*. Washington, D.C.: Government Printing Office.

Williams, Cynthia, ed. 1972. *Ohio Almanac*. 5th ed. Lorain, Ohio: Lorain Journal Co.

Suggested Readings

Introduction: The National Road and Its Landscapes

Perhaps the best way to become attuned to the vagaries of topography that National Road construction engineers had to contend with is to begin with William Thornbury's *Regional Geomorphology of the United States*.

Chapter 1. From Baltimore to Cumberland, Maryland

There are no literary works that relate directly to the National Road's eastern extension. Additional information must be filtered from broader frameworks that deal with a variety of chronological, topical, state, regional, and local studies. The best place to initiate this gleaning process is the extensive bibliographic essay in Robert J. Brugger, *Maryland: A Middle Temperament, 1634–1980* (Baltimore: Johns Hopkins University Press, 1988), 711–69.

Several studies relate more directly to the structure of this volume. Descriptions of National Road sections and related routes in Maryland may be drawn from *Maryland:*

A New Guide to the Old Line State, comp. and ed. Edward C. Papenfuse and others (Baltimore: Johns Hopkins University Press, 1976). This work is a worthy update of *Maryland: A Guide to the Old Line State* (New York: Oxford University Press, 1940), the celebrated product of the Maryland Writer's Project, and follows the same expanded "trip tick" format as its predecessor. Raphael Semmes's *Baltimore as Seen by Visitors, 1783–1860* (Baltimore: Maryland Historical Society, 1953) is a fine presentation of the many opinions of the culture, economy, physical appearance, and merits relative to other cities by travelers whom for the most part had only a passing acquaintance with the National Road's eastern terminus. Baltimore as the focus of expanding road systems, including the National Road, and the process of developing individual systems is presented in William Hollifield, *Difficulties Made Easy: History of the Turnpikes of Baltimore City and Country* (Baltimore: Baltimore County Historical Society, 1978).

Because landscape is the focus of this volume, three pictorial works are suggested. The magnificent photographs in Mame Warren and Marion E. Warren, *Maryland Time Exposures, 1840–1940* (Baltimore: Johns Hopkins University Press, 1984), are well organized—unusual for this genre—and are accompanied by a text. For the National Road, readers will need to make selections from "Central Maryland" (97–113), and "Western Maryland" (241–305). Joetta M. Cramm, *A Pictorial History, Howard County* (Norfolk: Donning Company, 1987), has photographs that relate to the National Road and to the rise of Ellicott City, but has much superfluous material, lacks organization, and tends to focus too much on the local elite. The reader must also be patient with Albert L. Feldstein, compiler and editor, *Downtown Cumberland, 1950–1980* (Cumberland: Commercial Printing Company, 1994). The lack of structure and explanatory text are frustrating, but the photographs poignantly chronicle the rapid decline of an American city as it "advances" into the postindustrial era.

Chapter 2. From Cumberland to Wheeling, West Virginia

Were it not for the Bicentennial spirit and monies, a great many local histories and surveys would never have gotten off the ground. Readers seeking more information about this region are indebted to that commemorative zeal. Maryland's Allegany and Garrett Counties are ably served by two Bicentennial treatments: *Allegany County: A History* by H. Stegmaier et al. and *Garrett County: A History of Maryland's Tableland* by S. Schlosnagle and others. McClain Printing Company of Parsons, West Virginia, published both books. Eugene Meyer provides a contemporary, newsy view of the state's diverse peoples and places in *Maryland: Lost and Found* (Baltimore: Johns Hopkins University Press, 1986).

The University of Pittsburgh Press has southwestern Pennsylvania covered. The region's aficionados can find books on everything from Braddock to the history of U.S. Air, from Mother Jones to deer hunting (yes, it is titled *Buck Fever*). Labor and industry issues, ethnicity, and eighteenth-century history are particularly well represented by the press. Much-loved regional novels include Marcia Davenport's *Valley of Decision* and Thomas Bell's *Out of This Furnace,* both written in the early 1940s. Both are multi-generational sagas; the first profiles a steelmill-owning family, the second vividly conveys the immigrant Slovak workers' perspectives. The book that most palpably portrays the Connellsville coke patch experience, however, while etching a haunting portrait of J. V. Thompson, is nonfiction: Muriel Sheppard Earley's *Cloud by Day.* It reads like a novel. Mystery writer K. C. Constantine has created a Serbian-Italian cop who operates in the patch landscapes in *The Rocksburg Railway Murders* and *Joey's Case.*

A *Guidebook to Historic Western Pennsylvania* by Smith and Swetnam provides site listings for twenty-six counties, including the three the Road traverses. First published in 1976 and revised in 1991, the book unfortunately still includes things that aren't there anymore and some misleading directions. Venerable county histories are available for the National Road counties of Somerset, Fayette, and Washington, and these are cited in Smith and Swetnam's bibliography.

No better introduction to West Virginia exists than John Alexander Williams's history published by Norton in 1976. By keying each chapter to an emblematic place—Point Pleasant, Harper's Ferry, Buffalo Creek, among others—Williams roots his chronology in the landscape. In the opening chapter on Point Pleasant, for example, land speculation, European powers, Amerinds, topography, route ways, and colonial politics are woven into the clearest interpretation of trans-Appalachian linkages to be found in thirty pages. Moundsville native Davis Grubb, author of the chilling *The Night of the Hunter,* fictionalizes his West Virginia hometown as "Glory" in several of his books, such as *The Voices of Glory.*

Chapter 3. From Wheeling to Columbus, Ohio

Ohio's Natural Heritage by Michael B. Lafferty (Columbus: Ohio Academy of Science, 1979) offers a well-illustrated, comprehensive survey of the state's natural landscape. Although it also touches on settlement, the book's focus is the land. The Ohio Country's early development, including its road system, is depicted in a collection of maps, charts, and plans entitled the *Mapping of Ohio* by Thomas H. Smith (Kent, Ohio: Kent State University Press, 1977). County histories offer detailed information about places and peoples along the National Road. Their genealogical descriptions are informative. One of the more comprehensive is *Stories of Guernsey County* by William G. Wolfe (Cambridge, Ohio: Published by the author, 1943). *Ohio Magazine* contains some of the best accounts of Ohioana, both past and present. And, for life in the hills of Ohio's Appalachia, there is no better account than *Out of the Red Bush* by Kermit Daugherty (1954; Rio Grande, Ohio: Rio Grande College, 1986). Although this autobiographical story is placed in Jackson County, it is representative of life and livelihood anywhere in the isolated Appalachian parts of the state.

Chapter 4. From Columbus to Richmond, Indiana

In addition to county histories, one may gain a flavor for the people and landscapes of western Ohio in several novels that employ the area as a backdrop. Allan Eckert's historical novels are based upon meticulous archival research. His *That Dark and Bloody River* (New York: Bantam Books, 1995) portrays frontier life in late-eighteenth century Ohio. A trilogy of books by Conrad Richter follows a Pennsylvania family to the Ohio frontier and, by studied use of nineteenth-century dialect, describes their transition from subsistence woodsfaring folk to settled farmers and townspeople. See his *The Trees* (New York: Knopf, 1940); *The Fields* (New York: Knopf, 1946); and *The Town* (New York: Knopf, 1950). In *Follow the River* (Garden City, N.Y.: Doubleday, 1969), Albert Mayer's character, Philadelphia school teacher Thomas Morrow, moves west to the Northwest Territory and follows the Ohio River to Fort Washington and Losantiville (Cincinnati), interacting with historical figures on the way. Sherwood Anderson drew upon his early years in Clyde, Ohio, to portray life in a small middlewestern town in *Winesburg, Ohio* (New York: B. W. Huebsch, 1919). Perhaps the most evocative of regional novels in portraying small-town life in Ohio are two books by Helen Hooven Santmyer, *Ohio Town* (Columbus: Ohio State University Press, 1962); and *". . . And Ladies of the Club"* (New York: Putnam, 1982).

Chapter 5. From Richmond to Terre Haute, Indiana

Various sources provide additional details about that part of US 40 which crosses Indiana from Richmond to Terre Haute. For a concise history of old National Road surveying and construction see Lee Burns, "The National Road in Indiana," *Indiana Historical Society Publications* 7 (1919): 210–37. A description of changing economic, social, and technological contexts in which the highway's visual attributes evolved is provided by Thomas J. Schlereth, *U.S. 40: A Roadscape of the American Experience* (Indianapolis: Indiana Historical Society, 1985). Accounts of all kinds of artifacts along the Road in Indiana are found in Robert M. Taylor Jr., Erroll Wayne Stevens, Mary Ann Ponder, and Paul Brockman, *Indiana: A New Historical Guide* (Indianapolis: Indiana Historical Society, 1989). Readers may want to consult additional references about Indianapolis. Two well-illustrated volumes are *Indianapolis Architecture* (Indiana Architectural Foundation, 1975), and David J. Bodenhamer, Lamont Hulse, and Elizabeth B. Monroe, *The Main Stem: The History and Architecture of North Meridian Street* (Indianapolis: Historic Landmarks Foundation of Indiana, 1992). The latter book describes the broader context in which this residential district developed.

Chapter 6. From Terre Haute to Vandalia, Illinois

Several sources can augment the serious traveler's experience along this segment. For land forms and living forms, see Illinois Nature Preserves Commission, *Comprehensive Plan for the Illinois Preserves System*, pt. 2, *The Natural Divisions of Illinois* (Springfield, Ill.: Illinois Nature Preserves Commission, 1973). William Henry Perrin, ed., *History of Crawford and Clark Counties* (Chicago: O. L. Baskin, 1883), is perhaps the best of the century-old county histories for the four counties astride the route. A descriptive adjunct for Marshall in the automobile age is easy reading in George T. Mitchell, *Dr. George: An Account of the Life of a Country Doctor* (Carbondale: Southern Illinois University Press, 1994). In an area deserving more study, Vandalia has drawn disproportionate attention. See Paul E. Stroble, *High on the Okaw's Western Bank: Vandalia, Illinois, 1819–1839* (Urbana: University of Illinois Press, 1992), for a scholarly treatment of the town in its capitol heyday, and Joseph P. Lyford, *The Talk of Vandalia: The Life of an American Town* (New York: Harper Colophon Books, 1965), for a journalist's report on more recent times.

Chapter 7. From Vandalia to East St. Louis and Alton, Illinois

Several sources enhance the experience of traveling this last Road section. For early nineteenth-century Illinois boosterism, see John M. Peck, *A Gazetteer of Illinois*, 2nd ed. (Philadelphia: Grigg & Elliot, 1837). Details on the physical environment can be found in Illinois Nature Preserves Commission, *Comprehensive Plan for the Illinois Preserves System*, pt. 2, *The Natural Divisions of Illinois* (Springfield: Illinois Nature Preserves Commission, 1973). Of the four counties along the proposed National Road corridor, Madison County would have most benefited from either the St. Louis or Alton terminus route. See *History of Madison County, Illinois* (Edwardsville, Ill.: W. R. Brink, 1882); and W. T. Norton, ed., *Centennial History of Madison County, Illinois and Its People, 1812–1912* (Chicago: Lewis Publishing, 1912). Thomas L. Hardin, "The National Road in Illinois," *Journal of the Illinois State Historical Society* 60 (Spring 1967): 5–22, is an interesting discussion of the Road and its termination at Vandalia. For a scholarly review of early nineteenth-century rivalry between St. Louis and Alton, and St. Louis's evolving hegemony, see Jeffrey S. Adler, *Yankee Merchants and the Making of the Urban West: The Rise and Fall of Antebellum St. Louis* (Cambridge: Cambridge University Press, 1991); and Timothy R. Mahoney, *River Towns in the Great West: The Structure of Provincial Urbanization in the American Midwest, 1820–1870* (Cambridge: Cambridge University Press, 1990).

Contributors

ROBERT W. BASTIAN received a Ph.D. from Indiana University in 1968, and has taught geography at Indiana State University since 1969. His research interests have focused upon architecture as a guide to traditional cultural regions, urban residential segregation, and the diffusion of popular culture in America. He is coauthor with John A. Jakle and Douglas K. Meyer of *Common Houses in American's Small Towns,* and his articles have appeared in *Geographical Review, Professional Geographer, Journal of Cultural Geography,* and a variety of other professional journals. He currently serves as a member of the Vigo County Preservation Alliance.

CHARLES J. FARMER, who earned a Ph.D. from the University of Maryland, was formerly a professor of geography at Frostburg State University, in Frostburg, Maryland. His research interests are focused primarily on the historical geography of the eighteenth-century and antebellum American South. He is the author of *In the Absence of Towns: Settlement and Country Trade in Southside Virginia, 1730–1800.*

John Jakle's interests spread across historical, cultural, and urban social geography with focus on interpreting the American landscape as built environment. Books include *Images of the Ohio Valley, The Tourist, The Visual Elements of Landscape, Common Houses in America's Small Towns* (coauthored with Robert W. Bastian and Douglas K. Meyer), and *Derelict Landscapes*. His most recent work, coauthored with Keith Sculle, is entitled *The Gas Station in America*. John received a Ph.D. degree from Indiana University. He taught at the University of Maine and at Western Michigan University before joining the faculty at the University of Illinois at Urbana-Champaign where he is currently professor of geography.

Artimus Keiffer, a Ph.D. candidate at Kent State University, has interests in cultural geography, especially utopian and illegal landscapes. His current research examines the role of technology in the design of residential architecture.

Karen Koegler received a Ph.D. in geography from the University of Kentucky where she has taught for over a decade. She also holds degrees in art history, library science, and historic preservation. An AAUW American Fellowship underwrote her dissertation research on material culture in southwestern Pennsylvania. She has published articles and presented papers interpreting the cultural landscape at a variety of scales. She perceives residing outside the greater Pittsburgh region as living in exile.

Douglas K. Meyer received a Ph.D. from Michigan State University in 1970 and is a professor of geography at Eastern Illinois University, at Charleston, Illinois. He is coauthor of *Common Houses in America's Small Towns*, with Robert W. Bastian and John A. Jakle.

Kenneth Pavelchak studied environmental design and historic presentation at Antioch College and Eastern Michigan University. He is currently pursuing a graduate degree in history at the University of Kentucky. During his nine-year tenure at the planning division of Lexington city government, he designed and illustrated publications on historic districts and coordinated production of the county's 1988 master land use plan. For the past four years he has spent all of his vacation time in southwestern Pennsylvania on or near US 40.

Karl Raitz grew up on the Upper Middle West's black dirt prairie and cultivated an interest in landscapes at the University of Minnesota where he received a Ph.D. in geography. As a member of the geography and anthropology faculties, he has taught at the University of Kentucky for over two decades and finds the Bluegrass Region in this border state an ideal base from which to explore the landscapes of eastern America.

Thomas J. Schlereth is professor of American studies and professor of history at the University of Notre Dame where he teaches American cultural, intellectual, architectural and landscape history in addition to material culture studies. He serves as a contributing editor for the *Journal of American History* and a general editor for the Midwest History and Culture series published by the Indiana University Press. His most recent book is *Victorian America: Transformations in Everyday Life, 1876–1915.*

KEITH A. SCULLE has studied the National Road, beginning with the Illinois Historic Landmarks Survey in 1972, for over twenty years in his native Illinois. Sculle is a landscape historian calling on interdisciplinary study to gain a fuller understanding and appreciation of his subjects than would be possible with but one of several disciplinary perspectives and their associated techniques. His is with the Illinois Historic Preservation Agency and is an adjunct professor of history at Sagamon State University.

HUBERT G. H. WILHELM is a native of Germany. He participated in a rural high school student exchange to the USA in 1950–51, and immigrated to the States in 1954. He received a M.A. degree from the University of Illinois in 1960 and completed a Ph.D. program at Louisiana State University in 1963. He is the author of numerous research papers on the rural American landscape.

Index

Frost, Josiah, 74, 101
Frost, Meshach, 76
Frostburg, Md., 74–77
Frostburg State University
  (Frostburg, Md.), 77
Fulton House/Moran House
  (Uniontown, Pa.), 97
Funkhouser, Ill., 297
Funkstown, Md., 50–51

Gager, Marvin, 190
"Galactic Metropolis," 43–44
Galbreath, John Wilmer, 184
Gallatin Hotel (Uniontown,
  Pa.), 97
Garlett's Garage (Brownsville,
  Pa.), 105
Garreau, Joel, 44
Garrett County, Md., 77–78,
  81
Gateway Arch (St. Louis), 347,
  350
Gehrig, Lou, 111
Gem, Ind., 242
General Braddock's Defeat
  (Deming), 21
*Genius of Universal Emancipa-
  tion,* 128
George Rogers Clark Park
  (Donnelsville, Ohio), 201
Georges Creek Coal Basin
  (Md.), 74
Georgesville, Ohio, 184
George Washington Hotel
  (Washington, Pa.), 111–12
German immigrants: in Illi-
  nois, 288, 291–92, 298, 330,
  337–38, 340; in Ohio, 171,
  194; in western Maryland,
  49, 70
German Village (Columbus,
  Ohio), 171
Gettysburg, Ohio, 219
Gilded Age, 86
Gist, Christopher, 91
Glaciers, 154, 156, 158, 201,
  206, 230
Glenn, John, 143–44
"Golden Mile" (Md.), 47

Goldman, Max, 105
Gorley's Lake Hotel (Fayette
  County, Pa.), 88
Graham, Thomas, 183
Grahamtown, Md., 77
Grain elevators, 291
Grantsville, Md., 81, 83
Granville, Ohio, 199
Gratiot, Charles, 154
Gratiot, Ohio, 154
Gravel pits, 230–31
Great Crossings stone bridge
  (Pa.), 84, 87
Great Miami River (Ohio),
  177, 206–7
Great Miami Valley (Ohio),
  206
Great Plains, 350
Great Southern Hotel
  (Columbus, Ohio), 171
Great Valley (Md.), 49, 53–54
Great Western School (Ohio),
  130
Greek Revival architecture,
  171
Greencastle, Ind., 252
Greene County, Pa., 112
Greenfield, Ind., 239–42
Green Ridge, Md., 62, 63
Greenup, Ill., 283–86, 293
Greenup, Ind., 50
Greenup, William C., 283–84,
  288, 306
Greenville, Ill., 310, 318–19,
  334–35
Greenville, Ohio, 177
Greenville, Treaty of (1795),
  176–77
Greenville College (Ill.), 334,
  335
Grey, Zane, 145
Groll, Theodore, 27

Hagarstown, Ill., 316–17
Hagerstown, Md., 45, 50,
  52–53
Hagerstown Speedway (Md.),
  56

Hair Tavern (Hopwood, Pa.),
  95
Hallofield, Md., 40
Hamel, Ill., 323
Hamilton, Ohio, 177
Hancock, Md., 58–59
Hancock County Courthouse
  (Greenfield, Ind.), 240
Hannaford, Sammuel, 261
Harmony, Ind., 254
Harmony, Ohio, 192
Harper, William Rainey, 143
Harrisburg, Ohio, 210
Harvey House (Sideling Hill,
  Md.), 59
Hawk's Creek (Ill.), 272, 273
Hayden building (Hopwood,
  Pa.), 95
Hayes Tavern (Middlebourne,
  Ohio), 135–36
Haystack Mountain (Md.), 71
Headley Inn (Zanesville,
  Ohio), 149–51
Hebron, Ohio, 159–60
Heller, John Matthew, 15, 30
Helvetia Milk Condensing
  Company: Greenville, Ill.,
  334; Highland, Ill., 339
Hendrysburg, Ohio, 133
Henninger, William, 316
Henry Clay Township, Pa., 87
Henry's Restaurant (West Jeff-
  erson, Ohio), 187
Henshaw House (Dunreith,
  Ind.), 235
Highland, Ill., 337–39
Highways: construction, 8–9;
  engineers, 8; numbering
  system, 24
Hillsboro, Ill., 319
Hill's Tavern (Scenery Hill,
  Pa.), 109
Hilltop Basic Resources (Enon,
  Ohio), 201
Hobbs, Howard, 112, 184, 193,
  204
Hobbs Road Guide, 84, 90, 93,
  105

ILLUSTRATION CREDITS

196 Bob Thall (1994).
197 Bob Thall (1994).
198 Charles Walters (1994).
200 Charles Walters (1994).
202 Charles Walters (1994).
203 Charles Walters (1994).
204 Gregory Conniff (1994).
209 Charles Walters (1994).
210 Gregory Conniff (1994).
212 Charles Walters (1994).
213 Charles Walters (1994).
216 Charles Walters (1994).
217 (*Above*) Charles Walters (1994); (*below*) Bob Thall (1994).
218 Bob Thall (1994).
220 Bob Thall (1994).
221 Bob Thall (1994).
226 Charles Walters (1994).
227 Charles Walters (1994).
228 Charles Walters (1994).
233 Bob Thall (1994).
234 Bob Thall (1994).
235 Charles Walters (1994).
236 Charles Walters (1994).
239 Charles Walters (1994).
240 Charles Walters (1994).
243 Bob Thall (1994).
244 Charles Walters (1994).
245 Bob Thall (1994).
246 Gregory Conniff (1994).
247 Charles Walters (1994).
248 Bob Thall (1994).
249 Gregory Conniff (1994).
250 Gregory Conniff (1994).
251 (*Above*) Bob Thall (1994); (*below*) Charles Walters (1994).
252 Gregory Conniff (1994).
253 Gregory Conniff (1994).
254 Gregory Conniff (1994).
255 Charles Walters (1994).
256 (*Above*) Bob Thall (1994); (*below*) Bob Thall: Seagram Bicentennial Project.
257 Charles Walters (1994).
258 Bob Thall (1994).
259 Bob Thall (1994).
260 Charles Walters (1994).
262 Charles Walters (1994).
263 Charles Walters (1994).
266 Bob Thall (1994).
267 (*Above left*) Charles Walters (1994); (*above right*)
     Bob Thall: Seagram Bicentennial Project; (*below*) Gregory Conniff (1994).
268 (*Above*) Gregory Conniff (1994); (*below*) Bob Thall (1994).
269 Bob Thall (1994).
270 Bob Thall (1994).
272 Charles Walters (1994).
275 Charles Walters (1994).
276 Gregory Conniff (1994).
277 Charles Walters (1994).
279 Charles Walters (1994).
280 Gregory Conniff (1994).
281 Gregory Conniff (1994).
282 Charles Walters (1994).
283 Charles Walters (1994).
285 Charles Walters (1994).
287 Gregory Conniff (1994).
288 Gregory Conniff (1994).
289 Gregory Conniff (1994).
290 Gregory Conniff (1994).
291 Charles Walters (1994).
292 Charles Walters (1994).
294 Charles Walters (1994).
295 Charles Walters (1994).
296 Charles Walters (1994).
298 Charles Walters (1994).
299 Charles Walters (1994).
300 Charles Walters (1994).
301 Charles Walters (1994).
302 Gregory Conniff (1994).
305 Charles Walters (1994).
315 Charles Walters (1994).
320 Gregory Conniff (1994).
321 Gregory Conniff (1994).
322 Gregory Conniff (1994).
323 Gregory Conniff (1994).
324 Gregory Conniff (1994).
325 Gregory Conniff (1994).
328 Gregory Conniff (1994).
329 Gregory Conniff (1994).
330 Gregory Conniff (1994).
331 Charles Walters (1994).
332 (*Above*) Gregory Conniff (1994); (*below*) Charles Walters (1994).
335 Gregory Conniff (1994).
343 Charles Walters (1994).
344 Charles Walters (1994).
345 Charles Walters (1994).
346 Charles Walters (1994).